The Powerful Ephemeral

SOUTH ASIA ACROSS THE DISCIPLINES

Edited by Dipesh Chakrabarty, Sheldon Pollock, and Sanjay Subrahmanyam

South Asia Across the Disciplines is a series devoted to publishing first books across a wide range of South Asian studies, including art, history, philology or textual studies, philosophy, religion, and interpretive social sciences. Contributors all share the goal of opening up new archives, especially in South Asian languages, and suggesting new methods and approaches, while demonstrating that South Asian scholarship can be at once deep in expertise and broad in appeal.

Funded by a grant from the Andrew W. Mellon Foundation and jointly published by the University of California Press, the University of Chicago Press, and Columbia University Press. Read more about the series at http://www.saacrossdisciplines.org.

Extreme Poetry: The South Asian Movement of Simultaneous Narration, by Yigal Bronner (Columbia University Press, 2010)

The Social Space of Language: Vernacular Culture in British Colonial Punjab, by Farina Mir (University of California Press, 2010)

Unifying Hinduism: The Philosophy of Vijnanabhiksu in Indian Intellectual History, by Andrew J. Nicholson (Columbia University Press, 2010)

Secularizing Islamists?: Jama'at-e-Islami and Jama 'at-ud-Da'wa in Urban Pakistan, by Humeira Iqtidar (University of Chicago Press, 2011)

Islam Translated: Literature, Conversion, and the Arabic Cosmopolis of South and Southeast Asia, by Ronit Ricci (University of Chicago Press, 2011)

Conjugations: Marriage and Form in New Bollywood Cinema, by Sangita Gopal (University of Chicago Press, 2011)

The Powerful Ephemeral: Everyday Healing in an Ambiguously Islamic Place, by Carla Bellamy (University of California Press, 2011)

The Powerful Ephemeral

Everyday Healing in an Ambiguously Islamic Place

Carla Bellamy

UNIVERSITY OF CALIFORNIA PRESS
Berkeley · Los Angeles · London

University of California Press, one of the most distinguished university presses in the United States, enriches lives around the world by advancing scholarship in the humanities, social sciences, and natural sciences. Its activities are supported by the UC Press Foundation and by philanthropic contributions from individuals and institutions. For more information, visit www.ucpress.edu.

University of California Press
Berkeley and Los Angeles, California

University of California Press, Ltd.
London, England

Library of Congress Cataloging-in-Publication Data
Bellamy, Carla, 1971–.
The powerful ephemeral : everyday healing in an ambiguously Islamic place / Carla Bellamy.
p. cm.
Includes bibliographical references and index.
ISBN 978-0-520-26280-5 (cloth : alk. paper)—
978-0-520-26281-2 (pbk. : alk. paper)
1. Healing—Religious aspects—Islam. 2. Spiritual healing—India. 3. Islamic shrines—India. 4. Sufism—India. I. Title.
BP189.65.F35B45 2011
297.4'3554—dc22 2010038918

Manufactured in the United States of America

20 19 18 17 16 15 14 13 12
10 9 8 7 6 5 4 3 2 1

The paper used in this publication meets the minimum requirements of ANSI/NISO Z39.48-1992 (R 1997) (*Permanence of Paper*).

This book is printed on Cascades Enviro 100, a 100% post consumer waste, recycled, de-inked fiber. FSC recycled certified and processed chlorine free. It is acid free, Ecologo certified, and manufactured by BioGas energy.

To Ḥusain Ṭekrī Sharīf

Contents

Illustrations

FIGURES

MAPS

Acknowledgments

This book would not have been possible without the participation and patience of what sometimes feels like the entire population of Jaora. First of all, I am extremely grateful to Haji Sarwar 'Ali Khan and Mr. M. K. Taimuri, respectively *mutavallī* and *waqf* board representative to Ḥusain Ṭekrī Sharīf during the period of my research. Without their support, this project would not have been possible. The entire staff at Ḥusain Ṭekrī was unfailingly gracious and helpful. Deep and heartfelt thanks to the Chippas, especially Farzana and Khadija, who made Jaora feel like home; their fabulous senses of humor made even really difficult days bearable. Thanks to Harun Chippa and the others at the milk stall for always giving me a comfortable place to sit with a cold drink, to Syed Nadir Shah for all the tea and insight, and to everyone at Fatima Guest House for providing a comfortable and cheerful place during my first visit to Ḥusain Ṭekrī and for enthusiastically maintaining an open door whenever I stopped by to interview their guests. Thanks also to all the shopkeepers of Ḥusain Ṭekrī for their time and willingness to share their knowledge, and heartfelt thanks to the countless pilgrims who shared their time and experiences with me. Special thanks to Suroor Kaif for his help in deciphering some challenging and poorly photocopied Urdu, and thanks to his family for opening their friendly home to me. I am grateful to H. E. Merchant in Bombay for his time and for making an extra effort to meet with me. For their openness and kindness I extend heartfelt thanks to the entire crew at Santa Cruz East—thanks especially to Babli, Muhammad, and 'Abid. In Delhi, I thank

Arjun Mahey and his parents, Kishori and Bharat, for their open-door policy during the period of my research and for the refuge I always found behind that door. Thank you to Father Lawrence Ober, S.J., for sharing his work on Jaora State. Most of all, to my main informants, especially Priya, Babli, Maya, and Nasim, I offer deep gratitude and admiration.

The initial research for this project was funded by a Junior Research Fellow grant from The American Institute of Indian Studies, and a vital year of advanced study of Hindi in Udaipur was supported by an AIIS Junior Language Fellowship. As I suspect anyone who does research in India knows, AIIS is a force of nature, and I am grateful for its financial, logistical, and general support. In particular, many thanks to Purnima Mehta and Mini Raji Kumar. Earlier study of Hindi in India was supported by a FLAS fellowship through the Southern Asian Institute at Columbia University; thanks to Phil Oldenberg for helping me put in place the paperwork necessary to use that funding at the Landour Language School. I am also grateful to Columbia University and its Department of Religion for awarding me a multiyear Mellon Foundation fellowship, without which it would not have been possible for me to pursue graduate work in religion.

For reading portions of this book and offering thoughtful and insightful comments, thanks to Jayson Beaster-Jones, Ashley Bristowe, Alexander Gardner, Teena Purohit, Sally Steindorf, and Andrea Pinkney. I am particularly grateful to Joyce Burkhalter Flueckiger, Joel Lee and Annabella Pitkin, all of whom read complete drafts of this book and offered detailed and often transformative comments and suggestions. Throughout the years it has taken to research and write this book, Todd Tarantino's logistical, intellectual, and emotional support has been instrumental; I am certain that he has read more drafts of this book than anyone other than myself, and the fact that I was able to complete this book during the first year of our daughter's life is better testament to his credentials as an ideal husband and coparent than anything I could say here.

Many thanks to Reed Malcolm, Kalicia Pivirotto, and Cindy Fulton, my editors at University of California Press: their professionalism and availability have made my first experience moving a manuscript through the publication process a pleasure. Thanks also to my copy editor, Sharron Wood, for her meticulous work and many spot-on comments and suggestions. Finally, I am extremely grateful to the anonymous readers of University of California Press for their thorough and insightful comments; the manuscript benefited significantly from their expertise and their suggestions for improvement. If any errors remain, I of course take full responsibility.

I have been blessed with many outstanding teachers and mentors.

Thanks to my parents Judy and Robert Bellamy, my first teachers, for raising me in a home filled with books and for instilling in me a love of ideas, and thanks to Nancy White for her friendship and her unwavering support. Thanks to Julie Galambush and John Barbour, whose teaching and mentoring motivated me to pursue graduate studies in religion; to Diana Eck for teaching the pilgrimage seminar at Harvard that set me on the path that led to this book; to Frances Pritchett for inspiring my love of Hindi and laying a firm foundation; and to Vidhu Chaturvedi both for being a gifted teacher and, together with his wife Neelam, providing wonderful company during my India-based Hindi study and thereafter. Most of all, I offer my gratitude to the scholars who attentively supervised, encouraged, and constructively criticized the initial research and writing on which this book is based: Jack Hawley, David Lelyveld, Rachel Fell McDermott, Michael Taussig, and Neguin Yavari. Particular thanks to Neguin Yavari for her constant efforts to make me careful and well informed in my attempts to discuss Islamic identity as such. Deep gratitude to Rachel McDermott for being a constant supporter, teacher, and mentor, and for offering detailed and extremely helpful comments on multiple drafts of this manuscript. And, finally, heartfelt thanks to Jack Hawley, without whose support, guidance, and encouragement this book would not have been possible, and whose own work has taught me that the best scholars do not forget their love of their subject in the course of critically engaging with it.

Note on Orthography

With a few exceptions that should be obvious to the specialist, historically Islamic place names, titles, festivals, objects, and religious actions have been transliterated according to the Urdu-to-English system employed by John Platts in his *A Dictionary of Urdū, Classical Hindī, and English.* Historically non-Muslim place names, titles, festivals, objects, and religious actions have been transliterated according to the Hindi-to-English system employed by R. S. McGregor in his *The Oxford Hindi-English Dictionary.* While many of these terms have origins in Arabic, Persian, and/or Sanskrit, in order to remain true to the sociolinguistic context under discussion, my transliterations reflect the vernacular rather than etymological origins. For the purposes of readability, I have not employed diacritics for people's names or for words from Hindi, Urdu, Sanskrit and Arabic that have come into English.

While Hindi and Urdu share a grammar and a basic vocabulary, they are written in different scripts and have, respectively, Sanskrit- and Arabic-influenced literary and formal vocabularies. In the context of everyday speech, however, distinguishing between Hindi and Urdu is a relative and highly politicized process, making transliteration of terms from oral sources challenging. In general, I have categorized spoken language as "Hindi" or "Urdu" based upon context, individuals' pronunciation, and the extent to which the speaker's language reflected Arabic or Sanskrit influence. Written sources have been transliterated in accordance with the script employed.

Prologue

I was led to the collection of shrines in northwestern India known as Ḥusain Ṭekrī, or Husain Hill, much in the same way as most of its pilgrims: through a series of coincidences—events and circumstances and opportunities—that some would say were not coincidences at all.

During a year of language study in the Indian city of Udaipur I lived as a paying guest in the home of a woman named Maya. Maya is a married Sindhi Hindu woman in her late fifties or perhaps early sixties who lives in one of the many suburbs that sprawl along National Highway 8, a world away from the tourist enclaves and narrow alleys of the historic old city. I chose to live with Maya simply because her home was a stone's throw from the language school, and, like all New Yorkers, I recognized the value of a short commute.

Maya's home is that of a typical working-class family: a poured concrete structure with a flat roof built around a small, breezy central courtyard. On one side of the courtyard, stairs lead to a second-story bedroom and bathroom built with a son's marriage in mind. Several months into my stay, however, it became clear that Maya's seemingly typical home was atypical beyond its resident foreign lady with her exotic American accent and ever-present stack of Hindi flashcards. At dusk on Thursdays, I noticed a steady stream of people pass by the door of my rented room. Curious, I followed them one evening to the roof, where I discovered Maya seated in a small shrine replete with recognizably Islamic iconography: a *panja*[1] and images of Zuljenah,[2] a photo of a local, recently deceased Sufi named Mastān Bābā,[3] colorful drawings of Mecca that Maya identified as depictions of Ḥusain Ṭekrī, and a Hindi Qur'an, wrapped in green cloth.[4]

Maya sat on the floor of the shrine, knees bent and feet tucked behind her. She was deep in hushed conversation with a young woman whose head was reverentially covered with her *dupaṭṭā;* those waiting to speak with her sat in a group on the other end of the roof. The shrine was positioned such that no one in the sitting area could see into it or hear the whispered conversations held within it, making individuals' interactions with Maya private affairs. Maya, it turns out, was offering healing and advice to pilgrims who had come to her home; her power comes from serving, on Thursday evenings, as the bodily host of the revered relatives of the Prophet Muhammad himself, Husain and 'Abbas, with whom she became acquainted many years ago, when she herself sought—and found—healing at Ḥusain Ṭekrī.[5]

In subsequent conversations with Maya, I learned that Ḥusain Ṭekrī is located in Jaora, a former Muslim princely state now part of modern Madhya Pradesh. Because of a longstanding interest in and affection for Muslim saint shrines, I decided to make a trip to Jaora to see what Ḥusain Ṭekrī was all about. This first visit to Jaora from Udaipur began with the only genuinely frightening overnight train ride I've ever experienced in India. The slow-moving narrow-gauge train was empty and dark, and when we pulled into Jaora, it was pitch-black night and the power was out, making it impossible to be certain of the station. The few people stumbling off the train assured me that this was in fact Jaora, and so I joined them, crossing over the platform and walking out to the road, where a handful of enterprising rickshaw-wālās were waiting for us. An older pilgrim, himself from Udaipur, correctly surmised that I was not a local and, after confirming that I was on my way to Ḥusain Ṭekrī, directed my rickshaw-wālā to one of Ḥusain Ṭekrī's many pilgrim guesthouses. Like many pilgrims, then, my initial visit to Ḥusain Ṭekrī was marked by feelings of disorientation, fear, and camaraderie. After this first visit, which mainly served to call into question most of what I knew about Muslim saint shrines, all I could say with certainty about Ḥusain Ṭekrī was that I wanted to go back.

And what *is* Ḥusain Ṭekrī? This is a reasonable question, since to anyone well versed in contemporary South Asian culture, it is clear that Ḥusain Ṭekrī does not quite fit into any of the categories—academic or popular—that are commonly used to describe and classify religious spaces in South Asia. Among pilgrims, Ḥusain Ṭekrī is often referred to as a *dargāḥ,* from a Persian word for threshold or court. In Urdu and Hindi, the primary meaning of *dargāḥ* is a royal court, but the word is also commonly used to describe the tomb of a Muslim saint.[6] Ḥusain Ṭekrī's shrines are domed, colorfully painted poured concrete buildings surrounded by courtyards; from the outside, they look very much like any of the thousands of structures called dargāḥs that are built to house the tombs of Muslim saints in India. Many of the shrines' daily ritual activities, shared by members of all the religious traditions of the subcontinent, also mirror those of dargāḥs: spirit possession practices of all kinds, the offering of money, sheets, and sweets inside the shrines, the burning of a particular form of incense known as lobān, and the weighing of children against sweets and fruit in large metal balances in the shrines' courtyards—a ritual often performed as a gesture of gratitude to the saint who is understood to have graced the family with much-petitioned-for progeny. Like some pilgrims to conventional dargāḥs, pilgrims to Ḥusain Ṭekrī come seeking healing of physical and mental illnesses, as well as solutions to financial and familial problems.

However, the interiors of the shrines at Ḥusain Ṭekrī tell a slightly different story: rather than the sheet-bedecked grave of a Muslim saint, the buildings of Ḥusain Ṭekrī contain *zarīḥ,* silver miniatures of the tombs of the major martyrs of Karbala, modeled on the actual tombs in the faraway Middle East. All are surrounded by metal latticework to which pilgrims cling as they offer their prayers and petitions.[7] *Zarīḥ* like these are normally housed in *imāmbāṛās,* shrines containing symbols representing the martyrs of Karbala, and in contemporary India, *imāmbāṛā*s are predominantly owned and operated by Shi'a communities. In this case, though, the heads of Ḥusain Ṭekrī's management board are Sunni descendants of the *nawāb*s of the former Muslim princely state of Jaora.

As structures marking a place understood to have been visited by a Muslim saint, the shrines of Ḥusain Ṭekrī are somewhat like *cillā*s, but neither texts nor pilgrims refer to them as such. *Cillā,* from the Persian for "forty," connotes the traditional number of days for Sufi acts of meditation and asceticism, and *cillā*s are so named in part because they are not only places of saintly visitation, but also places where saints performed acts of meditation and asceticism. However, there are no such acts associated with the stories of the visitation of Ḥusain Ṭekrī's saints.

In addition to using the term *dargāḥ,* pilgrims to Ḥusain Ṭekrī also commonly refer to its shrines as *rauẓa*s, an Arabic-derived Urdu term for a tomb or garden. While the shrines do not contain actual graves, and their courtyards lack gardens, two of the six rauẓas were constructed on top of or alongside springs that are said to have appeared during miraculous visitations of Husain and 'Ali, the grandson and cousin of the Prophet Muhammad, respectively. A third water source, a stepwell that stands next to a rauẓa recently constructed in memory of Fatima (the wife of 'Ali, mother of Husain,

FIGURE 1. The rauẓa of Maulā ʿAli.

and daughter of the Prophet Muhammad), is not associated with a miraculous visitation of Fatima or any other major Islamic figure, but it is understood to be a point of access to both Hindu and Islamic figures, among them a form of Devī, or the great Hindu goddess, and the *mahdī,* or Islamic messiah. A water source is the sine qua non of a garden, and with descriptions of the gardens of paradise spanning Islamicate literary expression from the Qur'an to Persian and Urdu poetry, it is not difficult to see that the symbolism operative in the shrines' identity as rauẓas participates in this greater tradition.

The well at the rauẓa of ʿAbbas is renowned for its healing properties, though it is nearly dry due to drought and is now enclosed in a locked building. Its current enclosure is symptomatic of the increased administrative control that inevitably follows the growing popularity of a pilgrimage center; what remains of its water is first mixed with water transported to the site by truck and then pumped into an adjacent public shower facility maintained by the shrines' management committee. The completely dry stepwell at the rauẓa of Fatima, while still a focus of prayer and veneration, was recently enclosed for similar reasons of administrative control.

Dargāḥ, zarīḥ, imāmbāṛā, cillā, rauẓa: the more closely we look at Ḥusain Ṭekrī, the more it seems that asking what, exactly, it *is* may be the wrong question. It is better, perhaps, to ask for whom it is what it is, and how it does what it does with such extraordinary success. As we seek answers to these questions, Ḥusain Ṭekrī becomes an open well again: its surface catches fragments of the world above, and those who look into it recognize pieces of themselves and the world they know, making it familiar, strangely, to everyone. This familiarity is not illusory: elementally, we have more of the well in us than anything else. Drop a bucket in the well: while the familiar reflection is momentarily shattered, what is brought from beneath the surface will be exactly what you need, though it may bear no discernable relationship to the surface image that drew you in. Try to show others what you see in the well: they won't see exactly what you see, even if you look over the edge with them, pointing to shapes on the shifting surface of the water.

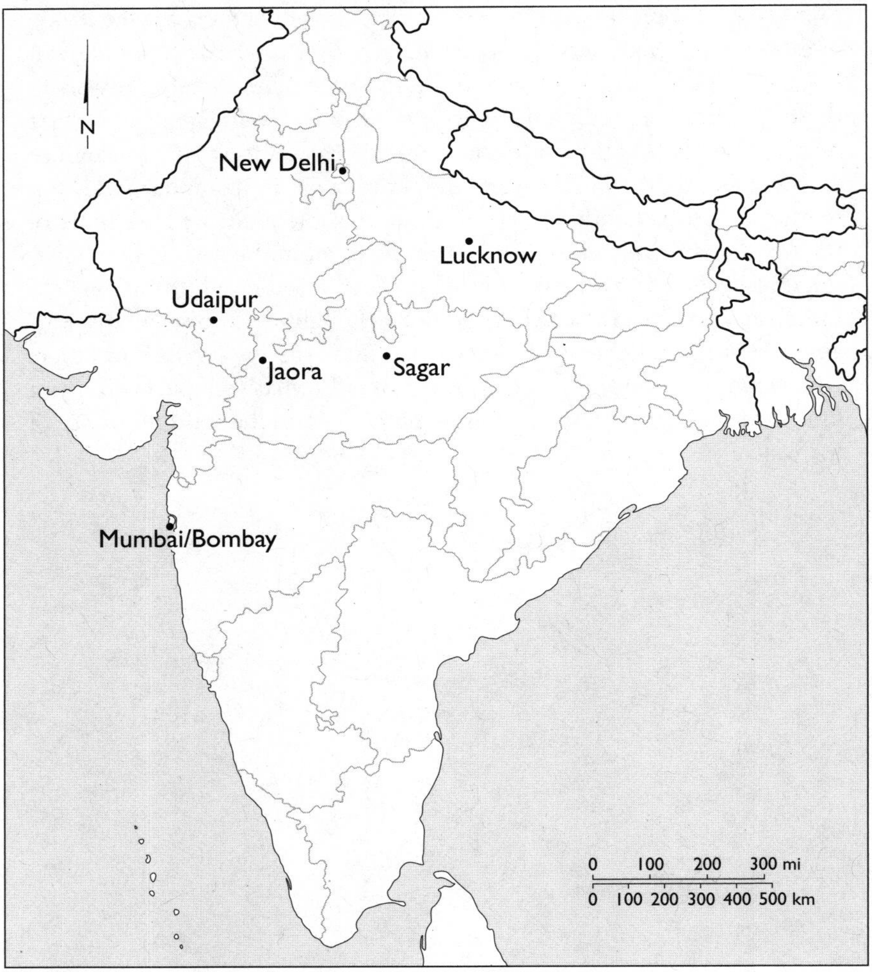

MAP 1. Jaora, India

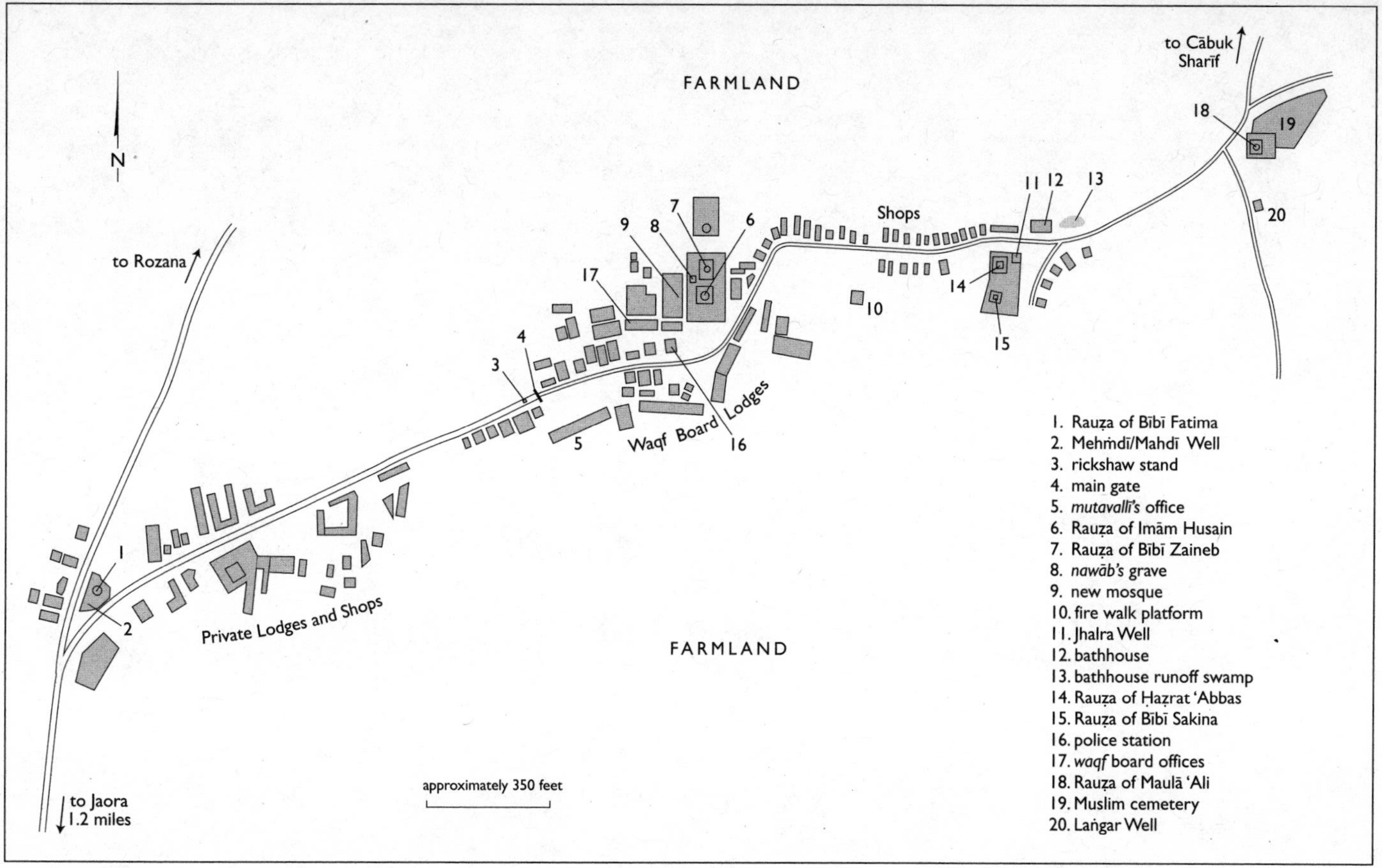
to Cābuk Sharīf
FARMLAND
N
to Rozana
Shops
Private Lodges and Shops
Waqf Board Lodges
FARMLAND
approximately 350 feet
to Jaora 1.2 miles
1. Rauẓa of Bībī Fatima
2. Mehṁdī/Mahdī Well
3. rickshaw stand
4. main gate
5. *mutavallī's* office
6. Rauẓa of Imām Husain
7. Rauẓa of Bībī Zaineb
8. *nawāb's* grave
9. new mosque
10. fire walk platform
11. Jhalra Well
12. bathhouse
13. bathhouse runoff swamp
14. Rauẓa of Ḥaẓrat 'Abbas
15. Rauẓa of Bībī Sakina
16. police station
17. *waqf* board offices
18. Rauẓa of Maulā 'Ali
19. Muslim cemetery
20. Laṅgar Well

MAP 2. Ḥusain Ṭekrī

INTRODUCTION

Ambiguity

Ḥusain Ṭekrī and Indian Dargāḥ Culture

This book is a description and interpretation of the everyday and ritual life of the collection of Muslim saint shrines that bear the name Ḥusain Ṭekrī; its primary texts include pilgrims' narratives as they have unfolded over many years, the shrines' major rituals, the bodies of pilgrims, local histories of Jaora state, and mass-produced pamphlets and books—on Islam, dargāḥs in general, and Ḥusain Ṭekrī in particular—written in Hindi and Urdu. Read carefully, I believe these texts help explain the cross-tradition popularity, power, and efficacy of Muslim saint shrines in India. As these shrines are places where psychological, physical, financial, and familial problems are resolved, their study can offer insight into South Asian perceptions of sickness, health, death, violence, justice, and personhood. Further, because elements of Ḥusain Ṭekrī's hybrid geography and ritual life are shared not only with many different types of Islamic memorial structures but also with non-Muslim sacred spaces, and because Muslim saint shrines in general are patronized by individuals of all religious backgrounds, ethnographic study of Ḥusain Ṭekrī in particular can provide a new, and I hope useful, vantage point for reconsidering debates about the nature of selfhood, religious identity, religious difference, and the nature of religion itself in contemporary India.

Because the act of naming reflects assumptions, observations, and conclusions, let me first explain some of my terminology and contextualize it in relation to previous historical and ethnographic study of dargāḥs. While it is certainly true that venerated Muslim teachers and healers are known by a wide range of honorifics, which may carry different meanings for different communities, in what follows I have purposefully used the term *saint* in place of many specific Urdu and Hindi terms and titles. Similarly, I have opted to use the word *shrine* in the place of a diverse range of Hindi and Urdu terms for memorial structures of revered Muslim saints. The most common titles of Muslim healers and teachers that I include in the category of "saint" are *walī* (pl. *auliyā*) and *k̲h̲wāja;* respectively, these terms connote friend (in this case, friend of God) and lord or master.[1] The category also includes *bābā* (father, grandfather, or old man), which is an extremely common title applied to venerated male healers and religious teachers of both Hindu and Muslim backgrounds.

While these terms connote elevated status, they are neither formal titles nor ritually bestowed by a Sufi order or other religious authorities, and they do not necessarily connote institutional power.[2] In general, then, these titles reflect the popular perception and acceptance of an individual's exceptional level of piety and morality, and as such, they derive their legitimacy from two sources: advanced age and/or closeness to God, the latter measured in terms of piety (arguably an observable and quantifiable set of behaviors) and love of God (a quality somewhat harder to observe and quantify).

Although these terms are commonly used at dargāḥs in general, Ḥusain Ṭekrī's pilgrims do not generally refer to Husain, 'Abbas, or 'Ali—the three male saints in whose memory the collection of shrines was built—as *auliyā* or *k̲h̲wāja.*[3] The neglect of these common titles may indicate that pilgrims generally recognize that these individuals—or their tombless shrines—are not of exactly the same type as those shrines built around the tombs of revered Sufis, whose relationships with Sufi lineages *(ṭarīqā*s*)* are often formalized and for whom the terms *auliyā* and *k̲h̲wājā* are in common use. Further, unlike many saints who are given the titles *auliyā* and *k̲h̲wāja,* the saints of Ḥusain Ṭekrī are associated with martyrdom: they are either martyrs themselves or close relatives of the martyrs, and this also sets them somewhat apart from many of the *auliyā* and *k̲h̲wāja* of the subcontinent.

Contrary to what one might expect, despite pilgrims' general awareness of the status of Husain and many of his companions as martyrs, the title *shahīd* (martyr) is not commonly used at Ḥusain Ṭekrī (as it is, for example, at the dargāḥ of Sarmad Shahīd, in Old Delhi). Rather, the full names (including titles) by which the saints of Ḥusain Ṭekrī are commonly known are Imām Husain, Ḥaẓrat 'Abbas (less commonly, Maulā 'Abbas), Maulā 'Ali, Bībī Fatima, Bībī Zaineb, and Bībī Sakina. Occasionally, *shāhzādī*—literally, from the Persian for female offspring of a king—is used by itself to refer to

Fatima or to any of the other female saints. *Bābā* is also a term applied to the male saints of Ḥusain Ṭekrī, particularly (though not exclusively) by Hindus.

While the title *ḥaẓrat,* meaning "excellence" or "highness," denotes temporal power, *maulā* and *imām* differ slightly from the more common terms *auliyā* and (to a lesser extent, perhaps) *k͟h͟wāja* in the sources of their authority. On the one hand, the term *imām,* like *auliyā,* derives its authority from the individual's piety and nearness to God; on the other hand, unlike *auliyā,* the titles *imām* and *maulā* also connote actual temporal power, responsibility, and authority.[4] In both Indian and extra-subcontinental contexts, *maulā* in particular is a title for a judge or a powerful landowner, and within Islamicate culture generally, an *imām* (literally, a leader) is both the title of the head of a particular mosque-centered community and the title given to the person who leads communal prayers.

In the Shiʿa context, the title of *imām* has an additional dimension, as ʿAli and Husain in particular are recognized by most Shiʿa as the first and third rightful *imāms,* or leaders, of the entire Islamic community. From a contemporary Shiʿa perspective, the legitimacy and authority of these and other Shiʿa *imāms* is complex. While valorized for their piety, closeness to God, and willingness to die for the protection of truth and justice, the Shiʿa *imāms* are also recognized as authoritative because they are descendants of Muhammad through ʿAli and Fatima. Further, they are understood by the majority of Shiʿa to be omniscient and to be created from the light of God *(nūr).* In this way, as *imāms,* they are possessed of a superhuman nature and God-given authority to lead the Muslim community.

On the one hand, the titles applied to the saints of Ḥusain Ṭekrī, whether related to their historical meaning or not, clearly reflect contemporary pilgrims' belief that these men, in addition to being lovers of God or chosen by God, also have the authority and the responsibility to rule justly and to lead actively; etymologically, these titles also have an administrative or organizational connotation that *bābā* and *auliyā* lack. On the other hand, the fact that the female saints of Ḥusain Ṭekrī, whose title *bībī* simply means "venerable woman," "lady," or "wife," function in exactly the same administrative and adjudicating capacity as those with the titles *maulā* and *imām* indicates that neither an explicitly administrative title, nor the status of a Shiʿa *imām,* nor the status of a martyr is a prerequisite for the type of work that Muslims saints do at saint shrines, specifically, acting in the capacity of a judge who offers healing through the disciplining or casting out of malevolent spirits.

Rather, whether male or female, friend of God or God's judge or representative, in the contemporary subcontinental context, a Muslim saint participates in a network that presumes a fundamental level of intimacy with divinity and both the capacity and the desire to intercede with the divine on behalf of pilgrims. For pilgrims seeking healing, all other distinctions between types of "saint" are secondary. Muslim saints' shrines, I suggest, are similarly interchangeable, despite the fact that the thousands of dargāḥs that dot the subcontinental landscape vary tremendously in size, type, and reputation. Some dargāḥs, like the dargāḥ of Muʿīn āl-dīn Chishtī in Ajmer, are pan-South Asian—or even global—places of pilgrimage. Others are humble graves—scattered across farmland, roadsides, crossroads, hilltops, and forests—known only to local residents. Many have regional reputations. Some allow women to enter the central shrine containing the grave of the saint and others do not. Some, like Ḥusain Ṭekrī, develop a reputation as places to go when radical and transgressive treatments are deemed necessary for healing, while others prohibit all but the most understated of ritual practices. Some house the graves of saints whose efficacy derives from their wild, wrathful temperaments, while others are built in memory of saints known for their mildness. All of them, however, are places where individuals of all religious backgrounds seek healing and succor.

I use the general terms "saint" and "shrine," therefore, because although they correspond neither with formal categories operative in institutional and extra-subcontinental Islamicate civilization nor with any single term in the Hindi or Urdu, they *do* accurately reflect the contemporary reality of popular culture at these memorial structures: pilgrims of all religious, caste, and class backgrounds recognize these edifices as being of the same fundamental type, and as fundamentally connected with one another. In other words, my choice of terminology reflects contemporary South Asia–specific usages of a range of terms and titles that can and do have different meanings in non–South Asian contexts and in orthodox or institutional Islamic contexts. Other scholars have documented a similar evolution of other extra-subcontinental Islamicate terms and systems of organization and power in the Indian cultural context: Muzaffar Alam, for example, has traced the transformation of the meaning and use of the term *sharīʿa* in Indo-Islamic culture,[5] and Joyce Burkhalter Flueckiger has discussed the tendency of contemporary Indian Muslim healers to identify as members of multiple Sufi lineages.[6]

While I am suggesting that in the modern South Asian context, Muslim saints have developed a particular and new level of connectedness and interchangeability, it is also true that certain extra-subcontinental Islamic concepts remain influential in the South Asian perception of Muslim saints, chief among them the major Islamic discourse of bearing witness. The term *shahīd,* or martyr, derives from an Arabic root meaning "to bear witness" (as does the Islamic declaration of faith, the *shahādah*), and by extension, the behavior of a Muslim pious enough to earn the titles of *auliyā* and *k̲h̲wājā* is itself a form of bearing witness to the greatness of God in the sense that a piously lived life is testament to the individual's recognition of the supremacy of God and his or her desire to draw ever closer to him.

If this notion of bearing witness is indeed part of what pilgrims of all religious backgrounds recognize as powerful and authoritative about Muslim saints, it follows that their shrines, or courts, would be places where testifying and bearing witness are particularly appropriate and effective. In fact, this is the case: at Ḥusain Ṭekrī and similar Muslim saint shrines throughout the subcontinent, by means of a practice called *ḥāẓirī,* pilgrims bear witness to the abuse they have suffered at the hands of others. This testimony is witnessed by fellow pilgrims as well as the saint, who is responsible for dispensing justice. The word *ḥāẓirī,* which translates literally as "presence," derives from Islamicate court culture, where it originally denoted an audience in a royal court. In the modern period, ḥāẓirī, which shares some characteristics with spirit possession and exorcism, is practiced by pilgrims of all religious backgrounds. Not all Muslim saint shrines host ḥāẓirī, and some explicitly discourage it, but even in these circumstances the culture of bearing witness exists in a less dramatic form, often through making the types petitions and vows that are also part of Ḥusain Ṭekrī's everyday and ritual life. In this way, the interchangeability and similarity of the authority and power of Muslim saint shrines in India—despite the diversity of honorifics and titles—also has roots in Islamicate culture's emphasis on bearing witness.

On the most basic level, then, I have chosen the term *Muslim saint shrines* because it accurately conveys the way in which pilgrims regard subcontinental Islamic memorial structures as connected and fundamentally interchangeable manifestations of a single type of power. Particular shrines develop particular reputations, of course, and pilgrims regularly speak of shrines as having hierarchal relationships, but there is no strong sense that visiting a shrine associated with one Sufi lineage or sectarian affiliation precludes visiting another with a different affiliation. The newly interchangeable character of Muslim saints and the resulting informal, nonsectarian relationships between shrines has several significant effects on pilgrims' experiences of healing. First, it contributes to what I describe as the cosmopolitan character of Ḥusain Ṭekrī, which is, I will argue, a foundational aspect of the appeal, power, and efficacy of this shrine and similar regionally or nationally famous Muslim saint shrines. Second, the very authority and power of Muslim saints and their shrines derives in large part from their participation in the network of shrines across the subcontinent that are home to this shared culture.

And what exactly is this culture? Simply put, I believe that dargāḥ culture is properly understood as a (religious) culture in and of itself, rather than a culture that draws its forms of authority and practice from Hinduism, Islam, or a syncretic combination of the two. Rather than "Hindu" or "Muslim," Indian dargāḥ culture is South Asian. In this regard, I partially agree with Peter van der Veer's claim that "Islam and Christianity in India are also Indian religions," particularly when one considers shared ritual practices.[7] Building on van der Veer's insight, however, I will argue that what makes dargāḥ culture both a unique (religious) culture and a particularly South Asian culture is not simply shared ritual practices, nor even shared ritual grammar. Further, I will claim that South Asian dargāḥ culture in particular offers a view beyond the category of religion as it is often assumed in statements like van der Veer's. Finally, I will suggest that Muslim saint shrines and the practices associated with them invite reexamination of many of the common categories of religious studies, including liminality and sacred space.

Of course, dargāḥs and similar Islamicate memorial structures exist in many areas of the world outside South Asia, where they are often associated with healing. In this regard, dargāḥ culture is not uniquely South Asian. However, in the context of South Asian culture in the Western diaspora, the fact that South Asian immigrants to Europe and North America do *not* habitually build shrines to Muslim saints even though they *do* build churches, mosques, temples, and *gurudwaras* (Sikh houses of worship) strongly indicates that Muslim saint shrine culture encompasses forms of religiosity, economy, legitimacy, and authority that are particular to South Asian culture as it exists in a *subcontinental* context rather than particular to exclusively Hindu, Muslim, Sikh, or Christian institutions.[8]

In what follows, drawing primarily on ethnographic fieldwork undertaken at Ḥusain Ṭekrī, I will identify the sources of Muslim saint shrines' authority and the elements that comprise their unique identity and function. I will argue that Muslim saint shrines are simultaneously local *and* cosmopolitan, and that they are fundamentally shaped by cross-tradition exchange. The culture I am describing is not, it is important to note, syncretism, which by definition involves the "synthesis" of elements of various traditions into a harmonious whole. Rather, I suggest that for pilgrims, the power and legitimacy of Ḥusain Ṭekrī derive in large part from the opportunity it affords them to encounter others in ways that are dangerous and transgressive on the one hand, and built around shared expressions of submission, devotion, and remembrance on the other. Together, these elements comprise Ḥusain Ṭekrī's ritual life and everyday culture and the source of its power and its legitimacy. As such, they constitute what Muslim saint shrines are uniquely able to contribute to South Asian religious life and notions of religious identity.

I am suggesting that much—though by no means all—of what is characteristic of contemporary Muslim saint shrine culture—dargāḥ culture—derives from sources other than dargāḥs' historic roots in the greater Islamic tradition. This assertion is not a variation on the old, racist, and historically untenable Orientalist distinction between rigid, legalistic Islam and the "tolerant" or "spiritual" Sufi tradition; nor does it participate in the similarly problematic distinction between "Aryan" and "Semitic" cultures. Rather, since ethnographic observation of dargāḥ culture plainly shows that the relationship between historically Islamic institutions and doctrines and contemporary dargāḥ life is exceedingly complex, the question of how Ḥusain Ṭekrī in particular—and Muslim saint shrines in general—do and do not derive their authority from their Islamic identity is necessarily a central issue in any discussion of dargāḥ culture.

Before turning to the larger topic of the contemporary life of Muslim saint shrines, I would first like to discuss briefly Muslim saint shrines' historical connection to Muslim rulers and institutions and Ḥusain Ṭekrī's historical relationship with the *nawāb*s of Jaora, since these connections help explain some aspects of Muslim saint shrine culture in the modern period, if not all pilgrims' perceptions of these aspects. Some historical studies of dargāḥs give the impression that dargāḥs' authority and legitimacy were unambiguously, if not exclusively, linked to Muslim rulers and institutions, and indeed, in the precolonial period, Muslim shrines *were* deeply implicated in the legitimation of Muslim rulers and in turn derived their own legitimacy from symbolic and actual association with those rulers. However, this picture is incomplete owing to historical studies' neglect of popular perceptions of the shrines and non-Muslim use of and contributions to the culture of these shrines. This is likely due in large part to a lack of sources: the experiences and contributions of non-Muslim pilgrims who visited Muslim saint shrines centuries or even just decades ago are generally not preserved in writing, and they simply have been lost with the passing of time.[9]

Muslim Shrines in India: Their Character, History, and Significance is a seminal and typical historical study of Indian dargāḥs: its authors analyze

Indian Muslim shrines' authority and legitimacy almost entirely by relating these shrines to imperial authority, extra-subcontinental individuals, or to Sufi terms, concepts, and institutions. The patronage and contributions of non-Muslims and subcontinental systems of thought and practice are not, however, central to the analysis offered by the articles.[10] Similarly, P. M. Currie's impressive *The Shrine and Cult of Mu'īn al-dīn Chishtī of Ajmer,* still one of the most comprehensive studies of what is arguably the most famous dargāḥ in India, is primarily concerned with the development of the religious and political authority of the dargāḥ of Ajmer in relation to Muslim (and particularly Mughal) rule; again, the participation of non-Muslims in the shrine's ritual life is neglected.[11]

Other significant historical studies of dargāḥ life have included subcontinental elements in their discussion of dargāḥs' legitimacy and authority. Richard Eaton's "Political and Religious Authority of the Shrine of Bābā Farīd" concerns itself with the question of how the early modern operators of Muslim shrines legitimated their authority over their patrons, suggesting that non-Muslim (in this case, *jāt*)[12] patronage of the shrine of Bābā Farīd was largely a response to the potential for social advancement offered by a non-Hindu institution; in particular, Eaton suggests that South Asian Muslim groups were drawn to such shrines because they offered a distinctly South Asian source of Islamic authority.[13] The shrine's governing family legitimated itself with pageantry and ceremony normally associated with Mughal or (more generally) Muslim courts, and the shrine itself served as a means to integrate heterogeneous people and subjects religiously, politically, and socially. Specifically, Eaton cites the ceremonial tying of a turban on the *dīwān,* or hereditary spiritual leader of the dargāḥ, as a defining moment in the ritual life of the shrine, stating that "the tying of the turban possessed a great symbolic repertoire: it defined relations of kinship between the shrine and subordinate clans, it symbolically conferred legitimacy on actual rulers in Delhi, and it conferred spiritual discipleship on the shrine itself."[14] Similarly, although a large portion of his project is concerned with other issues, speaking to the effect of dargāḥs upon non-Hindus, Carl Ernst's study of a major South Indian Sufi center suggests that during the centuries of Muslim rule in India, dargāḥs often employed symbolic language and rituals that brought together imperial, Sufi, and local signifiers of authority.[15] As such, they functioned as important places for the consolidation of temporal and spiritual authority for both rulers and the hereditary heads *(sajjādā naśīn)* of the shrines themselves.

Like many dargāḥs, Ḥusain Ṭekrī enjoyed an official affiliation with a Muslim ruler; its last royal patron was Nawāb Iftikar Ali Khan, who died in 1947. The collection of shrines was housed within and maintained by the Muslim princely state of Jaora until the state's dissolution in 1948, and as such it served to legitimate Muslim kingship in Jaora. The grave of Nawāb Muhammad Ismail Khan, the ruler at the time of Ḥusain Ṭekrī's founding in 1886, is located in the courtyard of the shrine built in memory of Imām Husain. In a Muslim saint shrine, it is common for the disciples and wife of an esteemed *pīr* to be buried in the courtyard of the shrine that houses the body of the *pīr* himself. At Ḥusain Ṭekrī, the location of the *nawāb*'s grave in the courtyard of the shrine of Imām Husain, the grandson of Muhammad, unambiguously places the *nawāb* in the lineage of the descendants of the only truly uncontroversial leader of the Muslim community: Muhammad himself.[16] Interestingly, in this case there is an inversion of the relationship between a dargāḥ's authority and the authority of the ruler: the ruler legitimates his authority by placing himself in relation to a long-dead martyr-saint who is also a close relative of Muhammad rather than in relation to a central Muslim ruler. Possibly the *nawāb* of Jaora legitimated himself in relation to a close relative of Muhammad at least in part because the central and dominant ruler was, in this case, the colonial government. In legitimating his rule by emphasizing his relationship to long-deceased relatives of Muhammad rather than a living Sufi saint or Sufi lineage, the *nawāb* of Jaora also effectively sidestepped potential power struggles or confrontations resulting from his management of the shrines and their revenue.

While the current *mutavallī* (manager) of Ḥusain Ṭekrī, Haji Sarwar 'Ali Khan, is a descendant of the *nawāb*s of Jaora, there is, of course, no longer a reigning Muslim ruler affiliated with the site.[17] However, while it is clear that Indian dargāḥs no longer have a ritual or administrative relationship with the modern government of India, it is also clear that, like other dargāḥs throughout the subcontinent, Ḥusain Ṭekrī's legitimacy continues to derive in part from its ongoing use of court symbols and legal language. Although the Urdu term dargāḥ historically connotes a royal court *(darbār)* rather than a legal court *('adālat),* contemporary pilgrims' understanding of dargāḥs as courts seems to encompass both of these meanings, with many of the aspects of registering a case at a dargāḥ also taking on characteristics of registering a case in a modern Indian government court.[18] A contemporary dargāḥ pilgrim's vocabulary is infused with legal language: in addition to *'arẓ* (petition) and *mannat* (vow), common terms include *ḥukm* (command), *'adālat* (court), *darbār* (court), *faislā* (the Hindi pronunciation of the Urdu *faiṣala,* or judgment), the borrowed English terms "court" and "case," and of course the word *dargāḥ* (royal court) itself.[19]

FIGURE 2. Pilgrims at the rauẓa of Imām Husain.

Contemporary pilgrims to Ḥusain Ṭekrī conceive of their petitions to the saints as cases filed in a court of law, and the standard procedure for lodging a case reflects notions of a royal court as well as actions that seem to be influenced by contemporary Indian court procedure. Upon arrival at the site, pilgrims purchase a length of mottled red-and-white cord that has been cut into two pieces; the shorter piece is tied to the metal latticework that covers the shrines' windows, and the longer one is tied around the petitioner's neck, right wrist, right arm, or waist.[20] While tying the cord to the latticework, the pilgrim offers his or her petition to the saint; most commonly, the petition is referred to as a *mannat, ʿarẓ,* or, in English, "case."[21] After making a petition, the pilgrim understands him- or herself to be available for ḥāẓirī (literally, presence).

Ḥāẓirī looks a great deal like a form of exorcism: the malevolent spirit speaks through the body of the pilgrim and is interrogated and physically disciplined by one of the saints of the shrine. To an outside observer, interrogation of the malevolent spirit appears to be a one-way conversation, since no one but the spirit can hear the voice of the saint. The saint's statements and actions can only be inferred by the statements made by the malevolent spiritual presence. Thus, for example, if a spiritual presence said,

"I'll never tell who did the magic that sent me, no matter how much you beat me!" and then the body of the person in ḥāẓirī was suddenly thrown onto the ground, an outside observer would understand that the saint was interrogating the spirit, attempting to elicit the information necessary to render a *faislā,* or judgment. In these interrogations, the generic honorifics *maulā* (lord) and *bībī* (lady) are most commonly used to address the saints. I will undertake a full analysis of the ritual life of Ḥusain Ṭekrī in chapters 3 and 4, but to understand dargāḥ culture as court culture, it is of primary significance that ḥāẓirī, observed as a performance, is conceptually and semantically embedded within the language of legal process.

In the contemporary period, these court-based rituals and symbols remain meaningful to pilgrims for two related reasons, neither of which is closely related to dargāḥs' historic relationship with Islamicate courts. First, they signal and substantiate Ḥusain Ṭekrī's membership in the endless network of Muslim saint shrines. Thus, while patronage of a particular Muslim saint shrine no longer relates saints, disciples, and pilgrims together in ways that are hierarchal and bound to a central Muslim temporal ruler (as was the case, Eaton argued, for Bābā Farīd's dargāḥ), patronage of a Muslim saint shrine and participation in its court-tinged rituals and vocabulary give contemporary pilgrims the in fact quite accurate sense that they are part of a pan-Indian community of dargāḥ patrons, imbuing visits to even the most humble of local dargāḥs with a sense that the pilgrim is cultivating a portion of his or her identity that transcends local social structures and restrictions. In other words, while the symbols and language of Muslim royal courts and legal courts remain powerful connective devices, in the contemporary period, they connect shrines to other shrines rather than to a ruler.

Second, dargāḥs wield substantive political authority, as the justice they offer petitioners often leads to actual change in individual lives. Like Hindu kings in the colonial period, dargāḥs in contemporary India possess a symbolic authority that lacks an institutionalized relationship with actual political authority.[22] However, while none of the pilgrims who come to the "court" of Ḥusain Ṭekrī explicitly assert that there is a relationship between the modern Indian state and the saints (indeed, pilgrims often dismiss the government of India and its courts as impotent), a decision in the court of Ḥusain Ṭekrī can be as binding and meaningful as a decision in a government court.[23] In fact, the legitimacy of the dargāḥ as an efficacious court is strengthened by the fact that state courts in contemporary India have a reputation for being corrupt and slow, making the opportunity to mobilize a legal discourse in an alternative and possibly more efficient and honest tribunal an extremely attractive option. The conceptual overlap between state courts and dargāḥs is also evidenced by the practice of tying photocopies of petitions to the latticework of the dargāḥ of Feroz Shah in Delhi, which parallels the necessity of making reproductions of documents when pursuing a case in a government court.[24]

In the modern period, the Indian dargāḥ has managed to retain both political and religious relevance: through the legitimizing personalities of its saints—none of whom are temporal rulers in the strictest sense—it retains authority that is remarkably political in nature on both the level of language and function. Widespread cross-tradition belief in the destructive potential of malevolent magic also contributes to the reputation of dargāḥs as effective courts, and not only among those too poor or uneducated to seek justice in government courts. For example, a middle-aged upper-caste Hindu man whom I met during both my initial and follow-up research at Ḥusain Ṭekrī explained to me that he was the victim of magic performed by an old woman who lived in a small village in rural Rajasthan. He had sought protection and justice by attempting to register his case with various human rights organizations in India, including, he said, Human Rights Watch, but he felt that his case had not been properly addressed. The man was absolutely in earnest; he had fliers with a description of his situation, and he took more hope than perhaps he should have from the fact that I interviewed him. Like countless pilgrims with whom I had conversations at Ḥusain Ṭekrī, this man recognized that this was the only institution that took his magic-generated problems seriously. Similarly, when an unfortunate confrontation at a Ḥusain Ṭekrī satellite *imāmbāṛā* in Bombay resulted in a police investigation, the family that owns the shrine made a significant effort to protect itself, hiring a photographer to take pictures of the daily routine at the shrine and seeking signatures on a petition that testified to the signers' voluntary participation in the ritual life of the *imāmbāṛā*. Members of this family freely acknowledged that the police "don't believe in magic," and they therefore felt the need to defend themselves. In both cases, the victims realized that magic could only be dealt with in a dargāḥ setting, making the dargāḥ court better than the government court.[25]

During the period of widespread Muslim rule in India, dargāḥs' legitimacy was linked explicitly with state power. However, the severing of those links in the contemporary period has not diminished the effectiveness of these dargāḥs as either *'adālat* or *darbār*. The dargāḥ's crown is not, it seems, hollow, and though it has changed in form from the colonial Muslim princely state to contemporary Indian contexts, the dargāḥ arguably has always offered pilgrims a means to seek justice and judgment with real-world consequences, whether an actual connection to the state exists or not. The contemporary legitimacy of the dargāḥ as a court has both historic elements and new ones: on the one hand, its authority is perpetuated in part through the continued use of legal language and rituals that evoke Muslim royal courts; on the other, its authority is perpetuated through the way that court-derived rituals and symbols substantiate each dargāḥ's participation in a newly unstructured, massive network of Muslim saint shrines: the dargāḥ's prestige exists in direct proportion to both its place in this larger-than-local-life network and the range of pilgrims it attracts. Thus, dargāḥs' authority in contemporary India is shaped in part by their historical connections to Muslim courts and in part by modern reconfigurations of the relationships between shrines and the resultant cosmopolitan culture.[26]

But do dargāḥs' historical connections with Islamic institutions and Muslim rulers and the resultant courtlike culture mean that, for contemporary pilgrims, dargāḥ culture in general and Ḥusain Ṭekrī's culture in particular is uncomplicatedly Islamic, or even uncomplicatedly Islamicate? The latter term, coined by the historian Marshall Hodgson, distinguishes itself from "Islam" by "refer[ring] not directly to the religion, Islam, itself, but to the social and cultural complex historically associated with Islam and the Muslims, both among Muslims themselves and even when found among non-Muslims."[27] A related methodological question would be whether or not this book, as a study of contemporary dargāḥ culture, is an anthropology of Islam. To answer these questions, it is worth recalling the seminal work of Talal Asad,[28] who is in large part responsible for the widespread recognition that "Islam" and "Islamic" are neither academic categories of analysis nor atemporal, autonomous, unchanging forces.[29] Rather, they are best understood as discursive fields.[30] In this regard, current trends in the study of religion in general and Islam in particular in part seek to correct earlier scholarship's conflation of the "universal" with the "textual," and its attendant failure to recognize that the spheres of "oral" and "written" are both mutually influential and often not operative categories in the culture under investigation.[31] Along these lines, Asad has argued that "if one wants to write an anthropology of Islam, one should begin, as Muslims do, from the concept of a discursive tradition that includes and relates itself to the founding texts."[32] Building on this initial trend, Varisco, in his comprehensive survey of anthropologies of Islam, has suggested that anthropologies of Islam document the process of "an islam defining itself as Islam."[33] As a discourse-focused approach, this involves study of the means used in particular cultural contexts to create meaningful connections between the founding texts of the Islamic tradition and local cultures and lives.[34]

Generally speaking, then, a discourse-based study of Islam involves identifying the ways in which principal Islamic texts—chiefly the Qur'an; *sīrah,* or biographies of the Prophet Muhammad; and hadith, or collections of Muhammad's sayings—become authoritative in particular local discourses and communities and documenting the ways in which local communities make explicit connections between their own situations and these founding texts. In both cases, the focus upon discourse involves analysis that takes both form and content into account. Specifically, a discourse-centered approach to the study of Islam ought to address all of the following: 1) whether a discourse references Islamic names or objects; 2) whether a discourse contains stories, themes, values, or worldviews that historically have been emphasized in founding Islamic texts; 3) whether elements of foundational Islamic texts are introduced into a culture and maintained within that culture by means that have precedent in Islamic communities; and 4) whether the elements of foundational Islamic texts derive their legitimacy in a community in ways that have precedent in the Islamic tradition.

Of these four areas, Ḥusain Ṭekrī's participation in Islamic and Islamicate culture derives primarily from the first and, to a lesser extent, the second, that is, from its association with Islamic names, objects, themes, and stories derived from the founding texts of the tradition. However, the sources of legitimacy of these objects, themes, and stories, as well as their means of introduction and transmission within the culture of Ḥusain Ṭekrī, do not derive exclusively (or in some cases at all) from Islamic precedents. Therefore, it seems that if the culture of the place is to be described as a whole, it cannot simply be described as an Islamic one: the culture's creators, many of whom are non-Muslim, do not uniformly seek to define "an islam as Isḷam"; nor do they regularly or explicitly relate the shrine to the founding texts of the Islamic tradition or consistently use historically Islamic means of introducing and maintaining relationships between dargāḥ culture and the founding texts and major concepts of the Islamic tradition.

Pilgrims' perceptions of the relationship between Ḥusain Ṭekrī and the founding texts of Islam are shaped in part by their religious backgrounds. In the context of the experiences, actions, and narratives that together comprise the healing processes of Ḥusain Ṭekrī's non-Muslim pilgrims, there is no widespread tendency to define the site *explicitly* as Islamic or Muslim or to relate it to the founding texts of the Islamic tradition. This is the case in large part because those with non-Muslim backgrounds lack the intention and expertise necessary to relate the shrines to the founding texts of Islam or to create connections between local relationships and an imagined translocal phenomenon of Islam. This is not to say, however, that Ḥusain Ṭekrī does not "read" as an Islamic space to its non-Muslim pilgrims, or that meaningful connections between Islamic texts (whether explicitly recognized as such or not) and local non-Muslim cultures and lives are not made by those pilgrims who are not Muslim. Though not made for the purposes of defining "an islam as Islam," such connections are certainly created and cultivated by non-Muslim pilgrims. Most important, the unstated but vitally operative recognition of Ḥusain Ṭekrī as an emphatically "other" space is, I suggest, central to non-Muslim pilgrims' healing processes there. Thus, for non-Muslim pilgrims, the appeal, authority, and legitimacy of the site derive in part from its identity as "other," specifically, its identity as "Islamic." This basic status as "other" has many consequences. For women in particular, because Muslim saint shrines are removed from the close relationship between religious and family life that exists in the Hindu tradition, they become attractive venues for healing when aspects of the pilgrim's illness are linked to broken family relationships.

The question of how *Muslim* pilgrims relate Ḥusain Ṭekrī to the founding texts of Islam is considerably more complicated, in part because within this community the diversity in levels of knowledge of these primary texts is significant. Generally speaking, the extent to which Muslim pilgrims do not *explicitly* reference the Qur'an is striking, though several stories with origins in the Qur'an and hadith collections are widely related by Muslim pilgrims when discussing the nature of Ḥusain Ṭekrī. Elements from these foundational Islamic texts that are invoked with some regularity include stories about the magic wielded by Pharaoh's magicians when confronted by Moses and the assertion that Muhammad had magic performed on him. The story about Moses and Pharaoh's magicians has Qur'anic origins[35] and was generally invoked by pilgrims to explain to me—presumably a skeptical Westerner—that magic is a real force in the world. Stories about magic being performed on the Prophet are not explicitly Qur'anic, though there are elements of the Qur'an that provoked later generations of Muslim scholars to speculate about Muhammad's vulnerability to magic; of these, the two final suras, or chapters, of the Qur'an are understood to have been given to Muhammad to protect him from magic and from resistance to his message during his lifetime. In contemporary India, framed calligraphic renderings of these two suras can be found on the walls of Muslim (and occasionally non-Muslim) homes and businesses; these suras are also commonly placed in *ta'vīẕ* (small metal boxes containing Qur'anic verses in Arabic, worn on a string around the neck or upper right arm). Notably, at Ḥusain Ṭekrī these stories about magic and Muhammad are not explicitly cited as "Qur'anic" or even "Muslim"; rather, they are authoritative and popular simply because they are stories about people whose lives provide answers to the types of questions with which pilgrims wrestle.

Stories about magic being performed on Muhammad are preserved in the hadith collections,[36] though none of the pilgrims who related this anecdote to me knew the specifics of the hadith, or even felt it necessary to legitimate the story with a *ṣaḥīḥ* (sound) pedigree. Rather, all that mattered was that Muhammad, by definition the most perfect of humans, had been hurt by magic. For the afflicted at Ḥusain Ṭekrī—the self-proclaimed *maʿṣūm,* or "innocent ones"—this is incredibly important: just as Muhammad suffered unjustly because of the magical machinations of others, so they suffer. This identity as an innocent victim combats other, less victim-friendly theories about magic and misfortune that circulate within contemporary South Asian culture, such as the idea that victims suffer because it is predestined, or because they have been remiss in their religious obligations, or because they have bad karma.

Again, to understand Ḥusain Ṭekrī's identity and appeal vis-à-vis its Islamic roots, it is important to recognize that these stories' authority and legitimacy derive from a combination of their ability to speak to the situation of Muslim and non-Muslim pilgrims, their fairly wide distribution, and their simple use of Muhammad's identity. Similarly, the relationship between the suffering of pilgrims and accounts of the suffering of the martyrs of Karbala is significant. Stories of Muhammad being a victim of magic, originally shared orally by Muslims, are also related and readily accepted by Hindus and other non-Muslims. In telling them, pilgrims are generally uninterested in making explicit connections between individual situations, local cultures, and founding texts of the Islamic tradition, and this being the case, it does not seem that the major project of pilgrims at Ḥusain Ṭekrī is to define "an islam as Islam," particularly if this process is understood as a self-conscious one. To be clear, then, Ḥusain Ṭekrī's pilgrims recognize stories about Muhammad, Husain, and other major Islamic figures as legitimate not simply because they are contained in a hadith collection or the Qur'an.[37] Rather, their authority derives in large part from other sources—sources that have far more to do with Indian subcontinental culture in general and the situation of pilgrims in particular.

Turning from pilgrims' use of Islamic texts, names, and stories to their engagement with forms of authority that have historically been recognized as *Islamic* within Islamicate cultures, there is no simple answer to the question of whether or not forms of legitimacy, transmission, and authority at Ḥusain Ṭekrī have Islamic precedent and/or "read" as Islamic in the same way and for the same reasons. If, for example, as Richard Bulliet has argued, hadith literature was generated from individual conversations about proper Islamic behavior, and reflects the concerns and anxieties of many non-Arab local cultures, at first glance it seems that a similar process marks the discourse of pilgrims at Ḥusain Ṭekrī; the stories about Muhammad that are frequently repeated are those that speak to the concerns of the local pilgrim population.[38] However, while both types of conversation are driven by the attempt to make the present meaningful by relating it to the past, the pilgrims' discourse is motivated not by the desire to become a better Muslim, but rather by the desire to make sense of and improve their often quite miserable situations. Here another aspect of the complex culture of Ḥusain Ṭekrī is in evidence: while pilgrims' use of narratives about Muhammad to make sense of their own situation is remarkably similar in form to the process that shaped the composition of hadith, the motivations behind these forms and processes are quite different. Further, in the case of the formation of hadith collections, stories were recognized as authoritative in part because of the person relating them (ultimately, this form of authority was inscribed in the *isnād,* or chain of transmission), whereas at Ḥusain Ṭekrī, the status of the teller is not a foundational aspect of the legitimacy of the story. Again, it is the content of the story itself—its message and its characters' Muslim identities—that seems to be the primary source of its power and authority among pilgrims.

Ḥusain Ṭekrī's culture participates in the tendency to locate authority in the spoken rather than the written word. In Islamicate culture, the authoritativeness of the spoken word is ultimately grounded in the aural nature of Qur'anic revelation, a primacy that is, as Brinkley Messick notes in his discussion of authority in Islam,[39] reinforced by the Arabic script itself: like other Semitic languages, Arabic records consonants but leaves vowels to be intuited by the individual reading the text. The attitude reflected in and reinforced by this script assumes intimacy with the text and suggests that the most complete and powerful form of the text is the recited one. Similarly, ḥāẓirī is predicated upon the primacy of the authority of the spoken word: the process of ḥāẓirī as well as the saints' eventual resolution of the problem (the *faislā*) are spoken. As was the case in the apparent parallel between the origin of hadith literature and the use of stories about Muhammad, here there seems to be a parallel between forms of authority that have historically been recognized as Islamic and forms of authority that are operative within the culture of Ḥusain Ṭekrī.

However, it is difficult, if not impossible, to make the case that this emphasis on the authority and power of the spoken word is a contribution of the Islamic tradition and Islamicate culture to South Asia: forms of the spoken word have long been recognized as authoritative in many of the traditions of the subcontinent, from the proper recitation of Vedic texts and mantras to the *satyakrīya,* or truth act, which entails the victim declaring that depending on the truth of his or her statements and his or her status as innocent, either the victim or his or her enemies will suffer dire consequences. Moreover, non-Muslim pilgrims' patterns of patronage and narratives show that contemporary dargāḥ culture in India overlaps with the culture of certain Hindu temples, particularly those to Hanumān, Devī, and Śani. Indeed, other scholars have discussed Hindu healing practices that seem to share some rituals and concepts with dargāḥs.[40] Consequently, some of Ḥusain Ṭekrī's forms of authority and rituals are easily recognizable by individuals with non-Muslim religious backgrounds, though these forms of authority and rituals are not consistently or explicitly equated with their non-Muslim counterparts. However, Hindu pilgrims to Ḥusain Ṭekrī often note the inability of Hindu deities to solve their problems, citing prior failed visits to temples dedicated to these deities. In this way, Ḥusain Ṭekrī participates in a larger culture that is also home to explicitly Hindu places and forms of authority and legitimacy.

In my analysis of Ḥusain Ṭekrī's sources of authority and legitimacy, I distinguish between a recognizably Islamic name or text (such as Fatima or the Qur'an) and a historically Islamic form of religious authority (recitation, for example). Of the former, there are ample examples at Ḥusain Ṭekrī; the shrines themselves are built in memory of major figures in Islamic history and culture. These Islamic names, however, do not make the site's authority uncomplicatedly Islamic in the second sense of the term, that is, on the level of historically Islamic forms of authority and sources of legitimacy. In this sense there is considerably more ambiguity about the religious identity of Ḥusain Ṭekrī's authority, since many of the major forms of religious authority there have clear analogues in both the greater Hindu and greater Islamic tradition. Thus, the sources of the site's authority are not fixed, but rather are determined by context, audience, and constantly changing combinations of Islamic names, narratives, and objects; these sources are in some cases historically Islamic, and in other cases equally at home in both the greater Islamic and greater Hindu traditions.

Beyond dargāḥ culture, general studies of Hindu-Muslim forms of religious life and interaction have shown that popular forms of religious expression, practice, and narrative are themselves the true bridges across traditions.[41] In other words, these studies have suggested that form rather than content facilitates cross-tradition exchange and participation. While I agree with this sentiment, I take it not as a conclusion but rather as my point of departure, since a simple coincidence of forms of religious expression alone cannot explain why it is that, if there is no shortage of Hindu temples, shrines, and religious professionals, so many Hindus and other non-Muslims continue to regard patronage of dargāḥs in particular as desirable and necessary.

In subsequent chapters I will show that the ambiguity inherent in Ḥusain Ṭekrī's culture and the use that all of its pilgrims make of this ambiguity—in both their own self-presentation and their interaction with others—are central elements in pilgrims' healing processes and experiences. I will also suggest that the related concept of otherness itself is central to both the culture of Muslim saint shrines and pilgrims' healing processes, and I will show that for both Muslim and non-Muslim pilgrims, this otherness is primarily couched in terms of religion and marked as transgressive, polluting/polluted, and dangerous. The dominance of discourses of religious identity in pilgrims' healing processes and narratives is one reason I am disinclined to classify Ḥusain Ṭekrī's culture as simply Islamicate, since that term was coined in part to shift scholarly focus from Islam as a religion (whatever that might be) to Islam as a civilizational force. Despite dargāḥs' clear historical and ongoing connections to Islamic institutions and forms of authority, I suggest that dargāḥ culture is neither Islamic nor Islamicate.

The idea that dargāḥ culture is neither Islamic nor Islamicate—if not my assertion that dargāḥ culture is both a distinct (religious) culture and particularly South Asian—is more readily seen in ethnographic and anthropological works on dargāḥs than it is in historical studies. Owing to the presence of many non-Muslim pilgrims at the shrines, ethnographic and anthropological studies of dargāḥ life, unlike historical studies, necessarily take the non-Muslim patronage of and contributions to the culture of Muslim saint shrines into account. As they grapple with the immediately observable reality of Muslim saint shrines' cross-tradition appeal, such studies tend to focus on the ways in which these shrines are shared or contested sites, emphasizing either their potential to bring individuals of diverse religious backgrounds together or (less commonly) their ability to tear them apart. Dargāḥs, these studies suggest, usually defy the increasing communalization of religious identity in contemporary India, but they may also serve as flashpoints.

The issue of religious identity is often a primary concern for those who work on Indian Islam generally and contemporary dargāḥ culture in particular.[42] Thus, it has been suggested that the simultaneous use of Muslim saint shrines by Hindus and non-Hindus is best understood as a cause of intra-Muslim conflict and that Hindu presence at the shrines is either a corruption of Islam or irrelevant;[43] as evidence of the fundamentally syncretic and, until recently, noncommunal culture of such shrines;[44] and as evidence that lived Indian religion organizes itself around shared ritual vocabulary, personages, and narratives rather than ideologically delineated, politicized notions of identity.[45] The contemporary identity of these shrines is seen by some scholars as increasingly marked by communalism,[46] though Yogindar Sikand rightly notes that dargāḥs are not unique in their status as contested religious spaces, since adherents of Brahminical Hinduism have been incorporating non-Brahminical traditions for many centuries.[47]

When arguing that dargāḥs are sites that defy communalism, some scholars emphasize the boundary-transcending nature of devotional religion in India. Thus, for example, Desiderio Pinto's discussion of pilgrims' devotional relationships with saints' shrines suggests (not incorrectly, though incompletely) that it is the pan-Indian phenomenon of devotional religion that accounts for the presence of non-Muslim petitioners to the shrines.[48] While this is partially true, Pinto makes no attempt to engage the question of what it means that non-Muslims would seek devotional relationships with saints who are explicitly Muslim. Paul Jackson's study of dargāḥs in the northern Indian city of Patna draws a similar conclusion; while his argument is not exclusively concerned with non-Muslim participation in dargāḥ life per se, it does note that the primary function of dargāḥs is to "bring them [Hindus and Muslims] together."[49] Along these lines, *Dargahs: Abodes of the Saints,* a collection of essays on the most renowned dargāḥs of the subcontinent written by major scholars for a popular audience, emphasizes the anticaste, devotional aspects of dargāḥ culture, linking this devotional culture with the legacies of the Sufi saints buried in them.[50]

In their quest to find alternative means to explain the cross-tradition appeal of dargāḥs, many scholars who reject the idea that devotional religion or shared forms of religious expression are the bedrock of dargāḥ culture take strong positions on the utility (or lack thereof) of the model of syncretism and Victor Turner's oft-critiqued and occasionally defended concepts of communitas and liminality. Of these, syncretism seems finally to have died an undignified death, the definitive blow being struck by Ernst, who succinctly argues that syncretism is inherently condescending and fundamentally flawed insofar as it necessarily posits ahistorical and pure categories, for example, Hindu and Muslim.[51] Along these lines, in his study of popular Muslim culture in the South Indian state of Karnataka, Jackie Assayag has rejected syncretism as a useful paradigm for understanding dargāḥ culture.[52]

In her study of dargāḥs in northwestern India, Shail Mayaram has proposed a variation on the Turnerian notion of communitas.[53] Following an argument originally made by the anthropologist Michael Lambeck, she suggests that dargāḥs are "microcosmic public spaces"; she argues that as individuals negotiate new identities in these spaces, they create a new type of communitas in which pilgrims are united by the desire to challenge socially sanctioned collective identities.[54] It is clear that Ḥusain Ṭekrī is both a microcosmic public space and a place where individuals, through participation in the ritual and everyday life of the shrines, develop new identities. However, as I explore pilgrims' narratives and experiences in subsequent chapters, I will show that this process of identity formation is less likely to develop the anticommunalist outlooks that Mayaram suggests, and in fact remains dependent upon a notion of others, and particularly religious others, as dangerous and potentially polluting.

While I do not think that communitas is a useful framework for understanding the healing experiences of Ḥusain Ṭekrī's pilgrims, I *do* think that dargāḥ life invites a reexamination of the Turnerian notion of liminality. Liminality, by definition an in-between place or state of mind, is meaningful only when placed in contrast with everyday society and consciousness. However, in dargāḥ culture this distinction is not absolute. Many Muslim saint shrines such as Ḥusain Ṭekrī have an ever-expanding network of affiliated satellite shrines, usually founded by individuals who have been healed at the original site. Maya and her rooftop shrine is a typical example of this phenomenon. Often a miraculous sign will authoritatively connect these far-flung shrines to Ḥusain Ṭekrī itself. Thus, for example, a satellite shrine presided over by a Hindu woman who lives in a village near Ḥusain Ṭekrī was founded after she had a dream in which she was shown that a *panja* (a hand-shaped symbol of the Five Pure Ones of the Islamic tradition: Muhammad, 'Ali, Hasan, Husain, and Fatima) was buried under a tree near a well on her family's property. The hand was subsequently found under the tree, and a shrine was built to house it. In a comparable circumstance, a miracle in which light was seen descending into two *panja* housed in a Ḥusain Ṭekrī–affiliated *imāmbāṛā* in Bombay is cited as the reason the *imāmbāṛā* is an effective place of healing.

On a related note, a Shi'a informant whom I have known for many years has been increasingly insistent that I take a *panja* back to the United States and open a "court," as she calls it, where Americans will be able to access the healing power of Ḥusain Ṭekrī. At the end of one of my visits to Ḥusain Ṭekrī, impatient with my apparent unwillingness to open a healing center in my New York apartment, she presented me with a bag containing incense and a *panja* that she said she had left in one of the rauẓas overnight.

This is a standard method for imbuing a *panja* with healing power, and pilgrims often take such *panjas* home with them. Her only instruction was a strong warning not to touch the *panja* during my menses.

In recognizing that the reach of Ḥusain Ṭekrī is extensive and that pilgrims see it as participant in a pan-Indian network of dargāḥs, the crucial point to highlight is that the practical result of this ever-expanding network of shrines is a strong, increasing, and theoretically endless interpenetration of liminal spaces with the "structured" societies within which they emerge. In the case of both the Bombay *imāmbāṛā* and my would-be New York healing center, the shrines exist (or, in my case, would exist) in domestic space, and the shrine founded in a village near Ḥusain Ṭekrī sits on the edge of the village, at the corner of a field near a well. Further, pilgrims' stories indicate that variations on the practice of *hāẓirī* are observed and experienced in both dargāḥs and domestic environments. In these cases, the distinction between ritual and nonritual actions and liminal and everyday spaces and states of being is fluid and relative. The many ways in which pilgrims temporarily assume new identities while at Ḥusain Ṭekrī, particularly when they pass as members of another religious community, are also liminal phenomena in the sense that practitioners regard them as alternative or temporary states. Here too the interpenetration of the liminal and the everyday is sustained by the continuance of practices, prayers, and rituals originally learned at Ḥusain Ṭekrī. This malleability of the boundary between liminal and everyday life, perhaps informed by a notion of immanence, is another aspect of dargāḥs' appeal and efficacy.

Texts are teleological: their pages march steadily toward an inexorable conclusion. It is therefore challenging to structure a book in a way that accurately conveys ambiguity, liminality, and context dependence. I hope that in what follows I have managed to strike a balance between providing necessary, straightforward orientation for readers and preserving the fluidity that sits at the core of pilgrims' experiences and dargāḥ culture itself. I begin in chapter 1 by detailing Ḥusain Ṭekrī's geography and highlighting major moments in its history as a changing Muslim pilgrimage center. With this context firmly in place, in chapter 2 I present the stories of four of my major informants: Maya, Priya, Babli, and Nasim.[55] Each of these women has an ongoing relationship with Ḥusain Ṭekrī: Maya, who was introduced earlier in this volume, has had a relationship with Ḥusain Ṭekrī for most of her adult life; Priya and Babli were resident at Ḥusain Ṭekrī during my major period of research, from January 2002 to 2003, as well as during my follow-up research in the summer of 2005; and Nasim was a regular Thursday visitor to Ḥusain Ṭekrī and was a resident there during the summer of 2005.

Like Maya, Nasim is a healer whose practices grew out of her relationship with the saints of Ḥusain Ṭekrī. As is necessarily the case in ethnographic research, the selection of these women as my main informants may be attributed to chance or, as they said, to fate. Nasim, Priya, and Babli happened to be long-term residents of Ḥusain Ṭekrī during my research and we simply had good chemistry. I got to know Maya, whose healing practice led me to Ḥusain Ṭekrī, simply because I lived as a paying guest in her home.

Though the fact that nearly all of my major informants were female might suggest otherwise, I did not embark upon this project intending to study women's religious practices in particular. Rather, the main reason for my focus on women's practices and narratives was cultural: in small-town and working-class India, it is unacceptable for men and women to be alone together or to form friendships. Thus, even if I had wanted to include men in my circle of close informants, it would have been very difficult to do so. Had my research been primarily or exclusively based upon formal interviews, this would not have been such a problem, and in fact, my conclusions do draw in part on many interviews that I conducted with men and entire families. However, because this book explores the efficacy of non-narrative, everyday, and hidden aspects of the culture of Muslim saint shrines, my research involved a great deal of informal contact and casual, unstructured time with my informants, both in their rented rooms and in the courtyards of the rauẓas.

Although, on the one hand, I had more freedom to speak with men because it was generally understood that, because I was a Westerner, my morals were different or debased, on the other hand, my relationships with male informants were often difficult to manage because of these very assumptions about my "Western" morals. Further, because I was living with a local Chippa family, I had to be mindful of my actions, since they would reflect on the family as a whole. Many people from both the town of Jaora and the Chippa *jāti* in particular had small businesses at Ḥusain Ṭekrī, making all of my actions there less anonymous than the average pilgrim's. For all of these reasons, my major informants are female. It is of course true that male researchers cannot develop close, time-intensive relationships with female informants, and they consequently produce work that is equally gendered, though their scholarship is often less inclined to acknowledge this fact or make it a central point of analysis. In any case, my intentions and limitations aside, it is important to note that my informants are predominantly but not exclusively women, and the conclusions reached in my work are predominantly but not exclusively representative of women's practices and religious lives.

My four major informants' stories are told primarily through statements that they made over the course of my research. In presenting many lengthy quotations from these women, I am not suggesting that the key to understanding the process of healing lies exclusively in understanding "native" experiences; nor do I presume that such an untainted and universally shared perspective exists; nor am I asserting that religious experience exists and can be conveyed beyond the experience of the individual; nor am I assuming that my informants' statements are unaltered by my translation and my use of them in the larger narrative of chapter 2. Rather, by presenting these women's statements and providing context about their lives and the moments in which their stories were told, chapter 2 offers a representative collection of the forms of story, anecdote, and narrative available in ambiguously Muslim spaces while at the same time illustrating how well suited these flexible, endlessly interpretable forms are to negotiating the situations in which pilgrims find themselves.

In presenting some of the stories these women related to me in their own (translated) words, I also hope to demonstrate that the experience of healing offered at dargāḥs is far more fraught with unknowing, retrogression, and ambiguity than the narratives of many "recovered" pilgrims would suggest. Pilgrims' experiences of illness and healing are not, in fact, well represented by Ḥusain Ṭekrī's dominant narrative of "I came, I prayed, I got better." According to this narrative, a pilgrim has an insurmountable problem; she comes to the shrines because she was called; she inhales the smoke of a type of incense known as lobān because it is known to be a cure; she is given a type of spirit possession known as ḥāẓirī in order to reveal the truth of what happened to her; she performs a wide range of actions that are understood to be commands *(ḥukm)* of the saints; the truth is revealed; the saints render a judgment *(faislā);* and the pilgrim leaves the shrine healed and whole. This dominant narrative is not difficult to come by: it is presented in all of the contemporary guidebooks, and without fail it was offered by pilgrims as either something that they had experienced or something they would someday experience.

This general, idealized narrative of healing at Ḥusain Ṭekrī sits in conversation with (and in opposition to) other forms and ways of speaking available at Ḥusain Ṭekrī, chief among them stories about Sufi saints and extra-subcontinental Muslim martyrs, but also narratives derived from dream visions, stories of the rauẓas' origins, stories of past lives, the language of law, and the fragmented utterances of *khulī ḥāẓirī.* Of the various forms of speech available at Ḥusain Ṭekrī, *khulī ḥāẓirī* is the most complex; on the one hand, it may be broken and incoherent or involve endless repetition of tropes and phrases, while on the other hand it generates the individual's version of the dominant narrative. In other words, in *khulī ḥāẓirī* the particulars of the individual's pathogenesis and treatment are revealed: who hired the magician, how the magic was done, how much was paid, and what must be done to eradicate the malevolent spirit that torments the victim. It is also a form of speech that exists within the embodied, often violent experience of interrogation at the hands of the saints.

Pilgrims feel deep ambivalence toward the dominant narrative of "I came, I prayed, I got better": depending on the circumstances, a pilgrim reproduces or resists it. Many competing and uncontrollable factors contribute to the difficult situations in which pilgrims find themselves. Therefore, narrative forms that allow for great flexibility are likely to be the most effective. Some of these forms are narratives that are created and sustained with words, such as stories about Sufi saints, and some are spoken but not linear, such as the collection of phrases and tropes that comprise the speech of an individual in *khulī ḥāẓirī*. Such forms, however, are not easily presented or examined in an analytic work such as a book because they are often fragmented or anecdotal in nature and are generally mobilized in a particular context; what makes them powerful is also what makes them challenging objects of inquiry.

As I relate the stories of Maya, Priya, Babli, and Nasim and show the ways in which the various forms of speech and narrative available at Ḥusain Ṭekrī facilitate the healing process, I also introduce categories and concepts that are central to pilgrims' actions and narratives. In no particular order, these concepts include healing, lack, place, mobility, hiddenness, unknowing, vision, debt, and sickness. These concepts, and in some cases their opposites, not only animate the narratives offered in chapter 2, but they are also operative in each of Ḥusain Ṭekrī's major rituals as well as in the origin stories of Ḥusain Ṭekrī itself.

Having explored the possibilities and limitations of the narrative aspects of pilgrims' healing processes, in chapter 3 I discuss the major healing practices of Ḥusain Ṭekrī, chief among them the ritual burning of lobān and the pilgrims' inhalation of its smoke. Drawing on pilgrims' narratives, a survey, and my own participant observation, this chapter offers an explanation for the popularity and efficacy of lobān as well as several other healing practices common at Ḥusain Ṭekrī. The chapter relies upon Mauss's influential discussion of gift exchange; specifically, it demonstrates that lobān, understood as a gift, corroborates Mauss's suggestion that gifts retain a trace of their giver, the giver in this case being either the saints of Ḥusain Ṭekrī or perhaps divinity itself.[56] Mauss's suggestion that all gifts create an obligation to reciprocate is borne out by the fact that, for reasons of both petition and gratitude, pilgrims regularly offer gifts to the shrines.[57] In the case of lobān, this notion of obligatory reciprocity is rendered more complex by virtue of the fact that much of the lobān burned at the shrines is either gifted to the shrines by pilgrims or purchased with money donated by pilgrims. On one level, the community of pilgrims functions as giver and as receiver, while on another lobān is sometimes understood to contain the power of either the saints or God, making lobān similar to the *prasād* offered in a Hindu temple: a divine gift, and therefore endlessly abundant. Contextualizing the lobān in the arena of pan–South Asian experience and culture provides insight into the ways in which lobān functions as a particularly effective source of healing.

The complex concept of ḥāẓirī is the exclusive focus of chapter 4. A central practice at Ḥusain Ṭekrī, ḥāẓirī has both narrative and nonnarrative aspects, and it is the medium within which pilgrims are granted what is ostensibly the goal of the healing process. In part, the challenge of this chapter is to categorize ḥāẓirī. The term, which literally means "presence," is used by pilgrims to describe actions that fit into the general category of ritual as well as nonobservable states of being. Ḥāẓirī is a series of actions that share many characteristics with exorcism (*khulī ḥāẓirī*, or "open presence"); it is a physically painful condition of being unwell that is not observable or known to anyone other than the sufferer (*gum ḥāẓirī*, or "hidden presence"); and it is a state of being (*ḥāẓirīwālā/ḥāẓirīwālī*, or a person primarily characterized by presence). Because the term *ḥāẓirī* represents states of being as well as ritual action, it participates in the phenomenon of spirit possession and the ritual of exorcism without being limited to them. Most important, perhaps, it seems to bridge the gap between ritual action and one's everyday state of being. Methodologically speaking, this means that while some aspects of ḥāẓirī can be analyzed as ritual and as a type of spirit possession, other aspects of ḥāẓirī cannot. *Gum ḥāẓirī* in particular, because it is a hidden, everyday experience and not a ritual action, calls into question the distinctions between ritual and everyday action, sacred space and profane space, and liminality and centrality that inform many analyses of religion in cultures and individual lives.

When analyzing ḥāẓirī as a ritual (and specifically when considering whether or not *khulī ḥāẓirī* is exorcism), I follow the perspective on ritual practice advocated in different ways by Bourdieu and Bell.[58] As Bell suggests, a person engaged in ritual is engaged in a practice that is "(1) situational; (2) strategic; (3) embedded in a misrecognition of what it is in fact doing; and (4) able to reproduce or reconfigure a vision of the order of power in the world."[59] Because spirit possession flouts attempts to assign agency to a single individual, self, or personality, it is debatable whether point three of Bell's description of ritual applies, but in the end, what is most important to understand in considering *khulī ḥāẓirī* as a ritual act is the fact that it is chosen and shaped by the individual practitioner.[60] In this regard, I use the phrases "spirit possession practice" and "ḥāẓirī practices" purposefully: in scholarship on religion, a practice is understood to be performed by a willing agent or petitioner. In contrast to this, in an exorcism the individual is at the mercy of the exorcist and the malevolent spirit. Properly understood, *khulī ḥāẓirī* is volitional and consciousness changing, just like many practices that are more readily recognized as "religious."

At Ḥusain Ṭekrī it is commonly accepted that an individual may tie a cord around the arm, waist, or neck as a physical expression of willingness to assume responsibility for one's own ḥāẓirī or, less frequently, another's. Here *khulī ḥāẓirī's* voluntary nature and its consciousness-changing potential give it the status of religious practice in a manner similar to meditation (the alteration of one's consciousness through breath and body control) or prayer (a request). Thus, given *khulī ḥāẓirī*'s voluntary nature, it would be limiting to class it as spirit possession or exorcism. In the context of the much larger debate over whether ritual activities are shaped by individuals and change to reflect changing power dynamics and struggles between dominant and subaltern groups or reflect and create systems of power that shape individuals, the chapter suggests that *khulī ḥāẓirī* is better understood as the former: a ritual that reflects the agency of its practitioners.

Further, in attempting to understand the efficacy of *khulī ḥāẓirī*, the chapter emphasizes that most days at Ḥusain Ṭekrī pass very slowly, punctuated by spasms of the incredible violence that characterizes *khulī ḥāẓirī*. Those who have written on spirit possession practices in India, even when they recognize the often coercive nature of many possession and exorcism practices, are inclined to focus their interpretive efforts on the moment of possession and exorcism and the rituals surrounding it without taking into account the equally significant extended noneventfulness of being unwell (in this case, of being a *ḥāẓirīwālā/ḥāẓirīwālī*).[61] *Khulī ḥāẓirī* is a significant moment in the healing process, but it is only a moment. As with the other narrative and nonnarrative aspects of pilgrims' experiences of healing, *khulī ḥāẓirī*'s power and its meaningfulness to its practitioners can only be understood if its greater context is taken into account.

In the final chapter I shift my focus from individual narratives, ritual practices, and experiences to the types of relationships that pilgrims develop at Ḥusain Ṭekrī. I suggest that Ḥusain Ṭekrī's power, like that of any dargāḥ, is in part derived from its unique ability to function as a place in which the other is encountered bodily, ritually, narratively, and in everyday life, and that through repeated encounters with others, the pilgrim's accumulated experience of becoming more than a narrowly or locally defined social being becomes a significant element in both the healing process and its occasional extension: the process of becoming a healer. In short, I suggest that a complex range of interactions that create what I term "imagined" and "actual" communities are central to the culture of dargāḥs. In my usage, imagined communities are those groups that afford pilgrims the opportunity to narrativize their current situations in relation to "others" without sustained personal contact with the members of the other community; actual communities are those that are created and sustained through self-conscious personal contact with members of one's own community and communities of others.

In the context of Indian notions of otherness and the relationship between otherness, magic, malevolent forces, and healing, Kakar has argued that spirit possession in India relies upon the notion of a dangerous or demonic religious other—hence Hindus are tormented by Muslim spirits, and vice versa.[62] In contrast to Kakar's interpretation of possession as an expression of and contribution to communalism, Mayaram, in an article based on fieldwork at a satellite site of Ḥusain Ṭekrī about eighty kilometers southwest of Ajmer in Rajasthan, refutes this notion, arguing that most spirit possession results from the spirits of close relatives of the victim.[63] While it is a commonplace of South Asian culture that the spirits of the untimely dead, including family members, *do* possess, I never met an individual at Ḥusain Ṭekrī whose malevolent possessing spirit was a family member who died an untimely or violent death, though it was almost always the case that the victim's family member had hired a magician to put a malevolent spirit into the victim's body. While this is by no means always the case, my research among pilgrims at Ḥusain Ṭekrī found that the malevolent possessing spirit was often from another religious community or, significantly, an untouchable. There was also agreement among most pilgrims that magic performed by untouchables and the spirits of untouchables is the most difficult type to eradicate.[64]

Mayaram has further suggested that the sorts of spirit possession–based healing practices that take place at dargāḥs in northwestern India "invert ethnicizing logic suggesting a reverse process by which an intimacy with the stranger, the ethnic other, can be established."[65] Again, she argues this in response to Kakar's above-mentioned thesis. On the one hand, I agree with much of what Kakar and Mayaram assert; on the other hand, I suggest that the interplay of the categories of self and other at dargāḥs is significantly more complicated than either Kakar or Mayaram's theory allows, and that while incorporation of the other is an important part of possession-based healing practices, possession and healing practices at dargāḥs are powerful in part because they retain a sense of others as dangerous. My categories of imagined and actual communities are central to this argument.

Finally, on the subject of narrative at Ḥusain Ṭekrī and the structure of this book, it is difficult to resist the "I came, I prayed, I got better" narrative that circulates at any dargāḥ. While I recognize that this idealized narrative has a certain value and meaning in dargāḥ culture in general and at Ḥusain Ṭekrī in particular, it is not the narrative in which healing takes place. It does not reflect the rhythms of the healing process—sometimes intense and sometimes completely uneventful—and does not reflect the fact that pilgrims to Ḥusain Ṭekrī often develop a lifelong relationship with it. Pilgrims' behavior suggests that they experience life as a chronic illness. Recurrent visits to one's chosen dargāḥ, whether to offer thanks, seek blessing, offer respect, or request help for an old or new problem, are necessary to keep the illness in remission. Health is not, in the end, the natural order of things, and consequently there can be no end to the narrative that is built over a lifetime of association with Ḥusain Ṭekrī. I have therefore tried to keep Ḥusain Ṭekrī's dominant narrative of recovery from exerting too strong an influence on the structure of my own narrative, seeking instead to mirror the markedly ongoing character of the relationships that pilgrims develop with the site, and the fragmented, ambiguous, ephemeral, and open-ended forms that facilitate their healing processes.

CHAPTER 1

Place

The Making of a Pilgrimage and a Pilgrimage Center

Jaora, the town in western Madhya Pradesh that is home to Ḥusain Ṭekrī, is almost well connected with the rest of India by rail. Although some say a major wide-gauge railway station will soon grace the outskirts of the town, significantly improving employment prospects for the economically depressed town's young men, for the time being, travelers from Rajasthan typically roll slowly into Jaora's narrow-gauge railway station. From Jaora the narrow-gauge line eventually makes its way to the renowned Chishtī dargāḥ in the city of Ajmer, making it convenient, and therefore common, for pilgrims to visit both the Chishtī shrine and the shrines of Ḥusain Ṭekrī in a single trip. For travelers from the rest of India, Jaora is most easily accessible from the city of Ratlam, a stop on all of the major routes on the Delhi-Bombay spoke of India Railways. Jaora is a bumpy one-hour bus ride from Ratlam station. Whether one arrives in Jaora by bus or train, options for the several-mile ride through the town to the shrines of Ḥusain Ṭekrī are limited to an auto rickshaw or the significantly cheaper, slower, and more pleasant horse-drawn tonga.

Sprawling out from the old part of town are Jaora's new poured-concrete suburbs; like suburbs everywhere, they are comfortable, lacking in deep history, affluent, and homogeneous. The route to Ḥusain Ṭekrī from the train and bus station bypasses the suburbs almost completely, instead passing through the winding streets of the old town's bazaars and whitewashed buildings with dilapidated wooden balconies. In these older neighborhoods, religious structures of all kinds are remarkably unobtrusive; as Catherine

Asher has shown in the context of Jaipur, Hindu and Jain temples built in the regional style often mimicked home or *havelī* (mansion) architecture.[1] Similarly, while modest minarets mark local mosques, *imāmbāṛās* built to contain each Muslim community's *ta'ziya,* or model of the tombs of the martyrs of Karbala, are unadorned and unobtrusive.

As the road to Ḥusain Ṭekrī passes over a bridge, the pilgrim is confronted with two uncharacteristically large religious buildings, unlike those in the old part of Jaora: on the left side of the river, a large Hindu temple topped with a massive *śikhara* towers over the crumbling old buildings that line the rest of the riverbank. Directly across the river, a brightly painted mosque known locally as the "government mosque" is small in comparison, but it has recently acquired backup: the massive half-finished poured-concrete minaret looming behind it stands as a relatively recent response to the towering white temple. To the right, on the other side of the bridge, the magnificent white *havelī* of the descendants of a Hindu Rajput *ṭhākur* (lord) who once donated land to Ḥusain Ṭekrī stands at the top of a cliff overlooking a water tank that, other than a few glorious weeks during a good monsoon season, is a cesspool of rank water used by local *dhobī*s (washermen).[2]

In conversations with me, Jaora residents often mentioned this cross-river conversation between temple and mosque as evidence of the religious tolerance that flourishes in their town. This very well may be the case. However, the *ṭhākur*'s monumental, whitewashed residence faces the temple across the water tank, and some now-defunct buildings bearing the seal of the former Muslim princely state of Jaora sit just downriver from the government mosque. Given their size and their proximity to buildings that, until Independence, were home to two rivals for power, it is also possible that these two religious structures could be read instead as expressions of communalism.

Just after the bridge, the road winds past a Bohra enclave and on to the small neighborhood of Chippapura, home to Jaora's Chippa Muslim community.[3] Religiously, Chippas self-identify as converts to Sunni Islam many generations ago; they still bear the *jāti* (birth-based community) name that indicates their traditional profession of block printing cloth.[4] Chippapura is my home in Jaora; an Internet search in 2002 put me in contact with Ghulam Chippa, a former resident of Chippapura who now works in Toronto as an engineer.[5] It was through Ghulam Chippa that I met his sister, Khadija, in whose home I lived during my initial and follow-up research.[6] I shared this space with an extended family of eight adults and four children aged three to twelve, to which a new daughter was added during my initial research, bringing the population of the home, including myself, to fourteen.

One of Khadija's married daughters, who, as is common among both Muslims and some Hindus, came back to her natal home for the birth of her first child, was also resident for several months. Further, as is usual in Indian households, visiting relatives are a fact of life, and so to this large family was added a steady stream of relatives from places as far-flung as Pakistan and as near as the cities of Mandsore (home to Khadija's oldest daughter) and Ahmedabad (which has a major Chippa population). The family is working class; Khadija's sons are local goods carriers and own two small trucks, the cabs of which are endearingly emblazoned with the motto "*sabr se*," or "with patience," a fine philosophy indeed for those who brave Indian roads.[7] The family income is supplemented by one of the sons, who has a part-time job as the driver for a local upper-class family, and until recently the youngest, just-married daughter was a teacher at a local elementary school, which is run by her uncle. The day-to-day experience of being part of this family's life significantly shaped my perspective on the everyday lives of the pilgrims whose healing processes I sought to understand.

Just beyond my home in Chippapura, the road passes through a small-scale version of the cross-river standoff: a diminutive green-tiled tomb of a local Sufi saint faces an equally diminutive Hindu temple to Hanumān directly across the road. Such pairings of Sufi shrines and temples to Hanumān or to the Goddess are not uncommon; as previous scholarship has demonstrated, Sufi saints can be associated with a local goddess through marriage, and more generally, goddesses, Hanumān, and Sufi saints often engage in the same kinds of healing work based on spirit possession.[8] Similar to the cross-river mosque-temple conversation as interpreted by Jaora's residents, these goddess/Hanumān/Sufi saint shrine confluences are popularly read as laudable expressions of religious tolerance.[9] Regarding a similar dargāḥ-temple confluence in a nearby village, Jaora's local newspaper ran a story with the following lengthy headline during my follow-up research: "One way, a dargāḥ, and the other way, Hanumān jī / Hindu worship and Muslim worship happen side by side / In the village of Lālākheṛī, the court of [sufi saint] Tāj ud Dīn / A rare example of Hindu-Muslim unity."[10] The story describes the apparently amicable relationship between the shrine to the saint Tāj ud Dīn and a shrine built to honor not just the Hindu god Hanumān, but also the goddess Ambemātā (Durgā). As does the general population, the popular press often chooses to read dargāḥs as geographies of tolerance. While some scholars also favor this interpretation, others suggest the opposite and instead read dargāḥs as geographies of communalism.[11] Neither interpretation, as I came to understand, tells the full story.

Soon after Jaora's own dargāḥ-temple cross-street conversation, the ragged, ever-expanding edge of the town dissolves, giving way to farmland sprinkled with shaggy date palms and the occasional majestic tree. From here, highlights on the road to Ḥusain Ṭekrī include a large cemetery and many of the less salubrious by-products of urban life: the town dump, a muddy swamp that occasionally offers respite from the heat to local water buffalo, and, finally, in disconcertingly close proximity to one another, a petrol pump and a local liquor store. The left fork in the road just after the petrol pump leads to Ḥusain Ṭekrī.

Ḥusain Ṭekrī has currently grown to a collection of six shrines, which pilgrims commonly refer to as rauẓas. Each rauẓa is erected in the name of an important member of the early Muslim community, all of whom date from the first Islamic century: 'Ali, Husain, 'Abbas, Sakina, Zaineb, and Fatima. Beyond these formally delineated religious spaces, it is difficult to know where or how to draw a line that circumscribes Ḥusain Ṭekrī's geography. At this point, Ḥusain Ṭekrī has all the makings of a town: it has a post office branch and a police *thānā* (station), and there are two "doctors" in residence who dispense medication and offer injections using needles of questionable cleanliness. Originally, Ḥusain Ṭekrī was founded as a Muslim charitable trust, or *waqf*. Recent *waqf* board documents claim ownership of seventeen lodges containing a total of 213 rooms that range in price from 5 to 100 rupees a night; the documents also claim a total of "230 homes and shops (including both concrete structures *[pakkā]* and shacks *[kaccā]*)," the proprietors of which pay rent to the *waqf* board. As a result of a major change of management several years ago, an old policy has been reinstituted to keep pilgrims from becoming permanent residents at Ḥusain Ṭekrī: after thirty-five days, the rent on the room increases by 50 percent; after sixty-five days, the original rent is doubled; and after this the pilgrim must leave *waqf* housing for eight days, at which point they can reenter at the original rent and begin a new cycle. Private lodges, of which there are about eighteen, have no formal residency policy; the pilgrim can stay as long as he or she is able to pay.

Though it is not noted in the *waqf* documentation, many of the temporary shops unofficially rent out their space to pilgrims, making the number of individuals resident at Ḥusain Ṭekrī at any time almost impossible to estimate, particularly since many pilgrims simply camp. Given the number of rooms in the *waqf* and private lodges, the stores' floor space, the fact that many individuals camp, and the fact that almost no one arrives alone (making each room home to a minimum of two people), it is certain that there are at least 750 people resident at Ḥusain Ṭekrī at any given time. In fact, a common lament is that in recent years Ḥusain Ṭekrī has become a small town *(qaṣbā),* and that this increase in population has reduced people's fear of the shrines, thus negatively impacting their efficacy.

While it is true that Ḥusain Ṭekrī has grown significantly in the past fifty years, it is unclear when, exactly, the majority of the growth took place. *Ĕʿjāz e Ḥusain* (The Miraculous Cure of Husain), a guidebook to Ḥusain Ṭekrī published in 1946 by a Hyderabad-based press, notes a total of forty-six lodge rooms, adding that an additional twenty rooms were due to be completed. This means that between 1946 and 2005, approximately 147 rooms were added. My own survey of the extant lodges suggested that all but twenty of the rooms were constructed fifty or more years ago, though the *waqf* board was unable to produce documentation of the exact date of construction of many of the lodges. If true, this means that there must have been an extraordinary building streak from 1945 to 1955. The *Ĕʿjāz e Ḥusain* also lists a three-tier rental policy identical to the one recently enforced by the new management of Ḥusain Ṭekrī, which suggests that despite current expressions of dismay about the "settled" character of Ḥusain Ṭekrī, the concern about individuals becoming permanent residents has been around for some time.

Compared to the *waqf*-owned lodges, the private lodges are a more recent phenomenon. Lodge owners were often reluctant to disclose information about their businesses, but the style and condition of the lodges suggest that they are fairly new, and the information I gathered confirmed this impression.[12] Of the thirteen owners whose information I was able to collect, one had built his lodge in 1984 and the rest had built theirs between 1990 and 2002. Reasons for building the lodges varied: six owners cited failed farms (largely due to prolonged drought); one indicated that the lodge was his legacy because he did not have children; one said that he had moved to Ḥusain Ṭekrī because the drug dealers in his old neighborhood in Jaora had made the neighborhood uninhabitable;[13] and the rest simply saw their lodges as businesses like any other. The private lodges, then, were built largely in response to changing financial circumstances. The growth in the number of shops that line the road that links the rauẓas is impossible to measure because most of them are ramshackle sheds, though the very fact that many of them are not permanent concrete structures suggests that the vast majority are recent constructions. Shopkeepers themselves overwhelmingly indicated that the most of the shops have sprung up in the past ten years or so.

The rauẓas also reflect Ḥusain Ṭekrī's slow expansion over time. According to a recent official *waqf* report, the largest rauẓa, that of Imām Husain (as it is formally known), was constructed in 1918 with funds donated by the Bombay-based merchant *(seṭh)* Haji Ismail Muhammad, and the rauẓa of Ḥaẓrat ʿAbbas (as it is formally known) was built in 1923 by a Bombay-based merchant known as Aladin Sahib. The most recent guidebook to Ḥusain Ṭekrī (published in 2003), citing the history *Tārīk̲h̲ e Jaora* (History of Jaora), credits the construction of both of these rauẓas to Ismail Muhammad, stating that their construction began in 1888.[14] The *Tārīk̲h̲ e Jaora* itself, which was originally published in Urdu in January 1947, notes 1888 as the date of the start of construction of a rauẓa, though it states neither the donors' names nor the names of the rauẓas.

In any case, it seems that by the early twentieth century, several rauẓas had been constructed next to the water sources where the miraculous events of Muharram in 1886 were understood to have taken place. The oldest record of Ḥusain Ṭekrī's founding comes from the *Tārīk̲h̲ e Yūsufī*, a history of the princely state of Jaora commissioned by the royal family and published in 1889. In this version of the story there is no mention of the construction of any rauẓas, and the discussion of Ḥusain Ṭekrī's origins ends almost immediately after it relates the events that led to the founding of Ḥusain Ṭekrī, which the text places in the year 1304 Hijri, or 1886.[15] By 1920, after the construction of the rauẓa of Imām Husain, the reputation of the site must have been well established: a letter housed in the National Archives in Delhi records a donation of land made by the *ṭhākur* Roop Singh of Shujaota to Ḥusain Ṭekrī Sharīf.[16] While British documents in the archive indicate that this donation was made as part of a resolution to a land dispute between the *ṭhākur* and the *nawāb* that had dragged on for several decades,[17] the *ṭhākur*'s letter of donation mentions none of this, instead stating that the *ṭhākur* "has heard that Ḥusain Ṭekrī Sharīf is in need of land for making additions, [and] because this humble petitioner has a special faith in Imām Husain, I wish to contribute to this worthy cause so that, by means of this gift, there may be blessing and plentitude."[18] Singh's descendants, who live in their ancestral home in Jaora, confirmed that the family had indeed donated to Ḥusain Ṭekrī, though they noted that their family made significant donations to *all* of Jaora's major religious institutions. As has been argued elsewhere,[19] many Indian "religious" institutions were important sites for displays of cross-tradition alliances; Ḥusain Ṭekrī was clearly part of this phenomenon.

It is certain that donors to the rauẓas of Imām Husain and Ḥaẓrat ʿAbbas were K̲h̲oja, a *jāti*-based community of Muslims. Interviews I conducted with some of the descendants of Ismail Muhammad confirm the scholarly consensus that the nineteenth century was a tumultuous time in the lives of Bombay Khojas; the arrival of the Aga Khan and his attempt to win the backing of the Ismaili community created divisions within the community, ultimately leading to a clear delineation of the three Khoja factions present in contemporary India: Ithna ʿAshari, Nizari Ismaili, and Sunni.[20] Thus, as Nazim Ismail, a descendant of Ismail Muhammad, explained to me in an interview conducted in Bombay in the summer of 2005, "Some of us became strong followers of the Aga Khan, and some of us did not."[21]

I was not able to determine definitively whether or not Ismail Muhammad responded to the situation within the Khoja community by aligning himself with the Nizari Ismaili supporters of the Aga Khan or the Ithna ʿAshari. Ismail Muhammad's grandson Husain Merchant, who lives in Bombay, identified his maternal grandmother—Ismail Muhammad's wife—as Ithna ʿAshari. For the purpose of understanding the development of Ḥusain Ṭekrī, however, in some ways it does not matter how Ismail Muhammad aligned himself. His decision to donate the rauẓa(s) and the lodge that bears his name to this day was in part related to his business interests. Husain Merchant explained to me that Ismail Muhammad had an extremely successful leather business, and he likely built the lodge that bears his name and the rauẓa of Imām Husain in Jaora because it was a good location from which he could oversee the collection of animal hides from the surrounding villages before shipping them back to Bombay. Nazim Ismail corroborated much of Husain's story, also emphasizing the usefulness of Jaora as a collection point. In the nineteenth century, Jaora was a small Muslim princely state surrounded by Hindu princely states, and it makes sense that it had appeal as a comfortable base of operations.[22] The possibility that a leather business would be considered problematically polluting by a Hindu majority or a Hindu-ruled principality should not be overplayed, but it is certainly true that this type of business would have been more or less a non-issue in a Muslim princely state.[23]

It is also worth noting that the Sunni identity of the *nawāb*s of Jaora and the Shiʿa identity of Ismail Muhammad—whether Ismaili or Ithna ʿAshari—was not a source of concern; in fact, Ismail Muhammad was clearly a generous donor to Ḥusain Ṭekrī. This is all the more striking given the fact that in Bombay, Islamic boundaries were being drawn in new ways as a result of the arrival of the Aga Khan, and, in India, Islamic reform movements were themselves implicitly (if not also explicitly) critical of many Shiʿa practices in particular, thus ultimately leading to stronger boundaries between Shiʿa and Sunni communities.[24] The history of Ḥusain Ṭekrī also reflects the notion of pan-Islamicism that was being propagated by both the Muslim League and the all-India Khalifat committee in the early to mid-twentieth century. Here, too, Jaora was participant in a Kẖoja- and Ismaili-dominated community that was central in the creation of the nation of Pakistan: the *zarīḥ* in the rauẓa of Imām Husain, for example, was donated by one of the founders of Habib Bank.[25] The relationship between Ḥusain Ṭekrī, Jaora, and Habib Bank was effectively severed at Partition, when the bank and its founding family emigrated to Pakistan, becoming a major influence in that new nation's life. This loss mirrors the major financial losses that the Indian Muslim community sustained in the wake of Partition.[26]

The strong historical connection between the Kẖoja community and Ḥusain Ṭekrī is maintained by the present-day community of Bombay-based Nizari Ismaili Kẖojas (originally from Kuch), also distantly related to Ismail Muhammad, who together oversee an annual fire walk at Ḥusain Ṭekrī that takes place forty days after the tenth of Muharram. They claim to have made the donations that resulted in the recent construction of the rauẓa of Bībī Sakina (daughter of Husain) next to the rauẓa of her paternal uncle 'Abbas and the rauẓa of Bībī Zaineb (daughter of 'Ali, sister of Husain and 'Abbas) next to the rauẓa of Imām Husain. Thus, the two oldest rauẓas at Ḥusain Ṭekrī were built in the early twentieth century with funds from the Bombay Kẖoja community, and two of the much more recently constructed rauẓas, each built next to one of the oldest rauẓas, were funded by members of the same extended family. In Jaora I knew many people who questioned the value of the newly constructed rauẓas: they are not affiliated with the original miracle, and therefore they are not seen as particularly important. In some cases they are even regarded as fakes.[27] Nevertheless, the rauẓas of Bībī Sakina and Bībī Zaineb are important expressions of devotion and gratitude for members of the contemporary Nizari Ismaili Kẖoja community, and generally speaking, most pilgrims simply accept them as authoritative because of their proximity to the other rauẓas.

Ḥusain Ṭekrī shares some aspects of the administrative structure common at many of the major dargāḥs of the subcontinent, though there are significant differences as well. The administration of these dargāḥs, as well as the sources of authority claimed by the administrators themselves, is complex and varies depending upon the period under consideration and the wealth and prestige of the dargāḥ. Historically, the major dargāḥs of the subcontinent enjoyed the patronage of local rulers, emperors, kings, and/or wealthy citizens; profits from donated property were used to pay the salaries of shrine workers, maintain and improve the shrine, or fund the dargāḥs' charitable activities. In this way the dargāḥ functioned as a center of alliance and exchange between many different communities on both local and translocal levels.

In contemporary India, the spiritual heads of older, well-known dargāḥs legitimate their authority by claiming to be direct patrilineal descendants of the saint buried in the shrine. In the case of the wealthy and famous Muʿīn āl-dīn Chishtī dargāḥ in Ajmer, for example, spiritual authority is fundamentally held by the *sajjāda nishīn* or *pīr,* understood to be a descendant of Muʿīn āl-dīn Chishtī, and the shrine is administered by *k̲h̲ādims*.[28] Originally *k̲h̲ādims* were appointed on the basis of being a devotee, a relative of the saint in whose memory the dargāḥ was constructed, and/or the member of a family seeking an affiliation with the shrine. In the contemporary period, however, these *k̲h̲ādims*, whose positions are hereditary, primarily self-identify as descendants of either the saint himself or his closest companions, and while these claims are not verifiable, they have been vigorously and fiercely defended by the present-day *k̲h̲ādims* in the face of legal action taken to disprove their status.[29]

Again in the context of the Chishtī dargāḥ at Ajmer, a later administrative role to be added was that of *mutavallī,* a position created by the Mughal emperor Akbar after his banishment of Shaykh Husain, the spiritual leader and chief administrator of the shrine in 1593–94. Currie's work on this moment in the shrine's history demonstrates that Akbar, concerned with the administration of imperial funds donated to the dargāḥ, initiated an investigation into the legitimacy of Shaykh Husain's claim of descent from Muʿīn āl-dīn Chishtī and, finding proof lacking, removed him from office and replaced him with a governmental representative with the title of *mutavallī.* The *mutavallī*'s right to administer the shrine thus derived solely from the fact that he had been appointed by the emperor. In the contemporary life of the Ajmer dargāḥ, the *sajjādā nishīn*'s title is held by an individual claiming descent from Muʿīn āl-dīn Chishtī; he has no administrative duties, but he leads the *samāʿ* and collects a salary from the shrine. His legitimacy derives from his ancestry.[30]

Thus, while the spiritual authority of the shrine remains officially concentrated in the person of the *sajjādā nishīn* and, ultimately, in the saint or martyr buried there, at large, well-endowed, famous dargāḥs as well as smaller shrines in contemporary India, it is often the *k̲h̲ādims* who serve as spiritual guides and mentors. In other cases, the role of spiritual guides and mentor falls to the *mujāvars* who have the responsibility of the day-to-day maintenance of the shrines; unlike the *sajjādā nishīn* or *pīr,* they need not have any familial relationship with the founding figure of the shrine, and their role may or may not be hereditary. In practice, for many pilgrims coming to a dargāḥ or similar shrine, it makes little difference if their spiritual guide is a *k̲h̲ādim, mujāvar,* or even a devotee who has chosen to settle nearby. In the eyes of pilgrims, the authority of such figures lies in a complex and changing mixture of ancestry, personal charisma, and simple physical proximity to or association with the shrines.

The administrative structure of Ḥusain Ṭekrī differs somewhat from the structure of the dargāḥ of Mu'īn āl-dīn Chishtī, though it is similar in that it has also been shaped by particular historical processes. Ḥusain Ṭekrī's current administrative structure affords the *mutavallī* a significant level of control over the management of the shrines, though, as is the case for all shrines in the wake of the *waqf* act of 1995, Ḥusain Ṭekrī's management now owes a higher level of financial accountability to the *waqf* board.[31] Mr. M. K. Taimuri, a member of the royal family of Jaora and retired from a Bhopal-based government job, is the *waqf* board representative at Ḥusain Ṭekrī, and since the late 1990s the *mutavallī*'s post has been occupied by Haji Sarwar 'Ali Khan, a lawyer and also a member of the royal family of Jaora.

Unlike the position of *mutavallī* as it was historically constituted and legitimated at the Chishtī dargāḥ in Ajmer, Khan's claim to the position of *mutavallī* is based on his status as the son of the brother of the last—and childless—*nawāb* of Jaora; according to Khan, a rival claimant had been forced out of office owing to a matrilineal rather than patrilineal claim to the position.[32] In this case, the title of *mutavallī* has been given a meaning that differs from the meaning of the term at the dargāḥ in Ajmer; as *mutavallī,* Khan derives his legitimacy through a hereditary process similar to that of a *k̲h̲ādim* or the *sajjāda nishīn,* though the lineage is traced not to the martyrs in whose memory the shrines were constructed, but rather to the *nawāb* of Jaora, under whose patronage Ḥusain Ṭekrī was founded.

The *mutavallī* at Ḥusain Ṭekrī does not, however, fulfill any ritual role or serve as a spiritual guide or mentor to pilgrims. His major public appearance each year is at the annual fire walk, at which he offers a short, polite speech welcoming everyone to the event. Neither Sarwar 'Ali Khan nor M. K. Taimuri participate in the fire walk; rather, after Khan's brief speech they retreat to the VIP area of the audience, where they join their extended family as well as members of the local and, occasionally, state government. Administered primarily by members of the Bombay K̲h̲oja Shi'a community, the fire walk is a source of tension for all involved: Shi'a participants suspect disapproval and mockery on the part of the Sunni royal family and VIP onlookers, and the Sunni onlookers, in part by virtue of not participating in the walk itself, express at best an ambivalent attitude toward the event.

The staff of Ḥusain Ṭekrī are all directly accountable to Khan and Taimuri; during my time at Ḥusain Ṭekrī, all hiring decisions were made by these two men. Employees, who are mainly Muslim but also Hindu, were dismissed for bad behavior (having designs on female pilgrims was an oft-cited reason for dismissal). *Mujāvar*s who were caught accepting money or valuable gifts from pilgrims (such things are offered in exchange for *taʿvīẕ* or other protective and curative objects) were also subject to disciplinary action and dismissal. Currently, some of the *mujāvar*s have served in that capacity for decades, having been appointed by the previous management. Others are more recent appointees of the current management.

All decisions about the management of the shrine are made by Sarwar ʿAli Khan and M. K. Taimuri, and it is clear that many of the major administrative policies are designed to keep the authority of the shrines firmly centered in the shrines themselves. As Sarwar ʿAli Khan acknowledged in one of our many conversations, the policy of rotating the *mujāvars* of each shrine several times each year is designed to prevent pilgrims from associating the charisma of a shrine with a particular attendant. This type of association is, of course, particularly likely (and therefore threatening) because many dargāḥ attendants, whether claiming the title *k̲h̲ādim* or *mujāvar,* are understood by pilgrims to be either descendants of the individual buried in the shrine, descendants of close companions of the saint, those who have been initiated into the lineage of the saint, or, at the very least, great devotees of the shrines. Earlier in Ḥusain Ṭekrī's history, the charisma inherent in proximity to the shrines was harnessed in a slightly different manner: the grave of *nawāb* Ismail ʿAli Khan is in the courtyard of the rauẓa of Imām Husain, along with the graves of some of his immediate descendants. Also in the courtyard is the grave of the Bombay-based K̲h̲oja, who donated the money for the rauẓas of Husain and ʿAbbas. Interestingly, and perhaps reflecting current and recent tensions between the K̲h̲ojas of Bombay and Ḥusain Ṭekrī's administration as well as tensions within the K̲h̲oja community itself, the grave of this significant donor was not only walled off from the main shrine but also overgrown with weeds and unmaintained.

An increased level of financial transparency—the result of both *waqf* law reform and the new management team—is most strikingly evidenced by the dramatic increase in the reported income of the shrines, which rose from 15,30,234 rupees in 1995 to 89,06,172 in 2001, the year in which the report containing these figures was submitted to the central *waqf* board.[33] The income of the shrines is derived from donations; rent paid by shopkeepers, private lodge owners, and people who have built private homes on Ḥusain Ṭekrī's land; the sale of crops grown on the surrounding farmland; and the rent paid by residents of the *waqf*-administered lodges.

The income derived from residents and owners of private lodges has been affected by the discovery of the original letter of *waqf* donation of land by a powerful local *ṭhākur* to Ḥusain Ṭekrī. In the period of colonial rule this document was kept by the British, and after Independence it somehow ended up in a file in the National Archives in New Delhi, where I found it. While the records kept by Ḥusain Ṭekrī management record the income derived from the donated land, until I found the original letter of donation in the archive, the record of the donation was missing. The letter has more than merely archival value due to the fact that, whether out of ignorance of or disregard for the fact that this land was donated in *waqf* and therefore not salable, a previous *mutavallī* of Ḥusain Ṭekrī had sold some of the land to some lodge owners and residents. With the change in management that brought Sarwar ʿAli Khan to the role of *mutavallī*, a number of legal cases were lodged in an attempt to collect back rent and enforce future rent payments. These cases, however, had been stalled by the failure of Ḥusain Ṭekrī's administration to produce the original letter of donation. Though I was aware that any documents about land ownership could have a significant effect on the current life of Ḥusain Ṭekrī, it did not seem to me that it was my right to withhold the letter of donation, and as a result of my decision, it seems to be only a matter of time before the various land cases are finally decided in favor of the administration of Ḥusain Ṭekrī. In this way, too, administrative control of the shrines remains firmly in the hands of Sarwar ʿAli Khan and M. K. Taimuri. Other major management positions at Ḥusain Ṭekrī include the several staff members in charge of keeping account of the shopkeepers and enforcing the three-month maximum residency policy for pilgrims who stay in the *waqf*-administered lodges.

This brief comparison between the current and past administrative structures of Ḥusain Ṭekrī and the Chishtī dargāḥ at Ajmer suggests that although a variety of titles is common at many dargāḥs, depending on political and other influences and interests, the sources of legitimacy and levels of control associated with particular titles (chief among them, *mutavallī, pīr, mujāvar, kḫādim, sajjāda nishīn*) vary. At Ḥusain Ṭekrī, the most significant practical consequence of the administrative decision to prevent long-term associations between *mujāvar*s and shrines is that pilgrims are afforded an opportunity to conceptualize their recovery in terms of a direct relationship with the saints rather than through the mediation and instruction of a *mujāvar.* While *mujāvar*s at Ḥusain Ṭekrī certainly do serve as spiritual guides and mentors to some pilgrims, they do not interfere with or attempt to regulate the process of *khulī ḥāẓirī*. Pilgrims themselves also directly participate in the administration of the shrine by volunteering to clean the courtyards, sweep, or assist in the distribution of lobān and water. Because the choice to offer one's services to the dargāḥ is normally the result of a command given by one of the saints through the medium of *khulī ḥāẓirī* or a dream, it is fair to say that even this level of involvement in the maintenance of the shrine is shaped by individual pilgrims' experiences and their direct relationship with the saints rather than by decisions made by the administrators of the shrines. Thus, in the context of contemporary Indian middle- and working-class culture, the atmosphere of Ḥusain Ṭekrī affords a significant and unique level of autonomy to its pilgrims and devotees.

This brings us to the question of how this particular piece of land came to be set apart. The story of Ḥusain Ṭekrī's origin has countless iterations, all of which include some type of miraculous event occurring on the eighth, ninth, or tenth day of the Islamic month of Muharram. All versions of the story also note some coincidence of the Hindu holiday of Daśahrā with these days. Of the various accounts, the earliest, contained in the *Tārīḵẖ e Yūsufī,* may date the founding of Ḥusain Ṭekrī most accurately, since it seems that in 1886 there *was* an actual concurrence of the eighth of Muharram and Daśahrā.[34] A full translation of the earliest account of the miraculous founding story (from *Tārīḵẖ e Yūsufī*) and the most recent (from *Ḥusain Ṭekrī kyā hai*) are presented in appendices A and B, respectively.[35]

According to the *Tārīḵẖ e Yūsufī,* the *nawāb* called in a regiment of mounted British soldiers to keep the peace during the concurrence of festivals; he also refused to forbid Hindus from observing Daśahrā. In Jaora state, as in much of India, observation of Muharram involves construction of models of the tombs of the martyrs of Karbala, or *ta'ziya,* and these *ta'ziya* are carried as a part of processions. To protest what they perceived as the *nawāb*'s failure to protect the interests of the Muslim community, the Muslim *ta'ziya* builders submerged the Jaora state *ta'ziya* in the river, effectively ending Muharram observances two days before the big procession of the tenth of Muharram. The practice of submerging the *ta'ziya* in water, called *ṭhaṇḍhā karnā,* or "cooling," is common in South Asian religious traditions, where religious objects used during a festival are often submerged into a ritually pure body of water at the end of the event.

This premature cooling of the *ta'ziya* prompted great consternation among the Muslims of Jaora, though the text emphasizes that riots did not occur owing to the presence of the British troops. The *nawāb* attempted to salvage the situation by giving the *ta'ziya* bearers money to reconstruct the models, which were ready just in time, by the evening of the ninth. The text then itemizes three miraculous events: first, villagers coming to Jaora to see the *ta'ziya* procession of the tenth saw, in the middle of the jungle outside town, horsemen and people on foot processing to the small hill where Ḥusain Ṭekrī now stands; second, people saw torches moving about in the woods (presumably, though the account is not specific, these torches were seen in the area in which the *taʿziya* and its mysterious bearers were seen); and third, on the place where the procession had stopped, a well that had been dry for a long time began to give water again, and this water became famous throughout India for its healing properties. The text then notes two major consequences of these events. First, the hill on which the procession had stopped was recognized as the place of Husain, and as such, the tradition of going to that hill to read *fātiḥa* (a recitation from the Qur'an, usually the eponymous first chapter, recited over food that is subsequently distributed), to offer *naẕr* (an offering, in this case, to a saint), to offer *niyāz* (a petition, usually to a saint), and to offer money "in the names of the *imāms*" was introduced. Second, the text notes that because of the miraculous power of the water of the well, individuals from distant places became "followers of Allah," and the names of Jaora and Ḥusain Ṭekrī became famous throughout India and the world.

Though similar to the stories that contemporary pilgrims relate, subsequent published versions of the story of the founding of Ḥusain Ṭekrī differ from the original in several ways. Most notably, in recent accounts two distinct stories have developed. In one narrative, the conflict between the events of Muharram and Daśahrā is related in terms of processions encountering one another on the road; the Hindu procession attempts to pass in front of the Muslim procession, and in response, the *taʿziya* of Jaora rises up into the air and floats to the *imāmbāṛā* located in the town of Jaora. In the second narrative, the miraculous events that take place on the land that is now known as Ḥusain Ṭekrī are less directly related to the events in the town of Jaora. Rather than a story in which the *taʿziya* of Jaora is borne through the jungle by a mysterious procession, in this version of the story, the villagers passing through the jungle on their way to the *taʿziya* procession see Husain himself (or someone who is very likely Husain); the supernatural water source is a spring that spontaneously erupts from the ground and provides water for the miraculous visitor to perform *wuẓū* (ritual ablutions) before performing *namāz* (prayer). The *nawāb* is eventually brought to the jungle, where a sweet smell is understood as evidence of the divine visitation; the *nawāb* orders the area protected and institutes the process of offering lobān.[36] These more recent versions of the origin story belie the influence of the present-day ritual life of Ḥusain Ṭekrī, particularly in the emphasis placed on offering lobān as opposed to bathing in the water of the miraculous well. The well itself is now completely enclosed, and its water is pumped into a bathing facility that was recently built with *waqf* funds. Indeed, many people assert that the well has completely dried up and that the water in the bathing facility is being supplied exclusively by tanker trucks.[37]

While the differences in these origin stories may tell us something about their historical and cultural contexts, it is important to note that for the most part, the details of the stories are not known by most pilgrims who visit the shrine, and, increasingly, the version of events published in several recent guidebooks (all of which closely follow the latter version, in which Husain himself visits Ḥusain Ṭekrī) is becoming the standard or authoritative version. For most pilgrims, even long-term residents, it is enough to know that the saints are present in the shrines: the origin stories of Ḥusain Ṭekrī are not, in other words, significant components of the authority and legitimacy of the present-day site, which centers on the notion that the rauẓas are places that channel the power of the saints to the pilgrims. In fact, it is striking the extent to which the trope of the land itself bearing witness to the power of the saints has been eclipsed by the shrines. A popular story that circulates at Ḥusain Ṭekrī—particularly among the Shiʿa urbanites who visit from Bombay—holds that the fields themselves used to yield sugar or a similar sweet substance *(misrī)*. However, as a result of an increase in population and a subsequent increase in filth and lack of fear that one might feel when alone in a strange, wild place, the fields have ceased to yield this miraculous sweetness.[38]

Like the sugar-bearing fields and the enclosed miraculous well at the rauẓa of ʿAbbas, the rauẓa constructed in memory of ʿAli is associated with divinely marked land: it is said that the shrine was built over a place that used to be a natural spring.[39] In this case, the origin of the spring is widely attributed to a miraculous visitation of Maulā ʿAli himself sometime in the twentieth century, well after the original saintly visitation of 1886. In all versions of this story, ʿAli appears because the shrines of ʿAbbas and Husain have been disrespected. Versions of this story contained in contemporary guidebooks and conveyed by pilgrims and shrine attendants mention one of two major sources of disrespect: either individuals (sometimes explicitly marked as Arabs or Saudis) express doubt about the power of the saints and their shrines, or they enter the shrines in a ritually impure state or without removing their shoes. In response to this ʿAli appears, mounted on his horse and bearing a whip that he uses to punish the disrespectful. In relating a version of this story, one pilgrim explained that when the doubter was whipped he lost consciousness; upon regaining consciousness, he had a handful of the soil of Karbala in his hand and a scar that never faded on his back.

The rauẓa's miraculous water source is understood to have sprung from a hoofprint of ʻAli's horse, making the nickname of the shrine Ṭāp Sharīf ([Place of the] blessed hoof). Today the rauẓa's floor has a removable central panel, and the soil under it is damp to the touch. The water that condenses inside of the central panel overnight is collected and distributed early in the morning to gender-segregated lines of waiting pilgrims. Like water from the well at the rauẓa of ʻAbbas, this water is understood to have healing properties. The courtyard of the rauẓa of ʻAli is surrounded by a wall and flanked by a small and crowded Muslim cemetery; of all the shrines it is the quietest, in large part because of its distance from the shrines of ʻAbbas and Husain. It is about an eight-minute walk from the rauẓa of ʻAli to the shrines of ʻAbbas and Husain, and, unlike the road connecting the rest of the rauẓas, this road is not lined with makeshift shops and homes but is instead flanked with farmland. Together with a nearby well popularly known as Laṅgaṛ Well, or the Well of Charitable Food Offering (so named because of popular stories that claim that, in less corrupt times, the well produced milk and/or food), Ṭāp Sharīf demarcates the farthest edge of Ḥusain Ṭekrī.

Taking the road that connects the rauẓas from Ṭāp Sharīf back toward Jaora, the pilgrim would first pass the rauẓas of ʻAbbas and Sakina and then those of Husain and Zaineb, around which are clustered shops, the *waqf* offices, most of the *waqf* lodges, the place set aside for the post-Muharram fire walk, and the corrugated-metal *imāmbāṛā,* in which the newly constructed *taʻziya* of Ḥusain Ṭekrī is stored. Beyond this oldest and most built-up part of the site, the pilgrim would pass private lodges and shops as well as the arch and gate that mark the old boundary of the site; on the other side of the gate is the main rickshaw and tonga stand. From here the road continues on to a large, recently constructed arch that signals the new entrance to Ḥusain Ṭekrī. This arch was doubtless deemed necessary in part because of the construction of the newest rauẓa of Ḥusain Ṭekrī, dedicated to Bībī Fatima, or Lady Fatima, daughter of the Prophet Muhammad and his first wife Khadija and the only female saint of Ḥusain Ṭekrī to have a rauẓa unchaperoned by a male saint. While each of the six rauẓas contains a model of the tomb of the saint whose name is associated with it, the models of the tombs of Fatima, Sakina, and Zaineb are kept in purdah, which in practice means that they are constantly covered with large, colorful pieces of fabric.

Fatima's shrine was built on the spot where, until a few years before I first visited Ḥusain Ṭekrī in 2000, an old woman had lived in a makeshift shack, maintaining a *taʻziya* that she had created herself. Fatima's shrine is a bit unusual in that it is said to house the *ta'ziya* that was built and maintained by this now deceased old woman, the location of whose grave is a subject of debate. Those who knew her—mainly those who have homes, shops, or lodges near the rauẓa of Fatima—had diverse opinions about who she was and where she came from: most agreed about her deep devotion to Husain and the other saints of Ḥusain Ṭekrī, but there was little agreement about any other details of her life or death.[40] Some said she was a Hindu Telī, while others said she was a Hindu who converted to Islam. Some said that her grave is a raised platform of concrete in the courtyard of the rauẓa of Fatima, while others maintained that her grave was actually in a nearby field. That grave is known as the grave of Dādī Ammā (literally, "grandmother mother"); the caretaker of the grave, however, does not identify Dādī Ammā as this recently deceased devotee of Ḥusain Ṭekrī, but rather as a member of "Husain's caravan": when Imām Husain visited, he asserted, he came with many members of his family, and this grave belongs to one of his entourage. All of these stories illustrate the two major ways in which a shrine's authority is legitimated: the land is rendered powerful either because of the visit of a saint, or because of the presence of the grave of an individual who exhibited a high level of devotion to a saint.

The rauẓa of Fatima shares a courtyard with a now-dry stepwell known to some as Mahdī Kuan, or Mahdī Well.[41] Ithna 'Ashari Shi'ite doctrine holds that the twelfth and final *imām,* the Mahdī, went into occultation; popularly he is understood to have disappeared after descending into a well, remaining hidden but accessible in dreams, and Ithna 'Ashari Shi'ite doctrine holds that he will emerge from hiding on judgment day. Thus, many pilgrims, particularly Shi'ites, revere the well. However, several Mehaṁdī trees grow by the well, and many Hindu pilgrims burn candles and offer flowers at the well in the name of Mehaṁdīwālī Mā, or Mehaṁdī Mother. Whether the near-homonymy between Mehaṁdī and Mahdī contributes to this confluence of identities is debatable, though over my time at Ḥusain Ṭekrī many Shi'ite pilgrims have explained that "simple" Hindus had misunderstood Mahdī and consequently took to worshipping the well as the abode of a goddess associated with the Mehaṁdī trees.

The ambiguity surrounding the rauẓa of Fatima has a contemporary communalist dimension as well; two years after my initial fieldwork, a pilgrim whom I had known for several years explained to me that at some point in the recent past someone had laid the foundation for a Hindu temple on the land where the rauẓa of Fatima currently stands, that is, the rauẓa is built atop the temple foundation. As evidence of the truth of this rumor, she cited the unique round shape of the shrine. There is, of course, no way to know if this rumor is true or not, but the sentiment was echoed in a frank conversation that I once had with a resident of Jaora; in a matter-of-fact manner, he explained that most new shrines—dargāḥs and temples alike—are simply attempts to appropriate land. Once the religious structure is in place, he concluded, it becomes difficult to remove it.

There is certainly truth to the statement that it is difficult to remove a religious space without prompting protest and retaliation, and it is also true that Mehaṁdī/Mahdī Well has inspired potentially territorial and communalist actions within the Muslim community: in 2005, the Sunni management of Ḥusain Ṭekrī had the well covered with grating similar to the latticework that covers the windows of the rauẓas; apparently, a woman in ḥāẓirī had fallen down the well and died. There is no doubt that the open well was dangerous, especially given the violent acrobatics of those in ḥāẓirī, though it is also true that an extended family of Persian-speaking Shiʿas who live in a home near the well once explained to me that the new management of the shrine had prevented them from placing a small shrine to the Twelfth Imām inside the (long-dry) well. In this case, the management may have been making an effort to maintain exclusive control of the shrine and its revenue-generating potential.

All of these stories about Ḥusain Ṭekrī contain communalist elements, and each could easily be read as representative of one of several major communalist discourses of Indian history of the past 125 years: Hindu/Muslim; Shiʿa/Sunni; Ithna ʿAshari / Nizari Ismaili. These shrines *are* contested places, and in this regard two things are worth noting: first, they have always been contested and will likely remain so; and second, and more importantly, it is in part these tensions that make dargāḥs such effective places of healing.[42]

CHAPTER 2

People

The Tale of the Four Virtuous Women

> What is involved, then, in that finding of the "true story," that discovery of the "real story" within or behind the events that come to us in the chaotic form of "historical records"? What wish is enacted, what desire is gratified, by the fantasy that real events are properly represented when they can be shown to display the formal coherency of a story? In the enigma of this wish, this desire, we catch a glimpse of the cultural function of narrativizing discourse in general, an intimation of the psychological impulse behind the apparently universal need not only to narrate but to give to events an aspect of narrativity.

In his influential volume *The Content of the Form,* Hayden White argues that, in the context of the writing of history, narrativity is both a universal human inclination and inseparable from "morality or a moralizing impulse."[1] In this chapter I present four Indian women's descriptions of their relationships with Ḥusain Ṭekrī, and I explicate how their healing processes are reconciled with the universal need to give events an aspect of narrativity. While these four individuals are not historians writing history, both their projects and my own involve, in one way or another, the use of narrative to render the past meaningful. The different forms of narrative that these four individuals use to negotiate their own pasts generally support White's assertion that narrativity is a universal human impulse and driven by morality in the broadest sense of the word, that is, driven by a desire to render the past comprehensible and acceptable.

In recording and analyzing their narratives, I seek to illuminate the morality that underlies them and to demonstrate narrative's unique ability to make this morality real, that is, to make it explicit, powerful, and authoritative in these four individuals' lives.[2] In addition to illustrating the place that narrative and narrativity hold in these individuals' understandings of their past and current relationships with Ḥusain Ṭekrī, these stories will also serve as a substantive foundation that can be built upon as subsequent chapters make new arguments and incorporate other written and oral sources. Perhaps most importantly, I hope that by recording and contexualizing these individuals' stories and uses of narrative, this book's narrative will be fundamentally shaped by them and therefore provide a true picture of the field of possibilities implicit in the narratives within and about Ḥusain Ṭekrī.

For pilgrims, the dominant narrative at Ḥusain Ṭekrī is one in which the etiology of the disease is revealed, the malevolent spirits eradicated, and the individual reintegrated into family and everyday society—in short, the dominant narrative is one of "I came, I prayed, I got better." An essential aspect of the healing process at Ḥusain Ṭekrī is the pilgrim's struggle to render this dominant narrative personally meaningful. The process by which this happens involves the use of a series of subnarratives, stories, anecdotes, and tropes. Rather than within the dominant narrative, it is through the recurrent, nonlinear use of these subnarratives, stories, anecdotes, and tropes—themselves always purposefully evoked to respond to a particular context—that the process of healing actually takes place. These elements must then be meaningfully connected with the dominant narrative, and it is the task of this chapter to demonstrate how this connection is created and to explain why it is necessary at all.

Pilgrims' journeys to meaningful acceptance of the dominant narrative pass through two phases. First, the pilgrim begins to develop literacy in a vast collection of stories and tropes that circulate within dargāḥ culture; these include anecdotes about the actions of Sufi saints and Muslim martyrs, stories of the founding of the shrines of Ḥusain Ṭekrī, stories of other pilgrims, and broken phrases and declarations characteristic of those with *khulī ḥāẓirī*. These fragments offer the storyteller the opportunity to express opinions and ideas that, for cultural reasons, cannot be explicitly stated. Additionally, these stories, like all good stories, resonate on levels that are not immediately conscious, allowing a pilgrim to experience multiple formulations of truth. These stories, tropes, and anecdotes do not comprise a linear narrative; rather, they are a well of resources that may be drawn upon as the need arises. It is important to recognize that in most cases, they are only meaningful in relation to the situation in which they are mobilized. The recovery process is, I suggest, the product of these contextualized moments.

The second phase of a pilgrim's recovery entails making a connection between all of these moments and the pilgrim's own narrative of illness and recovery. Most commonly, this connection is made through "successful" *khulī hāẓirī*. The process of *khulī hāẓirī* typically begins with the juxtaposition of general expressions of pain, protestation, and threat and incoherent cries of suffering and anger. It eventually gives way to specific declarations of who performed magic to send the spirit and how much was paid, or the motivations of the wandering spirit that has chosen to attach itself to the victim are revealed and the conditions that must be met for the spirit to leave are enumerated. The connection forged through the embodied process of *khulī ḥāẓirī* between the fragmented speech of ḥāẓirī and the eventual confession of the spirit is, admittedly, tenuous, but it is also necessary. The truth experienced in a context-dependent relation of fragmented stories, tropes, and anecdotes cannot be made social; it is not a universally recognized, coherent narrative, and thus it cannot be communicated to others.[3] Because it cannot be communicated to others, it is not powerful enough to reintegrate the pilgrim with family and society, thereby allowing them to resume their social roles. As I will discuss in subsequent chapters, pilgrims generally conceptualize healing in terms of the successful resumption of social roles.

As I present and analyze the following narratives, I will contextualize them in the lives of these pilgrims in order to begin to document the healing potential of the combination of the universal impulse toward narrative and the particular stories, rituals, tropes, and concepts that together comprise the culture of Muslim saint shrines in India. In exploring the relationship between context, form, and content in the healing processes of Ḥusain Ṭekrī's pilgrims, I suggest that not only do pilgrims' recovery processes develop out of many contextually meaningful, narratively unconnected experiences, stories, and ritual practices, but also that the power of these experiences, stories, and practices—nearly all of which are available only in the context of dargāḥ culture—derives in large part from their fragmented and open-ended nature.

HEALING, LACK, AND PLACE

The first of the four women I will discuss in this chapter is Maya, who introduced me to Ḥusain Ṭekrī and to whom the reader was introduced in this book's opening pages. Maya, it will be recalled, is a Sindhi Hindu woman who has had a relationship with Ḥusain Ṭekrī for nearly thirty years; until recently she maintained a possession-based healing practice in her home in Udaipur, serving as the bodily host for Husain and 'Abbas. Two years after the year I spent in her household, I sat down with her seeking a single narrative of how she came to be a healer. Maya began with a story about the problem of having had four daughters and no sons—a problem that I knew actually occurred quite late in her relationship with Ḥusain Ṭekrī. This tendency to discuss one's relationship with Ḥusain Ṭekrī in terms of the most recent visit or problem is fairly common among those who have a long history with the site; an initial conversation often creates the impression that the current visit is the first one, and even when explicitly asked when they first came to Ḥusain Ṭekrī, pilgrims may mention a visit that turns out not to have been their first time either. Like all of my primary informants' stories, then, Maya's story of her healing and recovery does not proceed linearly or even chronologically. Similarly, the recovery process has many twists and turns, and, in the end, it resolves itself without any crashing moment of revelation.[4] In other words, what makes for good recovery often makes for poor narrative.

During this interview with Maya, because of my long relationship with her, I knew that her problems originated earlier than her not having a son. I was seeking a more chronological narrative that would explain her possession practice, and at my prompting she obliged by momentarily abandoning the discussion of her immediate family and offering a much-abbreviated chronology of her healing process:

> *Maya:* His [my husband's] [maternal] grandfather arranged his [Maya's husband's] marriage. He arranged two marriages. That [first] wife died . . . there was a single daughter from that marriage—she lives in the house behind this one—you know the one—she's not officially mine; she's married, though—*I* arranged the marriage . . . anyway, I got married, and my health declined, so someone told me to go to Ḥusain Ṭekrī, and so I went there; and when I got there, I got much, much worse . . . and I cried and cried . . . and I lived there, and I found comfort *[ārām]* there.[5]

When chronology and Ḥusain Ṭekrī itself are made the organizing principles of remembering, a variation of the formulaic response above is typically offered. Not coincidentally, those at Ḥusain Ṭekrī who were most interested in convincing me of its prestige were most likely to offer narratives like these, since they showcase Ḥusain Ṭekrī *itself* rather than the *relationship* individuals have with it. The Ḥusain Ṭekrī–centered chronological narrative that I initially sought from pilgrims, in other words, is often fashioned only in response to questions that place Ḥusain Ṭekrī at the center. How, then, can centrality that is not narratively represented—arguably, this is the nature of the centrality of Ḥusain Ṭekrī in the lives of its pilgrims—be measured and understood?

Following Maya's abbreviated chronology, I steered the discussion back to one centered on human relationships, asking a variation on one of the first questions asked of me whenever I met new people at Ḥusain Ṭekrī.

Carla: Did you go there alone?

Maya: No, his [my husband's] [maternal] grandfather went there.

Carla: When?

Maya: Twenty-eight years ago. When the marriage was happening. So what I mean is that my illness happened at that time *[ṭabī'at k̲h̲arāb ho gayī]*. I spent *so* much time trying to get well in Udaipur. I went everywhere making inquiries, but my situation remained bad *[hālat k̲h̲arāb thī]*; nothing helped. Someone told me to go to Ḥusain Ṭekrī, so I went to Ḥusain Ṭekrī. And when I got there, I found comfort.

Carla: How long did you stay? Forty days? [Forty days is the officially prescribed period of time for healing at Ḥusain Ṭekrī according to guidebooks and many of the pilgrims.]

Maya: No, I went there a lot—altogether, I spent at least three years there. Then, in the end, I found comfort there. You know, during the big fire walk, or any of the big festivals, and also if my health declined, I went.

Carla: Did you do the fire walk? Because I thought that only people with ḥāẓirī did that. [The Bombay Shi'ite community facilitates a fire walk at Ḥusain Ṭekrī; it is generally understood to burn offending spirits out of victims' bodies.]

Maya: [I had] *such* ḥāẓirī. Yes—ḥāẓirī. I was sick, so ḥāẓirī came—regular [English word used]—I mean, I had ḥāẓirī for three years over there. I had the kind that made me roll; I shook and tore up huge trees—I had *such* ḥāẓirī. Three years. And then I got better. And then, the Master's *[mālik]* power *[kariśma]* manifest itself, and Bābā began coming to me. The one from Ḥusain Ṭekrī. So he started coming and he told me to make that little place that I have on the roof. So in that little place I've done service *[sevā]* for the past fourteen years—or maybe fifteen.

Carla: And in the beginning, did you know what was happening to you?

Maya: From the heart—I mean, ḥāẓirī came—in the beginning, the wife of my husband's elder brother lives over there, and . . . and I had a little bit of a fight with them. So I went there, and this anger *[krodh]* came into my body—so it was there that he came for the first time, the Master. He said, "My daughter, I have come for your protection." *[At this point Maya's voice is filled with emotion; she sounds near tears.]* And so he started coming.

Here it is clear that Maya associates the saints' power with anger and a taxing physical process; the latter characteristic is elaborated below, when Maya details the differences between the presence of Husain and the presence of 'Abbas. The main thing to note here is that both ḥāẓirī and the coming of the saints are violent experiences associated with the anger of a saint; the difference is only that in ḥāẓirī the violence comes from the saint's physical punishment of the malevolent possessing spirit and the host's body becomes a conduit for the outwardly directed expression of the anger—and therefore potency—of the saint himself. This potency is also protective, and it allows Maya to assert some substantive control in her relationship with her sister-in-law.

The conversation about the visitation of the saints continued:

Carla: Every Thursday?

Maya: Every Thursday. [Maya may have been politely echoing my words here; possibly this liturgical regularity is irrelevant to the narrative at this point.] So [anyway], I went to another temple *[mandir]* and again, he started coming to me. You know "Golden Vilas"? It's in Udaipur. There they've made [a] Ḥusain Ṭekrī.[6] And so I went there regularly. So there, my body started experiencing a lot of problems, and he [Master] told me, "Build a sitting place *[baiṭhak]* on the roof of your house." So I had one made, and my health improved, and my ḥāẓirī really finally ended.

Carla: Do you know the cause of your ḥāẓirī? Usually at Ḥusain Ṭekrī people say that someone did some kind of magic . . .

Maya: Something or other happened to me during my wedding. During my wedding, where I was married, you know, there was *that* sort of place *[sthān]* there. You know Surajpol Picture Palace, right? Across from that, in the neighborhood—it's called Vegar Colony—there's a house there, my house. I used to live there. And that's where my wedding happened. So the groom's procession came there, and it was too crowded. You know—there are a lot of houses where . . . there are countless houses like that, you know, you're there and your body gives you some kind of little trouble, where, you know, people have to go to the bathroom or they spit somewhere, and they don't know what is going on there—for example, there are [hidden] temples *[mandir]* around. You know, if you yourself went from here to there, you wouldn't necessarily know what kind of places you were passing. And there are a lot of places like this in Udaipur.

Carla: What? *[Not quite understanding Maya's description.]*

Maya: Look, what do I have upstairs? [That is, "Do I not have a shrine to Ḥusain Ṭekrī on my roof?"] I mean, there are lots in Udaipur, Jaipur, everywhere; there are a lot of places like that [like Maya's shrine]—not just in Udaipur, actually.

Here Maya is offering a perspective on ḥāẓirī widely shared across religious communities—that ḥāẓirī and physical illness can befall a person who inadvertently defiles any sort of sanctified place, including a temple that is housed in a home. In other words, Maya does not believe that anyone performed any sort of malevolent magic on her; rather, someone at her wedding likely inadvertently defiled a hidden or home-based temple or shrine.

Carla: *[after a longish pause]* So, I have seen a lot of ḥāẓirī at Ḥusain Ṭekrī . . .

Maya: In the very beginning, I went back and forth to Ḥusain Ṭekrī for months and months, and the only ḥāẓirī I had was hidden ḥāẓirī *[gum ḥāẓirī]*. I had so much pain in my body, and then I had open ḥāẓirī *[khulī ḥāẓirī]*. And then, there, it [the bad presence] was removed . . . they put it in a lemon there, or it comes out through the mouth, since it comes in through the mouth . . . that [a problem's final resolution, in which the offending magical item, often a lemon, is vomited out] happens, a lot happens at the fire walk—when is the fire walk happening?

Carla: It already happened this year.

Maya: It *happened?* It's just that it's the height of summer right now . . . before, huge numbers of people came, but now with the drought, who will go? If they go, they'll have a lot of trouble because of the water.

[An interlude during which Maya explains the fire walk to her granddaughter]

Maya: *[returning to her story]* So I had become very ill, I stopped eating and drinking . . . I was healed in Jaora.

Carla: And nowadays, do the people who come here on Thursday go to Ḥusain Ṭekrī?

Maya: The command [to send people to Ḥusain Ṭekrī] comes a lot. The work happens here, and I send them to Ḥusain Ṭekrī, and work is also accomplished here. The Master comes on his own; work more or less happens here . . . and then I *[ham]* say, go to Ḥusain Ṭekrī and offer your respects *[salām]*—it's necessary to pay respect, isn't it?[7] If you have a child, you need to get a blessing for pregnant mothers, and the tradition there is to weigh your child in sugar. And for the troubled who recover, still the command comes to go there [to Ḥusain Ṭekrī], and so I have to send them, don't I?

Carla: When the Master comes, do you remember what happens?

Maya: I have the strongest memories—he comes so forcefully. The first time he came, I was so troubled, my body suffered—I coughed, and my body hurt . . . when he first came, my eyes and everything got so heavy, and water came out of my eyes when he came, and after that, after sitting . . . then, the middle dargāḥ, the one to the Standard-bearer ['Abbas]—he's so powerful *[tez]*, and when he comes . . . it's . . . *[Overwhelmed, she trails off.]*

Carla: *Really* powerful?

Maya: . . . Really powerful. And the big one, the close one [Husain; here Maya is referring to the fact that the rauẓa of Husain is the largest and nearest to the main gate at Ḥusain Ṭekrī], he's a bit cooler *[ṭhaṇḍhā]*. If there is serious work to be done, the middle one comes [ʿAbbas—the middle rauẓa on the path that connects them]; for the rest, usually the big one.

Maya frames her relationship with the saints in terms of places rather than persons, so much so that the rauẓas themselves *are* the saints. This tendency to think in terms of place rather than chronological time influences Maya's way of organizing her narrative. Additionally, here Maya's description of the nature of serving as a healer suggests that, for her, being a healer means acceptance of the fact that the process itself will be physically demanding and even painful; in other words, it is not possible for the healer to make the power of the saints available without personal cost. In the remainder of the interview, Maya explains her inability to offer her healing practice regularly in terms of a lack of physical and economic resources—not, in other words, in terms of the climax of a lifelong narrative of healing.

Carla: Your brother-in-law told me that it's a *jinn* that comes to you. [Arab in origin, *jinn* are understood by some pilgrims to cause ḥāẓirī, though there is also a widespread sense that these spirits can be reformed and made servants of Husain.]

Maya: *[clearly a little perturbed]* It's *not* a *jinn*. The big one comes, and the middle one—Lord Husain, and the Standard-bearer. [Tellingly, she only offers a proper name when her legitimacy is being questioned; normally, of course, using a simple name would be a sign of disrespect.]

Significantly, the process of possession by Muslim saints is ambiguous enough that Maya and her brother-in-law would have different understandings of who comes to her. As I will further discuss in the case of the third woman considered in this chapter, this ambiguity, remarkably, is not an impediment to the formation of intimate and transformative relationships between the patient and the healer. In fact, the interchangeability of these saints constitutes part of their unique appeal and strength.

My conversation with Maya concluded with Maya's own understanding of the true nature of her relationship with Husain and ʿAbbas, and the connection between this relationship and her healing practice.

Carla: Your husband once told me that what you do for them [Husain and ʿAbbas] is service *[sevā]*.

Maya: *Sevā*—yes.

Maya's granddaughter: *[excited]* My grandma, every Thursday *[jummerāt]* . . .

Maya: He [Husain] has become a guru of our home; he's a guru, so we have to do service.

Maya's granddaughter: Every Thursday *[guruvār]* we wash him, and we offer a garland of red roses . . .

Significantly, Maya describes the saint of her home shrine as a *guru.* This title is notable for the fact that it derives its meaning from a private relationship between two individuals; the identity of both, and the power of the guru, derives primarily from the relationship itself rather than from outside, doctrinal, or institutional sources. Simple devotional actions give the relationship its substance. The discussion of service to a guru continued with Maya elaborating on her healing practice as another kind of *sevā.*

Maya: [interrupting] We do that *every* day. Before, I did a lot of service . . . and crowds came.

Maya's granddaughter: When grandma is seated up there, you know . . .

Carla: How many years ago are we talking about now?

Maya's granddaughter: Twenty-eight years!

Maya: Eight years ago, a lot of people came here. But now, for the past six months, or seven, I have stopped. My health isn't so good.

Maya's granddaughter: And Auntie Pinky [Maya's youngest daughter, recently married] . . .

Maya: [interrupting] I do service, of course—but I don't sit up there much anymore.

Maya's granddaughter: When Bābā [Husain] used to come here . . .

Maya: Now I do that very little. I'm alone now . . .

Maya's granddaughter: And the crowds were so big . . .

Maya: . . . And now, the cleaning, I have to do everything; people, they come and go. And everyone comes for their own selfish reasons *[matlab],* and they get what they want, and they go . . . The work happens regardless, of course, because the One from Jaora is a great being *[hastī].*

Carla: [returning to Maya's granddaughter's attempt to explain the situation] So that's the reason—Pinky is finally married and there is a lot of work here?

Maya: Work, yes, that's the problem: If someone comes, I have to give them time, and I don't have time. If someone comes and sits for an hour, and someone else for half an hour, I ought to speak with them, and I don't really have the resources to hire someone to do all the housework [that Pinky used to do]. It costs money to hire cleaning women and people like that . . .

Carla: But in *sevā* there is no cost, right?

Maya: No, no—not at all—what kind of cost could there be? [*Sevā* is] the lord's *[bhagavān kā]* . . . No, to get others to do the housework, that requires money. *[pause]* What I mean is that everything was resolved here, so they [pilgrims] offer some sheet, or some flowers, or sweets . . .

Maya's granddaughter: They put sweet-smelling [perfume] on grandma . . .

Maya: They offered [Bābā] the sweet smell [that is offered to him], you know? *[She is quiet.]*

Carla: So what do you do for *sevā* nowadays?

Maya: Flowers, and on Thursday *[jummerāt],* lobān in the morning at 8:30 [the time of the earliest lobān at Ḥusain Ṭekrī] . . . lobān, incense, flowers, perfume *['iṭr],* whatever is normally offered to the Master, that gets offered and I pay my respects *[salāmī denā].*

Maya's story features several elements typical of such narratives, such as troubles brought on by marriage, a recurring pattern of ḥāẓirī and visits to Ḥusain Ṭekrī, problems with children and the family, and, eventually, resolution. However, what seems to tie her narrative together is space and place rather than chronology; whether the visitation is that of Maya to Ḥusain Ṭekrī, pilgrims to Maya's shrine, or the saints to Maya's body itself, Maya's story is carried from one moment to another through movement in space rather than movement in time.

Maya's periodization of her life—her chronology, such as it is—is very broadly conceived, encompassing time spans that are too large to be meaningful on a day-to-day basis. For example, in a discussion with Maya about whether or not she wanted me to use her real name in publication, she said that because her troubles were behind her and her marriage and the marriage of her daughters was accomplished, there was no harm in her actual name being used. It seems that for Maya, the recovery process more or less spanned her entire married and maternal life and entered a final phase only upon the marriage of her last daughter. Healing, then, seems not to be conceived of on an individual level; rather, it is conceptualized and experienced through relationships with immediate and extended family members. In keeping with this understanding of healing, Maya also correctly speculated that the younger women at Ḥusain Ṭekrī whose stories I was following—two of whom are among those considered in this chapter—would likely not want their actual names used if they weren't married. Again, social integration seems to be a major measure of one's level of recovery; or, put slightly differently, recovery is only real when it is recognized and accepted by others.

MOBILE STORIES, MOBILIZING STORIES, MOBILE BODIES

Babli is a Sindhi Hindu woman from Udaipur who looks as if she is in her early thirties.[8] While her story and situation are uniquely her own, she is also representative of a particular type of Indian woman whom I often encountered at Ḥusain Ṭekrī and its satellite sites: urban women with working-class roots (in Babli's case, her father supported the family on small itinerant sales jobs; her brothers now run small shops in Udaipur) who have had some success in Hindi-medium school and subsequently find themselves torn between using their education to make their own money or getting married. This tension presents a challenge to urban working-class and lower-middle-class families with daughters, irrespective of their religious affiliation.[9] This tension between labor for one's own money and labor in marriage—a tension endured by lower-middle-class urban women—is uniquely addressed at the shrines of Muslim saints, and in some ways at Ḥusain Ṭekrī in particular.

Babli and I first met when I was conducting an interview with the manager of the lodge in which she was staying shortly after I returned from fieldwork at a Shiʿite *imāmbāṛā* in Bombay that affiliates itself with Ḥusain Ṭekrī. Over the year following our initial meeting and during my follow-up research, I visited her frequently, seeking to understand the relationship that Hindus have with Muslim shrines and to determine whether there are any significant differences between the relationships that Hindus and Muslims have with these shrines.

Over the course of our time together, Babli made a point of presenting herself as educated (which she is), still invested in learning (in the time I have known her, she has taught herself how to read the Arabic alphabet), cosmopolitan (which she is, particularly for a woman of her age and socioeconomic status, given the range of people she knows at Ḥusain Ṭekrī), and free to come and go as she pleases and to speak to anyone in the service of the furtherance of knowledge (which she is, within the rich network of dargāḥs in northwestern India). She also proved to be the informant least willing to be recorded. Often in the course of our conversations she would ask me to turn off my minidisc recorder, particularly on the somewhat rare occasions when she was talking explicitly about herself.[10]

My first extended conversation with Babli took place squatting outside the rauẓa of Maulā ʿAli at Ḥusain Ṭekrī. She and other young women had congregated outside the shrine and were waiting for lobān, which is distributed by attendants carrying wooden-handled metal dishes filled with red-hot coals, over which lobān is burned. Because she was present during an interview I was conducting with the manager of the lodge at which she was staying, Babli knew about my project; our conversation outside of Maulā ʿAli's shrine involved her sharing Shiʿite-generated stories about Karbala as well as the relationships between many of its martyrs. She related the names of the children who died at Karbala, the familial relationships between the martyrs of Karbala, and explained that a hand is the symbol of the *panj-e-pāk,* or the Five Pure Ones, because when Ḥaẓrat ʿAbbas was martyred it was his arm that was cut off first. She seamlessly moved from these stories of martyrdom to her version of the story of ʿAli's founding of a small shrine near Ḥusain Ṭekrī called Cābuk Sharīf, or [Place of the] Honorable Whip.[11]

The story about Cābuk Sharīf that Babli recounted was a version of a story that I heard from many pilgrims; a version also appears in some of the recently published guidebooks to Ḥusain Ṭekrī. In Babli's version, some local village men come to visit the shrines of Husain and ʿAbbas. One of them wore his dirty sandals inside the shrines and began to say wrong *[galat]* and obscene *[gandā]* things about ʿAbbas and Husain. He was warned to stop, but he continued. Eventually, when he and his friends were heading back to their village, they came to the place where Cābuk Sharīf now stands and were confronted by a man in white clothes (which in Babli's narrative was coded as Islamic through the use of the formal Urdu phrase *"safed libās"*). The man came out of the earth brandishing a whip, which he used to beat the offending young man to death. His friends took his body back to their village, and the shrine was built on the place where the man came out of the earth. Babli concluded the story by stating that the man who came out of the earth was none other than Maulā ʿAli himself.

While much could be said about this initial barrage of information, several points are particularly noteworthy. First, what allowed Babli to move effortlessly in time and space between stories about the origin of the shrines at Ḥusain Ṭekrī, the story of Karbala, and the doctrinally and devotionally significant configuration of the Five Pure Ones was a discourse of family. As the discussion of the geography of Ḥusain Ṭekrī in the first chapter has shown, this discourse of family is pervasive, undergirding how Muslim land becomes sacred; indeed, the discourse of family is one of the main means that pilgrims of all religious backgrounds employ in order to relate to one another and to the shrines. Second, in this initial extended conversation Babli had me fooled: by virtue of her nickname (common in both Hindu and Muslim communities),[12] her extensive knowledge of Muslim saints, and her region- and religion-neutral *salwar kameez,* she passed as Muslim—or at least I did not know for certain what her religious background was until, in response to my asking if she was Muslim, she said that she was Hindu, and by *jāti,* Sindhi.

I was not the only one who was fooled by Babli's devotion and knowledge of "Islamic" things; later that month, at the shrine dedicated to Bībī Fatima, a young Sunni woman watched Babli and a group of women reading a story about Fatima titled "The Tale of the Ten Virtuous Women." Readings of Shi'ite devotional stories are a regular feature of everyday life at Ḥusain Ṭekrī, and their significant contribution to its culture will be discussed in chapter 5. Babli concluded her reading with a series of typically Muslim devotional gestures, punctuated in the middle with a quick pan-Hindu *namaste.* This Sunni woman and I had just concluded a discussion wherein she had explained to me that the reason that Hindus become tormented by spirits *[bhūt-pret]* is because "those people [that is, Hindus] are dirty *[nāpāk].*" Perhaps confused by Babli's ambiguously Muslim actions and appearance, she asked Babli if she was Muslim *[musalmān].* Babli, clearly pleased at the confusion, replied that no, she was actually Sindhi, a Hindu. After this the two moved off together and became involved in a conversation that they clearly wanted to keep private. This culture of passing—or, more generally, this opportunity for anonymity—is another dominant and largely exclusive feature of the culture of Muslim saint shrines, and the consequences as well as possible causes of this will be further discussed in subsequent chapters.

Third, and most importantly, by telling the story of Cābuk Sharīf where and when she did, Babli was commenting on (and negotiating) her own life situation, as well as her immediate circumstances, through relating a story about a Muslim saint. The tendency of pilgrims to identify with Muslim saints or other characters in stories about these saints is central to the experience of pilgrims at Ḥusain Ṭekrī, and to the experiences that pilgrims have at Muslim shrines in general. In this case, on this particular day, Babli was menstruating and so could not enter the shrine to receive lobān; this was why she and the other women were squatting outside. A story about the dire importance of keeping a shrine pure, delivered as it was by a woman waiting outside the shrine because of her menstrual cycle, placed Babli in an elevated position despite her impure *[nāpāk]* status since she, unlike the unfortunate man of the story, knew better than to disrespect and pollute the shrine. Additionally, in telling this story Babli, an educated urban woman, was placing herself above ignorant village men. In doing so, she suggested there is endless opportunity for a woman to cultivate, refine, and educate herself in the service of the saints rather than in the service of her family or husband. Finally, it is likely that Babli related this story to me because she feared what a few other individuals, both Hindu and Muslim, explicitly related to me in our discussions of Ḥusain Ṭekrī: that as a barbaric Westerner I might actually walk right into the shrine during my menses. The fact that it was not immediately obvious to me why a group of women would be sitting together just outside the shrine—"Why don't you come on in to take lobān?" I asked, and they all smirked until I understood—probably only contributed to Babli's anxiety that I might bring the wrath of the saint down on myself, ultimately prompting her to relate the story of Cābuk Sharīf, several kilometers distant, rather than the story of the immediately present rauẓa of 'Ali. The point here is mainly that, once again, stories of Muslim saints gave Babli a way to assert her own honor and to comment on a situation without directly and therefore dangerously involving herself in it. Telling this story also placed Babli in the role of teacher, which is the first stage in a long process that may eventually result in Babli developing a healing practice of her own.

Following our first extended conversation at Maulā 'Ali's rauẓa, my subsequent conversations with Babli were shaped by our mutual desire to share information about spirits, ḥāẓirī, healing practices such as Maya's, and Babli's understanding of Sufi saints and Muslim martyrs. As time passed, however, it became increasingly striking that Babli neither spoke at length about herself nor had ḥāẓirī in my presence. Babli herself had once shyly observed that I had never seen her ḥāẓirī, and she wondered what I would think of her if I saw them because they were so fearsome.

One day in early November—quite late in our time together—Babli and I were enjoying a rare private moment sitting in the courtyard of her lodge. Babli shared that she was feeling much better of late—her body, she said, felt light (*halkā*, the typical adjective chosen to describe the body immediately after ḥāẓirī), and that she felt "*ekdam* normal" (absolutely normal). I expressed genuine happiness at the prospect that she was feeling so much better, and soon after this we went back to the lodge room where her father and brother were sitting. Almost immediately Babli was thrown into a bout of violent ḥāẓirī lasting about two minutes. She bent over and beat her back against the wall every time she straightened up, and her cries of pain were punctuated by entreaties to "*shāhzādī*"[13] to stop her torture, which is a fairly generic refrain in ḥāẓirī. As Babli struggled, her elderly father raised his hands above his head in a *namaste* gesture of gratitude, clearly delighted at the situation, and her brother grinned throughout the episode. The episode's end was signaled by Babli standing up straight, saying, "It's over now," and sitting down on the floor next to me.

In the moment, I made the decision not to ask her about the incident, since it seemed clear from her previous expression of concern about the fearsomeness of her ḥāẓirī and the fact that I had never seen her ḥāẓirī that she wanted to keep it from interfering with our "normal," even collegial, relationship. Two things about this episode, however, are notable. First, in Babli's experience (again, quite representative of the experience of nearly all the pilgrims I interviewed), while bodily sensations of pain can be trusted—in other words, pain is always evidence that something is wrong, and bodily feelings of disease and unease are never illusory—feelings of well-being are often misleading or have no relationship with the actual state of the individual. Healing, then, is not recognizable based upon how an individual feels; the measure of healing—both the medium of the experience of healing and the sources recognized as effecting the recovery—is not the body and cannot be the body, since, from the perspective of those with ḥāẓirī, the body is experienced as little more than a heap of vulnerabilities. This alone should give pause to researchers inclined to liken forms of spirit possession to forms of psychoanalysis or therapy; in ḥāẓirī, healing is a process of self-discipline and self-erasure, not conscious self-exploration. Further, the violence of ḥāẓirī is never understood as *damaging*, even though it is extremely physically taxing.

Often when I would visit Babli in her lodge room, both before and after this ḥāẓirī event, her father and brother (also a practitioner of *khulī ḥāẓirī*) passed the time by telling stories about Sufi saints and martyrs, and particularly stories about the recently deceased Mastān Bābā.[14] Babli remained much more inclined to relate stories about Muslim martyrs and saints—including stories about her own relationship with Mastān Bābā while he was still alive—than she was in directly relating the specifics of her own story, that is, her own story of suffering, ḥāẓirī, and healing at Ḥusain Ṭekrī. Almost without exception, she did not speak of her specific situation without my prompting. Likely this was in part a result of her desire to offer me useful information about "Islam," but it also speaks to certain tendencies that Babli shares with other pilgrims to Muslim saint shrines.

First, as was the case in her relating the story of the inception of Cābuk Sharīf, Babli's use of the stories of Muslim saints suggests that the interchangeable elements that fill stories of Muslim saints' and martyrs' lives offer pilgrims of all religious backgrounds an impersonal set of narratives and tropes that they can utilize to articulate and negotiate their own struggles and aspirations. In this way, Babli's stories of Mastān Bābā often allowed her to reflect upon and share her struggles without explicitly talking about herself. For example, one day in late November not too long after I first witnessed Babli's ḥāẓirī, in the midst of a series of stories about Mastān Bābā that Babli, her father, and her brother were exchanging as much, I think, for their own entertainment as for my information, Babli related the following:

Once a woman came to Mastān Bābā and asked him to help her free her two sons who had been wrongly imprisoned. Mastān Bābā told her to drop her *salwār* and her sons would be free.[15] At this point in the story Babli emphasized that the woman was actually wearing a long chemise with very shallow side slits and the *salwār* was actually a *cūṛīdār*—that is, a style that gathers into many tight pleats below the knee. Removing *cūṛīdār* is actually quite involved because of all the pleated fabric, and loosening the drawstring of a *cūṛīdār* results only in the waist falling no further than the knees. In relating these sartorial details, Babli's point was that while Mastān Bābā had asked the woman to do something that would normally be highly immodest, in this case, owing to the cut and style of the clothing, not an inch of unseemly flesh would have been revealed. However, the woman only dropped one pant leg. Soon after this, a man came and reported that one of her sons had been freed, but not the other. Eventually, Babli remarked, the other son was freed, but it took a lot of time and money.

In Babli's story the woman's trust in Mastān Bābā is not unconditional, and consequently it is not fully rewarded. This ideal of unconditional surrender to one's guru, *pīr,* or *murśid* is central to all of the devotional traditions of the subcontinent—recall, for example, Maya's veneration of Husain and 'Abbas as gurus. In this way, stories about Muslim saints have a pan-subcontinental appeal. The story's attractiveness—both to Babli and in general—also derives from the fact that it is driven by pan-subcontinental values, chief among them the fact that a woman's power and value derive from her chastity and her ability and willingness to support and protect her children and husband. In relating a story of a woman whose association with a Sufi saint appears to be causing her to lose her honor for the sake of her sons, Babli was speaking indirectly about herself, asserting that the morally suspect life of a single thirtysomething woman seeking the help of a Sufi saint was not compromising her value or her honor. The story also conveys another major aspect of pan-Indian perceptions of some Muslim saints that was also evident in Maya's description of the presence of Husain and 'Abbas: they are dangerous, often angry, and often transgressive, and therein lies their power.

Once again, the context in which stories about Muslim saints and martyrs are related is often as significant as the stories themselves. Babli shared this story with me after noting that her mother had initially forbidden her to visit Mastān Bābā, and that it was her brothers who had first smuggled her to see him. In telling this story, Babli was able to rebuke her mother's unspoken fears about her honor and to assert that while the crowds that Sufi saints in India attract are often rough and not strictly gender-segregated, a young woman like herself was absolutely not compromising her honor—and, therefore, her value—by becoming a devotee. The utility and necessity of making this point in such a seemingly roundabout way becomes clear when it is recognized that in most Indian contexts even explicitly denying wrongdoing related to one's honor as a woman is enough to taint one's name—that questions of honor are raised, even when innocence is proven, is still enough to damage most women's marriage prospects. Relating this story allowed Babli to defend her lifestyle at Ḥusain Ṭekrī without explicitly talking about herself and thereby calling her honor into question.

In addition to lending themselves to a wide variety of situations, stories of Muslim saints are uniquely portable. Much in the same way that Hindu goddesses, by virtue of their association with the feminine divine power known as *śakti*, are regarded as somewhat interchangeable, all Muslim saints—both their stories and their shrines—are regarded as connected and somewhat interchangeable.[16] Therefore, to begin a healing process with one Muslim saint creates the foundational relationship necessary for moving on to another saint as one's personal situation dictates. A close friend of Babli's, for example, once told me that her odyssey—by public bus—from her home in Maharashtra to Ḥusain Ṭekrī began with prayers to and subsequent visions of Sāī Bābā. The trip as she related it to me was full of miraculous occurrences and near disasters; whatever happened, the journey was no small event for a young Hindu woman who had never really traveled before, much less traveled with no one other than her two small children. In any case, although Sāī Bābā has no orthodox, specific, or lineage-based relationship with Ḥusain Ṭekrī, for this woman, both Sāī Bābā and the saints associated with Ḥusain Ṭekrī participate in the power associated with Muslim sainthood.[17] Similarly, Babli herself had been to some of the same home shrines in Udaipur that Maya had visited; she had also gone to Mīrā Dātār, a Muslim saint shrine in Gujarat.

Babli benefited from the flexibility of this network during a particularly difficult time, when her father's health deteriorated to the point where it was necessary for them to return to Udaipur for treatment. After this her own general health and situation deteriorated, and she took a number of typical ḥāẓirī-related actions that will be discussed in chapter 4. Following this turn of events, on Babli's request I visited her mother when I returned to Udaipur to see Maya. The visit was uneventful, though also somewhat sad. Over dinner Babli's mother reiterated something that Babli had once told me Mastān Bābā had said about her: that Babli needed to be married outside India to "a nice Sindhi or Punjabi boy who can understand what ḥāẓirī is." Babli's mother was understandably worried about Babli, and Babli, upon hearing my report, became increasingly worried about her mother, whom she could not visit because of the widely held belief that one cannot leave Ḥusain Ṭekrī without the permission of its saints.

Babli's concern about her mother sat in the background for several months, and then, in December, Babli told me that she had had a dream in which she was buying a book called *Mālik ke Phūl* (Flowers of the Lord). However, the next day, when she went looking for the book among Ḥusain Ṭekrī's booksellers, she was unable to find it. A second dream clarified that she was actually looking at the book at a stall in Ajmer, which resulted in the formulation of a travel plan that would allow her to take the narrow-gauge railway from Jaora to Udaipur, stop in and visit her mother, and then continue on the same railway line to Ajmer, where she would find the book she was looking for. The dense network of subcontinental Muslim shrines offers endless opportunities for individually tailored pilgrimages, so that problems that seem to be unsolvable at one shrine can be meaningfully transferred to others using, among other things, the notion of the interchangeability of Muslim saints, and therefore of Muslim saint shrines. In this case, the interconnectedness of Muslim shrines made Babli's visit home possible.

This network's viability is sustained by changes in transportation over the past century that have significantly increased the ability of most Indians to move from one shrine to another. Thus, places with a simple local following have become regional or national destinations, and the historical lineage-based relationships between distant Sufi shrines have taken on new lives as pilgrims to one shrine learn of a distant shrine of a student or devotee and, using a bus or train, manage to make a pilgrimage there as well. In the case of Ḥusain Ṭekrī, its position on the narrow-gauge railway to Ajmer means that although it has no historical or lineage-based relationship with the Chishtī order, many pilgrims of all religious backgrounds visit them both as part of a single pilgrimage.

Like Maya's narratives, Babli's are not linear. Instead of producing a straightforward chronology, conversations with Babli reveal a process that depends upon the constant cycling and recycling of stories of Sufi saints and Muslim martyrs. In a final example of the improvisatory range of associations and tales that Muslim shrines and saint stories uniquely offer to pilgrims, in the weeks immediately following Babli's ḥāẓirī, her father spoke about Babli's relationship with Mastān Bābā:

Taking [a garland] from his own neck, he put it on [Babli] right there in front of everyone. At that time, what was happening was the result of another magician, a sweeper *[bhaṅgī]* . . . [Mastān Bābā gave Babli the garland and said] "Go, my child. He [the sweeper] won't do anything, and he won't be able to say anything, and he won't be able to take this child's [Babli's] life *[jān]*." If he [Mastān Bābā] said that much, what more could anyone want? He [the magician] used to say, "I'll take that one's [Babli's] life in fifteen days, I'll take it in ten days . . . " But, sister [Carla], the savior *[bacānewāle]* is greater than the killers *[mārnewāle]*. And that's why we [as Hindus] believe *[bharosā karnā]* in him . . .

It is likely that Babli's father told this story in particular because earlier that day Babli had had an experience during her ḥāẓirī that had resulted in a garland of flowers being put around her neck. Soon after telling it, Babli entered the room wearing the garland.

Babli: In ḥāẓirī, the magician put a garland on the spirit *[pret]* . . . at Laṅgar Well *[Laṅgar kuāṁ]* very intense ḥāẓirī came.[18] The things that my spirit demanded last night at the *imāmbāṛā*, he got. [He demanded] *tabarruk*.[19] He demanded husked grain, one thing, and he got two things: the husked grain and *revṛī*.[20]

Carla: But why did he give the bad spirit these good things?

Babli: It's Bābā's condition, that you [the magician] aren't going to give this one [Babli] any trouble. And you won't keep this one from studying *[paṛhāī karnā]*, she's studying, that is, she's worshipping *['ibādat]*.

Carla: And the garland?

Babli: In ḥāẓirī, he picked it up, my spirit put it on, and swore . . . "I won't do magic anymore." . . . Someone left this garland as an offering, and Maulā's order happened: "Put it on," and then my magician—that *harijan* Mool Chand—picked it up and put it on. Now, when the flowers fall off, I'll cool them in water, and I'll keep the string around my neck.

Carla: [Seeking an explicit statement on the four players—the magician, Maulā, the spirit the magician put on Babli, and Babli herself—who all share Babli's body during her ḥāẓirī] Who put the garland on *whom?*

Babli: First he [the magician or the possessing spirit] took a lot of ḥāẓirī, and in ḥāẓirī he swore, "Oh 'Ali! Maulā 'Ali, I'm not going to do this anymore, I'm not going to cause any trouble." Then he put on the garland, and after that I fell down, unconscious.

Babli's story about being garlanded by Mastān Bābā (an experience that she related to me herself on a different occasion) was a significant moment in her healing process.[21] Being re-garlanded at Laṅgar Well provided her with a tangible reminder of her relationship with Mastān Bābā as well as a protective object. It is also evident that the repetition of the action of receiving a garland is part of a process of healing that is not based on linear narrative, but rather on the creative recycling of a pan-Indian trope of auspiciousness and honor. As is evident from her use of the term *Bābā* as well as the specific name of 'Ali, the interchangeable character of Muslim saints and martyrs also contributes to Babli's ability to connect past and present events meaningfully.

Finally, as is almost always the case when pilgrims use tropes to describe pivotal moments in their healing process, it very well may be the case that Babli herself never received any garland from Mastān Bābā. From the standpoint of power and efficacy, whether or not the trope-based event ever really occurred or not is irrelevant, particularly since she was given one in ḥāẓirī. While the fact that Babli's father independently related the story to me makes it more likely that the event happened at least once, it is also possible that Babli has simply internalized a story or event that she has been exposed to at some point in the past.

The relative unimportance of whether or not moments in the healing process physically occur is similarly displayed in a conversation that Babli and I had during my follow-up research. I believe that Babli was somewhat willing to have her story recorded in this instance because she regarded her problems as having been largely resolved (*ṭhaṇḍhā,* she said), and with the minidisc recorder going, she repeated her spontaneous and previously unrecorded telling of the following story:

Babli: In the last birth, [Babli's neighbor in this life] was a Muslim queen *[rānī],* and I was the servant *[kanīz]* of a queen who lived just across the street.

Carla: Both were Muslim?

Babli: Yes, both were Muslim. So she [the queen who was Babli's mistress] had gone to the bathroom, and her child, he was playing . . . and the queen who lived across the street came to kill the child. And I picked up the child and brought him to his mother. So my enemy was born. [The queen who had attempted to kill the child said to Babli], "Hey, you dog, I won't let you go even in the next life!" And so in this life, they had magic done on me for revenge.

Carla: So in the past life everyone was Muslim, and now everyone is Sindhi?

Babli: Yes, in the past life everyone was Muslim, and in this life they are Sindhi. But the magician, he's a *harijan.*[22] In a previous life, though, he was Muslim too, and I was his *potī* [paternal granddaughter] . . . *[Here Babli explains that this whole story is actually an old situation, and that it had been resolved when she had asked to be shown why the neighbors had done magic on her.]* In the last life, that magician was my paternal grandfather; Mastān Bābā showed him in a dream that in the last life, he was my paternal grandfather. Then the magician asked for forgiveness.

> [The magician became present in Babli's body through ḥāẓirī in the presence of Mastān Bābā and said], "I'm not going to do magic on my paternal granddaughter anymore. Please punish me with death. I didn't know that in a past life she was my paternal granddaughter, god *[k̲h̲udā]* forgive my sin *[gunāh]* . . . " and he asked Mastān Bābā for death.

There is much more to this complicated story, but here two final points should be made. First, Babli emphasized that this case had more or less resolved itself—literally, become cold *[ṭhaṇḍhā]*. This is likely why she was able to relate it to me in such detail; hindsight is twenty-twenty. The somewhat coherent morality, punishment, and cause-and-effect nature of this story is made possible and meaningful only because it is a story that now lives in the past. Second, it is significant that the story that Babli relates about her past life has several direct parallels with a similar story about 'Ali's martyrdom that Babli related much earlier in our relationship. She began this story with a somewhat breathless listing of the names and details of many of the martyrs of Karbala, and then moved to a more specific description of 'Ali's martyrdom in which the betrayal of his servant woman played a significant part.

> There were the Fourteen Innocent Ones, they died, and 272 total, 272 died. And Bībī Zaineb saw everything. She was Imām Husain's sister—her rauẓa is next to Bābā Husain's. And Sakina, she was 'Abbas's niece. They loved each other *[sneh]* very much, uncle and niece, so their rauẓas are next to each other. One brother [was killed] reading *namāz* and one was given poison . . . Hasan and Husain, they were brothers, and one was poisoned, and the other was beheaded. Bābā Husain, who is also called Imām Husain. And Bābā Maulā 'Ali, who was so beloved of Allah, he sat in worship *['ibādat]* twenty-four hours a day. No one could recognize him, and his body remained in iron twenty-four hours a day. Only when he read *namāz,* he would perform *wuẓū*, washing his face and mouth. At this time, he took on the form of a normal man *[ām insān ke rūp meṁ ho jāte the],* though the rest of the time he was made of iron. Bābā Maulā 'Ali, Hasan and Husain's father . . . his servant *[kanīz, naukrānī],* she went and met with the unbelievers *[kāfir]* . . . she was greedy, and she noted that it was possible to kill him when he performed *wuẓū,* so she told the *kāfir*s: "Before he reads *namāz* he washes his hands and face—performs *wuẓū*—at this moment, if you cut his neck, he'll die."[23]

Babli's narrative of her own past life as a servant who saves the life of a child sits in contrast to the servant who causes a life to be taken. Again, in a slightly different way, stories of Muslim saints and martyrs play a central role in Babli's recovery process. Their stories become the medium through which her own experiences are articulated and eventually narrativized and understood.

If Babli's tendency to relate stories of Muslim saints that in some way speak to her own experience is common among pilgrims to Muslim shrines, her means of describing what had happened to her was equally reliant upon pan-subcontinental tropes. Babli's first explicit discussion of her situation, which took place many months after our initial meeting, was only offered in response to my question of what, specifically, had been done to her. When I asked her what had caused her to seek refuge at Ḥusain Ṭekrī, she simply said, "My neighbors were jealous because I had eaten rice and milk." Eating rice and milk is a clear, simple way of saying that Babli's neighbors were jealous of her because she was healthy and prosperous, enjoying abundance (milk) and purity (whiteness). Babli's explanation of her neighbors' deceit is a variation on what is far and away the most common trope for magic *[jādū]* in India: the introduction of polluted substances into food that is ostensibly pure. The resulting illness and spirit possession is the reason that almost all pilgrims offer for why they have come to Ḥusain Ṭekrī, and, more generally, why one might visit Muslim saint shrines.

It is doubtful that Babli would have elaborated any further had she not been prompted by a visit from a neighbor in the lodge where she stayed. The woman, in the course of admiring the clothing of another young woman who was also visiting Babli, asked how much the clothing cost. This young woman had stopped by Babli's room to discuss the meaning a dream that she had had; dreams, along with Sufi saint stories, are one of the most significant ways to discuss and, in some ways, change one's situation.

After this young woman and the neighbor had left, Babli became visibly upset, explaining to me that it is acceptable to compliment someone but inappropriate to ask them how much things cost. To ask is to betray jealousy rather than innocent admiration. Angry about this apparent display of jealousy, Babli went on to say that her jealous neighbors had fed her vegetables and *khīr* (two foods that are far on the pure end of the Brahminical Hindu purity/pollution spectrum) into which they had mixed pig urine, which is polluting by any standard, and perhaps polluting in a particularly Islamic way, since Muslims are forbidden to eat pork. This type of polluting substance would then be particularly repugnant to the Muslim saints upon whom Babli is relying for her recovery, and, as was the case with Maya, the anger of the saint forms a significant part of his potency.

HIDDENNESS, PASSING, AND UNKNOWING

Priya is a Hindu Yadav woman in her mid-twenties from city of Sagar, in northern Madhya Pradesh.[24] We first met at the rauẓa of Bībī Fatima, where Priya was participating in a ritual reading of a Muslim devotional story known as "The Tale of the Ten Virtuous Women." When she saw me, she came over to talk, despite the protestations of the group. Priya was a regular participant in the reading of these stories. On the day we first spoke, however, she responded to the protestations of her companions by saying that she had had more than enough of the stories. In our initial meeting Priya talked about how hard it was to be a *ḥāẓirīwālī;* marriage prospects were doubtful, and she wondered out loud about her future. At the time of this meeting Priya had been resident at Ḥusain Ṭekrī for about three months. Because of our mutual interest in one another and her clear commitment to spending an extended amount of time at Ḥusain Ṭekrī, Priya became one of my primary informants.

Compared to Babli, Priya was more inclined to talk about her own feelings and experiences, though it is notable that she was never able to offer me the personal details that Babli eventually offered about the cause of her afflictions. Further, while she knew stories about Husain and 'Ali, she never developed the expertise that Babli attained, though she did develop other aspects of a Muslim identity that I will discuss as her story unfolds.

My initial formal interview with Priya took place in the presence of her mother; like everyone at Ḥusain Ṭekrī, Priya had a caretaker from home with her. The story began not with the onset of her affliction, as one might expect, but with a description of her relationship with a man named Salim:

> *Priya:* He works in a depot—the man at whose home I had ḥāẓirī. He works, too, and he has a family. You know, where they keep buses and all that—he repairs them. At his home he has all the dargāḥs and rauẓas in Jaora; the pictures *[tasvīr]* are all there, and *panja*—he has everything there.[25] And every Thursday, Bābā Sahib comes for him. And he's [Bābā Sahib] come countless times when I was in ḥāẓirī. The *bābās* of Ḥusain Ṭekrī, and his servants *[gulām]* have also come during my ḥāẓirī . . . for him, Salim, they come to him *[un ke pās pahunchte haiṁ]* . . .
>
> *Priya's mother:* In his body *[śarīr, tan]*.
>
> *Priya:* You've seen it, haven't you? Sometimes Bābā Sahib comes to someone—that's how it happens with Salim.
>
> *Priya's mother:* *[with feeling]* He's a really good man.
>
> *Priya:* I've had ḥāẓirī for two years, and all my bad spirit *[balā]* keeps saying is, "I'm going to take this innocent one and go."[26] And he keeps saying that, to this day. *[laughing]* This is my third round at Ḥusain Ṭekrī. The very first time I came for eight days—he [Salim] sent me to offer my greetings here *[salāmī denā]*. I came here and I had ḥāẓirī. Then I came for the fire walk, and I went across the coals.[27] I only stayed a day that time. And then I had a dream *[bishārat]*, it happened two or three times.

I saw all the rauẓas here at Ḥusain Ṭekrī, and strangers' faces, faces I didn't recognize. It's possible that your face was one of them. So I went and told him [Salim], and he said, "This one is having dreams about that [Ḥusain Ṭekrī] exactly. Take her there." So, for fifteen or twenty days, it went on like that. I had ḥāẓirī there [at Salim's], and I had ḥāẓirī at home, too. I just sat there, sometimes I was in ḥāẓirī for twenty-four hours, but those people [her family] couldn't possibly have understood what was happening. And to this day I still don't know who sent the bad spirit, or why, or what is happening. *[Priya is quiet.]*

Carla: And this has been the situation for two years? You said that you've had ḥāẓirī for two years.

Priya: I've had ḥāẓirī for two years, but maybe what has been done to me *[jo mere ūpar hai]* is really old; it's possible that it's eight or ten years old. But, when the secret is fully revealed, and my ḥāẓirī open completely, the bad spirit *[pret]* will say who sent it. This could take a year, or two, or maybe I'll just spend my life in ḥāẓirī. *(laughing)* But pray *[duā karnā]* that it won't take that long! *[She pauses.]*

Carla: So, you would go to Salim's—did you get ḥāẓirī the moment you came in the door?

Priya: There's so much *power* [English word used] that people with bad spirits are afraid to even go there. They can't manage to go inside. If they go, they get really restless *[becainī]*, they get so restless that they bolt. And once you sit there, you can't manage to stand up again. I used to say, let's go home, I'm hungry, I'm like this or that. That's all I would say the whole time I sat there. I would have ḥāẓirī like that for three or four hours—from seven to eleven or so. He [Salim] didn't call me on Thursdays at first, because the kind of ḥāẓirī I have requires so much space, but later I was allowed to come on Thursdays, and everyone there would pray that my decision *[faislā]* would come quickly.[28]

Carla: Has Salim come to Ḥusain Ṭekrī?

Priya: He's going to come. He hasn't been here yet, but I've come here, so he says that he will come now.

Priya's mother: He's got a job and he has a family, too. He has to wait until he gets a vacation.

Priya: He has a family, but he still gives time when people come with problems.

Priya's mother: But he doesn't take anything [he doesn't take money].

Priya: *[echoing her mother]* He doesn't take anything . . .

Carla: So when you go and sit with him, what kind of difference do you feel?

Priya: My ḥāẓirī start, and they go on, and until now—I mean . . . I haven't even seen that much, I haven't even seen that he's sitting in front of me. We've never sat facing one another. If I were to sit right in front of him, my ḥāẓirī start. I mean that to this day I haven't really looked at him properly, to see *how* he is. I mean he has *that much* power.

Carla: So, when you come and he's sitting there . . .

Priya: He doesn't sit—he moves around a lot, and when my ḥāẓirī start, then he doesn't come near me—he sits behind me, or far from me . . .

Priya's mother: He reads, and she has ḥāẓirī.

Priya: You know, the Holy Qur'an *[qur'an sharīf]*, he reads it, but he doesn't interfere with my ḥāẓirī *[bīc men nahīn āte haiṁ]*. When my ḥāẓirī calm down *[śānt hotī hai]*, he gives me flower petals, but even then, I can't manage to look at his face.

Priya's story continues, but at this point a few things ought to be emphasized. First, like Babli, it was a relationship with a charismatic local Muslim healer that led Priya to Ḥusain Ṭekrī, and, as was the case with Mastān Bābā, there is no familial or lineage-based relationship between Salim and Ḥusain Ṭekrī. Rather, the healers in each case are connected to Ḥusain Ṭekrī though a notion of pan-Islamic culture that is not grounded in doctrine or Tablighi Jama'at–style reformism and seems to be shared by Muslims and Hindus alike.

Second, more so than was the case for Babli, dreams are one of Priya's main means to move events in her life forward—dreams, for example, were what convinced her, her mother, and Salim that she should go to Ḥusain Ṭekrī. Just as dreams sent Babli from Ḥusain Ṭekrī on a visit to Ajmer, dreams sent Priya to Ḥusain Ṭekrī. Priya also uses dreams to make sense of past circumstances by relating them to the present. In other words, they become the points of connection in the unfolding narrative that Priya makes (or discovers) as she negotiates connections between her troubled past and her uncertain present. The unknown faces in Priya's dream, Priya speculates, may include my own. If Priya saw my face in her dream, it would perhaps be a sign to her that she was on the right track—that is, my otherwise somewhat inexplicable presence would be transformed into assurance that Priya is where she is supposed to be, or, at the very least, that things are unfolding according to a divinely sanctioned plan.

Finally, much in the spirit of the stories of Sufi saints that were so much a part of Babli's experience and imagination, Salim's efficacy as a healer is related to his fearsomeness—Priya can't bring herself to look at him. Salim's efficacy is also related to his recitation of the Qur'an, which is recognizable to Priya and her mother as a sign of his discipline and devotion as well as the power of recitation. Like Maya, Priya and her mother recognized the enormous demands that a healing practice places on an individual like Salim:

they were particularly grateful that a family man like him would give his time to the afflicted.

In this lengthy conversation, Priya moved from the subject of Salim to a discussion of the six locks and chains that she had wound tightly around her ankles, wrists, neck, and waist. This rite, universally observed at Ḥusain Ṭekrī, is practiced with a myriad of personal variations. Perhaps in keeping with the importance Priya affords her dreams and dream visions, she said that she had one chain for each of the visions *[bishārat]* she had experienced since coming to Ḥusain Ṭekrī three months earlier. These chains are a significant source of embarrassment for all involved; they are fearsome to look at, impossible to hide, and cannot be removed once the keys to the locks are irretrievably disposed of, which they always are, in a variety of places. When Priya displayed her chains, laughing, her mother, clearly flustered, hastened to make it clear that her daughter was once a normal and respectable girl:

Priya's mother: She was such a good girl—she had a good job with the Life Insurance Corporation of India.

Carla: Did you like the work?

Priya: I liked it a lot, because in this work too I got to meet lots and lots of different sorts of people. [At LIC] you have to have confidence because you have to learn how to talk with different kinds of people—just like you talk to lots of different people—not everyone can do that. I mean, I liked the work. I stayed there even after my health declined, but when it got really bad I stopped being able to go to the office at all. I mean, I stopped liking everything. If anyone called, I would ask, "Whose phone call is it?" . . . Sometimes I thought, "Heaven forbid that I actually go crazy *[pāgal]*." I stayed *mentally disturbed* [English phrase used] [. . .][29]

Carla: Did you go to anyone besides Salim?

Priya: No, no one else. At first we went to a hospital, to a doctor . . .

Priya's mother: No one else. Before Priya got sick, we didn't take any interest in things like this. It didn't seem to us that someone had had something done [that is, it didn't occur to them that someone had done magic].[30] We never said a bad word about anyone, so why would anyone say a bad word about us? But someone got jealous—she had a job, didn't she?

Priya then interrupted her mother to detail her education and professional life. She got a degree in electronics repair with a first-division pass and finished her B.A. She then took a year off and worked in a string factory in Bhopal before joining the Life Insurance Corporation of India. Prior to starting work in the factory she was invited to take a job in Noida, part of Delhi, but her family refused, saying, according to Priya, that "We don't send girls alone that far away."

Priya's weakness—an experience that she now counts as part of her ḥāẓirī—had been happening for the past five years, most of her professional life. Although she initially sought treatment in a hospital—which resulted in a fifteen-day admission—it was only later that she understood that her various physical symptoms were the result of the spirit that had been put in her. It is also worth noting that similar to Babli's experience, Priya's negotiation of young adulthood involves negotiation of the proper use of her education. While in Babli's case this struggle never moved beyond the trope of the neighbors being jealous of her success in school, in Priya's case, the situation seems to be glossed in two ways: in the above-quoted conversation, Priya's mother mobilizes the familiar trope of a neighbor's jealousy of Priya's job, but Priya herself is less committal, noting only that she was not allowed to take a job in Noida, and that she began to experience the physical distress that she now associates with ḥāẓirī when she was working in the string factory. Priya herself was clearly ambivalent about the job at the LIC; that is, despite her assertion that she liked the work, her delivery of the statement that one had to know how to talk with lots of people suggested that it was something that she learned on the job with some difficulty.

Another recurrent feature of Priya's discussion of her pre-ḥāẓirī life is her assertion that people really liked her, whether it was her teachers, her peers, or her managers at her LIC job. This emphasis on social location sits in rhetorical contrast to the often not explicitly articulated experience of social dislocation that those with ḥāẓirī experience. The feeling of dislocation is first noticed at home; in Priya's case, as in many, there was the feeling of alienation from family, expressed through physical and verbal fights that are later blamed on the malevolent possessing spirit.

Once, nearly two months after this conversation, Priya returned to the topic of her job at LIC. We were sitting on the roof of her lodge at dusk, alone. She shared with me a story of her former feelings of social location: one of her favorite (male) teachers and she got along so well that he always suggested that female members of his family go with her whenever they had to go to the bazaar. In contrast to this, she again brought up the fact that she had been so popular at the LIC that many of the managers would call her into their offices just to talk, but because she had learned how to deal with the many different kinds of people at her work, she had come to understand that there were certain managers who were best avoided, including the branch manager. Here something of the meaning behind Priya's initial description of her job is revealed; it was no small thing to learn how to avoid those in positions of authority in her office. Similar to Babli, who was reluctant to openly address issues of threats to her honor, Priya did not explicitly describe the potentially inappropriate behavior of her branch manager, but she contrasted him with the explicitly described honor-preserving behavior of her male teacher, who trusted Priya enough to accompany his female relatives to the bazaar. In this scenario Priya becomes something like another female relative of the teacher, under his protection.

Later that same evening Priya and I were sitting alone in the courtyard of the rauẓa of Imām Husain. The weather was cool and the crowds had gone home; that is, we were in a place of protection, relative privacy, and calm. Priya had finished her nightly routine of lighting candles at the doors of the shrines and reciting (in Arabic, which she does not understand) the *bismilla,* as she calls it, and the *durūd sharīf.*[31] Sitting down next to me, she produced a package of *guṭkhā,* a particularly strong processed form of chewing tobacco, and told me to promise not to tell her mother that she used it. She said that before she came to Ḥusain Ṭekrī, she used *guṭkhā* far more frequently and would, in fact, feel restless until she had some. She added that she uses significantly less of it at Ḥusain Ṭekrī, and that its effect on her is minimized because her possessing spirit consumes it. This last detail is in keeping with the widely held notion that possessing spirits eat the food ingested by their host, thriving while their host weakens. Priya said that it was her hope that when her *faislā* happens, she will stop consuming *guṭkhā* altogether; since her ḥāẓirī started she has begun taking it more regularly. Chewing on the *guṭkhā,* she told me that her *pret* [malevolent possessing spirit] had also begun to crave chicken, adding that chicken was not something she ever ate at home, but it was something that she ate working at the string factory in Bhopal. Still thinking about her *pret* and food, she added that the *mujāvar*—shrine attendant—from Sagar told her that the magic that had been put in her body was likely introduced through tainted milk sweets. Priya said that subsequent to this conversation she recalled a time that her father's elder brother came to their home and offered sweets that only she ate. Possibly, she speculated, part of her problems originated from this, though she suspected that more magic was done by unnamed individuals after this. Here again, Ḥusain Ṭekrī—through the person of the *mujāvar*—offers the pan-Indian tropes necessary for Priya to look at her past and to begin to understand, through a cause-and-effect narrative, what has brought her to the place that she now finds herself.

Very late in our time together, Priya offered me a somewhat more specific and decidedly unsupernatural reason for some of the sadness that she was experiencing at Ḥusain Ṭekrī. I think that she shared this with me because she felt it was safe to do so, knowing that I was leaving, that I did not share her culture's values with regard to the place of women and women's honor, and that she could trust me not to tell anyone. The details of what Priya shared with me are not important for the purposes of this study. What is important is to recognize that, first of all, there is no reason to suppose that these nonsupernatural, personal, and somewhat explicit statements have anything to do with the process of ḥāẓirī and *jādū*. Specifically, there is no reason to think that the "real" basis for Priya's trouble was the one that made the most sense to me. Alternatively, it is worth considering the possibility that in confiding in me the way that she did, Priya was not becoming more "honest" but was actually demonstrating an increasing level of literacy in the culture from which I come, and as a consequence was trying to explain at least part of her problems in terms that I would find meaningful.

Returning to Priya's initial interview, a final subject of discussion was Priya's relationship with temples and other aspects of Hindu orthodoxy. Priya's mother got a phone call and had to leave for a few minutes; I took this opportunity to ask Priya why she didn't seek help at a temple.

Priya: I've never gone to a temple.

Carla: You're Hindu, aren't you?

Priya: Yes, I'm Hindu. I don't ever go to temples. Temples, mosques, I didn't go anywhere at all; my heart wasn't in it *[merā dil nahīn kartā thā]*. For example, I'm sitting in the office, and some friend came by and said, "Come on, Priya—we're going to the temple and then we're going to Pīlī Goṭī." *[explaining]* Pīlī Goṭī means dargāḥ—there we say Pīlī Goṭī.[32] So I said, "You go. I don't need to go to a temple. Just from your talking, I'm mad, and troubled . . . " So the meaning is that this bad spirit [that is in her] was causing all these things to happen.

Carla: Maybe.

Priya: Not maybe! Now I've begun to understand, because these people used to take me to the temple by force, [saying], "You said you would go," but I stood outside [saying], "I will not go in the temple." I didn't go inside.

Carla: Has it been like this since you were a child?

Priya: *[laughing]* No, no—not since childhood. During Navratri, I would get up in the morning, bathe, put on nice clothes and go—it was a real pleasure *[śauq]* of mine. But it seems to me that when I was in the twelfth standard I became the way I am now. My soul stopped wanting things *[Man hat gayā thā, merā]*. I wasn't drawn to temples, or to mosques—wherever I went, I felt nothing but restlessness. I was always restless . . . and at home, I would turn on the TV and sit with the remote in my hand, and I didn't watch anything—nothing looked good to me. Some song would come on, and so I would watch the song, and I would change the channel—no matter what channel I watched . . .

Given how seamlessly she moved from temples and mosques to channel surfing, it can be deduced that for Priya, this problem of restlessness and of feeling cut off from the world, while it manifests itself in everyday moments in her life, is related to her participation—or lack thereof—in the mainstream orthodox expressions of the Hindu tradition, such as Navratri or visiting temples. In other words, Priya makes a distinction between orthodox institutions such as mosques and temples and, for lack of a better word, marginal institutions such as Salim's shrine and Ḥusain Ṭekrī. While it is true that in her initial example Priya refuses to visit both an orthodox temple and a marginal dargāḥ, her subsequent elaboration is focused on temples and her inability to enter them as being a recent problem. If Priya's malevolent spirit were removed, she would be able to enjoy temples and mainstream Hindu festivals again, and she would cease to visit marginal institutions regularly. It is clear here that the problem that Priya is negotiating is one that is in some way represented by religious orthodoxy, symbolized by her mention of the institutions of mosque and temple.

In contrast to this, Priya's alienation from orthodox Hindu institutions was articulated through ḥāẓirī, this time through an exhausting spell of ḥāẓirī that I did not see, though Priya's face wore the expression of disoriented weariness that was characteristic of her post-ḥāẓirī state. Priya's mother explained that day was Gyaras,[33] which she glossed as the date that their *kuldev* (family deity) wakes up after the rains, and which therefore marks the beginning of the time when marriages can take place. Significantly, Babli's above-mentioned ḥāẓirī—the first of hers that I witnessed—also took place on Gyaras. For these two Hindu women, it seems that marriage is closely associated with religious orthodoxy; thus, the fierce ḥāẓirī that both Babli and Priya experienced on Gyaras may reflect feelings of alienation from the orthodox Hindu tradition that both of them, for reasons private and complex, were likely experiencing with particular intensity on this day.

Interestingly, however, it was orthodox Islamic practices that eventually became a cornerstone of Priya's relationship with Ḥusain Ṭekrī, much in the same way that stories about Sufi saints and martyrs became a cornerstone of Babli's relationship with Ḥusain Ṭekrī. Priya's gradual incorporation of Islamic practice had several components. She first began learning to pray *namāz* through the instruction of one her neighbors in the lodge. Initially, she said that although she had learned the motions, she had not learned the words because her *balā* (malevolent possessing spirit) wouldn't let her learn to read Arabic. The inability to learn new things is actually a symptom commonly reported by ḥāẓirī sufferers.

Priya also kept a notebook in which she wrote the lyrics to the *munājāt* (lyrical prayers) that are popularly recited at the rauẓas. Additionally, several days after Gyaras, Priya modeled a head scarf that had been given to her by one of the *mujāvar*s at the rauẓa. Again, this was the *mujāvar* from Sagar, and perhaps in part because he came from her hometown and therefore symbolized a safe link to her former life, he became Priya's primary guide, interpreting her dreams and offering guidance. Priya explained that this *mujāvar* had told her that it was never excusable to have one's head uncovered in the rauẓas, even during ḥāẓirī, and so he had given her a *salwar kameez* and head scarf. When Priya tied it over her hair she looked immediately and strikingly Muslim. Judging by the expressions of her mother and her visiting older brother, Priya's sudden visual transformation into a Muslim was jarring to them as well. In addition to her participation in readings of "The Tale of the Ten Virtuous Women" and her experimentation with Muslim forms of dress, Priya also began attending afternoon *fariyād* sessions, which involved a regular group of Shiʿite women singing songs of petition at the rauẓas. With several other ḥāẓirī sufferers, Priya stood in the front of the group and engaged in silent ḥāẓirī, gripping the bars covering the closed door of the rauẓa and swinging back and forth slowly.

Three things about this "Islamic" behavior bear noting. First, on one level, Priya was anxious to appear Muslim. Her explicitly stated reason for this came in the form of a declaration of annoyance with her mother, whose *sindūr*-parted hair marked them both as unambiguously Hindu. Priya expressed frustration with her mother's appearance and concern that her mother's unambiguous identity as a Hindu would keep Priya from receiving preferential or "correct" treatment by the rauẓa attendants. Priya's sense was that while the rauẓa attendants certainly ministered to the Hindu population, there was something adulterated or altered in their message to Hindus that Priya herself wished to avoid, preferring the authentic and unadulterated—and likely more powerful—Islamic treatment. In addition to this concern, Priya's demeanor at the rauẓas suggested that like Babli, she truly enjoyed passing as a Muslim.

Second, Priya and her mother shared a belief that the more devotion and respect that they showed to the saints of Ḥusain Ṭekrī, the more the saints would reward them. Thus Priya's mother once explained to me that she went to light candles at the shrines in the evening much in the same way that she used to light small clay oil lanterns *(dīpikā)* in her home. When I asked her why she lit candles at the shrines, she said that she didn't know what other people prayed when they lit candles, but she prayed "Maulā, just as we bring light before you, so please bring light *[roshan]* to our house." There is a clear economy here, wherein the abundant power of the shrines is only accessible to the degree that it is solicited through the devotion of pilgrims and petitioners. Similarly, Priya once explained that the cloth covers that she had carefully made for her various collections of Islamic verses and devotional songs were her investment in what she perceived as a reciprocal relationship between herself and the saints of Ḥusain Ṭekrī; she explained that to the extent that she cares for the books *(ḥifāẓat karnā),* Maulā will take care of her. Priya's formulation of this notion of reciprocity is particularly powerful, since it essentially equates the religious texts and Priya herself.

Priya's other major orthodox Islamic practices developed during the year and a half between my initial and follow-up research. By the time I returned to Ḥusain Ṭekrī for my follow-up research, Priya had learned to read *namāz* regularly according to the daily schedule observed by Sunnis, reciting Arabic that she had memorized but which she did not completely understand. No doubt she saw this practice as having a positive effect on her, attesting with her mother, in the course of a follow-up interview, that one of the chains around her ankles had fallen off just as she stood up one day just after reading *namāz.* Another chain had fallen off soon after her return to Ḥusain Ṭekrī following a disastrous one-month visit to her home, thus perhaps signaling that she had done the right thing in returning to Ḥusain Ṭekrī. In both cases, it was not enough to trust that the chains had fallen off for the right reasons—the more common understanding is that the opening of the locks can only be performed by Maulā. Priya, on the other hand, feared that a *śaitān* (literally, "satan"; here, a demon) had opened them to lull her into a false sense of security. After voicing her concerns about the possibility that these chains had not fallen off on Maulā's orders, she concluded that because she had not been given a dream in which she saw herself with a new chain, she had not been commanded to put another one on, and so she had not replaced those that had fallen off.

In the course of a follow-up interview, after her discussion of reading *namāz,* Priya listed the various prayers that she learned to recite since her return to Ḥusain Ṭekrī, citing the sura Yā Sīn[34] and *durūd sharīf,* and then volunteered the following:

Priya: Then the veil *[naqāb]* dreams started happening; mom had one, and then I did, but we didn't get one. And then I had one again, and mom, and after this another lady started having dreams, too. These dreams had already happened two or three times.

Carla: Was this the lady who taught you how to pray *namāz?*

Priya: No, no [. . .] the lady [who had the dreams] was Hindu, and she told me, "I saw you at the Fatima's *jālī* in a burqa." So I told mom, and then [we understood it was] his *order* [English word]. So we called Bombay, and they brought it.

Carla: And they didn't take money?

Priya: No, they didn't take money . . . [the one who bought it], she's Shi'a, and I've made her my sister-in-law, and I put it on for the first time not on Holi, but on the day after Holi. *[confirms with her mother]* That's right, it came the day after Holi . . . and the day after Holi I had the dream to read *namāz,* and so I started reading *namāz,* and I observed the fast [Ramadan]. I read *namāz,* and I feel calm *[sukūn miltā hai].* If my health is declining *[ṭabī'at bigāṛ ho rahī hai]* I read *namāz* and it gets better *[sahī ho jatī hai]* . . .

Carla: And how does it feel to wear a burqa? Honestly, sometimes I really want to wear one when I go to the bazaar so that no one will know who I am.

Priya: I stay *safe;* I stay *free. [Safe rehtī hun; free rehtī hun.]* I mean, wherever I go, there's no reason for worry *[koī tensionwālī bāt nahī];* I don't have to take care that my *dupaṭṭā* is on properly—I don't have to take care of a thing.

Carla: [seeking a Hindi or Urdu term] So you feel *āzād?*

Priya: Yes, *free [using the English again, emphatically].* But, whoever wears one, the first time, it will seem really strange *[bahut ajīb-sā lagtā hai];* it's very confusing *[uljhan hotī hai]* . . . I mean, [you will think] I'm all closed in—I've always been open before. But, with me, nothing happened. I put it on, it felt great, I understood myself to be really safe, and *āzād [here Priya perhaps graciously concedes the Urdu word].* I can sit comfortably and hang onto the *jālī,* and I don't have to take care about anything. I don't have to take care of my *dupaṭṭā,* or this or that, and I don't have any tension at all. And also, I don't feel worried *[ghabrāhat]* or restless *[becainī]*, thinking, "I'm all closed in"—nothing like that at all. [. . .] And whoever finds out that I'm wearing one, they say it's very good, a burqa is a very honorable thing *[ādāb kī cīz]*—meaning nothing shows, hands, feet—nothing.

Priya's mother: [interrupting] Priya started having her ḥāẓirī again a few days after she started wearing a burqa.

Priya: [to her mother] Also, when I was in Farzana's burqa, at Mehaṁdī Well, and I had ḥāẓirī? Right. *[sighing, unhappy at the direction of the conversation]* Before this . . .

Priya's mother: And because of this, there was a revelation *[bayān].*[35]

Carla: So you put on the burqa and you had ḥāẓirī? [. . .]

Priya: In the room . . . He [her malevolent possessing spirit] said, "Maulā, you've kept [Priya] hidden from me, and I wanted to dishonor her." That's what happened; that's what was revealed, is all.[36]

For Priya, the burqa has a pan-Indian resonance beyond its Islamic one, as something that will protect her value as a young woman.[37] Like Babli,

Priya perceived her actions as expressions of devotion and discipline that would bring faster and better resolution of her problems. Among other pilgrims at Ḥusain Ṭekrī there was a general sense that actions like these were virtuous and protective, irrespective of whether the person performing them was Hindu or Muslim.

Broadly speaking, none of the Muslims I encountered who observed Hindus involved in Islamic practice said that these actions should not be performed by non-Muslims or that they would go unrewarded because the practitioners were not Muslim. Additionally, no Muslim volunteered that the combination of these actions was a sign that the practitioner had become Muslim, though some observed that the actions ultimately would or should make practitioners Muslim, or at the very least reflected a level of devotion that should put less devoted Muslims to shame. Here the ambiguity of religious identity in a South Asian context is clear: by orthodox standards, what would make a person Muslim if not daily prayer, fasting during Ramadan, and, in the case of women, the adoption of some form of hijab? One could argue that from an orthodox perspective declaration of the *shahādah* marks conversion, but in actuality, the only "converts" at Ḥusain Ṭekrī who were recognized as Muslim were those who had married Muslims. This suggests that religious identity is communal rather than individual: without some corroborating social relationship, individual conversion does not make sense.

Priya was clearly weary of her process at Ḥusain Ṭekrī; despite her best efforts, her ḥāẓirī had yet to develop into the open form, in which the spirit provides specific information about who did the magic, for what cost, and for what reason. On her current state, Priya observed:

> If I had *khulī ḥāẓirī* (open ḥāẓirī) my path would be easy. I would know that I had permission to leave, that the work at Ḥusain Ṭekrī would be accomplished, that at the fire walk I would get my *faislā*. I would know who had done something, and why; I would know everything. But in *gum ḥāẓirī* (hidden ḥāẓirī) there is much more trouble *[taklīf]*, and dreams [which substitute as the major medium of healing for those who do not have *khulī ḥāẓirī*] don't happen every day. Every fifteen days, every month, and then not all that clearly . . . If the dreams *[bishārat]* were clear, then I would know [for example] that it was *these* people, but to this day it hasn't been revealed in a dream why this was done. There is, of course, in my own mind the thought that *[apne dimāg se, soc ke, yeh ki]* they were thinking that I was studying, that I had a job, and so this is probably why they did it, because of jealousy. Okay, fine, there's that, but I have *gum ḥāẓirī,* and what's best is *khulī ḥāẓirī,* where every detail is revealed.

Here Priya, who had at that point been at Ḥusain Ṭekrī for almost two consecutive years, expressed discouragement but not hopelessness; her case, she acknowledged, could be solved without ever having open ḥāẓirī, but this path is far longer and more difficult. It is striking that even two years after arriving, the trope of jealousy, mentioned by her mother in her initial interview but largely ignored by Priya, has not become any more meaningful. She makes the distinction between divine inspiration and knowledge revealed in visions *(bishārat)*, and ideas that come merely from her own thinking *(apne dimāg se, soc ke, yeh ki . . .)*, dismissing the trope of jealousy as deriving from the latter, unimportant source. This notion of jealousy, in other words, does not, for whatever reason, provide Priya with what she needs to meaningfully narrativize her past and current situations.

Bored with Ḥusain Ṭekrī (and using the English word to describe her state), Priya was actively petitioning for permission to go home, which, she explained, would come in the form of a dream or vision in which she would see all her luggage packed, or a train. Priya would make her request like all petition processes at Ḥusain Ṭekrī, by tying a length of red twine to the grating that covers the windows of the rauẓas. She said that she tended to tie them on Sundays, Wednesdays, and Thursdays. When asked why, she said that people who knew about such things *(jānkār)* said that this was the best day to petition the shrines. Thursday is widely recognized as the best day of the week to visit a dargāḥ. In Hinduism, each day of the week is associated with particular deities, with Sunday being one of the days associated with the Goddess. Priya's statement suggests that there is a correlation between the Goddess (one of whose temple days is Sunday) and Muslim saints.

Priya's mother also once offered insight into the place within Hinduism that Muslim saints and martyrs seem to fit. When Priya was out of the room, she responded to my question of which temples they visited before going to Salim by saying that they had gone to a Hanumān temple and been told by an astrologer who read Priya's hand that both Priya and her younger sister had fallen under the inauspicious influence of Śani (Saturn, the planet-god who rules Saturday). To remedy this situation, they embarked on a six-month program of *pūjā* early every Saturday morning, which, according to Priya's mother, resulted in the improvement of her younger daughter but not Priya. Priya's mother speculated that Priya did not improve because she had not performed the *pūjā* properly and had refused to go to temples. In the middle of this observation, Priya returned to the room and, upon hearing her mother, rolled her eyes and made it clear that she thought her mother was a little bit ridiculous for thinking that her problems could have been solved through Śani *pūjā*. On the one hand, for some Hindus, at least, Muslim saints are particularly suited to the work of removing inauspicious influences. On the other hand, while there seem to be some tropes and characteristics that are shared by certain Hindu deities (chiefly Hanumān, Devī, and Bhairav) and Muslim saints, they are not interchangeable; for Priya, Hindu deities are useless.

Finally, it is significant that Priya's understanding of her earlier ḥāẓirī and of Salim changed as she became more familiar with the language and culture of Ḥusain Ṭekrī. Later on in our time together, when she was listening to my recordings of her initial interviews (at her request), she corrected herself, saying that it was not Husain himself who came into Salim's body but one of his servants. She further clarified that the other presence in Salim's body was a "Bābā from Nagpur" who was recognizable by his habits: smoking *bīṛī,* chewing tobacco, and a tendency to remain seated and shake on account of his very advanced age. The description of the "Bābā from Nagpur" (who is almost certainly Tāj ud Dīn Bābā, whose *cillā,* which Priya calls Pīlī Goṭī, is in Sagar) that Priya offers is likely simply an elaboration, since she did not initially mention him at all. It is more significant that she no longer understands that it is Husain himself that comes into Salim's body, but rather one of Husain's servants. This is important mainly because Priya's change in perception in no way undermines her faith in Salim's efficacy or her relationship with him. Here is further evidence that, from a Hindu perspective at least, Muslim saints of very different religious lineages and affiliations share in a pan-Islamic identity that, again, seems to have nothing to do with the major institutional means of creating affiliations between Muslim saints.

One might be tempted to argue that Priya's change of understanding also has something to do with her greater exposure to orthodox Muslim belief, which would only allow for possession by *jinn,* and it is possible that this is true, particularly given Priya's close relationship with the relatively orthodox *mujāvar* from Sagar. On the other hand, the last of the four women to be considered in this chapter is a Sunni Muslim who unapologetically serves as a conduit for Sakina, daughter of Husain. It seems, then, there is little use in attempting to understand the diversity of beliefs and practices associated with dargāḥs in terms of communal or orthodox religious boundaries. In support of the irrelevance of most forms of orthodox religious identity in the context of dargāḥs and shrines, Priya herself once responded with great frustration to my statement that many Muslims believe that Hindus' prayers are answered more quickly at dargāḥs because Maulā recognizes that they are not "his," and therefore that they are more likely to leave if they do not get an answer quickly. Arguing against this idea, Priya forcefully asserted that Maulā decided things on a "case" basis, irrespective of the religious affiliation of the individual.

VISION, DEBT, AND HEALING

Nasim is a young mother and a Sunni Muslim who lives in a town near Ḥusain Ṭekrī. When we were first getting to know one another, Nasim explained to me that her *jāti* was *"faqīr,"* and she added that she was not ashamed of her *jāti* because she came from one of its "original" families. This statement was likely made because of the widespread belief that many of those who call themselves *faqīr* are members of the *jāti* only by virtue of relatively recent conversion from the ranks of untouchables or very low-caste Hindus, though, as with most discussions of *jāti* and caste, especially in Muslim contexts, it is difficult to make any assertion that would stand up across the board. One of Nasim's attendants once explained that traditionally, Nasim's *jāti* sews mattresses.

Nasim is one of a handful of people who conduct charismatic healing practices in the courtyard of the rauẓas of Sakina and 'Abbas on Thursdays just after the dispensation of afternoon lobān. Simply put, Nasim's body becomes a conduit for Sakina, and pilgrims gather around her seeking resolution of physical, familial, and economic problems. Just before the lobān is dispensed, Nasim initiates her practice by pulling her *dupaṭṭā* over her face and securing it so that it will not become loose during her healing session. She then begins to make noises that sound somewhat like vomiting—a sound typical of some forms of ḥāẓirī—and then twists her left arm behind her back as though it were being forced there by an invisible hand. She raises her right hand in the air and then lowers it slowly, eventually lowering her body to the floor of the courtyard and bowing so that her forehead touches the floor in a gesture reminiscent of the *sujūd* (bowing posture) of *namāz.* An attendant then pours a small bottle of scented oil onto her *dupaṭṭā;* she inhales the scent deeply, at which point Bībī Sakina becomes available for questions. Throughout this process it is essential that a clear line of sight be maintained between 'Abbas's rauẓa and Nasim; attendants and pilgrims alike strictly observe and enforce this rule, and Bībī Sakina herself would occasionally express great anger if someone casually or unknowingly walked between her and the rauẓa of 'Abbas without acknowledging her.

Because Nasim did not live at Ḥusain Ṭekrī, our interactions were limited to the Thursdays when she came to Ḥusain Ṭekrī (a maximum of three a month). Further, because of the combined pressures of her work as a healer and the necessity of returning home in a timely manner to take care of cooking and childcare, it was difficult to have extended conversations with her. Additionally, when I initially met her, she was very reluctant to talk about herself and her practice. Family members who accompanied her to the shrines explained to me that she was a conduit for Bībī Sakina and that she had not been given this gift as a result of any recovery from ḥāẓirī or illness, but because of her great love of Sakina. She shunned any formal interview, though she was willing to talk with me while serving as a conduit for Sakina.[38] However, when I came back to do follow-up research, she was staying at Ḥusain Ṭekrī with two young women who had been put in her charge, and she was consequently much more available for interviews and conversation. The interviews are thus largely drawn from this later time.

In an initial attempt to explain the particulars of her practice, Nasim, who was discussing how the saints communicate with her, shared the following:

Carla: I go to school and learn; how do you learn from them [the saints of Ḥusain Ṭekrī]?

Nasim: At night I worship *[ʿibādat karnā]*. From nine to eleven at night, I sit in my room [. . .] I sit there, just like we're sitting face to face *[rū be rū]*, that's how they talk with me *[mujhse bāt hotī hai]*. Just like we're sitting here talking. I get answers for whatever work I am doing. [For example, they tell me,] "To accomplish this or that work, you need to do this, in the morning you need to do this, and at night you need to do that." This is how I work, and I don't want to do anything else. Not everyone has enough strength that they can look at them with no problem *[acche-se]*. And I look at them. We sit, and just like you and I are talking, we talk.

Carla: What do they look like? Are their faces hidden *[naqābposh]* or do you see their faces?

Nasim: I see their faces. The wives, they look like this *[she pulls her dupaṭṭā over her mouth, leaving her eyes and nose visible]*, and the rest—Maulā ʿAli and all—their faces are shown completely, without a veil *[naqāb]*.

Carla: So what are they like?

Nasim: They're middle-aged. ʿAli wears an *ijār*[39] and long kurta, and on top, only a jerkin [English word used]—black.

Carla: Jerkin? Is that foreign clothing?

Nasim: No, no, just old. He wears leather sandals, with stars on them. ʿAbbas ʿAlamdar wears white pajamas, and a green kurtī [short jacket]. [He wears] a long kurta, too, and ties a green ruby *[sic]* here [on the head]. [. . .] And Aga Husain wears a perfectly white kurta *[safed hī]* and white pajama. And on his shoulders he wears a small black blanket *[kālī kamlī]*.

Carla: And Bībī Fatima?

Nasim: Bībī Fatima wears a chadar *[cador uṛtī hai]*.

Carla: And Bībī Sakina?

Nasim: Bībī Sakina wears a *dupaṭṭā*—just like this—*[responding to Carla's question about whether Sakina's face shows]* so that her face shows.

Carla: Is she pretty *[khūbsūrat]?*

Nasim: She's very beautiful, *extremely* beautiful *[bahut hī zyādā]*—don't *ask* how beautiful she is. She wears a sparkling *[chamakī]* kurtī [short kameez]—you know the sort, don't you? And her *dupaṭṭā* is sparkling too. Her *salwar* is plain [English word].

In considering how Nasim's practice compares with Maya's, several things are worth noting. First of all, unlike Maya's practice, Nasim's is deeply rooted in extremely particular, detailed visions of 'Ali, 'Abbas, Husain, Fatima, and Sakina, and she revels in the details of their appearances rather than offering any justification for or defensiveness about her image-based form of practice. In form, Nasim's practice is both Sufi and shamanistic: it is particularly Sufi by virtue of its reliance upon transmissions from teacher *(pīr)* to disciple *(murid),* and both Sufi and shamanistic by virtue of the fact that Nasim claims the ability to travel to faraway places.

Additionally, judging by their appearances, the saints are unambiguously Indian; Sakina's outfit, in particular, could be worn by any young Indian woman on a special occasion, and it even reflects the trend toward shorter kameezes. Husain's adoption of a *kamlī,* the sort of blanket that in Indian iconography is associated with a beggar or ascetic, is particularly telling, demonstrating that an overlap between the categories of asceticism and martyrdom, present in Hindu descriptions of persons and rituals at Ḥusain Ṭekrī, is present in Muslim perspectives on Husain as well. The *kamlī* also has a pan-Islamic resonance, owing to the popularity of Urdu translations of the poem "The Mantle of the Prophet."[40] This poem was originally composed in Arabic in the late thirteenth century by the Egyptian poet al-Būṣīrī; in Urdu, the word used for mantle is *kamlī.* A pan-Islamic story holds that al-Būṣīrī was inspired to compose the poem after the Prophet cured him of an illness by placing his mantle on al-Būṣīrī's shoulders. Thus, in Nasim's vision, Husain is the heir of Muhammad, possessed of special power to heal.

The interview then moved to a discussion of the specifics of Nasim's conversations with the saints of Ḥusain Ṭekrī.

Carla: When you speak with them, do you call them, or do they come on their own?

Nasim: I burn incense, and I worship *['ibādat karnā],* and then they come.[41]

Carla: Do you recite anything in particular?

Nasim: No, I just say "Maulā 'Ali al-madad, 'Abbas 'Alamdar al-madad," and they come to help *[madad ke liye ā jāte haiṁ]*. [Then they say,] "What's the problem—why have you called us *[bulāyā]*?" Then, whatever the problem is, I place it before them, and I say, "I need this," or "You need to give this [thing] to so-and-so; you are responsible for my promise to heal."

Carla: What do you mean?

Nasim: I've said, "Tomorrow your work will be accomplished," so they have to do it, don't they? So they are the ones who are responsible for my promise to heal . . . I say, lord *[sarkār]*, you have to heal your servant *[gulām]*. Because I'm their [Nasim's clients'] servant.

This conversation illustrates the connection between sweet smells and saintly presence that will appear in many different guises in subsequent chapters. Further, it illustrates the way in which Nasim's honor is completely dependent upon the saints of Ḥusain Ṭekrī; she is only as good as her word, and her word is sustained by their gifts. In making promises to pilgrims, Nasim renders herself radically helpless. While it might seem that Nasim is engaging in a form of bargaining or even blackmail in her dealings with the saints, her methodology is reasonable and practical given the actualities of her practice; she must offer people answers when they come to her or they will be unlikely to return, which would both keep her from being able to help them further and effectively end her practice.

Interestingly, it seems that for Nasim, inhabiting the role of the healer necessarily involves placing oneself in an indebted state. In her case, her practice itself creates a debt that can only be paid by the saints. Thus, Nasim renders herself indebted whenever she makes a prediction or a promise to a client: indeed, a single promise renders her doubly indebted since she both owes results to her clients and needs a "handout" from the saints. This double debt of the healer is the only state that allows for the successful transfer of abundance from the saints to the petitioner; the healer embodies the two negatives that make a positive.

Nasim's debt is forgiven whenever the saints hear her request and fulfill her promises. What is particularly powerful about this practice is that the greater the debt, the greater the potential for Nasim to demonstrate her faith in the saints and for the saints to prove their power. Because both the indebtedness and the gift are voluntary, they can become powerful expressions of devotion and trust.

Nasim continued with a discussion of the inception of her role as a healer:

Carla: Before, did you have ḥāẓirī?

Nasim: No!

Carla: Before you told me you'd just come to Ḥusain Ṭekrī on pilgrimage *[ziyārat].*

Nasim: Right.

Carla: And Bībī Sakina came to you suddenly? I remember last year [during my research one and a half years earlier] you told me that you had such love for Bībī Sakina that she came to you.

Nasim: I came here for some work.[42] I thought to myself, "I'll come for pilgrimage, and also because I really have some work that needs doing." I tied a string, and [I prayed,] "Oh lord *[sarkār],* if I am a sinner *[gunāhgār],* punish me. And if I haven't done anything, free me *[mujhe barī karvānā. kisī kām se mujhe barī karvānā].* So I did this for the first Thursday, and the second Thursday, and the third Thursday, and then on the third Thursday, I had ḥāẓirī *[mujhe ḥāẓirī ā gayī];* and then I started to have the greeting of Bībī Sakina *[mujhe bībī sakīnā kī salāmī ā gayī].* Later I thought that someone had had something done.[43]

Carla: Later?

Nasim: When ḥāẓirī came, I thought that someone had had something done. Then Bībī Sahib came, and she said, "No one has done anything; our greeting *[salāmī]* is on you. Taking my name, put a string around the neck of anyone who comes with a petition, and their decision *[faislā]* will happen.[44] My name is Shāhzādī Sakina." So it's from this time that I have had all this knowledge of things that are far away. And everywhere that pilgrimage happens; any corner of this world where there is a temple *[mandir]* or a mosque, I can see it . . . closing my eyes.

Here the most striking thing to note is Nasim's confusion between the experiences of ḥāẓirī and receiving the *salāmī* of Bībī Sakina; indeed, when I first saw Nasim's practice in courtyard of the rauẓa of ʿAbbas, I was unsure as to what was happening because she seemed to be in the initial stages of a bout of ḥāẓirī, but her clean, nice clothes and the relatively large number of people watching her (most people with ḥāẓirī are more or less ignored by all but their caretakers) suggested that something else was going on. Specifically, for example, the bending of one's arm behind one's back as though it is being twisted and held there by an invisible force is a common gesture in ḥāẓirī, and it is one of the gestures that always seemed to mark the start of Nasim's practice. What is most significantly demonstrated here is that the experience of ḥāẓirī, whatever it may be, is not immediately comprehensible; in both Maya's case and in the case of Nasim, it is unclear what is happening until an explicit declaration is made on the part of the saint. Otherwise, the experience of physical stress associated with ḥāẓirī and that associated with the *salāmī* of a saint are similar enough to be confused with one another.

Just as ḥāẓirī and receiving a *salāmī* prompt confusingly similar feelings and sensations in the body, Nasim's healing practice shares some characteristics with its purported enemy, magic. Pan-Indian views on magic hold that the magician requires something from the victim's body (hair and fingernail clippings are two of the most commonly cited substances) and the victim's true name (the extreme reluctance of some pilgrims to give their real name is likely in part because of this understanding of magic). In participation with this discourse, Nasim's healing practice's efficacy and legitimacy derive from names and naming: she evokes the saints through a recitation of their names that parallels the recitation of the names of God common in Sufi forms of *dhikr;* Bībī Sakina seals her pact with Nasim by declaring her name; and the power of Nasim's practice derives from taking Sakina's name as she ties strings around the necks of pilgrims.

Additionally, Nasim exhibits characteristic reluctance to say that she came to Ḥusain Ṭekrī expecting ḥāẓirī; rather, she prefers to think of her visits as dedicated to worship and petition and not prompted by a suspicion that someone has performed magic on her. There is a certain shame in having ḥāẓirī, which Nasim neatly sidesteps in her description of her experience of coming to Ḥusain Ṭekrī. In another interview she shared specific information about what work needed to be done when she came to Ḥusain Ṭekrī and why she needed to be declared innocent:

Nasim: *[After asking some pilgrims at the rauẓa of ʿAli to move away and stop listening to our conversation]* My business, those who should hear it can hear it; no one else should hear it.

Carla: Of course—so what about these children [sitting with us]?

Nasim: Oh, they're with me. *[She reprimands them for not sitting nicely. There was then a lengthy interlude during which Nasim repeatedly shooed away people who were attracted to the spectacle of me and my minidisc recorder.*[45] *Finally we were alone, and the conversation continued.]*

Carla: So you told me that your mother and father passed away when you were very young?

Nasim: I was four.

Carla: Do you remember them?

Nasim: I don't remember either of them.

Carla: So where did you live?

Nasim: First, my mother passed away, so I lived with father *[baujī]*. Then, he got married a second time [and died soon thereafter]. So I lived with my second mother until I was twelve or thirteen years old . . . I got married in my twelfth or thirteenth year. So from the time I was thirteen, I lived at my in-laws' house.

Carla: And when did you first receive Bībī Sakina's *salāmī?*

Nasim: I had four children, and after this I had the operation done [so I wouldn't have any more children]. After this, four years after this, it happened. There was a false case [brought against me]. [. . .] Family members brought it [against me].

Carla: The court here? [Ḥusain Ṭekrī is often described as a court.] Or government *[sarkārī]* court?

Nasim: Government court. And my date for a trial was declared *[merī tārīkh lagī]*.

Carla: What did they say you had done?

Nasim: They said, " . . . she engaged my girl to someone else. And having arranged the engagement with someone else, she sent my girl there. And she [took] some 50,000 [rupees] in jewelry *[zevar]*." They brought such a big case against me that they had me sent to jail. So some people in my neighborhood said that possibly I could get a *faislā* from Ḥusain Ṭekrī. [They said,] "If you are truthful, then you will certainly find justice." So I came to Ḥusain Ṭekrī, and I tied a string on the *jālī,* and I said, "Lord *[sarkār],* if I've done anything, I need to be punished. And if I haven't done anything, free me" . . . So I did this, and I came for two Thursdays. On the third Thursday, Bībī Sakina's *salāmī* came. When it came, I started to cry. I thought, "Someone has done some magic or something, and now I have ḥāẓirī." On the first day, I didn't know that it is *[sic]* Bībī Sakina's *salāmī.* [. . .] So I cried constantly for two or four days; then Bībī Sahib came, cover ing her face like this, and she stood up, and she began to say, "No one has had anything done to you; my name is Shāhzādī Sakina, and my *salāmī* is upon you. Any pilgrim around whose neck you tie a string after taking my name will get what they ask for." So from this time, whenever I tie a string around a pilgrim's neck, they become well. [. . .] This happened three years ago . . . So Bībī Sahib gave me justice; she sat with me just like we're sitting, and said, "Don't worry; you're innocent *[begunāh],* and you'll be freed from this case." So my case went for a year, and then I was freed.

In this conversation, Nasim's description of receiving the *salāmī* of Bībī Sakina repeats nearly verbatim the description that she offered in her earlier discussion of her practice related above, and the ambiguity and traumatic nature of the experience is highlighted by Nasim's description of her tears, which is reminiscent of Maya's description of her own experience with ḥāẓirī. It also seems from Nasim's description that when Bībī Sakina made her declaration, she made it publicly, in the courtyard of the rauẓas of ʿAbbas and Sakina, through Nasim's body. This seems to have been a situation in which a young woman seemingly in ḥāẓirī suddenly covered her face—thus distinguishing herself from women actually in ḥāẓirī, whose *dupaṭṭās* are often disregarded and whose hair is unbound—and declared herself Sakina.

The significant addition to Nasim's earlier account of the start of her practice is the story about her trouble with the law, caused, it seems, by some sort of botched marriage arrangement. This is likely the reason that Nasim was so sensitive about the proximity of others during our conversation; even though she has been found innocent by both Bībī Sakina and the government court, Nasim is not willing to risk her name being is associated with any kind of scandal. Just as young unmarried women informants generally refrain from direct discussion of their pasts, even though they understand themselves as innocent, so Nasim has good reason to keep this story from public circulation, even though she holds that she did nothing wrong.

It is also significant that in the view of both Nasim and those in her neighborhood, the saints of Ḥusain Ṭekrī can override the government court and restore honor that has been called into question. The key here is whether, in their minds, there is any significant difference in the sort of authority wielded by a government court and the authority wielded by Ḥusain Ṭekrī's saints. It seems that both actually function on more or less the same level since they have the same practical effect: the establishment of guilt and innocence. The fact that many at Ḥusain Ṭekrī talk about "cases" being transferred from dargāḥ to dargāḥ suggests that for many pilgrims, the court represented by dargāḥs has the same weight as a government court, and is, in fact, often regarded as even more powerful because the sort of suffering caused by magic cannot be prosecuted in a government court. In short, one is only guilty or innocent if the community accepts one's guilt or innocence, and because of this, the authority of the saints, particularly in areas such as marriage, is the same in kind as the authority of a government court. Sacred and secular space, when considered from the standpoint of function and status in the community, are not rigidly separated. In this case, using similar tropes and narratives, the authority of the "sacred" court encompasses and, it seems, preempts the authority of the secular one. Justice in both cases derives from a single source: the saints in whose memory the shrines are constructed.

Though they differ in many significant and fascinating ways, the stories of Maya, Babli, Priya, and Nasim all show that healing at Ḥusain Ṭekrī and at similar Muslim saint shrines is in part the process of finding a way to make the dominant narrative of "I came, I prayed, I got better" personally meaningful.[46] In offering the words and stories of these four pilgrims, I have also attempted to demonstrate that this narrative is not itself a source of healing, and that its power derives from its wide acceptance rather than its actual ability to transform lives. Tales of Muslim saints, narratives derived from dream visions, stories of the rauẓas' origins, stories of past lives, and *khulī ḥāẓirī* are the major forms of context-dependent narrative within which the healing process occurs.

Within these types of narrative and the various healing practices particular to Muslim saint shrines lie fields of possibility: lack, place(ment), mobility, hiddenness, passing, unknowing, vision, debt, sickness, and healing. Unknowing, lack, sickness, hiddenness, and debt are among the reasons for making a pilgrimage. Physical suffering (Maya, Priya), inexplicable runs of misfortune (Nasim, Babli), and the need to ask the saints to intercede on behalf of pilgrims (Nasim) are all examples of these phenomena. At the dargāḥ, these negative conditions are addressed through dargāḥ-specific phenomena of mobility, placement, passing, and visions; all of these afford pilgrims the opportunity to be themselves elsewhere, or, even more radically, to become someone else elsewhere. The need that all of these individuals feel to be at Ḥusain Ṭekrī, Maya's ability to send others there to thank the saints for gifts bestowed through her, Nasim's ability to have visions of any place on earth, Babli's ability to move from one dargāḥ to another as dreams and personal necessity dictate, and Priya and Babli's ability to pass as Muslim are all examples of these dargāḥ-specific phenomena. I use the term *fields* to avoid an inaccurately linear image of a path that leads from sickness to healing: these fields truly overlap, and an individual may wander in one for a long time before suddenly finding herself in another. Narratively, healing is the goal, but in practice it is also a field; it overlaps with all the others, and a pilgrim may wander into it and back out again many times over the course of her life.

CHAPTER 3

Absence

Lobān, Volunteerism, and Abundance

On an average day in the courtyards of Ḥusain Ṭekrī's rauẓas, pilgrims may be observed performing a range of dargāḥ-specific healing practices. Of these, *khulī ḥāẓirī* is certainly the most eye-catching, but looking beyond this violent, fearsome spectacle a visitor may also observe pilgrims engaged in several other healing practices that are common at Muslim saint shrines: inhaling lobān (the Arabic-derived Urdu word for the smoke of a rocklike form of incense),[1] wrapping chains and locks around various parts of the body, hanging onto *jālī* (the metal or stone latticework that covers the windows of subcontinental Muslim tombs and shrines), and tying strings (commonly called *challā*) to *jālī*.[2] While most pilgrims' religious backgrounds are not easily deduced, some markers of religious identity are visible and obvious, making it clear that these practices are meaningful not just to Muslims, but also to Hindus, Sikhs, Christians, and Jains. What is it about these practices that allow them to transcend religious boundaries, and what might the answer to this question teach us about not only dargāḥ culture, but religion in South Asia in general?

Fundamental to this question is whether or not pilgrims generally regard Muslim saint shrines as Islamic places. It is certainly true—and important—that extra-subcontinental Islamic narratives and Arabic-derived names contribute an explicitly Islamic element to the popular perception of the tombs of subcontinental Muslim saints. Ḥusain Ṭekrī's rauẓas are marked as Islamic by their association with Islamic names and narratives of the deaths of Husain and his companions at Karbala. However, in what follows I will show that at Ḥusain Ṭekrī, these Islamicate markings are largely unrelated to the authority (and, hence, efficacy) of its major healing practices.

In addition to being authoritative and effective for reasons having little to do with their explicitly Islamic context, these common healing activities, though physically and psychologically demanding, fit neither of the two major categories of labor used by pilgrims in their narratives of healing: *sevā* and *kām*. In everyday conversation, *sevā* is generally used to describe a voluntary set of actions performed out of gratitude or devotion; nonreligious usage of the word connotes philanthropic volunteering. Somewhat like Hindu *pūjā, sevā* may also connote worship and caretaking. In all these usages, *sevā* is both offered from a position of comfort (or at least adequacy of resources) and predicated upon an abundance-based economy. Maya, for example, considered her healing practice *sevā,* and both she and Nasim only began their healing practices after the saints present in their bodies powerfully assured them that they indeed had the resources necessary to help others. Maya's subsequent turn to a form of *sevā* that simply involved offering lobān in her rooftop shrine reflected the fact that because of her daughter's marriage, she needed to spend more time maintaining her household, leaving less time and energy available for a healing practice.

In contrast to *sevā, kām,* literally "work," is the term used by Ḥusain Ṭekrī's pilgrims to describe the workings of magic or the hiring of someone to do magic. In this sense, *kām* is an illicit, usually secret action taken to achieve material gain: a jealous person, for example, may hire a magician to perform magic in order to obtain something that the victim possesses, and a magician performs the magic in exchange for money. In all of these cases, *kām* is an action taken from a position of lack and predicated on an economy in which resources are limited (hence the necessity of stealing). This dargāḥ-specific usage of the term *kām* parallels the more general use of the word to describe any type of work that provides a livelihood—action performed to survive in a money-based economy of lack.

Pilgrims to Ḥusain Ṭekrī don't merely *believe* that the work they perform at Ḥusain Ṭekrī is effective. They experience profound, demonstrable transformation as a result of participating in it. This means, among other things, that the inhalation of lobān, the practice of ḥāẓirī, hanging onto *jālī,* and tying *challā* must draw upon widely accepted forms of legitimacy and authority, making it all the more curious that they do not neatly fit into the common categories of *sevā* and *kām:* they are not simply a form of *sevā,* since pilgrims come to the shrines out of a profound sense of lack, but they are not exactly *kām* either, because while their practitioners have lost status, health, family, and property, they are not motivated by jealousy or even simple acquisitiveness.

If the power of these healing practices does not lie in an Islamic identity, and the practices do not fit easily into the categories of labor commonly used by pilgrims in their narratives of healing, what exactly *is* the source of these healing practices' cross-tradition appeal, authority, and efficacy? Let us first consider lobān, which is a ubiquitous feature of North Indian dargāḥ life, though the method of dispensing it differs from shrine to shrine and from region to region. At Ḥusain Ṭekrī lobān is burned and distributed to pilgrims eight times a day. Beginning at eight in the morning and again at three in the afternoon, it is burned at half hour intervals at each of the four major rauẓas. For both the morning and afternoon dispensations, the first offering is a mixture of lobān from the rauẓas of Sakina and 'Abbas, which share the same courtyard. According to a former *mujāvar*, until about six years ago the lobān burned in each of these rauẓas was offered separately to the crowds, but in recent years, to accommodate the increasing number of pilgrims, the offerings from the two shrines are mixed and then dispensed to the waiting crowd. Half an hour after the offering at the rauẓas of Sakina and 'Abbas, lobān is offered at the rauẓa of 'Ali, followed half an hour later by a dispensation of a mixture of lobān that has been offered in the rauẓas of Husain, Zaineb, and the shrine's *imāmbāṛā*, all of which share a large courtyard. In this case, the lobān has been consolidated for the same reasons as it was at the shrines of 'Abbas and Sakina. The final lobān is offered half an hour later at the rauẓa of Fatima. Thus, twice a day for two hours at a stretch, the geography of Ḥusain Ṭekrī is dominated by a flow of pilgrims moving together from rauẓa to rauẓa, following the dispensation of lobān.

Before beginning the process of offering prayers and burning lobān, the attendants bolt the door of the rauẓa; those with ḥāẓirī are not allowed inside, but their presence is attested to by their cries, which pierce the air throughout the offering. Inside the rauẓa, pilgrims are divided according to gender and a curtain is pulled between them. Everyone—Hindu, Muslim, Christian, ethnographer—then stands and assumes a pan-Islamic gesture of prayer: hands raised, held together, palms up. The *durūd sharīf* is sung, first by the pilgrims, and then at length by the *mujāvar*. After this, lobān is introduced to the metal container of glowing hot coals that will later be carried through the crowd and sweet-smelling smoke begins to fill the rauẓa's interior. The *mujāvar* then recites several portions of the Qur'an, including both the Sura Al-Fatiha and the Ayat Al-Kursi,[3] as well as the final suras, or chapters, of the Qur'an, which are widely used to ward off magic.

Then prayers are offered to the saints *(nazar karnā)*. As one *mujāvar* described this portion of the prayers:

> I pray to Allah, and I place all the prayers I have read in the care of the saints and martyrs of Karbala as a gift *[nazarāna]*,[4] that is, I ask that the benefit *[savāb]* of the prayers reach them. Then I pray, [saying,] "However many pilgrims are here, oh pure ones of Allah, by means of the blessing *[barkat]* of these prayers *[kalām-e-pāk]*, pray to Allah for them, that whatever magic, problems, illnesses, spirits and things like that may be there . . . I pray for healing [of these afflictions]."

In the rauẓa, this portion of the *mujāvar*'s prayer, delivered in Hindi-Urdu, is punctuated by repetitions of *"āmīn"* (so be it) by the standing pilgrims. Following this prayer the *ṣalvāt* (blessings upon the Prophet Muhammad and his family) is recited, and then the door to the rauẓa is opened and the pilgrims within file out, inhaling lobān as they pass the *mujāvar*.[5] This is a fairly standard procedure for prayer at Sufi saint tombs more generally: prayers are offered for the benefit of martyrs and saints, who in turn are asked to pray for the pilgrims.

The subsequent dispensation of lobān to those waiting outside the rauẓa is far less elaborate. After the prayers have been offered and the pilgrims inside the rauẓa have made their way outside, the *mujāvar* emerges from the shrine with a container of hot coals that still usually emits a bit of left-over smoke from lobān that was burned inside the shrine. While people occasionally fan the remnants of this smoke in their general direction, there is no special focus on it or reaction to it until it has been placed on the base of the standard of the shrine's principal saint, located in the shrine's courtyard. After this, lobān is reintroduced to the glowing coals and white smoke begins billowing in all directions. I have heard two explanations as to why lobān is offered at the standard of each shrine's saint; one holds that the standards are places as sacred to the saints as the rauẓas themselves and thus require a lobān offering, while the other holds that this is just a convenient place to mix the lobān that comes from different rauẓas, though this does not account for offerings made at the standards of 'Ali and Fatima, where no lobān mixing is necessary.

In any case, after pausing at the saint's standard, the attendant, accompanied by a pilgrim bearing a container of crushed lobān and a spoon, begins to make his way through the waiting double line of pilgrims. Together they move through the path created by the two lines, the assistant piling lobān on the hot coals in order to maintain the billowing smoke, which the attendant fans in all directions using a simple fan of woven palm fronds.[6] The smoke prompts cries of pain from those in ḥāẓirī: many are powerful, incomprehensible screams, and others lament the fact that they are "burning." After lobān has been dispensed, the leftovers are collected by waiting pilgrims to distribute among those too ill to leave their beds, and the attendants return to their seats next to the shrines.

The prayers and offerings performed inside the rauẓas by the attendant are experienced by a very small fraction of the pilgrim population, and by definition this population is not afflicted with ḥāẓirī, which renders its practitioners ritually impure and therefore barred from entry to the rauẓas.[7] For the vast majority of Ḥusain Ṭekrī's pilgrims, the lobān experience begins with lining up in the courtyards of the rauẓas. Pilgrims in need of healing often come with a member of their family who serves as a caretaker, and therefore, unlike the dispensation of lobān that takes place inside the rauẓas, the lines in the courtyard are not rigidly segregated by gender. Men, women, and children sit in two lines facing one another, with the space between these two lines creating the path in which the lobān will be distributed. There are many practices at Ḥusain Ṭekrī that are gender segregated, but this central and simple act of waiting for lobān is not one of them.

Menstruating women also manage to take lobān more or less in the shrines, usually by waiting just outside the walls of the courtyard for one of the self-appointed distributors to emerge with leftovers. In this way the experience of lobān at Ḥusain Ṭekrī subverts what is probably the South Asian gender trope par excellence—that is, menstrual prohibitions. Even more radically, during the period of my initial research, menstruating women awaiting lobān congregated on the bare ground just outside the most recently constructed rauẓa, a relatively underfunded tribute to Fatima. While its courtyard was paved, it lacked walls on all four sides, and this meant that practically speaking there was no division in the line as it snaked around and then outside the courtyard to the place where menstruating women waited in reasonably mixed company for the lobān to travel from the shrine itself through the line of pilgrims. By the time I returned to Ḥusain Ṭekrī for follow-up research, however, three walls had been built around the rauẓa's courtyard in an effort, according to the administrators, both to improve the overall aesthetic value of the shrine and to keep the neighbors' goats from urinating and defecating in the courtyard. Of course, in addition to keeping the goats out, the new wall has also facilitated greater administrative control over the rauẓa, which nevertheless remains the only one whose courtyard is not locked at night and which therefore continues to host late-night ḥāẓirī sessions and other healing practices.

The space in which lobān is distributed is defined and created by the two parallel lines of pilgrims. This is a unique way to create or define a space of divine efficacy—it is not, in other words, a space *to which* people come, as is the case with temples with their *mūrti* (divine image) or mosques with their *mihrāb* (a niche in a mosque wall that indicates the direction of Mecca). Rather, it is a space that is created simply by the presence of the pilgrims themselves. There are, of course, images and objects in the rauẓas—chiefly *zarīḥ*, or models of the tombs of the martyrs of Karbala that are a central part of Indian Shiʿite religious life—but they are not the focus of the pilgrims' attentions during lobān. During non-lobān times, pilgrims *do* engage in certain acts of reverence and petition with these *zarīḥ* as their focus, and lobān is first offered and burned in front of these *zarīḥ* before its distribution in the courtyard. However, what is unique about this most important and frequently enacted ritual activity at Ḥusain Ṭekrī—the act of receiving lobān—is that the moment of manifest power and efficacy is experienced first and foremost within space that is delineated by the bodies of the pilgrims themselves. In other words, the bodies of the pilgrims become ritually meaningful in relation to one another rather than in relation to a *mūrti,* the rauẓas, or the direction of Mecca.

If the most powerful space at Ḥusain Ṭekrī is the space created by the bodies of the pilgrims themselves, what can be said about these bodies? At Ḥusain Ṭekrī in general and during the moment of lobān in particular, pilgrims primarily self-identify as possessors of bodies that had or currently have serious problems. These problems can be broadly classed as either illness that doctors have been unable to treat or ḥāẓirī. Like menstruating women and anyone who has not bathed, people afflicted with ḥāẓirī are not supposed to enter the rauẓas because they are considered impure. What this means is that the space that the pilgrims' bodies create for lobān distribution is primarily characterized by all of the attributes that keep people from entering the rauẓas themselves. In fact, several of my Hindu informants cited these very attributes when asked why they could not get help from a temple. In short, the very thing that excludes individuals from more orthodox structures and practices makes them meaningful participants in the creation of a lobān space.

To the waiting pilgrim or participant observer, the distribution of lobān is initially a display of inevitability: the billowing whiteness advances steadily, completely obscuring both lines of pilgrims as it passes. When it finally arrives there is an experience of bright white blindness; eyes tear, throat and lungs burn, and the unmistakable scent of lobān—a smell inextricably associated with dargāḥs and the *faqīr*s who distribute it in the streets on Thursdays—lingers long after objects begin to become discernable in the dissipating smoke. In addition to momentarily erasing from view all the pilgrims it passes, lobān also briefly completely obscures the vision of each recipient. In this moment, it is often (though not always) the case

FIGURE 3. Waiting for lobān at the rauẓa of Imām Husain.

that those with some form of ḥāẓirī will fully manifest their particular practices; others swoon, and still others stand motionless, not breathing, holding the lobān in their lungs for as long as possible before exhaling. After the smoke passes, the lingering scent of lobān bears tangible and enduring witness to the transformative event.

FIGURE 4. Pilgrims engulfed in lobān.

On the level of physical experience, the moment of lobān is one in which the pilgrim is momentarily removed from others and his or her own self. It is a moment of negation, when the pilgrim, already significantly de-selfed by virtue of being largely ungendered, disappears from the view of others. It is also a moment during which the pilgrim is removed from him- or herself, often entering into *khulī ḥāẓirī,* for which no conscious memory remains.[8] It is, therefore, a moment of removal from community, waking consciousness, body, and gender identity. This moment of erasure, one of the most significant aspects of any pilgrim's experience of lobān, is radically different from many other popular South Asian religious practices, most of which locate the individual in relation to society.[9] In part, then, lobān's particular appeal may come from the fact that its moment of power is a moment of disappearance, disassociation, and negation.

Although the consumption of lobān is unique among popular South Asian religious practices by virtue of its negating character, it does participate in the major pan-Indian religious category *prasād,* or, in Urdu, *tabarruk.* There are some obvious simple parallels between lobān and the food-based form of *prasād* offered in temples, chiefly the fact that each is the primary and most significant consumable item available to pilgrims. Both lobān and the *prasād* available in a temple are also, albeit with different theological assumptions, offered first to the presence understood to preside in the space and then to the pilgrim population as a whole. Beyond these rough parallels, however, lobān becomes something else altogether.

What is lobān that Hindu temple *prasād* is not? Most significantly, it is something that can only be experienced in its ideal form if it is consumed *in the moment it is distributed.* Unlike *prasād,* which can be collected from a temple and later distributed among family members and friends, lobān requires the presence of the afflicted individual. At Ḥusain Ṭekrī, it is generally understood that lobān is best taken at the rauẓas rather than in the privacy of a lodge room or home.[10] Lobān therefore creates a paradoxical dialectic—it brings pilgrims together, and it manifests its power in a space that exists only because of the presence of the pilgrims, but its primary work is the temporary erasure of every pilgrim who has come to receive it. And here lies its genius: its form, because it is ephemeral, requires presence, but the most immediate reward for that presence is a moment of absence. And, arguably, what most pilgrims seek in coming to Ḥusain Ṭekrī is escape from sick bodies, distressed selves, trouble at home, or malevolent possessing spirits. Unlike *prasād,* lobān is in part a negating rather than a creative force, powerful for what it removes rather than for what it bestows.

By virtue of the fact that lobān and *prasād* are the primary consumable objects available in their respective settings of rauẓa and temple, it is worth pursuing lobān's parallel with *prasād* a bit further, building on the belief that the *prasād* offered in a temple takes on the presence and character of the deity whose temple has been visited. Analysis of lobān's *prasād* nature, in other words, may provide insight into how pilgrims to Ḥusain Ṭekrī conceptualize and experience divine intervention and efficacy.

Physically speaking, lobān is inevitable—the pilgrim need only show up, and this alone is enough for him or her to reap the benefits of lobān, which are as natural and necessary as breathing. This radical ritualization of the pilgrims' helplessness and the inevitable intercession by the power of Ḥusain Ṭekrī is likely what all pilgrims need, given the fact that they come to the site helpless with illness or as victims of labyrinthine family relationships that result in ḥāẓirī, over which they are equally helpless. Lobān is also inevitable when considered from the standpoint of its origin in fire: once a fire has started, it will take its natural course. That consumption of lobān is intimately related to breathing, a process that has been extensively analyzed in South Asian texts from the Upanishads to modern tracts on yoga and *dhikr,* also contributes to lobān's elemental and inevitable allure.

In addition to being inevitable, lobān by its very nature cannot be adulterated. Unlike foods, which are categorized in South Asia as pure or polluted, the smoke offered at the shrines is undoubtedly safe to consume. The lobān smoke, the product of fire, is ephemeral: no one can manipulate or pollute it, and so it can be trusted absolutely. On the other hand, in my experience, pilgrims at Ḥusain Ṭekrī trace almost all of their afflictions to the ingestion of magically tainted milk sweets and other sweet, traditionally "safe" foods that are often used for *prasād* and for entertaining guests. The idea that lobān imparts a benefit in the same manner as edible forms of *prasād* without the risk of eating actual food is in part affirmed by the fact that during the month of Ramadan, I noticed that many of the Muslim shrine workers bound cloth over their noses and mouths when distributing lobān, explaining that inhaling it would break their fasts.[11] No distinction was made between inhalation and ingestion, and this attitude was also reflected by Hindu pilgrims, who almost universally held that their participation in the Ramadan fast necessarily excluded them from consumption of lobān.[12]

On the topic of the purity of lobān and its affinity with *prasād,* Babli once explained to me that the reason that people would hold their amulets *(taʿvīẕ)* in the path of the lobān was to cleanse them of potential impurity. Should a *taʿvīẕ,* for example, be worn in a home where a woman is observing her post-birth period of seclusion, the *taʿvīẕ* would lose its power. It could, however, be revived: "Put it *[do]* in the lobān, or wash it *[dho]* in milk," she said, adding that it was also necessary to change the string, which, unlike the metal of the *taʿvīẕ,* cannot be purified once it has been defiled.[13] In this instance, the bright white smoke of lobān seems to outmilk milk itself: it is abundant, all-encompassing, uncorrupted, and possessed of a purifying whiteness. I will return to this significant parallel between lobān and milk shortly.

Finally, like the broader concept of *prasād,* lobān is radically abundant—and this characteristic in particular was emphasized by a young Shiʿite man who was a member of one of the boards that facilitate Muharram-related events at Ḥusain Ṭekrī.[14] Lobān, we agreed, is in theory endlessly consumable; unlike food or drink, lobān can never really make one "full." Further, by virtue of its nature, lobān contains in its unburned form the potential to fill a huge space. The Urdu word that conveys this concept of potentially endless abundance, *barkat,* was frequently used by members of both Shiʿite and Sunni communities whenever they wanted to convey to me the idea that something was greater than the sum of its parts.

But do pilgrims themselves describe lobān as an abundant yet negating presence? Is this the whole story? In fact, in both conversations with me and with one another, this ubiquitous practice goes relatively unmentioned. While this is in itself significant, I felt a responsibility to explore what pilgrims would explicitly articulate about the experience of receiving lobān, if given the opportunity. After initiating many informal conversations about lobān early in my research, I took what I had learned about pilgrims' beliefs and assumptions and used it to create a simple, informal survey that I administered among a random selection of ninety-one pilgrims during a subsequent visit to Ḥusain Ṭekrī. The survey, I hasten to add, was not a formal quantitative study and should be read as a distillation of the countless informal conversations about lobān that I initiated with pilgrims.

The survey was primarily conducted among pilgrims resident in the lodges maintained by the *waqf* board in charge of Ḥusain Ṭekrī's maintenance. These lodges have a tendency to attract a religiously and economically diverse range of pilgrims.[15] Private lodges, on the other hand, often have sectarian names and tend to attract concentrations of Hindu, Shiʿia, or Sunni pilgrims from a single income bracket. The simplest of the *waqf*-administered rooms are small, windowless, fanless cubicles, some with corrugated metal roofs, which start at two to five rupees per day. The most expensive accommodations offer comfort similar to that of a middle-class home and often include several rooms, fans, windows, basic furniture, and attached baths, at a cost of fifty rupees per day. Midrange rooms, some with running water and fans, range from ten to thirty-five rupees per day.[16] Consequently, like Ḥusain Ṭekrī's general population, those staying in *waqf* board housing are pilgrims from a broad range of economic backgrounds, and the population surveyed reflects this range.

The ninety-one individuals surveyed included thirty Hindus (nine male, twenty-one female), three Jains (one female, two male), two Sikhs (two female), and fifty-six Muslims (nineteen male, thirty-seven female), making the surveyed population 67 percent female, 33 percent male, 62 percent Muslim, 33 percent Hindu, 3 percent Jain, and 2 percent Sikh. My day-to-day experience at Ḥusain Ṭekrī and its satellite sites suggests that these numbers are an accurate representation of the gender ratio of petitioners at Muslim shrines. However, because I surveyed the resident rather than the transient population, my experience also suggests that the percentage of Hindus in this survey is a bit lower than the percentage who actually visit the shrine on any given day, and especially on Thursdays.

The survey indicated that approximately three-quarters of Ḥusain Ṭekrī's pilgrims had some experience with or knowledge of lobān prior to coming to Ḥusain Ṭekrī. Interestingly, this number was nearly the same in both Hindu and Muslim communities. Nearly all of the pilgrims who had previously taken lobān had done so in an Islamic context, including dargāḥs, *imāmbāṛās*, mosques, and in the presence of *pīr*s. When asked about their consumption of lobān at Ḥusain Ṭekrī, almost all of the surveyed pilgrims reported that they took lobān in the mornings and afternoons—both times that it is offered at Ḥusain Ṭekrī. This pattern of consumption was the same for those who had and had not heard of lobān before coming to Ḥusain Ṭekrī. The very few surveyed pilgrims who were not taking it regularly in the courtyards of Ḥusain Ṭekrī's rauẓas cited physical weakness as the main reason for their absence; in one case, an individual explained that her possessing spirit sometimes interfered with her ability to take lobān. In short, the survey confirmed that consumption of lobān is a central and widely practiced ritual activity at Ḥusain Ṭekrī, and it showed that irrespective of religious background, most pilgrims knew about lobān and had taken it in an explicitly Islamic context.

In an effort to determine how pilgrims experience lobān, I asked the surveyed pilgrims to reflect on their physical and mental state while taking lobān. They were presented with three questions: 1) Just before taking lobān, what do you experience? 2) Just as you take lobān, what do you experience? 3) Just after taking lobān, what do you experience?[17] The response options for each of the three questions were the same: happiness, fear, unconsciousness, sadness, peace, comfort, hope, anger, nothing, and something else (fill in blank).[18] Owing to the low literacy or illiteracy of many of the respondents, it was often necessary for me to read the options out loud, and this meant that the survey often led to an informal conversation about lobān in which other terms or frameworks were employed. In keeping with my hypothesis that one of the most powerful characteristics of lobān is its potential to be all things to all people, the responses to this series of questions were varied. Though the specifics varied considerably, most pilgrims experienced lobān as a catalyst for transformation of consciousness and physicality: pilgrims' responses to these three questions exhibit a general movement from feelings of bodily and emotional distress to feelings of well-being. Thus, of the ninety-one pilgrims surveyed, only six reported positive feelings immediately prior to taking lobān, as compared to twenty during and forty-four after, and conversely, while twenty-eight reported negative feelings before lobān, only seven experienced negative feelings during lobān, and only six after.

In keeping with this emphasis on bodily experience, the terms that pilgrims used to describe the experience of lobān consumption eschewed the more psychologically oriented vocabulary of the survey and instead specified whether the individual was conscious or unconscious, experiencing physical pain or pleasure, or in ḥāẓirī. In total, the number of informants who chose to describe their experience in these physical terms was thirty-three out of ninety-one before, thirty-nine during, and forty-two after.[19] Generally, then, pilgrims preferred to describe lobān in terms of its effect on the body rather than its effect on the psyche.

The range of positive physical sensations associated with lobān consumption included lightness *(halkāpan)* and a feeling of healing, which were commonly associated with the moments during and after consumption. The most common pleasurable feeling pilgrims reported was *ārām* (comfort), followed distantly by the less explicitly physical states of *sukūn* (peacefulness) and *acchā* (good). Unpleasurable physical reactions, concentrated before and during consumption, included burning, dizziness, intoxication, and a sensation of weakness in the hands and/or feet. The most common undesirable emotion was *krodh* (anger), followed by *ghabrāhaṭ* (confusion or agitation), and follow-up questions usually confirmed that respondents had offered the word "anger" as a description of their various possessing presences' feelings rather than their own.

During the use of lobān, ḥāẓirī and unconsciousness developed in inverse relationship with one another. Pilgrims reporting unconsciousness increased from four before lobān to six during to sixteen after, while pilgrims reporting ḥāẓirī decreased from sixteen before lobān to six during to only three after. As I interpreted the responses during the interviews themselves, neither the ḥāẓirī nor the unconsciousness that often manifest in the presence of lobān were considered positive or negative; they were, rather, inevitable physical consequences of taking lobān—automatic reactions, unwilled. Perhaps also significant in light of the hypothesis that lobān marks a moment of effacement, the number of respondents who were unable or unwilling to offer an answer for what they experienced was highest—seventeen—for the moment of consumption itself.[20] Finally, a very small number of pilgrims insisted they had no experience of any kind before, during, or after the consumption of lobān, using words like "normal" or explaining that it had no effect.

On the question of whether or not there is a divine or saintly presence in the lobān smoke itself, respondents' answers were, not surprisingly, varied. When asked if it seemed to them that a "great being" or "power" *(hastī)* was present in the smoke of lobān itself, twenty-six said no, sixty-two said yes, and three were not sure. *Hastī* is a word in somewhat common circulation at Ḥusain Ṭekrī to talk about a saint; I used it because I wanted a word that was ambiguous in its communal connotations. Again, in considering the range of response, it seems that lobān possesses a character that allows a range of interpretation in keeping with the particular situation of each individual who consumes it. Among pilgrims who indicated that no great being or power was present in the smoke itself, answers included the assertion that lobān is a kind of medicine or that it contains healing *(shifā)*. Others said it was only smoke, or that it simply burned, or that they couldn't say because they were either unconscious at the time it was administered or they did not have open ḥāẓirī and so could not know what was present in the smoke.

The "yes" answers were a bit more uniform: most said that the power of "Bābā" *(bābā kī śakti)* was present in the smoke, or that Husain himself used the smoke to heal pilgrims. Many emphasized that because they had seen an improvement in their situation there had to be something present in the smoke, overwhelmingly using the word *śakti* to describe this power, and many others explained that the fact that lobān induced ḥāẓirī was enough to show that some power or powerful individual was present in the smoke. Taking a similarly reasonable approach, a single pilgrim said that there had to be *some* reason so many people came to Ḥusain Ṭekrī. Several said that they did not have experiential knowledge, but that because the rauẓas were the place of Husain and the other saints, they had to believe that something was present in the smoke. Along these lines, a pilgrim emphasized that Mecca and Medina were both present at Ḥusain Ṭekrī. Results, reason, and faith: all of these resources, in short, were used in varying combinations to support an assertion of the presence of some kind of power or powerful individual in the smoke itself.[21]

A conversation with a young woman from Punjab offered yet another perspective: the *smoke* of lobān was not the location of saintly power. Notably, however, she still speaks in terms of bodily experience:

Young woman: You should have asked the question differently. You asked if it seems that there's someone with us [during lobān]. It has never seemed that way to me. Some people say that it seems that there's someone standing just behind them . . . but with me, it's happened countless times that it seems that there's something else *in* me, [something that is] not me. So you should have asked the question like that.

Carla: And you're talking about the saint *[hastī]*, not the bad spirit *[balā]*, right?

Young woman: That's right—because you can't see the saint *[hastī]*; you can only feel his presence.

Taking this young woman's observations into account, it is possible that the reason that so many respondents had difficulty with the series of questions on the experience of lobān has something to do with the fact that they associate the experience of the presence of the saints with sensations in their bodies rather than with the lobān itself.

Yet another perspective on the relationship between lobān and saintly presence was offered by Priya's mentor, the *mujāvar* from the city of Sagar in Madhya Pradesh. Regarding the special nature of lobān at Ḥusain Ṭekrī and Muslim shrines, he once explained the relationship between the martyrs and lobān through a discussion of the jinn under the saints' command:

Mujāvar: Ḥusain Ṭekrī's sepoys [English used] travel with the lobān container [as it is carried through the crowd], and they breathe on the patients *[marīẓ]*—and there's special power in that—and it's from this breath that the patients benefit. But the patients don't know that they're there. [. . .]

Carla: Are they present at other places where lobān is dispensed—Ajmer Sharīf or Māmū Sahib [a local dargāḥ]?

Mujāvar: Yes, but not [lobān that is given] at home, because they [saints] have jinn under their command, and they use these jinn to distribute their power *[fauj khilāte hain]*. [. . .] They don't have to work themselves—they [the saints] just give the command *[ḥukm]* and the sepoys do the work.

Unlike many of the other respondents, the *mujāvar* kept the power of lobān under the auspices of Islam. In fact, likely for similar reasons, this *mujāvar* also held that jinn were responsible for relaying the prayers that pilgrims offer to the saints of Ḥusain Ṭekrī as they tie *challā*.

The inhalation of lobān is also generally understood by pilgrims to be effective because its ephemeral form is most suited to combating the ephemeral, windlike form of spirits. The association between the two is such that in Hindi, the word for wind, *havā*, is also a common word for a spirit. In the words of Babli, "A [malevolent possessing] spirit, you know—it's like wind, so it's necessary to take lobān through the nose . . . and you'll help it reach the spirit—and really, you shouldn't take too much." *Havā kā cakkar* (literally, "wind-confusion"), a phrase commonly used at Ḥusain Ṭekrī to describe the cause of a health or spirit-related problem that may have been the result not of magic but of randomness, underscores the idea that malevolent presences come from, or are part of, air.

Lobān's power also derives in part from its ability to burn like fire. This source of lobān's efficacy is affirmed by the cries of spirits during ḥāẓirī, who often lament that they are being burned away as a result of the introduction of lobān into the body. This elemental power of fire seems to be largely unrelated to the pan–South Asian tendency to categorize consumables as "hot" or "cold." When given a choice between categorizing lobān as hot or cold, pilgrims' responses varied. When pilgrims described lobān in terms of "warming" or "cooling," its *efficacy* was often linked to its ability to burn offending malevolent spirits. At the same time, lobān's appeal was attributed to the cooling effect it has on the individual.[22] When the respondents who described lobān as cooling *(ṭhaṇḍhā)* chose to elaborate, they used positive adjectives such as *sukūn* (peacefulness) and *acchā* (good) to describe the coolness; they asserted that lobān was good because it did not burn. Like the smoke of lobān, its ashes (and those of incense sticks) were also cooling and therefore beneficial. In short, as is the case in all kinds of South Asian ritual and textual contexts, heat is powerful, change inducing, and dangerous, and coolness is sustaining and pleasant to experience.

The power of lobān's heating nature also derives from the ubiquitous association of heat, asceticism *(tapas)*, and power in South Asian culture. At Ḥusain Ṭekrī, for example, there is a great deal of emphasis placed on the suffering that pilgrims experience during their stay in the very basic accommodations. Thus, for example, two Agarwal sisters from Madhya Pradesh described their experience at Ḥusain Ṭekrī as a physical and emotional trial, noting that they were far from the comforts of their home and their urban Hindu community. Similarly, the wealthy Ḵhoja Shi'ite city dwellers who come to Ḥusain Ṭekrī for Muharram events often observe that Hindu devotees were more likely to find their requests granted than Muslims because of their superior practices of asceticism. The Shi'ite urbanites were referring to the pilgrims from villages who squat in makeshift tents on Ḥusain Ṭekrī's grounds, enduring the extremes of hot days and freezing nights, their mornings punctuated by cold-water baths. The Agarwal sisters, in fact, initially described the martyrdom of 'Abbas—specifically the severing of his hands—as part of his commitment to renunciation *(tyāg)*, also using the word *martyrdom (shahādat)*. 'Abbas, they held, was the most powerful *(jalālī)* of the martyrs because his martyrdom—part of his renunciation—was so gruesome. They went on to explain that the term *shahādat* was new to them, and that they had learned it and other Muslim terminology and ideology from a Jain family that had been in residence at Ḥusain Ṭekrī for more than ten years.

Recall, also, Nasim's description of Husain, in which he wears a small blanket associated with the clothing of an ascetic. In relation to lobān, it seems that the qualities of anger and asceticism that Husain and his fellow martyrs embody for all pilgrims are, to a certain extent, present in the heat of lobān itself. As one of my main Shi'ite informants from Bombay once explained to me, lobān offered during Muharram is especially potent because during the month that commemorates their suffering, Husain and the rest of the martyrs are particularly inclined to feel empathy for those who suffer from illness and ḥāẓirī and consequently have a strong desire to punish possessing spirits harshly. Here a fairly explicit connection is made between martyrdom, anger, and lobān. Along these lines, Ḥusain Ṭekrī's occasional midnight lobāns are regarded as especially effective because of the widely held belief that Husain and the rest of the martyrs are present in the rauẓas in the wee hours of the night: typically the rauẓas are closed well before midnight in order to protect pilgrims from the potentially angry saints.[23]

Returning to this chapter's guiding questions of why pilgrims regard Ḥusain Ṭekrī as powerful and why pilgrims experience their particular healing practices as effective, pilgrims' reflections on the nature of lobān and the often physically uncomfortable lifestyle of Ḥusain Ṭekrī suggest that the power of asceticism, which is universally recognized, irrespective of religious affiliation, is part of the way that pilgrims conceptualize their very presence at Ḥusain Ṭekrī, as well as their healing practices, and the power of its saints. I will further explore the concept of asceticism later in this chapter as I consider pilgrims' other major healing practices.

In contrast with pilgrims' varied opinions about the source of lobān's efficacy and its relationship with the presence of the saints, written accounts of Ḥusain Ṭekrī's origin, all of which have Muslim authors, are closer in spirit to the description provided by the *mujāvar* from Sagar in that they consistently link lobān with saintly presence. The version of Ḥusain Ṭekrī's origin below, taken from a popular guidebook written by a Shiʿite from Delhi, tells of a potential communal conflict on the tenth of Muharram in 1304/1886,[24] a subsequent miraculous visitation of Husain and several other major figures from early Islamic history to the princely state of Jaora, and, finally, the establishment of a ritual burning of lobān.

> Some people came from the village of Rozana to participate in the *taʿziya* procession.[25] When they were near Mehaṁdī Well, they saw a strange sight. Mehaṁdī Well was located in dense jungle; people saw lights in this jungle, and from the dense jungle lights came dazzling light. Every tree in the jungle was easily illuminated by the light. At first people were afraid and thought to themselves, "What is going on in this jungle? Even during the day people are afraid to come here; who would come at night?" Still, some people took the name of Maulā [Husain] on their lips and went forward. They saw that the *taʿziya* of Jaora was present. Here and there near the *taʿziya* they saw veiled people whose faces radiated light, and it was from this light that the jungle was illuminated. Some people saw this and stopped, but those people who wanted to see more went forward. They saw a beautiful old man with a radiant face who was seated in one place. In front of him, water was coming up from the ground as if from a pump, and he was using the water for *wuẓū* [the mandatory washing performed before *namāz*].
>
> Some people saw another old man with a luminous face offering *namāz* on a nearby hill on the place where the standard *[parcam]* of Imām Husain now waves and the rauẓa of Imām Husain now stands.

People had never seen anything like this before; after consulting with one another, they decided that the *nawāb* should be told about what had happened. It was late at night by that point, though, so everyone went home. First thing in the morning, they arrived at Nawāb Ismail Khan's bungalow. There were women and children in this group. They told the *nawāb*'s servants that they had come to see the *nawāb* because they had seen a strange sight on a hill the previous evening. They [the servants] told the *nawāb* and he told them to see to it that the people were seated comfortably with his permission. Immediately upon meeting the *nawāb,* the people told him about the miraculous things that they had seen. After listening carefully to what the people said to him, the *nawāb* said that he had seen in a dream exactly what the people had seen with their own eyes. It was also told [in the dream] that eyewitnesses would come and tell about this place. The *nawāb* said that this brilliant-faced old man had also said that he should go to this place and protect it. The *nawāb* sent the people to this place with his servants, and he himself arrived there soon thereafter. When the people arrived, the jungle was filled with a wonderful smell. It was revealed in a dream that "an enclosure should be created up to the point where the good smell has spread [because] we are pleased with this place." The *nawāb* also enclosed the place where water bubbled up from the ground. He made a big stepwell at this place. The place was named Jhālrā Sharīf (Blessed Spring).[26]

Some people came running from a hill and arrived in the presence of the *nawāb.* When the *nawāb* came to this hill with the people, there was an unearthly sweet smell in the air—better than aloe wood[27] and ambergris. The *nawāb* gave the order to enclose the entire area. Since this miracle happened on the tenth of Muharram and that day is the day of Imām Husain's martyrdom, the hill was associated with Husain and named Husain Hill. The *nawāb* appointed a man to take care of the place and to administer lobān in the morning and evening.[28]

In this story, as with the contemporary experience of lobān itself, the sweet smell experienced by the *nawāb* (who, significantly, did not see the visions himself) functions as the enduring witness to the transformative moment. It is also clear that the subsequent burning of lobān is meant as an offering to and an invocation of the saintly presence, since the sweet smell of the lobān is easily equated with the sweet smell that bore witness to the miraculous visitation. This connection between a sweet smell and a supernatural or saintly presence continues in the present-day life of Ḥusain Ṭekrī through the dispensation of lobān and in the healing practices of some of its recovered devotees. Thus, for example, Nasim begins her practice with an anointment with and inhalation of perfumed oil, and Maya, at her granddaughter's prompting, also acknowledged that pilgrims offered her sweet-smelling oil. Across religious traditions, sweet-smelling substances are strongly linked with transformative moments.

Ḥusain Ṭekrī's guidebooks speak more explicitly of lobān that do its pilgrims, which is in some ways not surprising because, like much popular literature at pilgrimage centers, guidebooks are written to "sell" their chosen place, and lobān, as the primary consumable object available at Ḥusain Ṭekrī, can certainly be controlled, if not actually sold.[29] Lobān, when it is given a name other than its own, is described as one of the chief "medicines" of Ḥusain Ṭekrī—the English word is often used. The English vocabulary and allopathic terminology might represent an attempt to speak about the power of Ḥusain Ṭekrī in a nonsectarian manner, which is necessary given that it attracts pilgrims from a broad range of religious backgrounds. According to *Ḥusain Ṭekrī kyā hai,* Ḥusain Ṭekrī is not a *religious* place at all, but rather "the biggest spiritual hospital in the world," and as such it is open to members of all religious backgrounds.[30]

On one level, marketing requires commodification, and allopathic medicine is inherently commodified and unlikely to alienate either a Hindu or Muslim clientele. On another level, this language of allopathy likely represents an attempt by the Muslim author of the guidebook to create a universal, nonsectarian language to describe the genuine gift that he sees Ḥusain Ṭekrī offering everyone, especially the poor and the suffering. In some ways echoing the sentiment that Ḥusain Ṭekrī should not be thought of in terms of "Hindu" or "Muslim," many a helpful pilgrim explained to me that if I really studied *religion,* I should go to a mosque, a temple, or, according to some Shi'a who were unhappy with the greater Sunni context of the *imāmbāṛā* at Ḥusain Ṭekrī, a *proper imāmbāṛā.*

However, despite the widely held view that Ḥusain Ṭekrī is not a conventional or orthodox religious place, pilgrims rarely adopted the guidebooks' strategy of describing lobān as medicine and Ḥusain Ṭekrī as a hospital, spiritual or otherwise. In fact, despite its centrality to most healing practices and to Ḥusain Ṭekrī's culture, pilgrims voluntarily discussed lobān so infrequently that I was compelled to make a special effort to supplement my own analysis of its physical characteristics by purposefully bringing it up in informal conversations with pilgrims and ultimately administering a survey about it. If pilgrims' own words are taken seriously and my observations about the physical experience of taking lobān are accurate, lobān's cross-tradition appeal is not the result of pilgrims conceptualizing it as nonreligious or allopathic. Rather, lobān's authority ultimately comes from the simple fact that it is particularly open to interpretation: if a pilgrim has a malevolent spirit, lobān can burn it; if the pilgrim has an illness, lobān can offer cooling and comfort; and if the pilgrim is unready or unwilling to enter into the healing process that lobān instigates and sustains, it is possible that he or she will find that lobān is simply smoke, sweetly scented and beneficial but not change inducing. On a biological level, regardless of individual interpretations of lobān's efficacy, the human sense of smell is such that transformative moments associated with the inhalation of lobān (whatever they may be) can easily be evoked anywhere: when pilgrims return home, the sweet smell of lobān—whether burned in a home-based shrine or at a nearby mosque or dargāḥ—will spontaneously induce memories of their healing experiences at Ḥusain Ṭekrī.[31]

I have suggested that dargāḥ culture is best conceptualized as a (religious) culture in and of itself rather than Hindu, Muslim, or even Islamicate; I have also suggested that this culture is particularly South Asian, by which I mean it is rooted in the subcontinental context rather than particular to South Asians as an ethnic group. As a product of this culture, lobān's white, hot, and abundant nature effectively synthesizes two major complementary religious discourses of the subcontinent: the radical abundance of divine love, often symbolized by milk (in lobān, its whiteness) and the power of asceticism (in lobān, its heat). The consumption of lobān allows pilgrims to absorb the potency of Husain and the other martyrs of Karbala: the heat of their martyrdom, asceticism, and wrath combined with the white abundance of the love that underlies the act of self-sacrifice. The milk-white, abundant, nurturing aspect of lobān sustains pilgrims, and the hot, wrathful, and martyrdom- and asceticism-driven element of lobān heals them. In addition to these aspects of its potency, lobān's essentially ephemeral, effacing, non-commodifiable form requires pilgrims to be physically present at Ḥusain Ṭekrī itself, thus forcing them to create communities outside any institutional structure (both familial and religious) while also affording them the opportunity to momentarily free themselves from all human relationships and suffering in the inevitable moment of erasure central to the physical experience of taking lobān.

While unburned lobān can be and in fact is sold at Ḥusain Ṭekrī and sustains commercial relationships between dargāḥs, the smoke of lobān cannot be owned, bottled, bought, sold, or otherwise introduced into a commercial economy where resources are limited. It is both endlessly available and inherently unpossessable.[32] This notion of absolute abundance is, I suggest, the foundation of the spiritual economy of Ḥusain Ṭekrī; its complement, paradoxically, is the notion of absence and absolute negation, and both of these elements are potentially present in the experience of taking lobān. Muslism and non-Muslim alike can agree that lobān is completely trustworthy: as a product of fire, it is a pure, sustaining and cleansing force. In short, lobān is an endlessly abundant source of all things to everyone: its very form affords it the ability to infuse any narrative with its power, and to be what pilgrims need when they need it. Lobān's physical nature makes it attractive and powerful to pilgrims of all religious backgrounds, and because lobān is primarily dispensed in Muslim places and by Muslim persons, pilgrims of all religious backgrounds associate it with places that are, like Ḥusain Ṭekrī, explicitly marked as Muslim.

Given lobān's ever-present yet unspoken nature, it is not surprising that songs that preface most daily dispensations of lobān at Ḥusain Ṭekrī—and always accompany the Thursday dispensation—contain few explicit references to the substance. However, they do offer some insight into another significant aspect of the culture of Muslim saint shrines: a discourse of command and volunteerism. The songs are often led by Mr. Chunnu Khan, a longtime resident of Ḥusain Ṭekrī who makes his living from voluntary offerings made by pilgrims as he sings. The unaccompanied songs operate in a call-and response manner; verses are led by Khan, with the gathering crowd of pilgrims joining in after a few repetitions of the simple lyrics. As he sings, Khan stands in each rauẓa's courtyard facing the rauẓa's front door, forming the center of a crowd of pilgrims that eventually grows to frame, on three sides, a space that opens immediately in front of the front door of the rauẓa. Persons in ḥāẓirī fill this space, pacing violently back and forth, tossing their heads in circles, and crying out in pain with increased vigor as the time for lobān approaches. As the distress of those in ḥāẓirī increases, the songs continue in an improvisational manner until the lobān emerges from the shrine, at which point the singing ends.

While singing, Mr. Khan offers occasional support to those in ḥāẓirī, catching them as they fall back or using his hand to briefly shake the unbound hair of women in ḥāẓirī, presumably to aid in the removal of the offending spirit, which is popularly understood to attach itself to women's hair. His singing and physical assistance of women together give Khan a healerlike status in the eyes of some pilgrims, though, as far as I was able to ascertain, he has no formal healing practice like that of Nasim and Maya.

As Khan sings, facing the shrine and, like the crowd of singing pilgrims, always standing, he often raises his right arm, palm upturned and arm outstretched in the direction of the shrine, in a gesture reminiscent of those made by *qawwals*. *Qawwali* itself is not at all a part of the ritual life of Ḥusain Ṭekrī, however; most pilgrims said they did not know why *qawwali* was not performed at Ḥusain Ṭekrī, though some local *qawwals* and several others explained to me that *qawwali* is an exuberant and joyful tradition and is therefore unsuited to Ḥusain Ṭekrī, which is home to saints whose gruesome and tragic martyrdoms are not properly remembered through ecstatic singing.

The following translation of the songs sung immediately prior to lobān dispensation is based on a live recording I made at one of the rauẓas dur-

FIGURE 5. Hāẓirī at the rauẓa of Bībī Fatima.

ing my time at Ḥusain Ṭekrī.[33] Khan has produced a studio version of these songs, and while the cassette insert lists four songs, my live recording captured a typically improvised compilation of these four songs. Of these songs, the only one with a markedly different tune is the one referred to in the cassette insert as "You called me here; if that isn't grace, what is?" My translation initially follows the live improvised lyrics and includes some repetition in order to provide a sense of the flow of the improvisation. Subsequently, ellipses mark the places of large sections of repeated verses. In between these repeated verses, I have translated the new verses in the order in which they were sung, and I have also noted the concluding verse, though it represents little more than the moment lobān was finally introduced to the waiting crowd. In general, the singing lasts about half an hour. Khan's solos are indicated by italics.

Lord *[āgā]* accept my salām
Oh my Master *[maulā]*, accept my salām

You've called
Everyone is standing here
Everyone is here
Oh Master, accept my salām.

Lord, accept my salām.
Everyone is standing here, salām!
Lord, accept my salām
Oh my Master, accept my salām

Oh my Master, you've called me here
You've called me here
If that's not grace, what is?

You called me here
You called me here
If that's not grace, what is?

You've called me here
If that's not grace, what is?

You've improved my lot in life
You've improved my lot in life
If that's not grace, what is?

You've improved my lot in life
You've improved my lot in life
If that's not grace, what is?

You called me here
You called me here
If that's not grace, what is?

You rebuilt my ruined home
You rebuilt my ruined home
If that's not grace, what is?

You called me here
You called me here
If that's not grace, what is?

Whether Hindu or Muslim
Your gaze rests on everyone.

Everyone has partaken of your offering
Everyone has partaken of your offering
If that's not grace, what is?

Everyone has partaken of your offering
Everyone has partaken of your offering
If that's not grace, what is?

You called me here
You called me here
If that's not grace, what is?

With great sadness my life was ending
My life, Lord.

You rebuilt my ruined home
You rebuilt my ruined home
If that's not grace, what is?
(repeat)

You called me here
You called me here
If that's not grace, what is?
(repeat)

Oh Sultan of Karbala
Lord, accept my salām.

Oh Sultan of Karbala
Lord, accept my salām.
(repeat 3 times)

Oh Sultan of Karbala
Lord, accept my salām.

Oh Sultan of Karbala
Lord, accept my salām.

Desired and extraordinary beloved
Desired and extraordinary beloved
Lord, accept my salām.

Desired and extraordinary beloved
Lord, accept my salām.

You, who bear with my whims
You, who preserve my honor.

You, who bear with my whims
You, who preserve my honor.

I'm your servant
I'm your servant.
Oh Lord, accept my salām.

You, who bear with my whims
You, who preserve my honor.

I'm your servant.
Oh Lord, accept my salām.

The oppressors of this age
What harm can they do?

The oppressors of this age
What harm can they do?

Oh Lord, accept my salām
Master, accept my salām.

My Lord is with me
My Lord is with me
Oh Lord, accept my salām.
(repeat)

I'm a servant of the Five Pure Ones
Who can cause my ruin?

I'm a servant of the Five Pure Ones
Who can cause my ruin?

They are shelter for my head
They are shelter for my head
Oh Lord, accept my salām.

They are shelter for my head
Oh Lord, accept my salām.

You, who bear with my whims
You, who preserve my honor.

You, who bear with my whims
You, who preserve my honor.

I'm your servant
I'm your servant
Oh Lord, accept my salām.

I'm your servant
Oh Lord, accept my salām.

Whoever meets with the servanthood of 'Abbas
(repeat)

He has attained greatness!
Oh Lord, accept my salām.
(repeat 3 times)

You, who bear with my whims
You, who preserve my honor.

You, who bear with my whims
You, who preserve my honor.

I'm your servant
I'm your servant
Oh Lord, accept my salām.

I'm your servant
Oh Lord, accept my salām.

If all the world opposes me
What harm can come to me?
(repeat)

My Lord is with me
My Lord is with me
Oh Lord, accept my salām.

The offering came at your beheading
[second line unclear]

You declare God's command
Oh Lord, accept my salām.
(repeat)
. . .
Oh Master, in lobān,
Burn away the magic and the evil spirits.
(repeat)

Every day the mad pray thus.
(repeat)
. . .
If I ever go to Medina,
I would tell the lord about this.
. . .
The oppressors of this age
What harm can they do?

The song is simple; while its audience is ostensibly the saints who are understood to be present in the shrines, the lyrics also strengthen the pilgrims' confidence in their own ability to heal at Ḥusain Ṭekrī. Most importantly, the song's refrain—"You called me here: if that's not grace, what is?"—reflects the fact that most pilgrims have no institutional, communal, orthodox, or family obligation–based reason for their presence at Ḥusain Ṭekrī. Various combinations of these reasons are, however, a significant element of the motivation for participating in the life of a temple or mosque, the two primary institutional and communal representations of orthodox

Hinduism and Islam. In contrast to this, the pilgrim's arrival at Ḥusain Ṭekrī is attributable solely to grace, which is my translation of the Arabic-derived "*karam*" of the original, and the lyrics efficiently equate this grace with the will of "*maulā*" or "*āgā*," which in the above are translated as "master" and "lord" respectively.

It is also important to clarify that here "grace" carries none of the connotations associated with Christian uses of this word, in which grace is offered to an undeserving sinner, irredeemably deep in spiritual debt. On the contrary, the most common way that those at Ḥusain Ṭekrī refer to themselves is "*ma'ṣūm*," or "innocent one": recall Priya's possessing spirit's repeated threat that he was going to "take this innocent one and go." Similarly, in the course of explaining the nature of ḥāẓirī, the most popular of the new guidebooks available for purchase at Ḥusain Ṭekrī explains that during ḥāẓirī, "whatever the person says is actually said by the [malevolent possessing spirit]. The person on whom the spirit has become present, he, that is, the innocent one, isn't the one speaking."[34] The grace offered at Ḥusain Ṭekrī, in other words, is freely given and provided to right wrongs rather than to release individuals from some sort of spiritual debt.[35]

Throughout, the song focuses on the voluntary nature of the relationship between pilgrims and Ḥusain Ṭekrī: Maulā was not obligated to call, the pilgrim was not compelled to come, and, along these lines, the shrine's martyrs were not forced to give up their lives. One of the major results of this fundamentally voluntary divine-human relationship is that other, socially sanctioned, obligation-based paradigms of the relationship between divinity and humanity—especially the categories of Hindu and Muslim—become less relevant because they are not popularly understood as identities entered into on an individual, voluntary basis. In India, religious identity in the formal sense (e.g., Hindu, Muslim, Sikh, or Christian) is community based and recognized rather than individually, consciously chosen. Because volunteerism is highly valued at Ḥusain Ṭekrī, these categories lose currency. In fact, at Ḥusain Ṭekrī, the only recognized conversions were those made in order to marry—individual, voluntary conversion to Hinduism or Islam simply made no sense, regardless of individual acts that might be recognizable as Hindu or Muslim. For example, Gayatri, a shrine worker, married a Muslim man whom she met at Ḥusain Ṭekrī—a not uncommon occurrence.[36] When we initially met, Gayatri was introduced with an explicitly Muslim name, which I never recorded in my field notes and cannot remember because, after this, Gayatri never used it again, either with me or with her friends and colleagues at the shrines. On a personal level, neither she nor her friends conceived of her identity as simply Muslim. However, everyone also understood that she was no longer straightforwardly Hindu because she had married a Muslim man. Gayatri's Hinduness, because it was not individually chosen, never completely left others' perceptions of her (or, indeed, her self-perception). At the same time, however, the socially significant act of marriage forced everyone to recognize that something fundamental about her identity had changed, and this is why, perhaps, she was initially introduced with her Muslim name.

Unlike the formal, socially constructed identities of Hindu, Muslim, Sikh, and Christian, which come with their attendant sets of obligations, pilgrims' relationships with Ḥusain Ṭekrī develop from the individual, voluntary nature of the initial encounter between the pilgrim and the rauẓas. This relationship is founded on the voluntary call and response as described in Khan's songs. The seal of this voluntary relationship is the tying of a *challā* to the *jālī* of the rauẓas.[37] This action is variously described as entering a "case" with the saints of Ḥusain Ṭekrī (the English word is often used), making a petition or vow *(mannat, murād),* or praying *(duā karnā).* The act of tying the *challā* is the outward expression of an inner willingness to submit to whatever is necessary to solve one's problems. Nasim's healing practice, for example, often involves assisting pilgrims as they tie their *challā,* which is an outward sign that a petition has been made. Comparably, the Hindi version of the popular guidebook *Ḥusain Ṭekrī kyā hai* states:

> First of all, pilgrims should go to the rauẓa of Ḥaẓrat ʿAbbas. To obtain release from illness and problems, you have to buy a string from the rauẓas. This string has two parts, one long and one short. Tie the shorter one on the rauẓa's *jālī* with the intention of having your requests fulfilled and your illnesses healed. As you tie the string, you should tell Maulā about your troubles and make your requests. After each request, tie a knot. After you tie the short string, tie the longer one around your neck. You should do this at every rauẓa, starting at the rauẓa of ʿAbbas the Martyr.[38]

Far from being confining, therefore, this literal binding of the individual with the saints of Ḥusain Ṭekrī has a fundamentally comforting rather than encumbering effect. By tying *a challā* to the *jālī,* a relationship is created between the individual and the rauẓa, and the *challā* tied around the neck is a visible sign to all that the individual wearing the string is struggling with some kind of problem. This is not always desirable: it was explained to me several times that the reason some individuals wore their *challā* on the upper part of their right arms, under their clothes, was to keep people from seeing that they had a problem.[39] Similarly, a woman buying string from one of the many vendors that line the main road connecting the rauẓas at Ḥusain Ṭekrī once told me that she was going to buy a black cord with decorative gold thread spun through it. The string would have the same protective qualities as the commonly used mottled red-and-white cotton string, but everyone would think she was wearing it for "*shauq*"—that is, for fun or fashion—rather than because she needed protection.

This woman's discussion of her choice of string highlights the popular understanding of the string's protective power. Babli, for example, in relating the sad story of her father's death (he passed away between the period of my initial and follow-up research), explained that the magician who had performed magic on her would be able to capture and manipulate the soul of her deceased father since, in addition to leaving the protective environment of Ḥusain Ṭekrī, he had taken off his protective *challā* in his death throes. Because the string no longer touched his body, he had lost the protection of the saints. The *challā* creates an enduring physical connection between the individual and the shrine. Therefore, it is not surprising that pilgrims would come to understand them as protective objects, and in some cases healing objects. I would even occasionally encounter a pilgrim who had tied one around his or her forehead to treat headaches.

This notion of the protective nature of *challā* was echoed in the statements of the matriarch of the Sunni family in whose home I lived when I was doing my research. She explained that she was not concerned about my bringing malevolent spirits home from Ḥusain Ṭekrī because everyone who goes there ties a *challā,* which effectively binds the spirits, confining them to Ḥusain Ṭekrī. Reflecting a similar belief about the binding power of the *challā,* a Muslim man who became friends with Priya once came to her room to consult with her about the meaning of his *challā* falling off while he was bathing. Pilgrims commonly believe that the moments spent bathing are among the most vulnerable of the day, and possessing spirits often seize individuals at this time. This being the case, it makes sense that the falling away of a *challā* during this time would be particularly worrisome.

Challā are also tied when an individual leaves Ḥusain Ṭekrī before being granted a *faislā* but intending to return. Recall, for example, Priya's desire to leave Ḥusain Ṭekrī. Because she did not trust her own desires and feelings, she was waiting for a dream that would signal that it was safe to leave. In such situations, if the dream comes, the individual ties the *challā* before leaving. It is also possible that in certain circumstances, such as when Babli's father's health was deteriorating, it becomes necessary to leave Ḥusain Ṭekrī without permission granted by a dream. Here again, tying a *challā* before leaving offers some security against further malevolent magic.

The *challā* creates and represents a protective and mutual but also binding relationship between the pilgrim and Ḥusain Ṭekrī: the tying is the act

FIGURE 6. Pilgrims hanging onto *challā*-covered *jālī*.

of voluntary submission necessary for subsequent progress and protection. So important is the intention with which the action is performed that it is possible to have someone else tie the *challā* as a proxy and deliver the other portion of the string to the person who has "commissioned" the tying.[40] Tying the *challā* and lobān consumption are the two ongoing, individual, voluntary, and necessary actions performed by pilgrims; they are the sine qua non of healing and recovery. Everything beneficial about Ḥusain Ṭekrī is contingent upon this initial voluntary relationship between the pilgrim and the saints of Ḥusain Ṭekrī, a relationship that formally begins with the tying of the *challā* and is sustained with the taking of lobān.

Once the pilgrim voluntarily submits to the saints' voluntarily offered invitation, however, the relationship that he or she has with Ḥusain Ṭekrī changes markedly from volunteerism to servitude, and commands *(ḥukm)* from Maulā to the pilgrims become the dominant mode of interaction. These commands are normally conveyed in ḥāẓirī and in dreams—often one's own, but also in the dreams or ḥāẓirī of others. Recall, for example, Priya's dreams about wearing a burqa being validated by a friend's similar dream.

So pronounced, deeply rooted, and widespread is the concept of *ḥukm* in the culture of Ḥusain Ṭekrī that a group of older women who often sat together in the doorway of the rauẓa of Husain once explained, in response to my question of what exactly they do all day, that they had a *baiṭhne kā ḥukm*, a command to sit. They elaborated by saying that Gayatri, who often spent her days cleaning the courtyard of the rauẓas—had a command to clean, and additionally she often served as a coordinator when women had dreams in which they were commanded to offer some service to the rauẓa. In some cases, the type of the service to the rauẓa does not matter as much as the willingness to obey the command to offer service. As a result, even sitting, which might otherwise look a great deal like loitering, can be service if it is performed as submission to a command.

These women's statements and actions exhibit an explicitly articulated spiritual economy according to which the grace of Maulā is available to all to the extent that they are willing to submit to him absolutely. Any subsequent improvement of the pilgrim's situation—be it recovering honor, home, health, or life—is the result of his or her absolute, individual, and voluntary submission to Maulā, surrendering his or her autonomy in order to become, to paraphrase the song, the servant of Maulā and of the Five Pure Ones.

Once bound to Maulā, pilgrims become open to commands less benign than sitting with one's friends in the cool of the rauẓas' courtyards. Commands to bathe in the water from the well at the rauẓa of 'Abbas or to bathe in the swamp of dirty water that flows out of the bathhouse constructed to distribute the well water will be considered in the next chapter because they fit into its larger discussion of magic. The command to bathe in dirty water is relatively uncommon; a far more common command—again, always given in a dream or in ḥāẓirī—entails binding one's hands and feet with chains, that is, a single chain is wound around a wrist, ankle, neck, or waist and secured with a lock. The size of the chains varies from delicate ones that are similar to jewelry to massive chains with links several inches in diameter; locks vary similarly in scale. So far as I was able to ascertain, chains are not put on with any special ceremony. In all my time at Ḥusain Ṭekrī, I never saw the moment of binding with lock and chain, and countless conversations with pilgrims yielded no more information than "I put on the locks." Babli once explained that she had wanted a particular brother to put locks on her, but he was unable to come to Ḥusain Ṭekrī so another brother had to do it instead. It is certainly possible that many lock bindings have this sort of personally meaningful formality about them, wherein players in the pilgrim's evolving narrative of healing are incorporated into the process through participating in the binding of the pilgrim.

The keys to the locks are irretrievably disposed of in a variety of protected places—that is, places under the jurisdiction of the saints, where no malevolent spirit or magician can hope to access them. Some pilgrims give their keys to the shrine attendants, who subsequently dispose of them; some put them in the offering boxes of the rauẓas; and many throw them into the large dry well next to the rauẓa of Bībī Fatima or into the still-functional Laṅgar Well, just beyond the rauẓa of 'Ali.

There is a widely held conviction that it is not possible to leave Ḥusain Ṭekrī safely until all of one's locks have fallen open. This spontaneous opening of the locks is meant to be a signal that some portion of the magic that has been performed on the individual has been destroyed by the saints. The opening of all of one's locks is one of several signs that a *faislā* has been attained. Leaving before these locks have opened—leaving without permission *(ijāzat),* as it is commonly called—renders the individual vulnerable to more malevolent magic.

However, the exact meaning of the spontaneous opening of individual locks is, significantly, open to individual interpretation. When the lock and chain on Babli's right wrist fell off, for example, it was considered a great mercy, because in addition to signaling the end of a spell, it made her preparation of meals significantly easier. Recall, too, Priya's uncertainty as to whether the opening of one of her locks could be trusted and her resort to the world of dreams for confirmation. Similarly, an acquaintance of mine at Ḥusain Ṭekrī once explained to me that a chain had fallen off a mutual acquaintance of ours who had been at the site for a very long time. However, our mutual acquaintance didn't want anyone to know, and rather than accepting her *faislā* and leaving right away, she was planning to wait an extra forty days before leaving Ḥusain Ṭekrī to see if anything else would happen. Forty is a ritually significant number in both the Islamic and Hindu traditions, and it is commonly used at Ḥusain Ṭekrī.[41] In all of these cases, different interpretations of the opening of the locks were possible and acceptable. Like inhaling lobān, the practice of binding one's body with locks and chains can and does accommodate a wide range of interpretations and narratives.

The action of locking up one's body in this way has a number of practical consequences, chief among them alerting everyone to the fact that the individual is struggling with some kind of malevolent spirit. For those with ḥāẓirī, coming as they do from a society in which the slightest possibility that something is "wrong" will negatively impact marriage options and future lives, there is a dramatic and powerful character to a public statement of suffering, even in a place as safe as Ḥusain Ṭekrī. Additionally, there is relief in performing an action that frees one of the responsibility of deciding when and how to return home. Finally, binding oneself in this way creates the possibility of a small, recognizable miracle: locks do not easily fall open of their own accord, and this miracle subsequently validates whatever narrative of healing each pilgrim creates around the meaning of the opening of the lock. As a concrete constraint to be negotiated, chains, locks, and the moments they open also afford pilgrims moments and objects upon which they can build the narrative that may eventually result in a *faislā*. This narrative is built, consciously and unconsciously, through ḥāẓirī, dreams, and the stories of fellow pilgrims and the lives of both the saints of Ḥusain Ṭekrī and other, mainly Sufi, saints.

Pilgrims are also commonly commanded to hang onto *jālī*. While this practice shares much with the use of lobān in both its physical nature and its effects, hanging onto *jālī* differs in that, like binding the body with locks and chains, it is normally performed in response to a command rather than voluntarily. Ideally, pilgrims with ḥāẓirī are supposed to spend several hours each day standing or sitting while holding onto the *jālī* that cover the windows of the rauẓas as well as the gates around the standards of each saint in each of the courtyards. In practice, however, spending this much time in the rauẓas is not practical, and so, while it is generally thought that hanging onto the *jālī* is beneficial in the same way that lobān is, it is not engaged in as regularly as lobān consumption. Usually those who sit in the courtyard of a rauẓa hanging onto the *jālī* are doing so in response to a command from Maulā.

A common explanation for the efficacy of clutching the *jālī* is that they contain a "current"—the English word is used—that only those with ḥāẓirī can feel. I never experienced any current in the *jālī*, though they do vibrate with the convulsions of those who hold them throughout bouts of violent ḥāẓirī. In pilgrims' discourse, the most significant characteristic of this current is its automatic nature; the reaction that those with ḥāẓirī have to it is not generally narrativized because it is an inevitable, natural, almost chemical response. The inevitability of the *jālī*'s effect on ḥāẓirī is mirrored by the inevitability of lobān's effect. Thus, it is not uncommon to see an individual grasp the *jālī* and be thrown into bouts of violent open ḥāẓirī, much in the same way that individuals react to lobān. Hanging onto the *jālī*, however, has a wider range of effects. One young woman explained to me that the *jālī* was the place where she received revelations about who had performed magic on her: the images of the guilty parties were revealed in the *jālī* itself, "just like a film." Priya reported a different use of the *jālī*, saying that early in her time at Ḥusain Ṭekrī she simply sat there because she was told to, but that later she used her time sitting as an opportunity to recite certain prayers in a meditative way.

Unlike consuming lobān, clutching *jālī* is a social activity: it is common

FIGURE 7. Hanging onto *jālī* at the rauẓa of Ḥaẓrat ʿAbbas. In the distance, the domes of the rauẓa of Bībī Zaineb and the half-finished minarets of the new mosque are visible.

to see groups of regulars sitting together talking in between bouts of ḥāẓirī. It seems that there would be a substantial benefit to allowing ḥāẓirī to disrupt otherwise normal conversations: suffering is not segregated, as it is in mainstream society. This group setting also affords pilgrims the opportunity to be exposed to a wide range of narratives of healing, thus increasing their literacy in the culture of Ḥusain Ṭekrī in a way that contributes to their own ability to develop personal narratives. In some cases the bouts of ḥāẓirī even develop entertainment value, breaking the monotony of hours and hours of uneventful sitting.

Like lobān and the binding of the body with locks and chains, the authority and efficacy of the *jālī* also derive in part from their physical nature: as does lobān, the *jālī* require the presence of the pilgrims in a radical and uncompromising way. Here again, this has the practical consequence of creating a community that has no familial, institutional, caste-based, or religion-based reason for existence, since the upshot of this requirement means that many unrelated individuals sit together around a window or door of the rauẓa for hours at a time. Unlike lobān consumption, however, hanging onto *jālī* is a gender-segregated practice, which, considering the crowding that it entails, makes good sense.

Finally, while it is neither immediately obvious nor explicitly described as such by pilgrims themselves, *jālī* share with lobān a strong association with air and the spirit world that lives within it: spirits move about in the air, lobān fills the air, and *jālī* frame the air and are largely defined by their relationship with it, as they allow air to pass through while catching less desirable materials—in this case, malevolent spirits—in their wake. As is universally the case with Indian Muslim tombs and shrines, the walls of Ḥusain Ṭekrī's rauẓas are filled with large screened windows.[42] Pilgrims' belief in the efficacy of the screens in the windows as well as those that surround the elevated platforms containing the saints' standards may also come from a notion that the shrines act as a sort of supernatural air filter; as such, the shrines' power would be most powerfully present in the screens on the windows, since these are the objects that do the actual work of catching spirits. This theory of the nature of the rauẓas' power is borne out by pilgrims' choice of terms to describe the saints' power over the spirit world: common words include *qaid* (imprisonment) and *qabẓā* (the forcible capture of spirits). The shrines' association with the bodies or presences of the saints (recall, for example, Maya distinguishing the saints of Ḥusain Ṭekrī through a description of the physicality of the rauẓas) renders the screens all the more potentially dangerous and powerful.

Taken together, pilgrims' perceptions of their healing practices—consuming lobān, hanging onto *jālī,* and binding their bodies with locks and chains—are not necessarily shaped primarily by their particular religious backgrounds. Instead, these nonnarrative elements of pilgrims' healing practices are authoritative, powerful, and effective because of their physical nature; their participation in subcontinental-specific types of power, including asceticism and notions of purity and pollution; and their openness to individual interpretation. Together with the culture of volunteerism and command that structures the daily lives of pilgrims at Ḥusain Ṭekrī, the interpretable nature of pilgrims' healing practices and the abundant yet effacing foundation of lobān create the conditions necessary for the construction of narratives of healing in dreams and in ḥāẓirī. It is in these narratives that the categories of Hindu and Muslim become meaningful again, though in ways that differ from the meaning that they carry in orthodox, institutional, and everyday contexts.

CHAPTER 4

Presence

The Work and Workings of Ḥāẓirī

On my first visit to Ḥusain Ṭekrī, the older man from Udaipur who had helped me make my way from the Jaora train station to Ḥusain Ṭekrī encouraged me to attend morning lobān. Using the English word, he assured me that during lobān, he would be changed "automatic," and I would see for myself the power of Ḥusain Ṭekrī. Sure enough, as the pilgrims gathered in front of the shrine of 'Abbas and began their songs, my acquaintance, his eyes closed and his hands raised, began shaking his head from side to side.

What I was seeing for the first time was *khulī ḥāẓirī.* Pilgrims make a distinction between *khulī ḥāẓirī* (literally, "open presence") and *gum ḥāẓirī* (literally, "hidden presence"), and so in what follows I will treat them separately. Of these two types, *khulī ḥāẓirī* is more common and desirable, so much so that often when speaking about their healing processes pilgrims simply use the term *ḥāẓirī* to describe what is specifically *khulī ḥāẓirī.*

In order to signal voluntary submission to the saints and willingness to endure ḥāẓirī, a pilgrim takes two lengths of cord *(challā)* and ties one piece to one of the metal screens *(jālī)* of the shrines of Ḥusain Ṭekrī and the other around his or her neck, waist, or arm. He or she then begins to consume lobān on a regular basis, quickly becoming a participant in the community of Ḥusain Ṭekrī. *Khulī ḥāẓirī* is the subsequent process by which the saint of the rauẓa calls the offending possessing spirit, or *pret,* contained in the body of the pilgrim into his or her presence for questioning, much in the manner of a judge in a court.[1] In questioning the *pret,* the saint seeks to elicit a confession of when, why, how, and by whom the *pret* was sent. The only participant in this interrogation that speaks audibly is the *pret* itself; through the body and voice of the victim, it responds to the saint's questions, which are audible only to the spirit. This means that in *khulī ḥāẓirī* there is no direct speech: the *pret* steals and alters the voice of the victim, the victim does not speak, and the saint speaks in a way that is only audible to the *pret.*[2] So, for example, if a *pret* says, through the voice of the possessed individual, "I'm never going to leave this body," it is understood to be responding to a statement by the saint ordering the *pret* to relinquish its claim on the body of the victim.

A person in *khulī ḥāẓirī* is often quite fearsome: her breathing is tortured, rapid, and rhythmic and interspersed with a gasping, grating staccato cry. She might throw her body to the floor with great force, roll on the ground, throw herself against walls, beat her face against the courtyard floor until she spits blood, repeatedly throw her head forward and back at great speed, toss her head around in violent circles, cry out in pain, scream in anger, and lend her voice to the malevolent spiritual presence inside her body, allowing it to verbally defy and insult the saint who inflicts this abuse on the body of the victim in order to elicit a confession from it. As the saint's interrogation progresses, she may recoil in a way that seems to respond to an invisible blow, perform flying somersaults, convulse on the ground, beat the tiles of the courtyard with her hands and feet, repeatedly bend and slam her back against the walls of a rauẓa, run across the rauẓas' courtyards at top speed, smashing into the courtyard walls as she goes, and roll around the rauẓa countless times.[3] Eventually she will fall to the ground, seemingly unconscious, and her caretaker will hurry to cover her face with a handkerchief or her *dupaṭṭā.*[4] In form, *khulī ḥāẓirī* seems to be a textbook case of spirit possession and exorcism: by accident, force, or the design of another, a spirit (human soul, demon, or deity) takes up residence in the body of an unwilling host, and through *khulī ḥāẓirī,* the pilgrim seeks the removal—or, in some cases, the reform—of the malevolent possessing presence. Is *khulī ḥāẓirī* a type of spirit possession, and even if it is, should it be analyzed as such?[5]

This question is fundamentally one of ḥāẓirī's nature and efficacy, and in what follows I will offer four possible answers. First, I suggest that despite the fact that ḥāẓirī entails the forcible entry of a spirit into the body of another, analyzing it exclusively as a form of spirit possession misrepresents its nature and misleadingly limits its range of influence. In making this argument, I am indebted to recent scholarship that has sought to remove spirit possession (and shamanism) from its phenomenological ghetto

FIGURE 8. Ḥāẓirī at Cābuk Sharīf.

and status as "folk," "low," or "popular" religion, placing it instead in conversation with global systems of power as well as global and text-based forms of religious traditions.[6] Some of the major aspects of the phenomenon of ḥāẓirī are *practices* like other (South Asian) religious practices in that they entail voluntary discipline of the body and mind; I suggest that in the South Asian context, ḥāẓirī, like many of the healing practices discussed in previous chapters, derives much of its power from its association with asceticism. Further, the language used to describe ḥāẓirī shows that it cannot be isolated (and therefore analyzed) as ritual behavior or action; *khulī ḥāẓirī* (open ḥāẓirī), *gum ḥāẓirī* (hidden ḥāẓirī), and *ḥāẓirīwālā/ ḥāẓirīwālī* respectively connote exorcism, painful illness or dis-ease, and a state of being. *Khulī ḥāẓirī* entails observable actions and audible statements, while *gum ḥāẓirī* entails symptoms that are silently contained within the body and therefore unobservable. *Ḥāẓirīwālā* and *ḥāẓirīwālī* (literally, "one with ḥāẓirī") are constructed with the common Hindi suffix "*wālā/wālī*," which can be attached to any adjective or noun to indicate that the object or person to which it refers is fundamentally characterized by the word to which the suffix is attached. In everyday conversations, words formed with this suffix are often used to alleviate confusion, as they allow the speaker to distinguish one thing from another. Taking this terminology seriously means that conceptualizing and analyzing ḥāẓirī cannot be limited to a discussion of "possession" or "exorcism."

Second, if, as I have argued, lobān represents the major nonnarrative source of curative power at Ḥusain Ṭekrī, then ḥāẓirī is the medium within which and from which *ḥāẓirīwāle* create their personal version of the dominant healing narrative. While producing an "I came, I prayed, I got better" narrative in *khulī ḥāẓirī* is usually a major part of the healing process of pilgrims at Ḥusain Ṭekrī, ḥāẓirī's efficacy derives in large part from the way that its narratives emerge from a potent combination of verbal and nonverbal elements. The narrative and verbal elements of ḥāẓirī may be separated from the greater process of *khulī ḥāẓirī* and, once extracted, they may be shaped by the pilgrim and his or her friends and family into meaningful and useful narratives of healing. However, the nonverbal elements of ḥāẓirī and their relationship with the verbal elements form their own reality and are an indispensable element of the meaningfulness of ḥāẓirī for both the *ḥāẓirīwālā /ī* and his or her caretaker.

Third, when considered in its greater South Asian cultural context, the transgressive, violent nature of *khulī ḥāẓirī* emerges as a key element of the legitimacy that *ḥāẓirīwāle* claim in their reintegration into their families and, for some, in developing healing practices. On one level, the violent actions of *khulī ḥāẓirī* seem to become irrelevant once a personal version of the dominant narrative of healing is extracted from the morass of cries and declarations of resistance characteristic of *khulī ḥāẓirī*. On another level, however, the body of the *ḥāẓirīwālā/ī* itself is the trace of this violence. This distinguishes the ḥāẓirī practitioner in ways that only he or she experiences and in ways that transform others' perspectives of his or her body, and by extension, his or her status in familial and societal contexts. In other words, especially in the case of those who move from the status of victim to that of healer, the violence and transgressiveness of *khulī ḥāẓirī* are preserved by the body of the *ḥāẓirīwālā/ī* and contribute to his or her legitimacy and authority.

Finally, linguistically oriented analysis of the term ḥāẓirī (literally "presence") affords great insight into ḥāẓirī's unique, and perhaps uniquely South Asian, efficacy as a form of justice and healing and offers Western scholars an alternative perspective on how the study of spirit possession itself might be framed. Ḥāẓirī is a particularly effective source of justice and healing because it reflects a notion of justice that is meaningful in a particular moment and in a particular place: ḥāẓirī-style justice, in other words, is local. This discussion of the fittingness of the justice offered by ḥāẓirī will include an account of its relationship with South Asian conceptions of magic *(jādū)*, purity and pollution, notions of fate *(qismat)*, and marriage in extended family situations.

Spirit possession and exorcism emerged as cross-tradition subjects in Western scholarship at least in part because, when viewed from the outside, a range of practices across cultures and continents appeared to share a characteristic that could not be taken at face value: the phenomenon of alien and wayward spirits invading the bodies of the living.[7] The isolation of spirit possession and exorcism as discrete objects of inquiry by Western academics was initially built on the assumption that spirit possession and exorcism are "popular," "folk," or "tribal" practices rather than "high" or "orthodox" ones, a distinction with diverse roots that often overlooked or ignored clear points of exchange and overlap between these two areas of human expression. In the context of South Asia, Frederick Smith's monumental *The Self Possessed* has convincingly demonstrated that spirit possession practices are as common in "high," Sanskritic, Brahminical Hinduism as they are in "folk," vernacular, non-Brahminical contexts, and that possession—permeable embodiment, as he puts it—sits at the very core of Indic religions.[8]

On the one hand, like other types of what is often considered spirit possession, ḥāẓirī participates in discourses that span both "high" and "folk" aspects of Indian religious expression and culture, including magic *(jādū)*, purity and pollution, and marriage in extended families. It should thus be considered in relation to these larger systems. On the other hand, one aspect of spirit possession's isolation as a distinct analytical category is valid and suggestive: there *is* something unique about a form of religious (or, perhaps, human) expression that derives its legitimacy primarily from its medium, in this case, the expression of an alien presence in a body. A significant consequence of this fact is that in the case of spirit possession, unlike other forms of religious expression, it is not possible to separate form from content, or medium from message. Compare spirit possession to other authoritative religious personages and objects: whether recited or written, the Qur'an retains authority because it is recognized as the actual word of God; whether evoked in a mantra or encountered through *darśan* (sight) in a temple, Siva is still a god. In these cases, authority and form are not inextricably linked, whereas the authority of spirit possession derives from the miraculous form of the utterances of the possessed, not from *what* is said or even *who* speaks. One significant consequence of this fact is that, unlike other forms of religious expression, possession has only a fleeting authority. After the spirit has been removed, it is only the surviving body that retains a trace of possession's authority.

Like spirit possession, ḥāẓirī derives its authority from its form: the spatially and temporally limited expression of things that are spatially or temporally out of place. At the same time, ḥāẓirī is more than spirit possession or exorcism: while *khulī ḥāẓirī* may fit into these categories, *gum ḥāẓirī* and *ḥāẓirīwālā/ḥāẓirīwālī* do not. *Gum ḥāẓirī* entails undramatic, nondiscursive, silent suffering, and *ḥāẓirīwālā/ḥāẓirīwālī* are constant states of being rather than events or practices. If the range of *khulī ḥāẓirī, gum ḥāẓirī,* and *ḥāẓirīwālā/ḥāẓirīwālī* is taken seriously, it is necessary to accept that ḥāẓirī is a conceptual category that does not fit within any of the usual academic categories, including spirit possession and exorcism.

If ḥāẓirī is something beyond spirit possession and exorcism, should it be analyzed as a form of therapy using a psychoanalytic model, given that its stated goal is healing? As Csordas has noted, "Therapeutic efficacy in religious healing is typically analyzed by extrapolating from ritual procedure to expected effect, without specifying conditions for success or failure in terms of the concrete experience[s] of participants. Taking such experiential data as primary in therapeutic process should allow for definition of minimal conditions of therapeutic efficacy, including incremental change and inconclusive results."[9] If one takes Csordas's statement to heart, a proper understanding of ḥāẓirī's therapeutic efficacy requires looking beyond the dominant narrative of "I came, I prayed, I got better" and instead starting with observation of the way in which ḥāẓirī functions as only one in a series of fragmented contributions to a socially constructed narrative of healing. This construction process is long and labor-intensive and involves many different contributors. When these factors are coupled with the fact that for ḥāẓirī practitioners there is no human exorcist, it is difficult to imagine how a standard psychoanalytic or therapeutic model, with its focus on the patient-healer relationship, is applicable. Further, unlike psychoanalytic and therapeutic models, the phenomenon of *gum ḥāẓirī* allows for the possibility of recovery without learning or consciously acknowledging the causes of the pilgrim's distress. As such, it seems that the therapeutic model of analysis is also lacking.[10]

Despite the fact that ḥāẓirī is a widespread practice at dargāḥs and *imāmbāṛās,* it has received very little scholarly attention, and the attention it has received has been primarily psychoanalytic and inclined to focus its interpretive efforts on the dominant narrative of "I came, I prayed, I got better" as it relates to the practice of *khulī ḥāẓirī* in particular. These studies also uniformly ignore the phenomenon of *gum ḥāẓirī* and the concept of *ḥāẓirīwālā/ī,* instead focusing exclusively upon the drama of *khulī ḥāẓirī.* This, too, undermines the usefulness of their analysis. Jackie Assayag describes *khulī ḥāẓirī* practices at a dargāḥ in Karnataka, though, as he notes, the term used at this dargāḥ is *ṭawāf,* or "circumambulation." Assayag states that the term is a reference to the counterclockwise circumambulation of the dargāḥ that is understood to induce the "trance" state, as he calls it; just as pilgrims circumambulate Mecca's Kaaba, so they circumambulate the saint's tomb, prompting the behaviors associated with *khulī ḥāẓirī.*[11] Assayag does not offer any analysis of *ṭawāf*/ḥāẓirī, and his description of the act is superficial and ultimately subsumed by the larger point of the work, which is a discussion of Hindu and Muslim demonology; hence, his discussion is primarily useful because it confirms that the phenomenon of ḥāẓirī is widespread.

Franck Rollier's discussion of *khulī ḥāẓirī* (also referred to as *ṭawāf* at the South Indian dargāḥ where he did his research) is an analysis of the practice using concepts drawn from Freud and Lacan in which he likens possession to Lacan's notion of *jouissance.* While his argument is suggestive, the use of psychoanalytic categories is problematic, in part because of its fundamental reliance upon the assumption that Lacan and Freud's theories reflect a notion of selfhood that is meaningful in India. Perhaps more importantly, his approach cannot account for the fact that the narratives that actually contribute to the healing process of pilgrims have many sources, of which the fragmented speech of *khulī ḥāẓirī* is only one. Further, as Rollier himself admits, this psychoanalytic discussion of *ṭawāf* does not explain why the phenomenon has authoritative meaning for anyone other than the individual who engages in it.[12] Similarly, Beatrix Pfleiderer's work on the dargāḥ of Mira Datar in Gujarat (part of the unofficial healing circuit that also includes Ḥusain Ṭekrī) describes *khulī ḥāẓirī* (though she fails to note the name), likening it to "therapy," and concludes that the practice must be effective because it is "a culture-specific illness theory: the possession of bhut."[13] Again, Pfleiderer does not state what this theory entails, though she notes parallels to Western psychotherapy throughout. On the other hand, while she does not elaborate, her suggestion that "patients seem, therefore, to have a curative influence on one another" is corroborated by this chapter's findings.[14] Another short article by Y. J. Shobha Devi and G. S. Bidarakoppa mentions the practice of ḥāẓirī by name and is useful only insofar as it demonstrates that ḥāẓirī is practiced in the central Indian city of Bijapur.[15]

Two psychoanalytically oriented studies of pilgrims at the Mehndipur Bālājī temple in Rajasthan, again part of the northern Indian healing circuit that includes Ḥusain Ṭekrī, further demonstrate the limits of analyzing ḥāẓirī in terms of a therapeutic practice.[16] The Bālājī temple is home to a practice known as *peśī*, and over my time at Ḥusain Ṭekrī I encountered many Hindu pilgrims who had previously sought a cure at Bālājī. Similar to ḥāẓirī, *peśī* translates as "presence," does not require a human exorcist, and carries an association with royal and legal courts.[17] Graham Dwyer's work on the Mehndipur Bālājī temple suggests that exorcism and psychotherapy share the result of "physical and psychological changes" and that in both types of "healing milieu" the "desired transformation itself is also said to be effected by engaging the emotions."[18] At the same time, Dwyer does concede that there are major differences between Indian and Western concepts of emotion, mainly that in an Indian context, emotion is conceptualized bodily.

At Ḥusain Ṭekrī, this is true: pilgrims usually (though not always) discuss their feelings about the consumption of lobān using terms that suggest a bodily aspect (i.e., *ārām, ṭhaṇḍhā, halkāpan*).[19] However, Dwyer still maintains that, these differences aside, using the Western lens of psychotherapy to understand the phenomenon of exorcism in Indian is useful and, indeed, mutually beneficial, because "much of what takes place in [Western psychotherapies] is similar to what occurs in exorcism." Thus, Dwyer concludes, "By understanding the first [Western psychotherapies], it may be possible to illuminate the second [exorcism] and vice versa."[20] This is a nice sentiment, but there is little evidence in Dwyer's text to suggest that the phenomenon of *peśī* has actually modified his psychoanalytic paradigm. Further, and more important, such a project does not do very much to explain why people engage in *peśī* in particular and, by extension, what this practice suggests about larger issues such as South Asian notions of religious identity and selfhood.

This psychoanalytic approach to the study of South Asian spirit possession–based forms of healing has an earlier incarnation in the work of Sudhir Kakar, a psychologist whose work on the Bālājī temple Dwyer critiques for "failing to take adequate account of the cultural construction of illness and cure."[21] Specifically, he takes issue with Kakar's suggestion that one of his subjects is "addicted to *peśī*," and he suggests that Kakar's assumption that this subject exhibits a "hysteric personality" fails to take into account the value system of the temple itself, in which it is held that without *peśī*, there can be no cure.[22] Perhaps aware of his limitations, in another chapter in the same volume, Kakar does, for example, conclude his description of a Delhi-based Sufi healer's practice with the following sentence: "Both of us [Kakar and the Muslim healer] were silent for a while as we sat there companionably, contemplating the limits of our respective healing traditions."[23] Some of the potential for mutual critique inherent in Dwyer's "vice versa" is in evidence here, but again, Kakar's work, while respectful in its description of his relationship with the Muslim healer as a collegial one, does not in the end offer much more than a study of the places where Freudian concepts seem to parallel the Muslim healer's methods. Where the parallels end, Kakar pleads "confusionism," which, while clever, again suggests that apparent parallels between apparently similar processes eventually break down under the weight of the assumptions that undergird them.[24]

In contrast to this individually oriented psychoanalytic approach, in his insightful study of the Bālājī temple,[25] Antti Pakaslahti, a psychologist, emphasizes the communal nature of illness, recovery, and cure by including in his analysis the ways in which families participate in and are changed by the possession-based healing processes available and widely practiced at the temple.[26] Pakaslahti rightly observes that the therapeutic value of *peśī* is not conceptualized on the level of individual benefit and recovery; specifically, he argues that it cannot be reduced to the physical experience of the trance states achieved by certain individuals in the context of their "spirit possession," since these individuals often take on the possessing spirits of family members and later report that their relatives' condition has improved as a result of their proxy possession practices.[27] The phenomenon of proxy possession is also part of the practice of ḥāẓirī at Ḥusain Ṭekrī, further suggesting that something beyond individually oriented self-help is happening in ḥāẓirī.

A combination of these perspectives on the individual and communal aspects of healing is most useful. On the one hand, those with ḥāẓirī of course see themselves as individual victims, and their desire for recovery has an intensely personal aspect: they suffer bodily and mentally. On the other hand, the cure they seek is itself regarded as a healing of the family, and this does not necessarily result in the sacrifice of the selfhood of the individual with ḥāẓirī. On the contrary, the healing of the individual with ḥāẓirī is understood to extend beyond the family to society as a whole.

In part because ḥāẓirī lacks both a regimented ritual structure and a human exorcist, the narratives produced within the embodied process of ḥāẓirī also develop different and differently useful meanings for practitioners and their friends and families as they are shared and developed in conversation. This is the case because the person in ḥāẓirī almost never retains a waking memory of what is said during ḥāẓirī and thus is necessarily reliant upon reports from caretakers and bystanders. The narratives of healing that are developed from the process of ḥāẓirī, in other words, become meaningful as they become *shared* narratives, negotiated and interpreted among the person with ḥāẓirī, their caretaker(s), and their fellow pilgrims.[28] Given the social nature of the narratives that are developed in ḥāẓirī, the larger goal of ḥāẓirī is, in part, the healing of a community rather than just an individual. Here again, strict adherence to psychological and therapeutic models that concern themselves with individual recovery is inappropriate. Further, psychoanalytic approaches usually frame illness and recovery in terms of an individual's self-conscious perception of him- or herself. As such, these approaches still implicitly participate in a perspective framed by individual subjectivity.

Finally, the use of a psychoanalytically based system is also misguided because such systems rely heavily upon insight into an individual's past.[29] Of course, the dominant form of a ḥāẓirī narrative is the assertion that a neighbor, friend, or relative was jealous of the victim's property, family, beauty, or success and thus performed magic to either obtain these things or, at the very least, to take them away from the victim. However, ḥāẓirī is a system that has the capacity to be meaningful even without the revelation of a specific, personal cause of one's problems. In Maya's case, for example, recall that she attributed her ḥāẓirī to inadvertent pollution of a hidden temple. For her, a widely circulated, nonspecific (that is, impersonal) trope was enough to lead to recovery and eventually to her developing her own healing practice. An even more extreme example of this phenomenon is evident in Priya's case: she suggested that her own problems were unlikely to be resolved through *khulī ḥāẓirī,* and she spoke about the suffering and difficulty that were a necessary part of resolving a case through *gum ḥāẓirī* alone. In Priya's case, even the impersonal causality that the trope of jealousy offered was not meaningful; as she said, she had often thought to herself that the jealousy of a neighbor or relative might have been the cause of her ḥāẓirī, but, aside from her own personal musings on the subject, which she obviously did not trust or value, she asserted that she had never felt divine or saintly endorsement of this generally acceptable and widely circulated trope. While the situation could certainly change, Priya, more than two years into the exploration of her problems within the idiom of ḥāẓirī, had resigned herself to *gum ḥāẓirī.* In both of these cases, the origins of each of these women's problems are not narrativized in the specific, personal, clearly causal manner afforded by ḥāẓirī-based narratives.

Recall also that in ḥāẓirī, self-evaluation is not to be trusted: both Priya and Babli were disinclined to trust their desires, judgments, or physical feelings of wellness; leaving Ḥusain Ṭekrī, as well as many of the major measures in the recovery process, is unrelated to feelings, thoughts, will, or self-knowledge. Instead, it is widely believed at Ḥusain Ṭekrī that one can leave only with permission, not when one feels like it or feels well. Progress, instead of being revealed through self-knowledge or experience, is instead marked by a dream or the falling open of a lock. The greater system of which ḥāẓirī is a part locates truth in areas that are clearly outside the (conscious) control of the individual, in items such as locks, chains, and dreams, all of which can acquire meaning without specific reference to past events.

Thus, while Western psychoanalysis, therapy, and various forms of exorcism seem to do the same type of work, there are several problems with using a Western psychoanalytic or therapeutic model to analyze ḥāẓirī: such models presume that illness and health are individually experienced and individually regulated states; they presume that selfhood is similarly conceptualized in Indian and Western contexts; they presume that recovery requires knowledge of the causes of distress; and they lack a means to incorporate bodily experience into the healing process. Taking the language of ḥāẓirī at face value also requires recognizing that the spirits that speak during ḥāẓirī lack a Western analogue. Contemporary Western Christian English-speaking environments' instances of spirit possession—whether at a Pentecostal church or in the form of a Catholic exorcism—lack both a concept and a word for the spirit of a deceased person that has the ability to possess an individual.[30] The spirits that *possess* are demons or, in the Pentecostal context, the Christian Holy Spirit; the spirits that *haunt* houses and other spaces are lost human souls.[31] This is not the case in the Indian context, where the spirits of the dead both haunt places and possess human hosts.[32]

This distinction in the capacities of the spirits of the dead is in keeping with the influential typology developed by anthropologist Erika Bourguignon, according to which possession by the spirits of the dead is common in cultures that have extended families and a jurisdictional hierarchy above the local level and that practice bride price, polygamous marriages, and slavery. The meaning of and reasons for this correlation are debatable. With the possible exception of polygamous marriages, many of the above practices represent commodification of the individual in one way or another: obviously, slavery, bride price, and extended family structures are part of systems within which money and persons are exchanged, and from the perspective of an individual, nonlocal jurisdictional hierarchies can and do rob individuals and groups of their autonomy, handing down life-altering decisions without the direct involvement of the individual or the local community. In societies with these practices, bodies are sellable, stealable objects. It follows that in such societies souls deprived of a full life and spirits subjected to a violent death would continue to participate in this economy, naturally feeling entitled to seize the desirable body of a living human. If humans can buy, sell, or otherwise dominate the body of another human, wayward human souls should be able to do the same thing.

In analyzing so-called "spirit possession" in a South Asian context, it is also important to recognize that the English terms "spirit" and "soul" must be used with care since notions of selfhood in life and afterlife vary significantly according to cultural and historical context.[33] Technically, in Hindu funerary contexts, *pret* is used to refer to the spirit of the deceased prior to the performance of funeral rites.[34] At Ḥusain Ṭekrī, one of the most common words for "spirit" is *pret;* its use there indicates conversation with those aspects of the Hindu tradition that deal with the spirits of the deceased as individuals or persons, rather than those that conceptualize a person primarily in terms of karma.[35] Ḥusain Ṭekrī's pilgrims commonly use the term *pret* generically, without reference to caste, religion, gender, and (if relevant) the nature of the deceased's untimely death. The term is, however, flexible, since pilgrims also use it to refer to specific possessing spirits. At Ḥusain Ṭekrī, *pret* have memories, enduring family ties, and personalities; they are not mere amalgams of impersonal karma.

When speaking generally about the phenomenon of malevolent possessing spirits, Ḥusain Ṭekrī's pilgrims commonly compound *bhūt* with *pret* to form the term *bhūt-pret.*[36] In spoken Hindi, *bhūt* is popularly used to mean "ghost," and it can also be translated literally as "been," the past participle of the verb "to be."[37] However, *bhūt* and *bhūt-pret* are rarely employed when an individual speaks about his or her own malevolent possessing spirit; in this context, the simple term *pret* is often used. The other term commonly used by an individual describing his or her malevolent possessing presence is the Arabic-derived *balā,* which in the Hindi-Urdu can mean both "misfortune" and "evil spirit." While it is my sense that in common speech *balā* is slightly more removed from the notion of something with human origins than the terms *bhūt* and *pret,* at Ḥusain Ṭekrī, *balā* still connotes a liminal, out-of-place being. Because English lacks a word that conveys the full meaning of the most commonly used terms *bhūt* and *pret*—that is, a term that encompasses a ghost's status as a liminal, lost soul with the ability to possess a human host—the untranslated word *pret* will be used throughout this chapter to refer to malevolent noncorporeal presences that speak through the victim during ḥāẓirī.

In the context of ḥāẓirī, the *pret* that has taken up residence in the pilgrim's body is understood to be there for one of three reasons. First, the *pret* may attach itself to an individual because it has been forced to do so by a magician (most commonly a *jādūgar,* or practitioner of Tantra). This magic is often understood to have been done at the behest of a family member or neighbor, usually because he or she is jealous of the success or beauty of the victim. While such things are impossible to quantify, in my experience, this is by far the most commonly cited cause of possession at Ḥusain Ṭekrī. A *pret* may also attach itself to an individual who is impure in some way: by birth (i.e., a *dalit*/untouchable or Shudra), because of gender (women are said to be more vulnerable because they menstruate, which is regarded as a ritually polluting process by all religious traditions of the subcontinent), or because of physical uncleanliness. Alternatively, a *pret* may choose a victim because he or she is beautiful, sweet smelling, or has something of which the *pret* is jealous. Thus, for example, one of my main informants in Bombay, whose family operates a Ḥusain Ṭekrī–affiliated *imāmbāṛā,* once explained that her ḥāẓirī was caused by the *pret* of a woman who had died in childbirth in the hospital where my informant had her first child; the woman's *pret* was jealous of her son.

Magic, when confessed to in *khulī ḥāẓirī,* is categorized in two ways: in terms of the number of spells and the number of *pret* placed in the individual. Sometimes the magic is understood to have a time limit. An informant once explained that she had learned in *khulī ḥāẓirī* that the magic that had been done on her was intended to kill her in seven years. By the time she learned this fact, five years had passed, and thus she had been given this life-saving information just in the nick of time. Regardless of the number of spells or *pret,* magic is almost always intended to lead to death; the stakes are understood to be that high.

Magic as described by pilgrims often involves the introduction of ritually polluting substances—menstrual blood, urine, feces, ashes from a crematorium, and human bones are among the most common objects—into food intended for the victim or brought into the victim's home. Alternatively, magic can be performed on a hair, fingernail, or toenail of the victim. In the parlance of those at Ḥusain Ṭekrī, the consumption of impure substances is synonymous with the introduction of a *pret* into the body. In other words, when Babli, for example, explained that she had been fed *khīr* polluted with pig urine, it was understood that this substance facilitated the introduction of a *pret* into her body. It is possible that the concept of pollution is often related to the introduction of a *pret* into a body because pollution has the ability to function as a conceptual link between corporeal and noncorporeal realms: it is an abstract and a physically based concept, operative both in the construction of the caste system and the designation of certain physical substances—for example, pig urine—as harmful. In addition to being a way to talk about the presence and placement of a *pret*, the impure substances are also considered a source of harm in and of themselves, and their removal during *khulī ḥāẓirī* is widely understood to involve vomiting. As a result, stories about vomiting snakes, salamanders, and sharp objects such as broken glass, pins, and nails are common. Vomiting these and other objects is understood to be a sign of progress.[38] In addition to introducing polluted substances into the body, magic, it is also commonly reported, can be enacted by driving pins into small dolls *(putlā)*. It is difficult to know the source of this description of malevolent magic, since documentaries of African religious practices, including Vodou, that were broadcast on the Discovery Channel and National Geographic Channel were often described to me as evidence that magic as a global phenomenon *does* exist and is practiced with particular efficacy in Africa.[39]

Often, stories of a *pret*'s attachment to a human host will contain a combination of these elements. A Muslim informant, for example, once explained the ḥāẓirī of his wife by suggesting that a spirit had seen her washing her hair at a public water pipe when she was a young girl and had attached himself to her hair.[40] Much has been written about hair—and women's hair in particular—in South Asian cultural contexts: it is a polluting object, a sexual object, and an object on which malevolent magic can be performed. Another Muslim informant, in relating a story about a distant relative who had a possession-based healing practice, explained that her relative probably acquired her spirit on a trip to the outhouse on her wedding night, suggesting that the jasmine in the bride's hair likely attracted the spirit. Here again, the sexual, pure, beautiful, and polluting are all potential elements of a woman's appeal and vulnerability. Not surprisingly, therefore, hair figures prominently into ḥāẓirī: as was noted above, the shaking of unbound hair is commonly part of the process of *khulī ḥāẓirī,* and cutting a lock of the *ḥāẓirīwālī*'s hair and nailing it to a tree with a lemon is also an element of the process for trapping the *pret* after its removal from the body of the victim.

In the case of the new bride whose sweet-smelling hair proved too attractive to resist, the spirit in question was actually not a *pret* but a *jinn*. In pan-Islamic culture—both textual and experiential—*jinn* are not the souls of the dead but their own class of beings, created, Islamic tradition holds, from fire. Unlike a *pret,* which is a liminal, illegitimate, and therefore dangerously manipulatable entity, *jinn* are their own agents; like humans, *jinn* can choose to accept or reject Islam and they can exert either a good or a bad influence on an individual. While Muslim informants generally saw *jinn* as an entirely separate class of being, Hindus either conflated them with *pret* or held the Islamic perspective. For the purposes of understanding ḥāẓirī it does not matter if Muslims and Hindus have markedly similar or completely dissimilar perspectives on the differences between *jinn* and *pret* because, by and large, *pret* and *jinn* are able to perform the same tasks. *Pret* are capable of offering beneficial healing power in a manner similar to that of a *jinn:* the process of *khulī ḥāẓirī* can result in either the "reform" or replacement of the malevolent *pret* with one that has become a *gulām,* or slave, of the saints of Ḥusain Ṭekrī. In the case of reform, subdued by the saints of Ḥusain Ṭekrī, the *pret* is given back to the individual in its rehabilitated state, transformed into an agent of Maulā, who, in collaboration with its human host, offers healing and advice to petitioners. In the case of replacement, the offending sprit is substituted with a "pure" one. Along these lines, one woman I met told me she was a host to both malevolent and benevolent spirits, which again highlights ḥāẓirī's unique and pronounced ability to accommodate a wide range of interpretations and variations.

The only truly unambiguous aspect of *khulī ḥāẓirī* is its violence, and it is this violence that is a vital part of the healing process of pilgrims. In this regard, it is worth noting that the saints' methodology—torture—is acceptable to pilgrims because, despite the fact that Ḥusain Ṭekrī is understood as a court, the defendants—that is, the malevolent spirit, the magician, and the neighbor or family member who hired the magician—are understood to be guilty. Therefore, the interrogation process at Ḥusain Ṭekrī is a process of eliciting a confession, not determining guilt or innocence. The saints are not conventional judges; they are *sources* of justice rather than arbitrators of the law.

Pret do not respond meekly to the saints' violent interrogation methods. Rather than submitting or confessing, the *pret* refuses to offer revelations that would lead to a *faislā,* and a common refrain that drifts through the rauẓas is, "I won't tell, I won't ever tell."[41] *Pret* are notorious liars, in

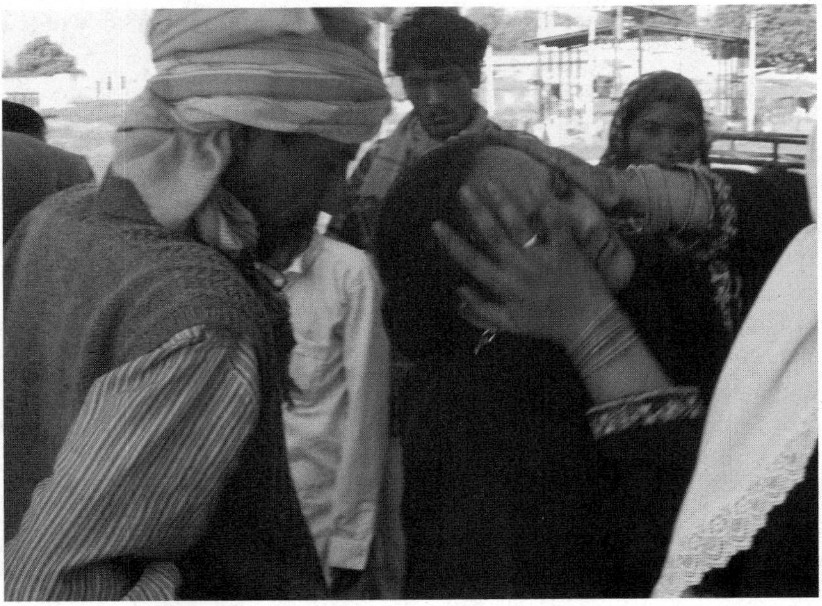

FIGURE 9. A woman in ḥāẓirī.

any case; their eventual confessions and expression of willingness to finally leave the body are often subsequently found to be untrue or half truths; a person may discover, in the course of a *khulī ḥāẓirī* session, that while one magical spell was in fact broken, he or she is actually the victim of a number of different spells, all of which need to be given individual *faislā*s.[42] The very real possibility of a false *faislā* is reflected in two common terms: *kaccā faislā*, literally, "unripe decision," and *jhūṭhā faislā*, literally, "false decision." As with all other aspects of the experience of ḥāẓirī, by including the possibility that a *faislā* is incomplete or even untrue, the declaration of a particular *faislā* also affords individuals the opportunity to experience a narrative before definitively accepting it as part of their own understanding of their predicament.

When the *pret* finally confesses, it does so with a description of who hired the magician, the sort of magic that was done, the amount of money that was paid, and, in some cases, the motivation of whomever hired the magician. Sometimes the amount of money paid is astronomical, amounting to *lakhs* of rupees.[43] In *khulī ḥāẓirī* (though not in *gum ḥāẓirī*), this information is considered a necessary element of the healing process. Conventionally speaking, in the context of *khulī ḥāẓirī*, a *faislā* comes when this information is offered and the *pret* makes a promise to leave the victim's body. Following a confession like this, a common procedure for ensuring that the *pret* will not return is to take a lock of the victim's hair, a lemon, and a long iron nail and to nail the hair and the lemon to a large dead tree that stands outside the rauẓas of 'Abbas and Sakina.[44] This process traps the *pret* in the lemon, ensuring that it cannot be recaptured and deployed by a magician.

Whether or not the fearsome acrobatics that are commonly practiced by those in *khulī ḥāẓirī* convince the skeptical onlooker of the veracity of the possession, it is impossible to ignore the fact that those in *khulī ḥāẓirī* seem to be invulnerable to the extreme heat of the rauẓas' courtyards, a feat that was often cited by pilgrims as evidence of the authenticity of *khulī ḥāẓirī*. Especially during the summer, the stone floors of the rauẓas' courtyards become dangerously hot. Recently erected courtyard roofs offer respite for some, but during the distribution of lobān the crowds are such that many pilgrims have no choice but to wait in the sun on the blisteringly hot courtyard floor. At the height of summer the tile in the open part of the courtyards becomes so phenomenally hot that I couldn't walk on it: upon shedding my shoes and entering the rauẓas, I made a run for the shade, much to the amusement of many. Pilgrims often assured me that they didn't feel the heat of the tiles because they had developed a habit *('ādat)* of tolerance. How exactly this "habit" develops, I am not sure, but in any case, pilgrims' own *'ādat* was not interpreted as being supernatural in origin. If anything, it was a discipline that was developed over time, or even a form of asceticism.

The extreme nature of the physical pain caused by ḥāẓirī's violence is cited by pilgrims as evidence of the reality of ḥāẓirī. This violence is rendered all the more miraculous by the fact that pilgrims unanimously agree that the guilty-until-proven-guilty *pret* rather than the victim him- or herself experiences it. It is true that pilgrims who have become particularly ill or weak are often offered a dispensation to be excused from *khulī ḥāẓirī* for a time because they are not strong enough to bear it, but this is an issue of bodily strength and capacity (or lack thereof) rather than an inability to bear the actual pain of ḥāẓirī.

The violence of ḥāẓirī is therefore essential for several reasons, some stated and some unstated. Since violence of ḥāẓirī is the primary indicator of the genuineness, or lack thereof, of the possession, the body of the possessed individual becomes powerful only insofar as it serves as a theater of (in)subordination and submission to the saint. Further, because so much of the discourse around magic is not based upon provable cause-and-effect relationships, the clarity of the cause-and-effect violence of *khulī ḥāẓirī* is a necessary foundation of the movement from *jādū* to resolution. This clarity stands in contrast to the narratives of punishment that pilgrims create on their own, which usually involve their own interpretation of misfortune experienced by their oppressors. For example a Shi'a woman from Bombay once explained to me that her sister's mother-in-law had done magic on her sister, resulting in the sister's untimely death. A number of years later the mother-in-law died a horrible death. Her death, my informant concluded, must have been part of the justice administered by the saints of Ḥusain Ṭekrī.

Outside the medium of *khulī ḥāẓirī,* misfortune can be interpreted as justice or as victimhood, but the indisputable disclosure of the truth and the meting out of punishment—often a necessary (if not sufficient) part of the equation—is rendered substantive through the clear cause-and-effect nature of the violence and submission that are embodied and enacted in *khulī ḥāẓirī.* For most pilgrims at Ḥusain Ṭekrī, this type of obvious narrative, in which questions are answered and facts obtained, is legitimated in part through the clarity of cause and effect inherent in the violence of *khulī ḥāẓirī.* In this way, justice is not possible—that is, it is not recognizable and therefore authoritative—without violence.

Khulī ḥāẓirī's power has several undramatic, nonverbal, and therefore easily overlooked aspects, chief among them the relationship it creates between the individual in ḥāẓirī and his or her caretaker, who is almost without exception a relative. As they care for a woman during an episode of *khulī ḥāẓirī,* the caretakers generally aim to protect her modesty and, by extension, her value. While the spirit insists, through the voice of the woman, that it will take the woman's honor and even her very life, the caretaker, in small and persistent ways, both practical and symbolic, repeatedly protects—and even asserts—the honor and value of the *ḥāẓirīwālī* by keeping her body properly covered and protecting her *dupaṭṭā* by either holding it or, if a woman's *khulī ḥāẓirī* is not too severe, keeping it draped on her shoulders. The *dupaṭṭā*'s function as a symbol of the value of a woman is so ubiquitous in contemporary South Asian culture as to not even warrant a list of examples; as a symbol of a woman's honor, it spans religions, genres, and centuries.

When I asked pilgrims why the faces of those with ḥāẓirī were covered during the unconsciousness that generally follows *khulī ḥāẓirī,* it was often explained to me that women's faces in particular were covered to protect them from the potentially lecherous gaze of men in the rauẓas. This is surely one of its practical functions, though the fact that men's faces are also covered when they fall unconscious strongly suggests that the act has other meanings as well. Covering the face could enact the symbolic death of the individual; it could represent the beating of the *pret* into submission; or it could reflect a desire to hide or make private the transformation from *khulī ḥāẓirī* to normal waking consciousness.[45]

For both the *ḥāẓirīwāle* and their caretakers, this unspoken, physically enacted resistance to *prets*' constant threatening statements and convulsions forms a silent counternarrative: the *pret* insists that he or she will kill the victim; the victim's caretaker either redrapes or holds the victim's *dupaṭṭā;* the *pret* boasts that he or she has killed thousands of people before the current victim; the victim's caretaker clears the area where the victim rolls, making sure that no one interferes with the process of ḥāẓirī; the *pret* insists that he or she will never disclose the name of the magician who did the magic and the victim falls to the ground, unconscious; and the caretaker covers the victim's face and sits with her, waiting quietly at her side until she regains consciousness. In addition to performing these simple protective and even nurturing acts, the caretaker necessarily witnesses all that happens in the victim's *khulī ḥāẓirī;* both share the burden of the adversity that is made substantive in *khulī ḥāẓirī* and the everyday asceticism that they practice as residents of Ḥusain Ṭekrī.[46]

It is inevitable that, over time, the repeated experience of having one's honor protected, as well as the repeated action of protecting the honor of the victim, will create a new set of experiences and memories that may, by virtue of their experiential nature, become a meaningful, positive correction of a past failure, when the honor of the *ḥāẓirīwālī* was not guarded by the family. The extended family is conceived of as a structure that will ideally preserve and maintain the value of each of its members. When that system fails, *khulī ḥāẓirī* offers the opportunity to construct a nonverbal but very real counternarrative: this narrative holds that the victim is valuable and should be protected, and that the caretaker has the ability and the desire to protect the victim effectively. Thus, for both the victim and the caretaker, the process of the dual narrative of *khulī ḥāẓirī* can be understood as an opportunity to remake the past. This remade past is rendered meaningful through repetition of the experiences of violence and protection.

At the same time, the explicit verbal narrative constructed within and from declarations made during *khulī ḥāẓirī* is unambiguously concerned with justice, to be sure, but since family reconstruction is a central goal of ḥāẓirī, these specific narratives of justice cannot be carried back to the family. Consider, for example, this bit of conversation between two women who were sitting together in the courtyard of the rauẓa of 'Abbas:

Young Hindu woman: [In ḥāẓirī I have learned that] three or four people had magic done on me, including the older sister of my mother-in-law and the people in my neighborhood . . .

Older woman: Did you go there and confront them? [That is, having learned the truth in ḥāẓirī, did you leave Ḥusain Ṭekrī to confront them?]

Young Hindu woman: Bābā [i.e., Husain or 'Ali] will punish them—what am I supposed to do? I shouldn't do anything; Bābā will punish them. What would I do after confronting them? Whatever pain and suffering I experience [in life and in ḥāẓirī], Bābā will give them exactly the same suffering . . . so that they will know what it means to give someone's daughter the sort of suffering I have experienced, and what kind of punishment they deserve . . . I am not a fighter *[laṛāī karnī lāyaq]*—what would I do, having fought with someone?

For this young woman, justice is achieved specifically during ḥāẓirī, not in the direct confrontation of individuals outside ḥāẓirī. Additionally, this woman asserts her legitimacy and honor in the non-ḥāẓirī world through a discourse of family—she is "someone's daughter." In the non-ḥāẓirī world, for both women and men, legitimacy continues to be closely allied with family relationships. In short, a Western notion of justice cannot restore honor because in everyday Indian life, an individual's honor is preserved and protected only through properly functioning family relationships. While pilgrims at Ḥusain Ṭekrī certainly desire a form of justice that bears some resemblance to the popularly conceived, individually oriented Western model of public declaration of guilt and subsequent punishment, they also clearly recognize the folly of pursuing it through direct, narrative-based means beyond the bounds of Ḥusain Ṭekrī.

Rather than from a clear, specific revelation of guilt, motivation, and punishment, the efficacy of *khulī ḥāẓirī*'s verbal elements comes from their broken, fragmented character. Below is a translation of a typical ḥāẓirī speech delivered by a woman at the rauẓa of 'Abbas:

> I dance, I dance; I do everything; come on! Come on Bābā! I want to go in the dirty water! Oh 'Alamdār ['Abbas], I'm going to take your innocent one *[ma'ṣūm]* and go; your innocent one is so precious *[pyārī];* I'm going to take your innocent one and go; oh Bābā, oh Bābā [unclear speech and the frenzied breathing pattern typical of *khulī ḥāẓirī*], I need a *faislā* . . .

In this rapid-fire series of statements, the *pret* vacillates between aggressively asserting that he will kill the woman and take her honor and asking for further punishment in the dirty water.[47] The request to bathe in dirty water could be either a display of bravado in the face of punishment, or it could reflect a wish to expedite the process of receiving a *faislā,* which is requested at the end of this quotation, after the flurry of aggressive statements have been made. Additionally, the *pret*'s dancing, manifest by the woman running slowly in place, forward and backward, tossing her head around, may be seen as either punishment or a form of rebellion in the face of the authority of the saint.

As this quotation shows, ḥāẓirī speech typically strings together its various tropes and stock phrases in any order. Further, this utterance shows how the various elements of ḥāẓirī speech are learned and shared in the context of Ḥusain Ṭekrī. The phrase "I'm going to take this innocent one and go" was, for example, also a dominant refrain in Priya's ḥāẓirī. *Khulī ḥāẓirī* speech is also typically punctuated with a particular deep and rapid breathing pattern, yelling, and crying, and, except for the relatively rare moments of explicit declaration of some piece of information about *jādū,* it lacks narrative climax and resolution. Instead, one trope moves seamlessly into another, connected by the state of ḥāẓirī itself rather than narrative meaning. Continuity of speech derives from the experience of violence: violence will engender declarations of pain, and extreme violence will prompt screams, frenzied breathing, and the punctuation of each word with a rasping inhalation. Verbal narrative emerges only rarely.

Repeated bouts of *khulī ḥāẓirī* can and do extend for months or years. It is the work of the *ḥāẓirīwāle,* together with the community of pilgrims and their own caretakers, to speculate on the progress that each bout of *khulī ḥāẓirī* represents, and to place *khulī ḥāẓirī* declarations in meaningful relationship with other resources for narrative creation such as dreams and the miraculous opening of locks and chains. Formally, these disconnected figures of speech create a template that may eventually be filled with each victim's specific information: which neighbor or family member, what kind of magic, and how much was paid. The often explicitly articulated hope of the community of caretakers as well as the *ḥāẓirīwāle* themselves when they are not in *khulī ḥāẓirī* is that these general tropes will eventually yield specific information about the cause of the *ḥāẓirīwālī/ā*'s distress. The fact that caretakers have nothing more than the narrative aspect of ḥāẓirī by which to gauge the process makes their investment in narrative progress considerably more marked than the investment of those who practice ḥāẓirī. Recall, for example, that Priya's mother was much more enthusiastic than Priya about a *bayān* (revelation) that had happened the first time Priya wore a burqa.

To be clear, in order to understand how practices like ḥāẓirī heal, it is necessary to recognize that if a specific causal narrative is created during the process, this narrative is created in response to expectations; it is a learned narrative, and it does not reflect the efficacy of the *process* of ḥāẓirī itself, but rather the *ḥāẓirīwālā*'s knowledge of the society of ḥāẓirī. When a specific linear, causal narrative is finally offered, the *pret* has admitted defeat and the process of *khulī ḥāẓirī* is understood to be over. While on the one hand, the declaration of the truth has a positive effect on all involved, on the other hand, most of ḥāẓirī's efficacy lies in its broken speech and physical process—the violence, the time, the dislocation, the relationship between the caretaker and the *ḥāẓirīwālī,* and ungovernable elements like dreams and the opening of locks. If recovery came solely from *khulī ḥāẓirī*–derived narratives, it would not be possible to recover without a causal *jādū*-based narrative, as Priya, for example, expects to accomplish through *gum ḥāẓirī,* or as Maya claims to have accomplished.[48] Individuals and caretakers may *desire* the clarity of a specific narrative, but because of the nonnarrative ways that ḥāẓirī actually works—through violence, dislocation, and the passage of time—they do not *need* it.

The common term for a person with *khulī ḥāẓirī* or *gum ḥāẓirī* is simply *ḥāẓirīwālā/ḥāẓirīwālī,* literally, "one with presence."[49] Conversationally, the generic plural *ḥāẓirīwāle* is used most often to talk about the community of resident pilgrims. Variations on the phrases "We *ḥāẓirīwāle* don't know what will happen to us" and "*Ḥāẓirīwāle* can't enter the rauẓas" are common refrains, reflecting the uncertainty and outsider status of those who practice *khulī ḥāẓirī* or *gum ḥāẓirī.* This term reflects an important but easily overlooked aspect of ḥāẓirī: although studies of spirit possession tend to focus on the violent, active moments of the possession, the phenomenon is best understood more broadly as an enduring state of being rather than a fleeting one. It is significant that of the wide range of terms that pilgrims might use to describe themselves at Ḥusain Ṭekrī, the term in common usage brands them as persons who are not quite right, who suffer ḥāẓirī at every moment regardless of whether or not they are having an explicit bout of *khulī ḥāẓirī.* The only other term that rivals *ḥāẓirīwāle* in frequency of use is *marīẓ,* or patient; here, too the term conveys the sense of someone who is unwell.

In addition to a constant feeling of out-of-placeness characteristic of the daily experience of being at Ḥusain Ṭekrī, much of life there is marked by incredibly undramatic slowness—hours sitting in the courtyards of the rauẓas, waiting in line for kerosene for the stove, cooking food, and sweating one's way through constant power outages, the frequency and duration of which are new to many of the city- and town-dwelling pilgrims. At Ḥusain Ṭekrī, pilgrims experience an undramatic but powerful asceticism of everyday life.

Further, the novelty for Indians of a life lived largely apart from most of one's extended family as well as neighbors and friends has both positive and negative consequences. It is clearly freeing and exciting, as pilgrims meet others with problems similar to their own and together develop the shared narratives that often lead to healing, but at the same time it is also stifling: the relationships formed at Ḥusain Ṭekrī, while perhaps significantly comforting, will not advance the individual in the outside world, where marriage and family are the basis of stability and security. Thus, the constant social and geographic out-of-placeness that pilgrims experience is also part of the reason that they self-identify as *ḥāẓirīwāle.*

Once, for example, when I was walking through the date palm–studded farmland that stretches out in all directions from the rauẓas of Ḥusain Ṭekrī, I asked the elderly man who was taking me to visit his brother Ẕākir Mohib—a major personality at Ḥusain Ṭekrī and author of one of its guidebooks—about a young girl who was following us. In explaining who she was, he simply said, "*Voh bāhar kī hai, voh yahāṁ kī hai,*" or, "She's from outside, she's from here." While the statement seems like a meaningless contradiction, in fact it perfectly describes the liminal existence of pilgrims who live at Ḥusain Ṭekrī. They live at Ḥusain Ṭekrī, but it is not their home; neither, however, can their home be home. At its most basic level, ḥāẓirī is a state of being, and specifically it is a condition of being out of place; it is not simply a moment of overt spirit possession.

So who holds the power in ḥāẓirī? On one level, the power in ḥāẓirī comes from the saints of Ḥusain Ṭekrī. Certainly, that is the location of power that pilgrims cite, and it is clear that shared assumptions about the nature of the saints of Ḥusain Ṭekrī—and Sufi saints—are necessary elements in the construction of individual narratives of healing. The meaning of ḥāẓirī derives in part from the fact that dargāḥs in the subcontinent historically maintained a ritual and institutional life that self-consciously imitated the ritual and institutional life of Muslim rulers. In this context, ḥāẓirī has an earlier meaning of presence or attendance at a court. Thus, in terms of pilgrims' explicitly stated beliefs and the dominant narrative of Ḥusain Ṭekrī, the power in ḥāẓirī rests with the saints themselves.

Practically speaking, however, power in ḥāẓirī is complexly distributed: It is in the *pret,* whose noncorporeal form makes him or her uniquely qualified to physically torment a human being; it is in the magician, whose skill allows for the manipulation and command of the *pret;* it is in the money that is paid to the magician, without which he or she would not do the work; it is in the saints of Ḥusain Ṭekrī, who have the power to beat and otherwise discipline the *pret* until it confesses who sent it and why; and finally and perhaps most importantly, it is in the victim, whose body is the medium within which all of the above sources of power are able to express and assert themselves, and whose body may eventually endure as the surviving—and therefore most powerful—participant in the process of ḥāẓirī. In addition to the power of narrative, my discussion of the verbal and nonverbal elements of ḥāẓirī has also located elements of its power in the violence of the physical process of *khulī ḥāẓirī,* and in the fact that ḥāẓirī is fundamentally a displaced and time-consuming state of being.

In addition to all of these aspects of ḥāẓirī's power, the term *ḥāẓirī* itself contains a meaning that indicates a different location of power, a location that is not a body, a narrative, or a relationship but rather a time and a place. Recall that ḥāẓirī literally means "presence." Given the interest in the issues of power, selfhood, and agency that has directly informed much scholarship on religion over the past several decades as well as the tendency of spirit possession practices to prompt scholarly focus on questions of agency and power, this term is most notable for its agentless, power-neutral connotations: specifically, unlike the term *possession, presence* offers no perspective on who controls what, and in this way it is, arguably and amazingly, a power-neutral term.

The words used to relate ḥāẓirī to the *ḥāẓirīwāle* are equally unhelpful in delineating relationships of agents, agency, or power. A common way to describe the process of ḥāẓirī is simply to say that the person in question is "in" ḥāẓirī *(ḥāẓirī meṁ)*—the language is locative. Of the verbs used in relation to ḥāẓirī, one often hears the Hindi word *calnā,* which is most appropriately translated as "going on," as in *"Us kī ḥāẓirī cal rahī hai,"* or "His ḥāẓirī is going on." The literal translation of *calnā* is "to move." Again, the language refuses to assign agency to an individual, as the verb is intransitive. To say that presence is "going on" denies clarity about who or what is driving the action, or even what direction the action is moving. Similarly, some pilgrims also use the verb *ānā* (to come) to describe the onset of ḥāẓirī. Also used in conjunction with ḥāẓirī is *bharnā,* which literally means "to fill." The phrase *"Voh ḥāẓirī bhar rahā hai"* is thus translated literally as "He is filling presence"; a nonliteral translation that captures the sense of the phrase is "doing time."

No one I asked about the use of *bharnā* was able to offer an explanation for the term's use. One Muslim shopkeeper who had been at Ḥusain Ṭekrī for years suggested that the term was used by less educated individuals who spend a lot of time at Ḥusain Ṭekrī, and he also rightly noted that the term *ḥāẓirī* is also used in formal Urdu with the verb *deṇā* (to give) to describe visiting a dargāḥ for simple reasons of faith *('aqīda).* The phrase *ḥāẓirī bharnā* conveys a sense of indebtedness and captivity that stands in marked contrast to the effortless abundance of lobān and the voluntary nature of each pilgrim's response to the "call" from the saints to come to Ḥusain Ṭekrī in the first place. While the *ḥāẓirīwāle* are self-proclaimed innocents *(ma'ṣūm),* the state of ḥāẓirī itself is predicated on the notion of debt. *Time* and *presence* are owed, and these debts cannot be bought out or otherwise bargained away: they must be paid in full and in proper kind. Coming to Ḥusain Ṭekrī may be voluntary and lobān may be endlessly abundant, but *khulī ḥāẓirī* is a command-based discourse, and, as a state of being, ḥāẓirī holds that the individual is not in control of his or her comings and goings from Ḥusain Ṭekrī: without a *faislā,* one can only leave with special permission. This permission is usually given in a dream, and before leaving the pilgrim is required to tie a *challā* on the *jālī* as a promise to return. The power of ḥāẓirī, in other words, also derives from paying a debt through placement, specifically, placing one's body in the presence of the saint-judges of Ḥusain Ṭekrī and their court.

This notion of paying a debt through placement has other manifestations, among them the widely practiced tradition of weighing a prayed-for child in sugar, sweets, coconuts, or fruit in a large balance that is often kept in the courtyard of dargāḥs. After the weighing, the sweets are distributed to the poor, which in practical terms means anyone sitting in the courtyard. I also know two young men who were weighed in sugar on the occasion of their marriages. In both cases a promise had been made to weigh them when they were infants, but for various reasons it had not been accomplished. In weighing these young men immediately prior to their weddings, both families hoped to appease the saints of Ḥusain Ṭekrī so that their sons would not be in their debt as they began married life. While weighing children is generally described as being done voluntarily, out of happiness *(k̲h̲uśī se)* and as an expression of gratitude,[50] the fact that the child is *weighed*—a more fundamentally transactional act is hard to imagine—suggests that something more than voluntary gratitude is being expressed: the child is being bought back from the saint, ounce for ounce.

The body of the *ḥāẓirīwālī* is similarly contingent upon its presence: it is powerful in the present moment of having *khulī ḥāẓirī,* in its presentness at Ḥusain Ṭekrī, and in being in the presence of Maulā and Bībī. Theorizing the subjectivity of the possessed, the goal of much feminist, postcolonial, and psychoanalytic scholarship on spirit possession, generally emphasizes personhood or relationships between persons rather than placeness.[51] In fact, in ḥāẓirī the reverse is true: efficacy derives from placeness, not personhood, and healing in ḥāẓirī develops out of displacement rather than from any sort of enduring self-assertion on the part of the women themselves. However well-intentioned, any attempt to locate agency and power exclusively in the person in ḥāẓirī would miss what is most powerful about the practice: in leaving home, coming to Ḥusain Ṭekrī, and bringing the case before the saints, the person with ḥāẓirī is disassociated from the life that he or she has left behind. For all that *ḥāẓirīwāle* have suffered as the result of jealousy and magic, they understand themselves to be *maʿṣūm,* innocent, and because of this they seek justice in addition to escape. There is nothing that they themselves can do to better their situation, and there is nothing that they should do; the body that participates in ḥāẓirī is not powerful for what it is or for what is in it or for the relationship between the two, but rather for where it is and when it is. *Khulī ḥāẓirī* is an event; it takes place, and as such its power comes from time and place rather than persons or personalities.

Ḥāẓirī is a truth-seeking, justice-meting, narrative-creating process; it is a liminal state of being that temporarily becomes an individual's foundational identity, and it is a nonverbal means of creating a set of experiences that restore broken familial relationships and compensate for past injustices. How and why does ḥāẓirī then serve as a gateway—and often, a sine qua non—for becoming a healer like Maya? Because ḥāẓirī is a process with so many potential avenues of meaning making, it follows that the stories of healers that I collected over my time at Ḥusain Ṭekrī are varied. However, healers' stories often shared certain assumptions and tropes, many of which figure prominently into the story of a young woman with ḥāẓirī whose tale was largely related to me by her husband and mother-in-law. Her story reflects the expectations and assumptions of family members in addition to her own.

The main spokesperson for the family was a middle-aged Sunni woman whom I will call Bilkis—she explained that she and her family were *"shaikh̲"* by *jāti*—who had come to Ḥusain Ṭekrī with her daughter-in-law and son. They were all staying in the shack of one of the vendors near the rauẓa of Fatima, which is common practice for poorer pilgrims. Because the vendors are not officially permitted by the *waqf* board to take boarders (indeed, while I was there, there was a very hush-hush crackdown on this practice because of allegations that these shacks were functioning as brothels), vendors allow pilgrims to sleep on the shacks' dirt floors in exchange for their exclusive business whenever they buy flowers, incense, or lobān to offer in the rauẓas. In this way, they circumvent the rule that forbids them from renting their shacks as lodges.

Bilkis explained that prior to their arrival at Ḥusain Ṭekrī, they had spent two and a half months at another popular healing dargāḥ, that of Sailani Bābā in Madhya Pradesh.[52] This dargāḥ, mentioned by many at Ḥusain Ṭekrī, is a part of the network of healing shrines that also includes Ḥusain Ṭekrī. Bilkis told me that while at Sailani Bābā's dargāḥ, there was a revelation *(bayān)* about who had performed the magic on her daughter-in-law. It was revealed (likely in *khulī ḥāẓirī,* but also possibly in a dream—she did not specify) that the young woman's maternal aunt had paid two thousand rupees to perform magic that would eventually kill the young woman, and that a further one thousand had been promised to the magician upon the young woman's death. Bilkis emphasized that it was particularly tragic that the magic had been paid for by a family member rather than a total stranger.[53]

She then explained that a Hindu man at Sailani Bābā who has a possession-based healing practice *(bābā kī salāmī)* had performed a form of exorcism on her daughter-in-law using lemons *(nimbū caṛhānā),*[54] and that because of the improvement that this procedure elicited, the magician who had performed the original magic was hired again, which resulted in a regression in the daughter-in-law's condition. *Bābā kī salāmī,* literally "father's greeting," is a fairly common term at Ḥusain Ṭekrī for a benevolent spirit possession–based healing practice. More generally, in the idiom common at dargāḥs, *salāmī* functions as a nonliteral shorthand for the presence of a person in a place: often, pilgrims explain their visits to Ḥusain Ṭekrī as *salāmī dene ke liye,* or as offering a greeting, usually out of gratitude for relief from a problem or for a wedding. This motivation for visiting a dargāḥ is also often glossed as *k̲h̲uśī se,* from "happiness."

After the daughter-in-law became victim to a second round of magic, the decree came from Sailani Bābā—again, likely in ḥāẓirī but also possibly in a dream—that the family's case had been transferred to Ḥusain Ṭekrī, and so the family went there. (In describing this transfer, Bilkis used the English word *case,* which is common in pilgrims' discussions of their situations.) She repeatedly emphasized that they had not gone home in the interim and that they would not leave Ḥusain Ṭekrī until they received a *faislā.*

Speaking of his wife's ḥāẓirī, Bilkis's son told me that his wife had received an order to drink from a filthy swamp that is on the side of the road that connects Ḥusain Ṭekrī with the dargāḥ of Māmū Sahib, one of the major dargāḥs of the town of Jaora proper. It is common for pilgrims to walk the mile and a half from Ḥusain Ṭekrī to Māmū Sahib (Respected Maternal Uncle) every evening after the final lobān to eat the *laṅgar* (charitable meals) offered there. Because of prolonged drought conditions, this swamp is one of the very few places where Jaora's water buffalo can wallow com-

FIGURE 10. *Ḥāẓirīwāle* bathing in dirty water.

fortably. In other words, the water there is truly and visibly filthy. The husband's explanation of the benefit of drinking dirty water was the one most commonly offered by pilgrims, primarily those who observe the consumption of dirty water, but also those who consume and bathe in it: that drinking it was a command *(ḥukm),* and that the water had the ability to destroy the *jādū* and to cause the *pret* enough stress to prompt a *bayān* and subsequent removal of the *pret.*

Bathing in or drinking dirty water is a less common command *(ḥukm)* than, for example, binding one's body with locks, but neither is it unheard of. Generally, pilgrims at Ḥusain Ṭekrī who receive a command to bathe in or drink dirty water do so in a swamp behind the public bathhouse just across from the rauẓas of Sakina and 'Abbas. The water in the public bathhouse is understood to come from a well that came into existence during the miraculous visitation of Husain and his companions. The runoff from the shower area collects in a pit behind the building, and any day of the week a number of people can be seen bathing in the resultant swamp or burying themselves in its mud after having dug themselves into grave-shaped holes. As they bathe, they engage in the usual range of *khulī ḥāẓirī* actions and declarations.

A *mujāvar* of Ḥusain Ṭekrī, in an attempt to convey the full strength of this practice in terms that he thought I would understand, likened the sort of suffering that the dirty water caused the *pret* to harsh punishments of the colonial era such as hanging or exile to an island labor camp. Pilgrims at Ḥusain Ṭekrī offer two somewhat conflicting explanations for these activities: some say that the filth is punishment and torture directed at the possessing *pret*, and, like the violence of *khulī ḥāẓirī* as practiced in the rauẓa courtyards, will eventually result in the surrender and subsequent expulsion of the *pret* from the body of the victim. If pressed on why this dirty water in particular is effective, some say that if the magic performed is "dirty," dirty substances are needed to remove it. Similarly, magic performed by an untouchable, the most dangerous and difficult to remove, may require dirty means.

In contrast to this view, a man who happened by the cart of a bookseller I knew quite well volunteered that those who bathed in dirty water were actually low-born individuals—not, he elaborated, a Sayyid (blood descendant of the Prophet) such as the bookseller. After he walked away, I turned to the bookseller and incredulously observed that the man had assumed that she was a Sayyid when in fact she was a Hindu. His confusion was somewhat understandable. This woman, whose husband had been healed at Ḥusain Ṭekrī many years earlier, made a point of dressing in a neutral way so that, she said, she would get business from both Muslims and Hindus. She also explained that she felt that she would have more legitimacy if she looked Muslim because the books she sold were Islamic texts.

The salient point in considering the man's observation that the Hindu bookseller was a Sayyid is that those who are of a higher social or caste status are more inclined to interpret bathing in dirty water as something done by lower-caste or poorer individuals, although in my experience the activity attracted a range of individuals. In any case, bathing in dirty water is significantly less common than consuming lobān, and, unlike the consumption of lobān, it is only engaged in when a *ḥukm* is given.

Even within the practice of bathing or drinking dirty water, there remains room for the negotiation and formation of individual narratives that are characteristic of ḥāẓirī and healing at Ḥusain Ṭekrī more generally. Another woman who spoke with me told me that although she had been given a command to drink dirty water, she was going to wait until her *faislā* to do it. This seems to conflict with the widely held notion that the command facilitates obtaining a *faislā*, for what is the use of drinking dirty water once the *pret* has been subdued? On one level, such seeming irrationality remains mysterious; on another, it participates in general assumptions about purity and pollution and the nature of a *ḥukm*. This woman explained that she was in the habit of eating the *laṅgar* at Māmū Sahib, and because of the benefit of eating this food, she was not going to stop eating it until she received her *faislā*. In the meantime, from her perspective, it was decidedly wrong to put the dirty water on top of the pure food of *laṅgar*, mixing them in her body. The power of *ḥukm* is such that even the discourse of ḥāẓirī does not allow for its outright dismissal; once it is received, it may be negotiated but it cannot be ignored. However, while the *ḥukm* must be obeyed, other standards—in this case, taking care not to pollute a pure substance—must also be maintained. This conflict of interests mirrors the very nature of ḥāẓirī. It is a practice of negotiating pan-Indian values and culture systems with very few resources and many physical constraints.

Other pilgrims and residents had mixed feelings about the efficacy of bathing in and drinking dirty water. A shopkeeper who has been in residence at Ḥusain Ṭekrī for more than forty years often used the example of people bathing in dirty water as evidence that Ḥusain Ṭekrī had become less powerful and wonderful than it had been earlier in its history. In lamenting this decline, her common refrain was "They used to bathe in clean water, and now they bathe in filthy water." Whenever she mentioned bathing in dirty water, which she said was a very recent development, she would briefly touch her earlobes and mouth in a common Muslim gesture for asking forgiveness for having said something unspeakable or reprehensible.[55] While the logic of the benefit of bathing in dirty water was lost on her, her shocked response to the practice was shared by just about anyone who sees or talks about these bathers, whether they accept the activity's healing properties or not.

A friend from Jaora once highlighted the shocking nature of this practice by telling me in confidence that he was certain that the new management of Ḥusain Ṭekrī had hired people to bathe in the dirty water. When I asked him what the use of this would be and how he knew, he explained that he knew several of the bathers, who were residents of a neighborhood adjacent to his and were known to be very poor. He said that it struck him as suspicious that one day they were fine and the next they were bathing in the dirty water at Ḥusain Ṭekrī. To explain this sudden anomalous behavior, he speculated that the management had offered to pay them to bathe in the water because it would attract more people to Ḥusain Ṭekrī in order to see this sensational practice for themselves. True or not, this rumor participates in the general opinion that the practices of drinking and bathing in dirty water are radical, transgressive, and shocking.

In the case of Bilkis's daughter-in-law, it is significant that the husband emphasized this aspect of his wife's ḥāẓirī. In part because they are command-based rather than a voluntary actions, bathing in and consuming dirty water are relatively uncommon and radical practices, and in eagerly offering this detail, it seemed to me that the husband very much wanted to give me a good interview—something that I often sensed from pilgrims, many of whom were remarkably open about their suffering and who often told me that they hoped that my research on ḥāẓirī would lend legitimacy to their practices, since, as they were well aware, many people dismiss their problems as being merely "psychological" or "mental."

This explicit rejection of the category of mental illness by those with ḥāẓirī is yet another reason I am disinclined to apply psychoanalytic models of analysis. Beyond cross-cultural differences in notions of selfhood, if the discourse of ḥāẓirī is made meaningful to some of its practitioners in part through explicitly contrasting it with "mental problems," using a psychological lens without offering a compelling reason is perhaps presumptuous. If a pilgrim asserts that ḥāẓirī is not a mental illness *even though it may look like one,* it seems that in urgently emphasizing this distinction, ḥāẓirī practitioners are making a statement about the source of their problems: they are making the vital assertion that they are reacting to outside forces and systems, be they spirits, magic, or mothers-in-law. The problems that prompt ḥāẓirī are not simply in their heads and cannot be solved there. Because the problems are external and social, truly effective solutions are also necessarily social, and ḥāẓirī is a social process.

Bilkis elaborated on her daughter-in-law's extreme ḥāẓirī by explaining that the daughter-in-law also had a *ḥukm* to roll from the rauẓa of 'Ali to the rauẓa of Fatima, a distance that can be covered by a twenty-minute walk. I saw the daughter-in-law do this myself and was actually encouraged by the mother-in-law and the husband to take pictures and video footage. Because of the physical distress that the *pret* was experiencing as a result of the marathon rolling sessions and the bathing in dirty water, both Bilkis and her son were optimistic that a *bayān* was imminent. After the revelation about the nature of the magic, Bilkis said, it was likely that the *pret* would request to be contained in a lemon and nailed to the tree near the rauẓa of 'Abbas used for this purpose. The final *faislā,* Bilkis concluded, would come during the *holī* fire walk at Ḥusain Ṭekrī. The *holī* fire walk is not to be confused with the one held forty days after the tenth of Muharram. These events, which have very different narratives attached, are understood by some to burn *pret* out of the body once and for all. The *holī* fire walk is also, strictly speaking, not exactly a fire walk. Although it is held on the same raised platform that hosts the post-Muharram event, the *holī* fire can only be seen and experienced by *pret*. Attendees of the *holī* fire walk will observe *ḥāẓirīwāle* making their way across an empty platform, rolling, swaying, and writhing as the *pret* cry out in agony, protesting that they are burning.

Bilkis's expectation that her daughter-in-law's *pret* would request a *faislā* and specify his final resting place is common; *pret* beg *(māṁgnā)* for a *faislā* in order to end the physical violence that they endure during ḥāẓirī. Further, she elaborated that after the case was completely resolved her daughter-in-law would be given *bābā kī salāmī* and thereafter become an arbiter and mediator in family quarrels and problems. She emphasized that this gift would be used exclusively with family members, since those who extended their role as charismatic healers beyond the bounds of family often opened themselves up to ridicule or accusations of fraud, resulting, Bilkis said, in *badnāmī*, or "disgrace" (literally, "bad-name-ness") for the family.

For Bilkis, the legitimate place for an individual claiming to have *bābā kī salāmī* lies within the family, though this legitimacy is often metaphorically extended beyond blood relatives by the use of family language, most obviously in the use of the title *bābā* (father) for many healers and Muslim saints. However, while necessary, family language is not a sufficient element in the legitimacy that healers claim for themselves, especially given that many of the healers I interviewed, including Maya, treat those outside their immediate family or community. In these cases, it seems to me that it is the fearsome, transgressive, and violent nature of the activities engaged in by *ḥāẓirīwāle* that lends legitimacy to their status as healers. In Bilkis's story, her daughter-in-law's commentary is relatively absent. This was in part a function of the daughter-in-law's personality: she was exceptionally shy. However, I did notice that this young woman would sit with her eyes downcast and a half smile on her face as her husband and mother-in-law described her formidable, transgressive acts. There was, for lack of a better word, a machismo about her, as though she were proud of the extremity and ferocity of her ḥāẓirī. Over my time at Ḥusain Ṭekrī I met many individuals who were similarly proud of their fearsome ḥāẓirī and who were uninhibited and even enthusiastic in detailing the violent, frightening nature of their experiences.

What might it be possible to conclude if smiling silence and the tendency to emphasize the radical actions of *khulī ḥāẓirī* together encompass everything that a *ḥāẓirīwālī* needs to convey to the world? If a woman who was a *ḥāẓirīwālī* becomes a healer, narratively—that is to say, explicitly—all power is attributed to "*bābā*." Without discounting the power and legitimacy inherent in lineage and shared narratives, it is also true that many healers who employ this language are dismissed as frauds; simply claiming to have a particular lineage is, in other words, contestable. In contrast to narrative- and lineage-based claims, on a nonnarrative level, the body of the woman—the body that has overcome acts of incredible violence and pollution—functions as fearsome, enduring, and largely irrefutable evidence of its own power and authority, and by extension, its ability to command and remove illnesses and *pret.*

Whether the woman's body derives its power and authority from being exceptionally transgressive or from being pure enough to overcome transgressive and polluting acts is not clear, and if other phenomena at Ḥusain Ṭekrī are any indication, it is likely that both assumptions are operative, depending on an individual's personal history and his or her regional and religious background. On the one hand, in the spirit of the common saying "*Lohā lohe se kāṭnā*" (cut iron with iron), it has been amply documented in studies of South Asian religion that the village goddesses Kālī and Śītalā are regarded as quite dangerous; their power is associated with transgressive activities such as blood sacrifice, and specifically in the case of Śītalā, the Goddess can bring illness. Because goddess temples, along with Hanumān temples, are a major site of charismatic healing and exorcism, and because it is clear that some goddesses derive their power in part from transgression (most strikingly in the contemporary popular association of Kālī and Tantric practice) and impurity (most strikingly in the preference some have for blood sacrifice), it is clear that transgression itself must constitute one aspect of the power and legitimacy that I am suggesting that women cultivate through ḥāẓirī.

On the other hand, popular Indian culture also contains the notion of feminine power derived from auspiciousness, and specifically the auspiciousness of a married woman. This auspiciousness, associated with the category *sat* (literally "honor" or "truth"), is popularly displayed in the character of the epic heroine Sītā, whose chastity and loyalty to her husband Rāma is proven through the famous fire ordeal. Even before Doordarshan's phenomenally successful Ramayana television series, stories of Sītā and Rāma formed a major element of popular cultural and religious expressions.[56] While *sat* is understood to form the basis of a married woman's power, in the context of debates about *satī* (the practice of a Hindu widow voluntarily burning herself alive on her husband's funeral pyre) in contemporary Indian communities, *sat* is also evidenced in ways that are reminiscent of practices associated with ḥāẓirī. In an article on Indian women's attitudes toward *sat* and its relation to the practice of *satī,* a Bania widow noted the opinion of women who visited her small shop: "The women also said that they had heard that when a woman is possessed by *sat* her miraculous powers are so strong that locked doors open on their own and her body catches fire on its own." Similarly, a Brahmin widow from the same region elaborated on the question of whether a particular instance of *satī* was voluntary or coerced by saying, "If [the young woman's] family members felt that her *sat* was true, they should have tried to lock her and checked whether the locks open . . ." (ellipsis in original).[57] Particularly given the fact that the women interviewed in this article come from the same culture area as Ḥusain Ṭekrī (Marwari- and Mewari-speaking areas with strong Rajput influence), it is very likely that the locks with which many female sufferers of ḥāẓirī bind their bodies are understood to open for the same reasons; the power of their *sat* is responsible. *Ḥāẓirīwālī* may appear to be inauspicious women, either because they are unmarried or because they come from a failed marriage or broken family, but the breaking of the locks that bind them is a clear testament to their honor, paralleling exactly the honor of a widow who proves her fitness for the sacrifice of *satī* by breaking through physical constraints that would stand between her and the act of self-sacrifice to which she is entitled because of her high level of *sat*. The transgressive and violent practices associated with *khulī ḥāẓirī* are also understood to test the measure of a woman's *sat*, or auspiciousness: the more her body can take, the greater her *sat*, and, subsequently, the greater her legitimacy and power.

Powerful actions and objects are powerful in part because have the capacity to index many potential sources of power and systems of meaning. In *khulī ḥāẓirī*, power and authority derive from the body of the woman itself: if these women become healers, whether their power is transgressive or auspicious, people recognize the power of these women because their still-living bodies themselves bear witness to something about them that is more powerful than illness, pollution, or *pret*. One could speculate that the process of *khulī ḥāẓirī* has other benefits: the opportunity it affords women to express verbal and physical violence may offer them the only opportunity they will ever have to release rage, for example, but among other challenges to such psychologically driven interpretations, this sort of interpretation of ḥāẓirī is by nature completely speculative (it assumes much about a woman's past and her desires for the future) and presumes a more individually focused and nonphysical psychologically driven model of selfhood than is operative in South Asian culture.[58]

The idea that the body itself is the chief legitimating element of healers is further substantiated by a story related to me by the same Muslim woman who related the story of a *jinn* attaching himself to a female relative while she was on her way to an outhouse on her wedding night. Subsequently, this female relative developed a charismatic healing practice. After hearing this I related Maya's story because I was curious to see what sort of reaction a story about Husain and 'Abbas possessing a Hindu woman would provoke. Interestingly, my informant did not take issue with the idea that Husain or 'Abbas would *themselves* possess Maya, which would technically offend orthodox Muslim sensibilities. Rather, she took issue with the fact that Maya was Hindu. According to my informant, the problem had little to do with Hindu doctrine or religious practice; rather, she insisted that it had to do with the fact that Hindus have "dirty" bodies and therefore couldn't possibly be vehicles for Husain and 'Abbas. When I asked what she meant, she elaborated that on long bus trips, she had seen Hindus urinate on the side of the road and then simply stand up and go on their way, without using water to clean themselves afterward. Thus, Hindus were ritually impure and could not possibly serve as conduits for Husain and 'Abbas.

Finally, in addition to healers' bodies serving as the basis of their power both in their own eyes and the eyes of others, I also collected many other instances of individuals describing the superhuman transgressive acts of ḥāẓirī as evidence that the *pret* had to be real. One of the two young Punjabi women cited in the description of lobān in chapter 3, for example, once said to me that anyone who thought that those in ḥāẓirī were somehow faking it should try rolling around the rauẓa for hours, as she herself did as part of her ḥāẓirī, and learn for themselves that no one in her right mind could do such a thing. Similarly, a local schoolteacher once elaborated on a case of ḥāẓirī he witnessed in a daughter from a "good family" (again, this marker of status is not meaningful in the ḥāẓirī world). She bathed in and drank dirty water and claimed to have no memory of doing so once the bout of ḥāẓirī ended. The schoolteacher concluded that some of what happens in ḥāẓirī *had* to be real because no one in a normal state of consciousness could do what this woman had done.

I have suggested that ḥāẓirī is powerful and widespread because its violent, transgressive, frightening nature evidences the extreme purity (or, perhaps, potent pollutedness) of the body of the *ḥāẓirīwālī/ā* and because the fleeting and context-dependent justice it offers is culturally appropriate and therefore meaningful to its practitioners. However, my argument has yet to take into account pilgrims' own interpretations of the reasons for the practice's violent form. In order to understand pilgrims' own explanations of why the process of ḥāẓirī is time-consuming and painful, I thought it would be instructive to ask pilgrims why, if the saints are powerful enough to remove offending *pret,* those in ḥāẓirī have to endure so much time in exile and suffering. Why is justice not as simple as a prayer, exorcism, and vindication? If the saints are as powerful as everyone says, why the lengthy, messy, uncertain process of ḥāẓirī? In posing this series of questions, I also asked pilgrims to place the concept of *jādū* in conversation with either Muslim notions of free will or divine omniscience or Hindu notions of karma, since these are the systems that each tradition has generated to prevent the possibility of the suffering of innocents. As innocents *(ma'ṣūm),* why, I asked, do *ḥāẓirīwāle* suffer?

Not surprisingly, the reasons given for the suffering of the innocent *ḥāẓirīwāle* varied, and those that were not grounded in formal Islamic or Hindu theodicy centered on the capacities of the body itself. Farhat, one of the members of an extended Shi'a family that operates a Bombay-based Ḥusain Ṭekrī–affiliated public *imāmbāṛā,* offered this perspective. She herself did not suffer from ḥāẓirī, though she saw it every day and had two sisters with histories of ḥāẓirī, and as such she had thought about the process more than most nonsufferers. In the quotation below, the slowness of ḥāẓirī is deemed necessary because of the limitations of the body and the demands that are placed upon it.

> *Carla:* Before, you said that if Maulā ['Ali or 'Abbas] were to remove the magic from a person quickly, he or she would die?
>
> *Farhat:* You won't *die,* but you'll suffer a lot physically *(śarīr meṁ zyādā taklīf),* and it's for this reason that Maulā takes [the magic] out very slowly, so that the body doesn't suffer, and we can do our work, and take care of our families; [magic is removed slowly so that] we'll be able to bear it, and that thing [the magic] *will* come out, slowly.

In addition to being necessarily linked to the passage of time, ḥāẓirī is also conceptualized as a form of labor, specifically, as a time-consuming, physically demanding, accomplishment-oriented activity. Ideally, the work of ḥāẓirī ought not to interfere with the family-oriented work performed by women. Indeed, ḥāẓirī's purpose is to reestablish an individual's ability to perform family-sustaining work. A similar assumption is evident in a statement made by Farhat's brother-in-law Salim, who sells the usual assortment of offerings outside their *imāmbāṛā.* Salim once explained that it was much more common to see women at the *imāmbāṛā* because they could take the time to come and have ḥāẓirī. Unlike men, whose occupations often require being present at a job for a full day, women can leave home for a few hours to have *ḥāẓirī.* An unemployed man, he concluded, would be more likely to have ḥāẓirī than an employed one because it would not interfere with his work.[59]

In both of these statements there is also a sense that ḥāẓirī, as a process administered by Muslim saints, has a compassionate—even merciful—character: it is uniquely equipped to address the fundamentally unavoidable problems that arise from magic, and it is uniquely sensitive to the weaknesses and vulnerabilities of the human body and the varied labor demands that are placed on men and women. In fact, it is the obvious weakness and vulnerability of the human body that render theodicy-oriented questions meaningless; ḥāẓirī provides incontrovertible physical evidence that humans *can* and *do* manipulate circumstances to their advantage, and this has palpable effects on the frail human body. Therefore, asking why an all-powerful god or a powerful martyr cannot immediately remove an offending *pret* is nonsensical because the healing process is constrained by the limitations of the body.

On why magic happens in the first place and why innocent people suffer ḥāẓirī, Farhat offered this explanation: magic is equated with human nature, which is understood to tend strongly toward negative actions and emotions, chiefly, jealousy. In other words, there is an ideal way that the world should be, and magic interferes with that natural order. Without exception, pilgrims to Ḥusain Ṭekrī understood magic to be performed because of jealousy, so in this way Farhat's response is representative, though her subsequent discussion of conscience and divine will is more specifically Muslim and literate.

Carla: So why does magic *[jādū]* happen? Before I thought you said something about jealousy being a "fact of being human" *[insān kā fact]*.

Farhat: Right . . . [A person may think] they have a lot of money, and I should have money too; they have everything, and I have nothing; and because I have nothing, they shouldn't have good things either. And so people do magic. So it's not at all the case that God and Maulā command us to be jealous of things; they teach us a good path. But those who do magic, they understand that what they are doing is wrong, but still, because they are jealous, they do magic. And they'll be punished.

Carla: But does Maulā give them *permission* to do magic?

Farhat: *No!* He tells them what's right and what's wrong. But humans need to think for themselves—think about what is right and what is wrong—and they should recognize that magic is wrong. But they don't think like that, and they don't go on the right path. They do magic because of their own jealousy.

According to Farhat, the natural order of things is a moral code revealed by God: magic is a human-made deviation from that order. A similar, more textually based response to the same question was offered by Maulānā

'Abbas, who regularly led *majlis* at the Bombay *imāmbāṛā*. In keeping with the observations offered by Salim and Farhat, his explanations for why magic exists were grounded in the concepts of self-awareness and labor. He began, sermon-style, by citing examples of magic from the Qur'an, a common tactic of many Muslim Ḥusain Ṭekrī pilgrims who sought to explain magic to me:

> Moses had a staff—it was made of wood. He threw it on the ground. And he threw it on the ground to show Pharaoh that he was a messenger. When he let go of the stick, it became a snake, and the snake moved toward Pharaoh. So Pharaoh was afraid, and then Moses caught it and it became wood again. So Pharaoh said to his advisors, "That's really serious magic—let's call our magicians and compare them to him." So they called all their magicians, and then they called Moses back in. So Moses said, "Show me what kind of magic you can do." The magicians had all these little pieces of string, and when they released them they became snakes. So Moses threw down his staff, and it became a big snake that ate all the other snakes. So after that all the magicians recognized Moses, and they said that they now believed in [his] God. They declared their faith in Allah and became Muslims. But Pharaoh didn't believe and he had the magicians punished, tearing them apart. That's the story. But the Pharaoh *should* have believed in Moses when he saw the staff turn into a snake. It's important to realize that Moses had power, but Moses wasn't using magic—it was a miracle that had come from Allah—Allah had given him the power. And why? Because Allah knew that the Pharaoh had magicians, and that he would use them to fight. Isn't it true that the magicians used their magic in front of Moses, and this prompted him to use his miracle? [And wasn't it this miracle that led them to the truth?] So from this we can conclude that Allah never punishes people without giving them an opportunity to recognize the truth. Allah is all-powerful . . . Allah still has power today, just like then, but suppose there is a magician—he works his entire life studying magic. If Maulā doesn't allow him to use his magic, his study is useless.

Two elements of this story echo Farhat's ideas. First, the natural order of things is a divinely ordained moral order, and magic is thus a force that derives from people following their own will; it is unnatural in the sense that it is a deviation. This is why it was important to Maulānā 'Abbas to distinguish between Moses's action and that of the Pharaoh's magicians: they commanded power that deviated from God's will, whereas Moses's power was given by God and not something for which he labored. Second, there is a sense in this story that the magician is entitled to the fruits of his labor and that it is not the place of God to withhold the results of individual effort. Human labor *necessarily* produces results; this is not a moral issue, nor a process that requires a narrative explanation. Similarly, ḥāẓirī, by virtue of its character as time-consuming labor, will necessarily produce results.

The importance of making a clear distinction between divine will and human will is also why, at this point in his narrative, Maulānā 'Abbas paused to clarify the relationship between 'Ali, 'Abbas, and Allah—again, his explanation echoes Farhat's notion that deviation from divine order is what lies at the root of *all* problems, not only magic. The point here is that 'Ali and 'Abbas's power over magic is not magical power, but, like Moses, a miraculous power compliant with divine will. Maulānā 'Abbas continued:

> Maulā does what Allah wants, of course—that's also very important. What he wants and what Allah wants are the same. Maulā doesn't do things that he wants, but rather what Allah wants.

Having clarified this, Maulānā 'Abbas addressed the question of why innocent individuals suffer from magic by moving the conversation from an acknowledgement of cause and effect to an expansive moral narrative:

> Imagine that your clothing could talk—it would say, "Hey, you wore me, but then you washed me and dried me and put a really hot iron all over me—why did you do all this work? What did I do to deserve this treatment?" Now, that's just an example to make a point, but people are like clothes—Allah sends them into the world absolutely clean and without sin, but they get dirty as they get older—they might lie, or steal something—and each sin is a flaw. Allah loves his servants *[bande]*, and he wants to call them back to him. But when he calls us back, he wants us as clean as when he sent us into the world. In this world, whatever sin is committed is punished, and from punishment, the sin is erased. It's not possible for an innocent person to suffer from magic. *Ever.* So when people say that magic was done on the Prophet in his lifetime, that's not true. People only said that to give him a bad reputation.

This seems to conflict with one of the cornerstones of the ḥāẓirī process: *ḥāẓirīwāle* understand themselves to be innocent victims, as do their caretakers. However, while it is the case that men and upper-caste or upper-class individuals sometimes made the argument that people only fall victim to magic if they do not practice their religion properly, Maulānā 'Abbas had a different intention. Eventually, he put a finer point on his definition of "innocent," in part to clarify why it was not possible that the Prophet had been a victim of magic:

> It's human nature to know the business of others but not understand one's own nature. The prophet said that the person who has recognized *[pahcānā]* himself has recognized Allah. And when a person doesn't recognize himself, he doesn't understand if something is right or wrong. Because later, after making some mistake, when he's feeling regret, that's the proof that he didn't really know himself, or he wouldn't have made the mistake. That's the difference between an innocent person and a regular person—a truly innocent person understands

> himself completely, and therefore he can't possibly do anything wrong. Those who don't recognize themselves, *they* make mistakes.

This is a somewhat more sophisticated notion of "innocent" than the one in common usage at Ḥusain Ṭekrī, which simply holds that the *ḥāẓirīwālā* did nothing wrong and so does not deserve to suffer because of the jealousy-motivated magic of another. Based on his own sense of the word *innocent,* Maulānā 'Abbas maintained that there is no such thing as suffering that is not divinely sanctioned, suggesting, first, that even a generally moral, religiously observant person might still harbor some sins that need to be punished, and, second, that in some cases the suffering caused by magic functions as a test of faith. He concluded by summarizing these three potential reasons that a person might suffer from *jādū:* the amoral acknowledgment that any labor necessarily produces results, and the two morally oriented narratives that attribute suffering from magic to either a cleansing process or a divine test of faith. While the morally oriented narratives offered by Maulānā 'Abbas clearly—and, given his position as a representative of orthodoxy—predictably do not allow for meaningless suffering, his recognition of the amoral principle that all labor necessarily produces results is shared by ḥāẓirī practitioners, who implicitly and explicitly recognize that in addition to being an unequivocally moral discourse of justice and punishment, ḥāẓirī is also physical labor that counteracts the labor of magic.

In the Hindu context, the issue of ḥāẓirī's place in the larger order of things was once explained by Priya's mother in relation to fate *(qismat).* I asked her if magic was part of an individual's fate or interfered with it. She explained that as she understood it, fate is predetermined and moves with a person *(ātmā)* from one birth to the next. Magic, she clarified, only has an effect on one birth. She elaborated on this by saying that it was done on someone's name, which is in part chosen according to the time and place of one's birth as detailed in *kuṇḍalī,* or horoscopes, that Hindus commission on the birth of a child.[60] The interference of magic derives from explicitly commercial labor: jealousy may be the motivation, but jealousy alone will not destroy its intended victim. For this, money must be paid and magic must be enacted:

> Just like you and I study books, some people study magic *[tāntrik-vidyā];* and then, if they need money, they do magic, and they get paid.

Priya's explicit thoughts on magic and fate echoed those of her mother. An individual's fate can be good or bad, but it is not something that human efforts to perform magic ultimately can alter:

They study magic *[tāntrik-vidyā]*, and then, after they've learned it, they use it on people. So that means that magic is outside of fate *[qismat]*. If magic is done on someone's name, just as it's happened from my name, magic affects me. But slowly, its effect *[aṣar]* will extend to my whole family—because I talk with my family, slowly, it will affect them all . . . But I think my fate is good, because I came here. If my fate was bad, I wouldn't have come here, and I would have just wandered from one place to another.

In addition to corroborating the idea that the effects and eradication of magic as manifest in ḥāẓirī are a family-centered phenomenon, Priya's statements also affirm the notion that magic derives its power from human labor—in this case, study. Similarly, she uses the image of wandering to convey purposeless exertion; just as a *pret* wanders aimlessly, so a person with bad fate will futilely expend all his or her efforts.

When asked what controls fate, Priya simply replied *"ūparwālā,"* literally, "the one up there," a common expression for a very unspecific notion of some kind of divine overseer. On an abstract level, Priya and her mother seem to hold that magic is generated by and for humans, and that fate is a nonhuman momentum that moves an *ātmā* through one life and onto another. Like my Muslim informants, then, Priya and her mother regard *jādū* and ḥāẓirī as aberrations, ultimately incompatible with an orthodox Hindu or Muslim worldview.

This distinction between magic and fate extends to individuals' discussions of physical illness and healing. While some pilgrims make distinctions between physical and mental illnesses, they universally hold that an illness with a magical origin cannot be healed through human means, that is, through allopathy. In an interview with me, Safdar Rizvi, a New Delhi–based journalist and author of one of the most popular local guidebooks for Ḥusain Ṭekrī, explained the difference between magical and mundane illnesses:

AIIMS [is the] biggest hospital in India, very famous; I went there and tried to be healed *[ilāj karvāyā]*, and there was no use. So I went to Ḥusain Ṭekrī, and there I found relief *[fāydā]*. But the role of medical science is still very important. If you have an injury, you do everything you can to heal it. If there is no magic involved in the wound, medical science is sufficient. But, for example, you break your finger, medical science fixes it. If you break it again, it can be fixed again. But magic is just the sort of thing *[yantra]*, it's an instrument [English word used] that can really wreck things that have been caused to be made *[banvāyī cīz]*, and for this reason medical science is rendered completely useless. Otherwise, medical science is very powerful and sufficient.

There is a vital distinction between an illness with an ordinary physical cause and a physical illness with a magical cause. Yet again, magic is understood as a form of labor that has the capacity to counteract the mundane natural order of things, in this case, the expected efficacy of allopathic treatment.

In chapter 2 I introduced the various idioms, tropes, and narrative strategies adopted by four individuals in the course of their relationship with Ḥusain Ṭekrī. Besides introducing many of the major aspects of the ritual and social life of shrines, the primary goal of the chapter was to understand something of the process of healing at Ḥusain Ṭekrī as individual experiences are slowly incorporated into (and shaped by) the different narratives, idioms, and tropes that are available there. The chapter also demonstrated how these conventions allow pilgrims to come to terms with otherwise inexplicable or painful aspects of their lives. In chapters 3 and 4 I examined the nature, power, uses, and narratives attached to and generated by the major healing practices of Ḥusain Ṭekrī: the nonnarrative experiences of consuming of lobān, hanging onto *jālī,* bathing in dirty water, and binding the body with locks and chains, as well as the narrative-building practice of ḥāẓirī. Guiding both of these examinations has been the question of how each process works, with reference to both the physical experience of each of these practices and how pilgrims speak about these physical experiences.

Often, in order to understand why the narratives offered by pilgrims take the form that they do, I have contextualized them within major pan-Indian cultural systems, including magic *(jādū),* purity and pollution, notions of fate, and marriage in extended family situations. In the course of discussing both the unstated reasons for the efficacy of these activities, narratives, and actions and the reasons that are offered by pilgrims, chapters 2, 3, and 4 have also offered a picture of a pan-Indian understanding of the self, framed primarily in terms of health and illness. In part, I have shown that at Ḥusain Ṭekrī an individual's health is gauged by the extent to which he or she is able to perform his or her familial duties, whether that is earning money, providing a dowry, or having a son. Because the stated and operative purpose of all ritual life at Ḥusain Ṭekrī is to eradicate *jādū,* to heal sickness, and thereby restore broken families, it follows that sickness and magic often strike during fleeting moments of vulnerable isolation and subsequently cause long-term isolation and alienation from one's home and family.

Being alone, whether physically or psychologically, is regarded as dangerous. Recall, for example, the several instances mentioned in this book of individuals who became victims of magic or attacks by *jinn* when they were alone bathing or on their way to the bathroom. Attacks can also happen when traveling solo or when working alone in the fields. Similarly, sleeping by oneself in a private room is unheard of in all but upper-class Indian communities. With the exception of time spent in the bathroom, it is more or less impossible to be alone in working-class and middle-class urban India, and this may be why moments of bathing and of urinating or defecating are often cited as the times when a person is most susceptible to malign influences.

The danger, vulnerability, and illness-provoking potential of solitude is perhaps best evidenced by the cries of a woman whose particularly violent ḥāẓirī I witnessed at the rauẓas of ʿAbbas and Sakina. Her *pret* confessed that the magic that had been done on her was *tanhāī kā jādū* and *akelāpan kā jādū* (magic of loneliness). In other words, the intention of the magic was to place this young woman in complete isolation, which would lead to her eventual undoing.[61] Paradoxically, being alone is also popularly understood as the time when a person is most likely to experience divine revelation, and instances and consequences of this phenomenon, particularly as it relates to the stories of Ḥusain Ṭekrī's founding, are evident in the origin story found in Appendix B, in which a single village woman who goes out into the jungle alone witnesses the miraculous visitation of Husain. When people related this story to me, they often noted that this woman was going out to relieve herself. This detail, however, is omitted from written versions.

Thus far, I have sought to explain why it is that the various major ritual activities at Ḥusain Ṭekrī work as well as they do, offering a culturally grounded account of how Ḥusain Ṭekrī and dargāḥs like it function as effective cross-tradition places of healing. The focus of the following chapter shifts from individual experience and the use of rituals associated with dargāḥs to the communal narratives that are created about and within Ḥusain Ṭekrī, as well as how the communities that form there contribute to the healing processes of its pilgrims. Here, finally, the categories of Hindu, Muslim, Sikh, and Christian are operative, albeit in unexpected ways.

CHAPTER 5

Personae

Transgression, Otherness, Cosmopolitanism, and Kinship

Analysis of religious and caste identity in India is, to say the least, fraught: a colonial legacy, ongoing communal violence, and the tenor of some public conversations about terrorism have all contributed to an academic climate of concern, caution, and careful introspection. In response to this situation, some recent scholarship on South Asian religion has critically reexamined the categories of Hindu, Muslim, and Christian and suggested that they are neither fixed nor foundational elements of South Asian individuals' senses of self and community.[1] More generally, scholarship on Indian society and religion has long grappled with the question of the extent to which individual identity is shaped by group identity, and whether or not the relationship between individual and group identity differs in Indian and non-Indian contexts.[2] I have not yet related group identity or communalist discourses to pilgrims' experiences at Ḥusain Ṭekrī in part because, as I have argued in preceding chapters, there is no consistent correlation between religious or caste identity and the ways in which the major ritual activities of Ḥusain Ṭekrī are practiced and understood. Pilgrims engage in the same practices regardless of background, and members of all communities exhibit a similar range of understandings about the efficacy of these practices. In fact, as chapters 3 and 4 in particular have shown, Ḥusain Ṭekrī's major ritual activities have a strong dissociative effect on their practitioners, in which the physical and mental identities of the individual are either effaced (as in the consumption of lobān) or fragmented (as in the practice of *khulī ḥāẓirī*). Further, I have suggested that pilgrims at Ḥusain

Ṭekrī overwhelmingly experience ḥāẓirī as an existential and liminal state; to be a *ḥāẓirīwālā/ī* is to exist apart—to be fundamentally unable to meet familial obligations or participate in orthodox, institutional religious life.

At the same time, however, it is clear that during their time at Ḥusain Ṭekrī and thereafter, pilgrims create, participate in, and strategically deploy a range of community identities and communalist discourses. Among these, the most common are those that articulate explicit religious identities and those grounded in the language of devotion and family. While these notions of group identity do not significantly shape pilgrims' perspectives on lobān, ḥāẓirī, and other healing practices common at Ḥusain Ṭekrī, they are essential elements of pilgrims' narratively expressed understandings of how magic is performed and, by extension, how healing occurs. Identifying the role of community identity and communalist discourse at Ḥusain Ṭekrī is the final necessary step in understanding how it functions as a successful place of healing. However, as is commonly the case in cosmopolitan cultures, at Ḥusain Ṭekrī the meaning and meaningfulness of different community identities varies according to context, making it impossible to argue that one group or community identity or another is universally meaningful or consistently operative. Therefore, using any of the range of common subcontinental community identities—for example, religion, caste, or class—as categories of analysis is potentially misleading or, at the very least, confusing and unnecessarily complicated, since these common categories presume a level of consistency that is simply not present in the ways they are used by pilgrims at Ḥusain Ṭekrī.

What *is* consistent at Ḥusain Ṭekrī is the utility of a basic notion of otherness: in different ways, otherness is a foundational concept in conceptualizations of both illness and healing. This category of otherness is manifest in two broad types of communities that I have termed "imagined" and "actual." The term "imagined communities" was coined by anthropologist Benedict Anderson to describe new conceptions of nation as they emerged in the formerly colonized world. In my usage, which differs from that of Anderson, imagined communities are those that afford pilgrims the opportunity to narrativize their current situations in relation to "others" without sustained, personal contact with members of that community. Actual communities are those that are created and sustained through self-conscious personal contact with others, including members of a community that is marked as "other" in terms of religion, caste, or class.[3] Because these categories are defined according to function, any of the major sources of community identity in South Asia—religion, caste, and class—can and do fall into either of these categories, depending upon the context.[4] At Ḥusain

Ṭekrī, all other means of creating group identities can be placed in one of these two categories.

At Ḥusain Ṭekrī, imagined communities are often described in terms of "Hindu," "Muslim," and "Christian"—in other words, the "imagined" communities are often religious ones.[5] Media of all types—television, films, radio, and books—greatly contribute to the development of imagined communities, which are used in both narratives of affliction (in particular, stories about *jādū*, or magic) and narratives of healing. Actual communities, on the other hand, are less dependent upon dualism (i.e., Hindu versus Muslim) and are instead conceptualized within discourses of devotion and family. In general, at Ḥusain Ṭekrī explicit sectarian religious identities are most present in the healing narratives and processes of pilgrims when they are being used rhetorically, to make a point about community, politics, or cosmology, while devotional and family-based idioms are used to name, experience, and build relationships that pilgrims actively cultivate. Even these tendencies are not, of course, completely consistent, and I will discuss exceptions as they occur.

Pilgrims' experience of otherness on both an imagined and actual level is a necessary part of the healing process. Returning to the larger foundational question of why Muslim saint shrines in particular have such a pronounced cross-tradition reputation for healing, it is significant that Muslim saint shrines are places in which both kinds of "other" communities—the imagined and the actual—function in a simultaneous and mutually influential manner. On a practical level, this is due in part to the fact that in India, Muslim saint shrines are the only religious places—and arguably, one of the only places—that afford men and women of all religious backgrounds, castes, classes, and ages the opportunity to mingle in a relatively unregulated fashion. This situation is attributable to two related factors. First, unlike major temples and mosques, Muslim saint shrines are officially open to everyone, irrespective of caste, gender, and religion. Thus, everyone can visit.[6] Second, Muslims have no reason to visit Hindu temples, and indeed, in my experience, it is a commonplace of Indian Islamic culture that a building that contains images of deities is not an appropriate destination for the offering of prayers or vows. However, the reverse is not true: Hindus of all types, as well as Adivasi and other non-Hindu populations, are not subject to explicitly stated doctrinal injunctions against visiting nontemple environments to offer prayers or vows.[7] These two general facts together form the conditions necessary for the diversity of pilgrims at Muslim saint shrines.

Further, if this official—and, in my experience, actual—openness of Muslim saint shrines is coupled with the fact that some of these shrines attract large nonlocal populations of pilgrims, it is clear that some Muslim shrines offer an opportunity for anonymity unparalleled in South Asian culture, and this anonymity allows for freer interaction between (and the creation of) imagined and actual communities. Additionally, the endless network of Muslim saint shrines affords pilgrims the possibility of moving on and continuing their healing process anonymously in a new place, should personal relations at one shrine deteriorate to the point that it becomes necessary to leave. As I have already discussed, the interchangeability of Muslim saints gives pilgrims the option of creating a healing program that is sensitive to familial and other personal responsibilities and constraints.[8]

Muslim shrines afford pilgrims an opportunity to craft an individual identity independent from group affiliation that is unparalleled in any environment other than, perhaps, modern Western cities. Even in these cities, this freedom is very much the privilege of the middle and upper classes, whereas at Indian Muslim saint shrines, poor and working-class individuals are equally able to function autonomously and anonymously. In other words, though Ḥusain Ṭekrī may initially strike many of its pilgrims (and, perhaps, its researcher) as being at the absolute end of the earth, by virtue of the diversity of its pilgrim population and the anonymity that they enjoy, it is in reality a profoundly cosmopolitan island in rural Madhya Pradesh, and it therefore offers pilgrims a unique opportunity to develop a self-understanding that is not fundamentally rooted in class, family of origin, *jāti,* or orthodox religious institutions. Of course, I am not arguing that these factors cease to exist or cease to exercise a certain influence; rather, I am simply suggesting that these factors become less influential when a pilgrim is removed from his or her home. In what follows, I will use the categories of otherness and imagined/actual communities to elucidate the healing process at Ḥusain Ṭekrī and the cross-tradition appeal of Muslim saint shrines in general. I will suggest that by virtue of their anonymity, cosmopolitanism, and otherness-centered culture, Ḥusain Ṭekrī and similar Indian Muslim saint shrines are environments uniquely equipped to allow for the simultaneous, mutually influential development of various imagined and actual communities, and that this capacity is a significant aspect of pilgrims' healing processes.

Rumor is a major medium for the construction of imagined communities. Rumor-stories about imagined communities, which are usually couched in religious language, form a necessary half of the dialectic operative in healing processes as they take place at Ḥusain Ṭekrī: in order for the formation of actual relationships with the other to have a powerful effect—that is, to create the experience of becoming more than one's caste-

and religion-based identity—it is necessary to develop personal relationships with members of a community that, on the level of rumor, has a dangerous or transgressive character.[9]

Incorporating rumor into academic analysis is challenging; it lacks ritual, definitive texts, institutions, an explicitly defined community, and official caretakers. In substance, it is often morally suspect or even xenophobic and dangerous, and thus it perhaps does not bear repeating. It is exceedingly difficult to "collect," since it is offered at unexpected and unguarded moments, and it cannot be elicited though direct questions or interviews. It is also inconsistently maintained. Informants may share a rumor one day and not remember it when the researcher brings it up weeks or months later. They may deny having made an earlier statement because they have genuinely forgotten about it, or because they do not wish to be represented as a person with irrational or discriminatory beliefs.[10]

In public, governmental, and "on the record" discourse, refutation of xenophobic rumors rarely involves restating the rumor. Thus, for example, a rickshaw may bear the slogan *"ham sab ek haiṁ"* (we are all one), and Indian citizens and politicians alike will point with pride to the fact that the constitution of India was written by an "untouchable." Both of these attempts to repudiate caste- or religion-based forms of xenophobia, discrimination, and violence do not actively engage the language of purity, pollution, or spiritual danger, but the discriminatory structures that they condemn are fueled by narratives and rumors founded on these very concepts. Political efforts to eradicate caste-, religion-, and gender-based discrimination and violence necessarily engage with institutions such as law and caste, but they cannot engage with the narratives and ideas that circulate in the form of rumors. Rumor, owing to its ephemeral form and its assumptions about the less-than-human nature of other communities, seems impossible to engage, and yet it remains a major force in contemporary Indian attitudes towards caste-, religion- and gender-based difference. It is, in other words, a major element in the construction of otherness.

In the following stories and anecdotes, most collected during my time at Ḥusain Ṭekrī, the other is dangerous, transgressive, and, most significantly, in some cases, not properly human insofar as the other is conceived of as incapable of proper care of both living bodies and corpses.[11] While clearly in conversation with the more general standardized structures of caste and purity and pollution, these rumor-stories reflect attitudes that have not been systematized or made into concrete social systems or cultural products. Rather, these are ideas and attitudes that float through the air like so many *bhūt-pret,* possessing vulnerable individuals and manipulated by magician-politicians. Like *bhūt-pret,* rumor has bona fide negative effects and human origins but no corporeal presence.

Rumor is difficult to capture. Often, when people made such statements, my minidisc recorder was not on, and attempting to gain permission to record the conversation and set up the recorder would have been an absurd exercise in breaking the flow of the conversation. All of the following examples of rumor are based on descriptions I wrote my field notes after the fact. Dates of the original declarations are provided in the notes. In reproducing these rumors as re-created direct speech, I believe I come closer to depicting their nature and influence than if I were to relate them in my own academic prose. They are not presented in any particular order.

A Muslim man: I once knew this man who moved from Pakistan to Canada to be with his son. When it got to be winter there, he was excited to see the snow. One day, though, he asked his son what they did about burying bodies in the winter, and as a joke, his son said to him that they just kept all the bodies in the hospital for six months, waiting for spring. His son was just joking, but the man got really upset and eventually he got so sick that they sent him back to Pakistan. His family there placed him under the care of a psychologist. When he explained that he was horrified by the idea that a dead body would just be kept in the hospital for six months, the psychologist was able to convince him that his son had just been joking. After a while, the man got better.[12]

A Hindu Brahmin woman: Don't go to the Bohra neighborhood by yourself![13] They all live together with all those narrow alleys so that they can trap others and drag them down into a network of tunnels under their houses. Down there, no one can hear you scream, and they'll chop you up and share the meat with one another and eat it.[14]

Sunni Muslim woman: Hindus are dirty because they drink cow urine. Our Prophet taught us the right way to live—we aren't supposed to put dirty things in our bodies, like alcohol.[15]

A Jain woman, in front of her two young daughters: No, I've never been to Ḥusain Ṭekrī, even though it's nearby. I'm afraid of Muslims.[16]

A Shi'a cleric of Indian origin who had been trained in Iran: My faith wasn't really firm until I came to Ḥusain Ṭekrī and saw non-Muslims benefiting from being here. In response to your question about whether or not there is magic in Iran, I would say that in India there are polytheists and it's also very easy to find alcohol, whereas in Iran, you could search with a sieve and still not find any.[17]

Hindu woman: You know, when Muslims die, they become *bhūt.* That's why I'm here: our house was haunted by the spirit of a dead Muslim girl.

Second woman: That's right. When Muslims die, they become *bhūt.*

Young man of indeterminate religious background: No they don't! What are you talking about?[18]

Hindu woman: If I'm healed at Ḥusain Ṭekrī, I've made a vow that I'll start wearing a cross.

Shi'a woman: No, no: the difference between Christians and Muslims is that Christians think Jesus was God and Muslims recognize him as a prophet.

Hindu woman: Right, okay. I'll wear a cross if my prayer is answered here.[19]

Shi'a woman: [to me] You, come over here—further. Okay, now listen. I saw you talking with those Hindus and I wanted to tell you that I'm a Sayyid, and because I'm a Sayyid, I could never sit down and eat with Hindus. I may be poor, but I'm a Sayyid.[20]

Muslim woman: The reason that *bhūt* and magicians can possess Hindus is because Hindus exist in an impure state.[21]

Hindu woman: [to me] The [Hindu] owners of our lodge have said we can't have you as a guest in our room anymore; they're afraid that you're gathering information to take their land away. And also, some people are saying that you are going to steal the power of Ḥusain Ṭekrī like the British stole from India, because you are working for the American government. Also, they say you are doing *jādū*.[22]

Shi'a woman from Bhopal: It's the Sunnis who killed Husain, and they only call on him when they're in trouble. Otherwise, they don't care about him.[23]

Sunni woman from Jaipur: [observing a Shi'a procession and mātam session] They're beating themselves like that because they are trying to tell Maulā ['Ali] that they are sorry for killing Husain. They killed Husain, and when they beat themselves, they're saying they're sorry.[24]

Sunni Muslim man: [laughing, in reference to a Hindu man who had just left] He's a very good friend of mine, and he always comes here on 'Id to have some *khīr* [rice pudding], but you can see that he didn't eat very much because he's worried that the dish we used to serve the *khīr* once contained beef and might still contain traces of beef.[25]

In addition to these subcontinentally generated rumors, pilgrims at Ḥusain Ṭekrī also commonly cited various television documentaries to support their arguments that certain groups in Indian (and global) society were particularly responsible for much magic. American and British documentaries (usually on the Discovery and National Geographic channels) on Haitian Vodou and African religions were often mentioned, as were Indian-made documentaries on the practices of the Aghori, a group whose Tantric ritual practices are popularly understood to include frequenting cremation grounds, collecting human bones and ashes, and eating human remains. Television shows that document supernatural events, which are increasingly popular, were also cited.[26]

Often the magician named in bouts of *khulī ḥāẓirī* is identified as a practitioner of Tantra or a member of the so-called "untouchable" *jāti*s. In both cases, magical abilities are in part equated with bodies that are transgressive and polluted.[27] Thus, as in everyday Indian society, so too in the society of *ḥāẓirīwāle:* an improperly maintained body, living or dead, is a potential source of corruption and danger. The husband of a Shi'a woman who had a "seven- or eight-year" relationship with Ḥusain Ṭekrī provided further evidence of the belief in the inherently dangerous nature of the souls of members of other religious communities. The attitude of this Shi'a man about the dead of other religious communities was also reflected in other conversations I had over the course of my fieldwork. In his description of the nature of magic, this man explained his own invulnerability to the wiles of magicians:

Shi'a man I read *namāz* regularly, and so magicians can't take my soul after I die.

Carla: But Hindus don't read *namāz.*

Shi'a man: That's right, and so it's no problem for a magician to capture their soul after they die.

While belief in the menace of the bodies and spirits of religious others is common, over my time at Ḥusain Ṭekrī I also encountered some Muslims who suggested that Hindus who observed their religion properly would also be protected from the machinations of magicians. Once, for example, I heard a Shi'a healer from Kashmir (Srinagar) who regularly visits Ḥusain Ṭekrī reprimanding a Hindu woman for not maintaining a regular regimen of goddess worship. He explained that if she had performed *pūjā* regularly, she would not have become afflicted by a *pret.*

On the whole, however, the attitude about members of other religious communities reflected in the quotation above was more common. In this case, the Shi'a man had come to Ḥusain Ṭekrī with his wife, whose story also reflects a fear of the dead of another community, in this case, Christian. While the portion of her story presented here focuses on an earlier set of problems, it is worth noting that she felt that she had made an almost complete recovery because she had successfully married and had a child; in her words, she had finally achieved a normal life. As usual, recovery is equated with social integration. In the following excerpt from a much longer interview, the wife, whom I will call Halima, discusses the nature of the magic that caused her ḥāẓirī.

Halima: My aunt took a *ta'vīẕ* and buried it in a Christian graveyard . . . and so I fell under the influence of this spell . . . One day, I saw this man, wearing pants and a shirt and a black hat—I saw him the same way I can see you sitting in front of me: he was really there.

Carla: How old were you when all this started?

Halima: I must have been twenty-one. So I saw this man and I thought to myself, "Who's that?" And then this man came and he stood in front of me and he said, "Hello." So I ran away and I said to my mother, "I saw this man standing in front of me, with pants and a shirt and a hat—a Dracula-type man—he looked just like Dracula."[28] My mother said that I was crazy and that I hadn't seen anything. Then I went to sleep and had a dream. In the dream I saw lots and lots of white *[aṁgrez]* girls[29]—girls and boys—and I was dancing in the middle of them . . . and when I woke up, I decided that Christian people were the best. I told my mother that Christian people were the best, and they were like this and they were like that, and so on. What it meant was I wanted to break with my own people. And the thing that was put on me, well, it was Christian, wasn't it? And so it was decided that I should come here, though at that point no one suspected that magic had been done.

Carla: If you didn't know it was magic, why did you know to come to Ḥusain Ṭekrī?

Halima: Ever since I was a little girl I've had health problems, but no matter what I did, the doctors couldn't find any cause for my problems—I had x-rays, ultrasounds, everything, and no one could say what was wrong. They would say I was fine, but I was in so much pain . . . I had a cousin who said that I should go to Ḥusain Ṭekrī . . . My mother prayed *namāz* every day, and she prayed *[duā karnā]* that I would get better, but I remained sick. One night I had a dream where a veiled woman came to me and said, "Come to Ḥusain Ṭekrī." [. . .][30] And so I told my mother about it, and we came here. But I didn't tie a string on the rauẓas, like most people do. My mother went and prayed by the standard of ʿAbbas here at Ḥusain Ṭekrī [at the rauẓa of ʿAbbas], and after she prayed, I started to have ḥāẓirī.[31] During ḥāẓirī, everyone who had hurt me—my aunt, my cousins, and the magician who was hired—all of them became present and confessed to what they had done to me.[32]

In the comments of Halima and her husband, it is clear that the spirits of the dead of other communities are dangerous: the *taʿvīẕ* is buried in a Christian cemetery, the subsequent spiritual threat is a Christian one, and the nature of the magic is to disassociate this young woman from her own (Shiʿa) community.[33] Similarly, the husband explicitly states that the spirits of practicing Muslims cannot be manipulated after death, but those of Hindus are vulnerable.

Most of these rumors and stories turn on notions of others who cause serious or fatal bodily harm, others who do not maintain their own bodies properly, or others who do not treat the bodies of the dead properly. Because others fail to dispose of bodies in a nonpolluting manner, their *pret* become a particular threat to the world of the living. In addition to the universally held notion that spirits of those who have died violent or untimely deaths can be captured and manipulated by magicians, among pilgrims at Ḥusain Ṭekrī there is also a pronounced, though not universal, tendency to regard the spirits of the dead of other communities as dangerous.

The logic underlying this tendency is clear enough: if it is universally held that the *ātmā* or *rūḥ* of those who have died untimely or particularly violent deaths wander the earth until they are captured and used by magicians, it follows that the *rūḥ* or *ātmā* of a body that has not been disposed of properly will also be subject to wandering and eventual capture by a magician. Thus, the dead of other religious communities are potentially much more dangerous than the dead of one's own community. This belief is not explicitly stated very often, but it seems to drive many of the above comments, and it is an inevitable consequence of belief systems that hold that certain things must be done to ensure that the *ātmā* or *rūḥ* of an individual moves on to its proper location after death.

In fact, in all my years of research at Ḥusain Ṭekrī, the *only* completely consistently held belief I found was that a lack of ritual purity can instigate or sustain the problems that result in ḥāẓirī. On this very basic level, then, other religious communities have a danger and menace about them.[34] These rumors also suggest that some of the most dangerous others are the *aṁgrez,* or "white," non-Indians: the girls who haunt the young woman in her dreams are *aṁgrez,* and it is in an *aṁgrez* hospital in the *aṁgrez* country of Canada that corpses are potentially treated in a profoundly inappropriate manner. Similarly, because I am an *aṁgrez,* some people at Ḥusain Ṭekrī saw me as a threat to the power of the place.

It is impossible to prove that this attitude about the dangerousness of other communities is consistently held by all Indians, or even by all pilgrims to Muslim saint shrines. As the examples above suggest, however, it is clearly in the air, and the simple fact of the existence of this attitude is foundational to what I am arguing. Because each community is aware that other communities are held by some to be dangerous, it follows that even if an individual does not consistently or actively believe that others are "dirty" or dangerous, because such rumors and attitudes are in wide circulation, developing a relationship with members of other religious traditions is always a transgressive act.[35]

As this relates to their healing process, pilgrims at Ḥusain Ṭekrī endure the physical experience of being tormented by a *pret* that might have its origin in another religious community while simultaneously forming personal relationships with members of other communities. This is a powerful physical, intellectual, and emotional experience: to suffer bodily torment in ḥāẓirī, which is widely understood to be caused by transgressive others, while at the same time sharing narratives, meals, rituals, healing processes, lodges, taxis to nearby shrines, bathing facilities, and friendships with members of these very communities. Earlier I suggested that by coming to Ḥusain Ṭekrī pilgrims have the opportunity to become something more than their caste-, *jāti*-, and class-based identities. Here I suggest that as part of this process, individuals in ḥāẓirī have an opportunity to physically and self-consciously experience overcoming all that is potentially wrong or out of place in society as their bodies are invaded by *pret* associated with transgressive others or simply *pret* associated with transgression. On an undeniable, painful, physical level, for the *ḥāzirīwālī,* these forces are real and deeply dangerous. As the pilgrim's body lives every moment with unarticulatable knowledge of the power of these transgressive (and therefore dangerous) forces, the pilgrim wills, chooses, and experiences relationships of all kinds with members of other communities. As a result of these two processes, if a pilgrim at Ḥusain Ṭekrī is healed, otherness, with its inherently transgressive nature, is doubly defeated: it is physically fought with and destroyed in the body, and it is intellectually and emotionally erased in the many cross-tradition friendships (and occasional marriages) that develop at the shrines themselves. While social integration and reunion with one's one familial, caste, and religious community is the measure of healing, in the process of recovery, the healed individual has become something more than a narrowly social being.

On the one hand, otherness, conceived of as religion, caste, or race, is the source of all that is out of place, debased, and potentially dangerous. On the other hand, the language of religious otherness at Ḥusain Ṭekrī is also part of the healing process. What this means, in part, is that the attractiveness of Ḥusain Ṭekrī and similar Muslim saint shrines for Hindus derives from these shrines' explicit Islamic identity. While dargāḥs' sources of authority are subcontinental and multivalent, their *identity* is explicitly Islamic, and in recent years this Islamic identity has become increasingly communalist and exclusive in tone. Dominque-Sila Khan, for example, has documented the increasing tendency to mark roadside and other minor shrines as Hindu or Muslim, most dramatically in the shift from whitewash to brilliant green or saffron paint, with accompanying banners in similarly lurid tones.[36] The construction of a massive new mosque at Ḥusain Ṭekrī is also a testament to this trend: the minarets of the Sunni mosque tower emphatically over the domes of the rauẓas. Now, as a pilgrim's tonga or rickshaw rolls through the farmland that surrounds Ḥusain Ṭekrī, there is no doubt that he or she is approaching a Muslim place.

Khan regards these changes to dargāḥ life as necessarily communalist and exclusionary, and certainly this is part of the picture. At Ḥusain Ṭekrī, for example, a habitually cantankerous low-caste Hindu (Telī) lodge owner responded to my questions about Ḥusain Ṭekrī with anger, saying he had nothing to do with "Urdu matters" *(māmle)*. Commonly, "Urdu" is used to refer to anything written in derivations of Perso-Arabic script. In popular religion the script itself is understood to have powerful properties, and anything on which it is written immediately acquires new authority and an Islamic sheen if not identity.[37] While this lodge owner's statement may seem aggressively communal, upon further conversation it became clear that he was reacting to the explicit Islamization of Ḥusain Ṭekrī, and thus the seizure of a shrine that had once been as much Telī as Muslim. As evidence of what he regarded as a hostile, politicized takeover of Ḥusain Ṭekrī, he cited the Urdu- and Arabic-inscribed archway that had recently been built over the main road leading to the rauẓas. He also asserted that formerly the rauẓas were referred to simply as the "big" and "little" rauẓa, whereas now they are also referred to as the rauẓas of Imām Husain and Ḥaẓrat 'Abbas. His claim is corroborated by Maya's discussion of Ḥusain Ṭekrī, which draws on experience from many years ago and tends to describe the rauẓas as "big" and "little." Such feelings of alienation aside, I suggest that the explicit and pronounced identity of dargāḥs as Islamic is part of what makes them attractive to Hindu pilgrims.

Several arguments have been advanced to explain the nature of the Hindus' attraction to the explicitly Islamic identity of Muslim saint shrines. Gottschalk has demonstrated that Muslim saints are understood to have jurisdiction and power over Muslim *pret*,[38] and van der Veer has speculated that Muslim shrines are considered "dirty" by Hindus and therefore well equipped to deal with "dirty" spirits.[39] Flueckiger has suggested that the written aspect of some Islamic healers' practices makes them particularly attractive, though her text also emphasizes the importance of gender as a determining factor in an individual's choice of healers.[40] These reasons are represented in the attitudes and statements of some pilgrims at Ḥusain Ṭekrī and its satellite sites. Along these lines, for example, a Hindu family that had come to Ḥusain Ṭekrī after repeated attempts to heal their daughter through petitions to various goddesses explained that they had finally come to Ḥusain Ṭekrī because there was nothing in their daughter's *kuṇḍalī* (horoscope) that would indicate that she was destined to endure such suffering. They elaborated by saying that there was no explanation for her troubles other than the possibility that something from the "air" had attached itself to her, and for such problems it was necessary to come to a dargāḥ. *Pret* are universally understood to float through the air, which again points to the notion that the spirits of other communities' dead, who would by definition be doomed to a life of wandering, are especially threatening.[41] This is not quite the same thing as suggesting that Muslim saints are uniquely equipped to deal with *pret* problems because they are dirty or because Muslim *pret* are under their jurisdiction; rather, it simply indicates that the troubles being experienced by this young woman were more or less inexplicable within an orthodox, regulated Hindu context, and therefore needed to be addressed in a context that was clearly "not Hindu."

In addition to these reasons for Hindu attraction to Muslim religious spaces, Muslim saint shrines' explicit and even communal Islamic identity may be particularly appealing to Hindu women. Because most women in South Asia consider religious and family life to be inextricably linked, if it becomes necessary to solve a family-related problem, seeking help at an explicitly Hindu place may be unappealing, impossible, or ineffectual. That is, if a woman feels significant estrangement from her family (which is almost universally the case among female sufferers of ḥāẓirī), because of the linkage between family and religion, she will feel estrangement from Hindu places. In the following excerpts from an interview with a young Hindu woman from Jaipur who often lived at Ḥusain Ṭekrī, the attractiveness of particularly Muslim places of pilgrimage to Hindu women is particularly evident. This woman's explicit evaluation of her situation is mirrored in the stories and actions of many Hindu women I interviewed at Ḥusain Ṭekrī.

Sunila is a woman in her thirties who identified herself as an "Udichi Brahmin," specifically, the daughter of a *pujārī* (priest) at a Jaipur-based Ganesh temple.[42] In a lengthy interview she described her situation and her ten-year relationship with Ḥusain Ṭekrī. Sunila emphasized that the site was responsible for her recovery to date. Specifically, she attributed her continued recovery to an exceptionally grueling regimen of dietary restrictions and physical labor. She was convinced that by eating husked *mūṁg kī dāl* (a particular lentil preparation) once a day and sweeping the road that connects the rauẓas, she was slowly making progress.

To explain the benefit of and need for this regimen, she said that what would have been revealed in her *khulī ḥāẓirī* was so awful that she suffered with *gum ḥāẓirī* instead. Specifically, she remarked that Maulā had told her that she would never be given *khulī ḥāẓirī* because the magic that had done on her had been "naked magic," and that if she were to be given *khulī ḥāẓirī*, she would be given the command to remove all her clothes, which would be unacceptable. Sunila's statement suggests that forcing a *pret* to act out the nature of the magic performed is part of the process of offering a confession and possibly also part of the *pret*'s punishment. The magic that is performed on the victim is effectively reperformed on the *pret* through the body of the victim.

Eventually Sunila found that she could not bear the strain of *gum ḥāẓirī*, and so she told Maulā that she needed relief. Sunila explained that Maulā responded by giving her a command to sweep the road, and Sunila claimed that as long as she does the work she does not suffer physically. She elaborated:

> I've still got *gum ḥāẓirī* going on inside of me, but I don't have pain anymore. If you have *gum ḥāẓirī* but you don't sweep or do some kind of work, then you'll have a lot of pain. Why? Because people who don't do work for Maulā ['Ali] are the ones who suffer pain.

In keeping with general attitudes at Ḥusain Ṭekrī, Sunila regards *khulī ḥāẓirī* as hard labor, making the labor involved in sweeping the street an effective substitute. In the case of *khulī ḥāẓirī*, efficacy derives in part from the corporal punishment that the body of the *ḥāẓirīwālī/ā* is forced to bear; in the case of sweeping the road, Sunila claimed that the power of the *pret* dissipates into the garbage that she sweeps.

Further substantiating an equivalence of the labor of sweeping and the labor of *khulī ḥāẓirī*, Sunila maintained that as she sweeps the spirit that torments her suffers, in part because she performs this activity on an empty stomach:

> I go along, sweeping on an empty stomach. And when I go on like that, sweeping while I'm hungry, the *pret* is beaten and punished. And his effect on me is removed, and his strength fades.

Sunila also maintained this austere diet because she found that eating any food that caused her blood to "increase" actually caused her possessing *pret* to thrive, because, she explained, they feed on her blood. She described a situation that took place two years earlier, when she went home to study for an exam related to her career as a schoolteacher. During this time she took to drinking tea and eating tomatoes, and she accepted papaya from her father. (Papaya in particular is widely understood to make blood.) Sunila explained that when she ate this food the *pret* became stronger because it had blood to drink again, and it was once more able to torment her with what she described as "*sex kī ḥāẓirī*."[43] Many individuals in ḥāẓirī engage in actions that mimic aspects of the act of intercourse, so it is possible that

Sunila's exceptionally open statements about the violating sexual nature of her possessing *pret*'s actions are shared by some who suffer in *khulī ḥāẓirī*. In any case, Sunila found the combination of reducing her body and performing polluting labor as effective as *khulī ḥāẓirī* in lessening the hold of the *pret* on her body.[44]

Thus far Sunila's story fits within the broad parameters of the process of ḥāẓirī at Ḥusain Ṭekrī. Also typically, Sunila explained that the magic that had been done on her had been performed by an uncle for the usual reason: to create unrest in the family. Her uncle hoped that her father, the eldest brother in the family, would expend all his resources trying to solve the problem and finally have no choice but to turn the temple over to her uncle. In a dramatic and explicit way, then, Sunila's family life and her religious identity are inextricably linked. Thus, when problems erupted in her family, it would have been ineffectual to pursue a solution within Hindu rituals or spaces. When explicitly asked why she did not seek a solution in a temple, Sunila replied:

> I've run all the way from the temple *[mandir]* to the mosque *[masjid]*. I was born at a pilgrimage center, in the midst of consecrated temple images of gods *[mūrti]*, the daughter of a *pujarī*. I lived in a temple, but because of this suffering I've come from the temple to the mosque. In the very temple where I grew up my uncle had magic done, and in order to rid myself of this magic, I've come all the way to the mosque. And in doing this I've improved, though I'm not completely recovered yet.[45] But I have hope that I will recover completely.[46]

Strictly speaking, Ḥusain Ṭekrī and similar Muslim saint shrines are not mosques; it seems that Sunila uses the terms *temple* and *mosque* rhetorically to represent two different religious communities. As is vividly illustrated in Sunila's case, for Hindu women, religious life is dramatically inseparable from family life, and specifically the roles of mother, sister, and/or wife.[47] If serious problems erupt in a familial context, a young woman may find herself so fundamentally alienated from her own religious tradition that she will feel she has no choice but to seek a remedy elsewhere. If this is the case, it seems that unless a dargāḥ's management aggressively enforces exclusion of Hindus, the more explicit and even communal the Islamic identity of the shrine, the greater its potential appeal to non-Muslim women.

This equation of religious and family life is not experienced exclusively by women, though women, because they often lack the ability to support themselves or to live in or near their natal home indefinitely, are more likely to equate the two than Hindu men. Still, many non-Muslim men are also resident at Ḥusain Ṭekrī, and in my experience their choice to come to a

Muslim saint shrine also depended in part on feeling alienated from their families and, in turn, alienated from the greater Hindu tradition. The case of a young Hindu Rajasthani man with ḥāẓirī who had come to Ḥusain Ṭekrī with several female relatives contains elements of the various stories related above while also containing characteristics that reflect his *jāti* and the fact that Ḥusain Ṭekrī, itself very near the Rajasthani border, participates in Rajput/Marwari/Mewari cultural conceits. His case further substantiates my claim that unambiguous communal Islamic identity has particular appeal to non-Muslims.

This man and his female family members explained that they were from an oft-touristed town in Rajasthan that is home to a famous goddess temple populated by a thriving rat population.[48] They explained that this goddess is their *būā,* or paternal aunt, and that all the rats in the temple will eventually be reincarnated as members of their *jāti.* On the subject of this goddess (their *kuldevī*), one afternoon, while we were sitting in the courtyard of the rauẓa of Fatima waiting for lobān, this man asked me if I knew the name of the large bird of prey that was circling in the sky above the rauẓa. I correctly identified the bird as a *cīl* (kite), which delighted them; they explained to me that their *kuldevī* sometimes took the form of a *cīl.* At the mention of their *kuldevī,* I asked them why, if their *kuldevī* was as beloved and powerful as they claimed, she was unable to help them. His wife explained that the man had become lazy in performing *pūjā* to their *kuldevī,* and as a result he had been stricken by something from the air and become truly helpless. Her meaning was, I gathered, that because the man had not met his kinship-based obligations to the goddess, the goddess had ceased to protect him and he had become vulnerable to random wandering spirits. However, despite their current state of alienation, they explained that they when they go to the rauẓas they burn incense (sticks, not lobān) as an offering to their *kuldevī* in an effort to maintain peace with her, and perhaps, eventually, to receive assistance from her again. Because of this unfortunate estrangement from their *kuldevī,* they said that every morning, when they wake up and see the *cīl* circling above Ḥusain Ṭekrī they feel happy and protected. They seemed to take the presence of the *cīl* as a sign that their relationship with their *kuldevī* was healing through their devotion to the saints at Ḥusain Ṭekrī.

Four aspects of this Rajput family's situation bear highlighting. First, the explicitly Islamic Ḥusain Ṭekrī is appealing and effective because it is removed from the Hindu world, which is by definition inextricably linked to family life and obligations. Second, like the Hindu family whose daughter was seeking relief and healing at Ḥusain Ṭekrī, this man attributed his problems to an affliction carried by the "air"; again, his problems have both an origin and, consequently, a cure that cannot be found in a Hindu context. Third, as chapters 3 and 4 have shown, shared ritual forms (such as fasting, *pūjā*, and *prasād*) allow individuals to perform meaningful rituals from their home tradition in a new place.

Fourth, this story is an excellent example of the way that local culture influences cross-tradition use of Muslim shrines. As Lindsey Harlan has discussed, in Rajput culture it is common to identify the Goddess as a *cīl*. Rajput oral traditions hold that the Goddess takes this form in order to consume the bodies of Rajput soldier-martyrs killed in battle; soldiers who die the death of a martyr become sacrificial victims, worthy of consumption by the Goddess. If non-Muslim pilgrims know anything about the saints of the rauẓas (and there is a tremendous range in their level of knowledge), they know that they died in battle defending their families, or, in the case of Husain, they know that he was beheaded. The notion of the beheaded martyr in particular is prominent in Hindu-Rajput understandings of soldiers who sacrifice themselves to the Goddess, and it therefore makes a great deal of sense that this family from Rajasthan would have no problem at all offering incense to their goddess at the rauẓas: if the saints at Ḥusain Ṭekrī are understood by these Rajasthani pilgrims as the martyrs that they in fact are, it easily follows that they could be understood as bodily offerings to the Goddess, her devoted sacrificial victims. Similarly, for these Rajasthani pilgrims it makes perfect sense that the Goddess would circle over the shrines of martyrs in her form as a *cīl*. Her hovering above the martyrs' shrines evokes her presumed consumption of their martyred corpses, as she is described doing in local epics.[49]

The importance of local culture is worth emphasizing since much of my argument about Muslim saint shrines' appeal and authority has centered on their transregional draw and the anonymity that they offer pilgrims who come from great distances. If the history of Ḥusain Ṭekrī is any indication, it seems likely that until the advent of cheap public transit, most Muslim saint shrines were largely defined by local economies and relationships. In recent years, however, the culture of some Muslim saint shrines has become transregional as a result of advances in transportation networks and media.[50] Thus, what was once addressed in local contexts can now be addressed anonymously, far from home. In this way the culture of Ḥusain Ṭekrī and similar Muslim saint shrines is new: it is a combination of local, regional, and media-driven pan-Islamic elements.

Whether Muslim saint shrines like Ḥusain Ṭekrī are understood as being "not Hindu" or "Muslim," their religious—or even communal—identity as Islamic is a significant aspect of their appeal to non-Muslims. While other scholars have suggested that this attraction is attributable to the belief that Muslim spaces and saints are either dirty or administratively responsible for the management of Muslim *pret,* the stories of Ḥusain Ṭekrī's pilgrims show that beyond these reasons, non-Muslims seeking a solution to family problems will almost certainly find something immensely powerful about a place that they have come to voluntarily, as outsiders. In this context, it is worth remembering that the notion of volunteerism is central to pilgrims' understanding of how they came to Ḥusain Ṭekrī: the saints may call, but pilgrims *choose* to heed this call. Ḥusain Ṭekrī is attractive because many of its non-Muslim pilgrims have no familial or explicitly religious connection with it: for non-Muslims, dargāḥs are powerful because they are not-Hindu, not-Christian, and not-Sikh.[51]

Anonymity is the natural consequence of the tendency of Ḥusain Ṭekrī and similar Muslim saint shrines to attract individuals from distant places who have no preexisting relationship with it. When this opportunity for anonymity is combined with the fact that the dense network of Muslim saint shrines allows for an endless variety of individually tailored pilgrimages, the result is a place that allows both male and female pilgrims to address familial and financial concerns without the knowledge of other family members, friends, or neighbors. Over the years that I have spent visiting Ḥusain Ṭekrī and related shrines, the existence and value of the anonymity offered has been repeatedly affirmed. For example, in the courtyard of the rauẓa of Imām Husain I once got into a conversation with a Mumbai-based Shi'a family about the nature of the problems that had brought them to Ḥusain Ṭekrī. When they were approached by a Shi'a woman from Mumbai who is fairly well known at Ḥusain Ṭekrī, however, they changed their story completely, saying that they had only come for *'ibādat* (worship), and they explicitly denied any family or financial problems. This family came to Ḥusain Ṭekrī because it gave them the opportunity to work out their various issues in relative anonymity. When that anonymity was threatened, they could convincingly say that they had come to Ḥusain Ṭekrī simply to offer their respects to its saints.

Similarly, during a visit to a nearby dargāḥ in Jaora with some local friends, I witnessed a conversation in which one of my friends asked another local woman if her health was bad or whether there was some other problem, since the woman was visiting the dargāḥ. The woman made a point of denying that she had any problems, saying that she had simply come to pay her respects and to spend some time relaxing in the dargāḥ's courtyard. Priya also explicitly stated that she did not visit the local dargāḥ, because then all of her problems (as potentially revealed in ḥāẓirī) would have been on display for the entire community. Similarly, Babli's mother was opposed to her daughter visiting Mastān Bābā because of what it might have done to her reputation.

In short, because it is culturally acceptable to travel some distance to visit a Muslim saint shrine, dargāḥs provide pilgrims with a unique context in which they can deal with serious problems without undue damage to their reputations. At the same time, owing to the existence of Ḥusain Ṭekrī outposts like Maya's, as well as the presumed connection that any Muslim healer or dargāḥ has with any other Islamic place, experiences that one has far away from home remain anchored in one's home. Upon return, it is possible to maintain a relationship with Ḥusain Ṭekrī through visiting its outpost or any Islamic space that is not a mosque. Given that successful reintegration into family life is a major characteristic of pilgrims' visions of healing, a relatively anonymous context is essential. In the interest of protecting family reputation, it can always be claimed that the visit to the dargāḥ is for devotional reasons rather than in response to problem. Should a longer stay at a distant dargāḥ be required, the victim and his or her caretakers can rest assured that the often shocking process of healing will not have an overly negative impact upon the rest of his or her life.

Otherness alone cannot sustain a relationship, however: once in a Muslim space a non-Muslim individual must find idioms, symbols, tropes, and/or narratives that resonate with his or her own systems of meaning. This brings us to the question of which idioms and narratives non-Muslims find meaningful when they come to a place like Ḥusain Ṭekrī, and why these idioms and narratives are meaningful. Nonnarrative aspects of the cross-tradition appeal of lobān and ḥāẓirī have been discussed in previous chapters, but the nature of shared narratives has yet to be explored. I have already begun to discuss this topic in offering an account of the Rajasthani family: here martyrdom reads powerfully across religious traditions, and in a particular manner in the context of Rajput culture.

There are, however, several other major aspects of the appeal of Muslim saint shrines. Among female pilgrims to Ḥusain Ṭekrī, a structured source of narrative-based cross-tradition community formation is the recitation of "The Tale of the Ten Virtuous Women" *(Das Bībīyoṁ kī Kahānī).* Both Priya and Babli participated in the reading of this story at Ḥusain Ṭekrī.[52] Leaving the tale's content aside for the moment, it is important to recognize that in simply gathering to participate in its recitation, female pilgrims at Ḥusain Ṭekrī create actual cross-tradition and cross-*jāti* communities that develop over time. Most significantly, through the power that is understood to be inherent in the act of recitation, pilgrims bring themselves into the imagined community of virtuous women whose stories they relate. This reciting oneself into an imaginary community is in part possible because within the structure of the story are descriptions of women who themselves recite the story of the ten virtuous women, and who subsequently reap the benefits of this recitation. Women at Ḥusain Ṭekrī who recite the story thus see and hear their own actions being enacted in their own recitation.

"The Tale of the Ten Virtuous Women" is widespread. A May 2006 trip to a New York City shop run by Pakistani immigrants and selling Pakistani and Indian books, music, and films turned up an Urdu copy of the tale that had been printed in Karachi. The shopkeeper refused to charge me for it, an action reminiscent of Priya's statement that the woman who brought her a burqa from Bombay refused to charge her for it. Giving non-Muslims items that will foster virtuous behavior is popularly understood to be a laudable act of grace *(faiẓ)* that also imparts *faiẓ* to the giver. In the summer of 2008 I also witnessed a young female visitor to a small dargāḥ in the southern city of Mysore request and purchase a copy of "The Tale of the Ten Virtuous Women" from a local bookseller.[53]

At Ḥusain Ṭekrī this story is ritually recited by groups of female pilgrims over a ten-day period. At the tenth recitation a special type of *laḍḍū* is prepared by one of the members of the group and distributed to the readers of the story and their friends and family. Two types of recitation take place: private ones held in lodge rooms and public ones held in the courtyard of the rauẓa of Fatima. Because its courtyard is open on one side, the rauẓa of Fatima is by default the only public space at Ḥusain Ṭekrī that stays open all night, allowing groups of women to gather long after the shrine attendant has gone home for the evening. The shrine of Fatima has quite a nightlife; people have ḥāẓirī until the wee hours, some pilgrims sleep in the courtyard, and members of the Shi'a community in particular hold *majlis* there as well. It is easily the least regulated of the rauẓas. In most cases, women involved in the recitation heard about the events informally from fellow lodge residents or acquaintances. During my time at Ḥusain Ṭekrī I attended both public and private recitations.[54]

The version of "The Tale of the Ten Virtuous Women" translated below is available for purchase at Ḥusain Ṭekrī in a Devanagari-script pamphlet and was recited by Babli and a group of women at the rauẓa of Fatima.[55]

Bismilla . . .

First, recite two *rakats* of *namāz.*

Two brothers lived in the same city. The older brother was a man of wealth and status *[raīs]* and the younger brother was poor *[nādār]*. The poor brother was very bothered by his older brother's prosperous state, and so one day he said to his wife, "How much longer are we going to be able to bear all this hunger and poverty *[muhtājī]*? I'm going to go abroad. Maybe I'll manage to get some kind of work and finally put an end to our suffering." And so, having taken leave of his wife, this man went looking for work in another city. After the departure of her husband, the wife's troubles became truly unbearable. In her heart, she cried out, "Oh Lord who protects us *[pālnewālā rab]*, only you can truly sustain us. Now I'm alone—even my husband is gone. Who is going to feed me?" When this believer *[mominā]* had become truly helpless, she went to her husband's older brother and, crying, she said:

"Oh brother, what should I do and where should I go? Your brother has left me to go and find work abroad. Now, other than your home, where can I go? *You* are truly my only support." Now, that rich man said to his wife, "This is my young sister-in-law. Have her do your housework and take care of your children. For food, you can give her your leftovers."

In short, this believer endured the blow of doing work there. She had no choice but to take care of her sister-in-law's children as well as all her housework. As if this weren't enough, her rich sister-in-law taunted her and fed her polluted leftovers. By the grace of God, this poor woman was able to endure all of these troubles. She didn't have a minute of rest. At night, thinking of her ruin and loss of honor, she wept tears of blood. Things went on like this for a very long time. All night long she would fill the time with prayers, and, crying, she would pray for the return of her husband. One night this believer cried herself to sleep and she had a dream *[k̲h̲vāb; sapnā]*. In this dream a virtuous woman wearing a veil came to her and said *[farmāyā]*, "Oh believer! You shouldn't be this bereft over your husband! God willing, your husband will return to you safe and sound *[sahī aur salāmat]*. On Thursday listen to "The Tale of the Ten Virtuous Women." In order to banish troubles, listen to "The Tale of the Ten Virtuous Women." A lot of beneficial [things] and trials have happened.

In the beneficent, world-sustaining Qur'an, it is stated: "Oh, Mary! God has chosen you *[barguzīdā karnā]* and kept you pure and clean, free of all sins and faults. According to his purpose, he has chosen you from among all women in this world." From this *ayat* it is clear that Mary's time was momentous and important. In Islam, there are four women whose examples cannot be equaled. The great and blessed Fatima, descendant of Muhammad, is first among these women. The second is the blessed Hagar; the third is Asiya, Pharaoh's wife. Asiya was a daughter of the family of Isra'il.[56] Her father's name was Maraham and was from the line of blessed Abraham. As a child, she was taught to be God-fearing. Somehow, a woman as pure as Asiya was married to a man as base as Pharaoh. Perhaps this happened because God knew that Moses and Aaron would be raised by her, since of course the prophets of God should never be raised by unbelievers.

Before getting married Pharaoh was a man like other men. Later, puffed up with pride over his wealth and his power, he began to think of himself as God. One day he said to Asiya, "You've seemed a bit off to me for a while. What's going on?" Asiya replied, "It pains me to see you thinking of yourself as God." Hearing this, Pharaoh demanded, "Have you gone and accepted the God of Moses and Aaron?" To this, Asiya simply said, "As of today it's been forty years since I accepted their God." Amazed, Pharaoh asked, "Aren't you afraid of me at all?" to which Asiya replied, "I'm much more afraid of God *[k̲h̲udā]* than I am of you." Hearing this, Pharaoh flew into a fiery whirlwind of rage, and, throwing Asiya on the ground, he had her hands and feet pierced with nails. Any other woman would have cried in pain, but she preferred death to the company of unbelievers. Praise Allah—what can be said about the glory of Asiya?

The fourth virtuous woman is the blessed Hagar, whom blessed Abraham left on a hill.[57] Alone with her child, she didn't lose heart because she understood her situation to be nothing but the will of Allah. She didn't have anything but God—she didn't even have water. Leaving her child in the care of God, she circled the mountain seven times looking for water, with her child crying the whole time. When she was concerned about her child, she went up the mountain to get him, and when she was concerned about thirst, she went looking for water. In the end, though, God took care of everything.

The marks that her child's heels made as he crawled in the dirt in agony turned into the spring Zum Zum,[58] which has the ability to quench the thirst of the entire world. Because of Zum Zum, that place became settled and became a great city. And later, when blessed Abraham went to sacrifice *[jibah karnā]* Ismail, Satan took on the guise of a person and said, "Hey woman, blessed Abraham is coming here to sacrifice your child." Hearing this, she said, "You must be none other than Satan himself, come to trouble me—everyone knows that the prophets of God are flawless. Blessed Abraham couldn't possibly sacrifice his own son." And so these are the four flawless women, whose praises both God and all the prophets sing.

Life may leave you; comfort and pleasure may leave you; but faith ought not leave you. Now, blessed Zaineb, the wealth of Karbala, consumed by sorrow, blessed Kulsum, mourner of the seventy-two martyrs, and blessed Sugra all suffered the worst sort of separation from their family: they were never reunited. After hearing news of their father and brothers, they spent the rest of their days in restlessness. Remember blessed Sakina, the wealth of Karbala, mourner of her loved ones: think how much torture she endured, and still she couldn't overcome the burden of being an orphan. She was so consumed with longing for her father's deliverance that she perished while still imprisoned. Picture all of their suffering and, with tears in your eyes, read this story. Look with awe upon the wonder of divine beneficence.

That story is this:

One day blessed ʿAli was preparing to host blessed Muhammad in his home; however, he had no food in his house. Blessed ʿAli borrowed a bit of barley and gave it to his wife, blessed Fatima, saying, "Today your father is my guest." Fatima ground up the barley and made three *roṭīs*. When the Prophet of God returned from evening prayers, he took his grandsons and his cousin and sat down to dinner. Fatima gave one *roṭī* to her female servant, blessed Fiza, and to the Five Pure Ones.[59] Later, after she was finished in the kitchen, Fatima asked her father if he would honor her with his presence tomorrow.

The Prophet accepted her invitation, and so it was that Hasan and Husain hosted a dinner for their grandfather. Every day ʿAli would borrow whatever was needed for the dinner. ʿAli brought barley, and Fatima ground it and made it into six *roṭī*s: one for Fiza and five for the Five Pure Ones. When Muhammad was on his way to help blessed Imām Ḥusain, he saw Fiza standing in the doorway. He asked her, "Is there something you want to say?" Hoping that she too could offer him a meal, blessed Fiza said, "I'm not worthy of troubling you at all, but I am still hopeful." Understanding her desire to offer him a meal, Muhammad accepted her offer. Fiza had not been able to gather anything together because of her poverty.

After his prayers, the Prophet arrived at the home of ʿAli. Everyone stood out of respect for him. Blessed Fiza hadn't mentioned to anyone that he was coming, so no one knew that she had invited him. The Prophet said, "Today I am Fiza's guest."

ʿAli said, "Fiza, if you had let us know ahead of time, I would have brought food." Fiza replied, "Please don't worry; Allah is the great provider."

Fiza retreated to a corner of the house, fell to her knees, and cried, "Oh, provider of what is needed! You are the support of the world in the midst of this poverty and want! I've invited your friend here as a guest. Please do something about blessed Muhammad and his descendants so that I'm not humiliated!" She looked up and saw that the floor had been completely filled with abundance from heaven. She brought everything to the Prophet and placed it before him. He offered it to the rest of the family, ate, and then he asked, "Where did this come from?" Blessed Muhammad asked this even though the angel Gabriel had told him the origin of the food. This all happened so that blessed Muhammad could convey to them that even their servant woman was so beloved of God that he couldn't possibly deny her request. If you have true devotion and faith, there's nothing you can't obtain. There are no shortages in God's treasury.

[At this point the text returns to the initial story of the poor sister's dream. The veiled woman, soon to be explicitly identified as Fatima, is speaking.]

For ten days, in a place where you pray *[jā-e-namāz]*, having performed ritual ablutions and with pure intention, sit [and remember this story]. And when your husband comes to you, make ten *laḍḍū*s from a sweet *roṭī* mixture, and make an offering in the name of these ten women.

The believer asked, "Who are you? What is your name? And who are these ten women in whose name I should make this offering?" And blessed Fatima replied, "1) My name is Fatima Zahra, daughter of the Prophet Muhammad, and these are the names of the nine others—remember them well! 2) Blessed Sara, 3) Blessed Hagar, 4) Blessed Mary, 5) Blessed Asiya. After this, my two daughters, 6) Blessed Fatima Sugara,[60] and 7) Blessed Zaineb, and then 8) Blessed Fatima Kubra [daughter of Husain], 9) Blessed Umme Kulsum [daughter of ʿAli and Fatima], and 10) Blessed Sakina [daughter of Husain]. Bearers of hardship and troubles, who took the suffering of Karbala with her wherever they went, and these women were all patient, even as they endured prison and beatings. If you reverently call to mind the suffering of these ten women and ask earnestly for relief from your suffering, in ten days, whoever you may be, your wishes will be granted, God willing."

When this believer woke up, it was Friday. She went out into her neighborhood and began telling her friends about her dream, saying, "I had this dream where I was commanded to gather you together and tell blessed Fatima's story."

The women of the neighborhood gathered at this believer's house, and she began to tell them the story of the ten virtuous women. Nine days passed. On the tenth day, what do you know—this woman's husband showed up on their doorstep, arms full of gold and other treasures. So the people of the neighborhood went running to find this believer, saying, "Hey—your husband's back, and he's brought lots of stuff with him!" She was overjoyed and immediately took a bath.[61] After this she gathered together pure water and a new clay vessel, and in the clay vessel she mixed up ghee, sugar, and flour, which she had asked someone to bring. She made sweet *roṭī* and then she crushed the *roṭī* and used them to make *laḍḍū*. Then everything was ready, and so she made an offering in the name of the ten wives. She gave some of the *laḍḍū*s to her friends, who accepted them with great honor and reverence. After this she went to her sister-in-law and said, "I've listened to the ten virtuous women's story and my wish has been granted. My husband has returned, and I've made this offering in gratitude. I've brought this portion of the *laḍḍū*s for you."

But the sister-in-law was a proud and haughty woman, and she gave the *laḍḍū*s back, saying, "I don't eat disgusting food like this—it would be like putting rocks or bricks in my stomach! Get out of here and take your filthy *laḍḍū*s with you!" And so the poor thing had no choice but to take back her *laḍḍū*s and leave. She ate the portion of the *laḍḍū*s that had been intended for her sister-in-law, and even in this situation she thanked God.

Now, listen to what happened to that miserable sister-in-law! That night she fell asleep as usual, but when she woke up in the morning she saw that her children had died! When there was nothing at all in her house, not even her beloved children, she went out of her mind. Both she and her husband cried and cried—there was nothing else they could do. And so they went on like this for days and days. One day the wife said, "Oh Allah! I'm starving! What can I do? There's not a thing to eat in the house but chaff." She made up her mind to try to cook something from the chaff, but the moment she touched it she saw that it was filled with worms, and so she had no choice but to throw it away immediately. When her husband saw all this, he said, "Let's go to my sister's house: we can get food there, and my brother-in-law can offer us some work." They put a lock on the door and headed out even though they didn't have any of the things that are necessary for a journey. As they walked on and on, their feet became blistered. Soon, they came to a field of chickpeas, and the husband said, "Wait here and I'll go gather some of the green chickpeas. If we eat them and drink some water, we'll have the strength to continue the journey."

Her husband gathered together some bits of chickpeas and gave them to her, but, to her horror, the moment she touched them they immediately shriveled up and became useless fodder. And so she and her husband had to throw the food away and continue without anything to eat.

They came to a field full of ripe sugarcane and her husband was beside himself with hunger and thirst. When he saw the sugarcane he became hopeful. He took some from the field and gave it to her and said, "Now we can live. Eat this sugarcane so that we will have the strength to go on."

But the moment she laid a hand on the sugarcane it dried up, and they had no choice but to throw it away then and there and continue on their way. And so after a lot of struggle, they finally arrived at the husband's sister's home. She immediately brought them a cot, and they sat down. She cooked food and she and her family members ate. Then she remembered her brother and sister-in-law, and so she said to her servant, "If there is any food left, gather it together and give it to my in-laws." And so the servant got a container, gathered the left-overs, and gave them to those two. But what do you know—that miserable woman washed her hands and got ready to eat, but the moment she touched the *roṭī,* the room was filled with a foul stench because the food had suddenly spoiled. At this they wrung their hands and said, "Oh Allah! How long is this going to go on? We're going to die of hunger and thirst!" The wretched sister-in-law dug a hole and buried the spoiled food, and both of them went to bed with empty stomachs.

In the morning the husband said to his wife, "The ruler of these parts is my friend; let's go to him and see if he can do anything to help us." They went to the court of the local ruler and told the servant that they had come. The servant went to the ruler and said, "If it please the king, a man and a woman have come here to see you—they're in really bad shape. Will you see them?" The ruler had his servant bring them in, and when he saw them, he recognized them as his friends. He had a separate room prepared for them, saying, "Have a bath and rest." Then he went to the kitchen staff and said, "Prepare the best meal you can and bring it to my friends." Food was prepared according to his command and brought to the husband and wife. When the husband saw the food he was thrilled, and he said to his wife, "This has been given to us by the grace of Allah!" His wife went and washed her hands and then sat down to enjoy the meal, but whatever she touched immediately became spoiled. In short, the entire meal was ruined. Her husband was astonished, and he became worried, saying, "If we complain about this to the king, he'll get really angry and think that we've said that he sent bad food in order to ruin his reputation. What are we going to do with all of this rotten food? If he finds out about this, he's sure to ask what kind of magic we've done."

In the end, the two snuck outside and buried the rotten food and they told the servants to remove the empty dishes. The husband was beside himself and cried out, "Oh Allah! Why are we in such a sorry state?" At this, his wife became upset and went to sit in the courtyard of the house.

While all this was going on, the king's wife decided that she was going to have a bath, and her daughter decided that she would also bathe. They both hung their sandalwood necklaces on pegs, but when they did, the strangest thing happened: the pegs swallowed the necklaces. Of course the queen and the princess were astonished by this, but the woman, sitting there in the courtyard, was alarmed too. She went to her husband and said, "What will God do next?" "What happened now?" her husband asked, and she proceeded to tell him the story of the pegs swallowing up the sandalwood necklaces. "We should get out of here right away," she concluded, "before the king accuses us of causing all these things to happen and has us thrown in jail—or even executed!" And so without telling the king, the two of them left.

Eventually they came to a river, and, unable to go any farther, they sat on its bank. The husband turned to his wife and said, "I can't imagine what we've done that has made us so unfortunate." His wife said, "Well, I am sure that I've committed at least one sin." "What sin?" said her husband. And so the wife explained, "Do you remember when your younger brother went abroad looking for work and he didn't have any idea how much trouble his wife had while he was gone? Well, while she was staying with us, she dreamt of a veiled woman who came and told her to listen to "The Tale of the Ten Virtuous Women," and on the tenth day, this veiled woman promised that your younger brother would return to his home with lots of gold and other treasures. So on a Friday your sister-in-law listened to "The Tale of the Ten Virtuous Women" and sure enough, your brother came home. Then she bathed and prepared *laḍḍū*s made from sweet *roṭī*s and made an offering of them in the name of the ten wives. Your sister-in-law shared the *laḍḍū*s with everyone, and she brought me my portion, but I refused to eat it, and I said that I wouldn't eat disgusting food that would just sit in my stomach like bricks and rocks! This sin was mine and mine alone, and since that time we've found ourselves in this sorry state." Hearing this story, the husband said, "You wretch! You spoke with pride and disrespect! Hurry and beg for forgiveness so that we have some hope of escaping this misery!"

So the wife got up from where they were sitting and bathed in a nearby irrigation channel. She performed *vuzū,* read *namāz,* and, breaking down in tears, she prayed, "Oh blessed daughter of the most blessed Prophet! Save me from this miserable situation!" Her husband burst into tears and said, "We have nothing. Tell us how we can make an offering." His wife took some sand from the riverbank, made it into *laḍḍū*s, and made an offering in the name of the ten virtuous women. By the miraculous power of blessed Zaineb, the blessed Kulsum, and the blessed Sakina, the sand *laḍḍū*s were transformed into real, sweet *laḍḍū*s, and when this happened the husband and wife recited the *durūd sharīf.* Then the husband and wife had five *laḍḍū*s each, and they drank some water, and so God's will was accomplished. The husband said, "Our sin has been forgiven—let's hurry home! And when they arrived at home, what do you think they saw? Everything was just as it had been before all the trouble had started—their storehouse was full of grain, and their children were busy reading the blessed Qur'an. The children were overjoyed to see their parents, and of course their mother and father were overjoyed to see them, and so the two of them recited the *durūd sharīf* at the top of their lungs: [*durūd sharīf* in Arabic transliterated into Devanagari]

Oh, my beloved ten virtuous women! Just as Allah forgave this woman's sin, forgive the sins of all believers, and fulfill their wishes! Amen.

On the level of substance, the appeal of "The Tale of the Ten Virtuous Women" to female pilgrims who come to Ḥusain Ṭekrī is clear: basically, the entire recitation offers an account of how two women are saved from wretched situations involving alienation from family and prosperity. In form, however, this story possesses some uniquely powerful characteristics, most importantly, perhaps, its self-conscious narrative within a narrative within a narrative: the stories related in "The Tale of the Ten Virtuous Women" describe women in difficult situations being called upon to remember other women who were themselves in difficult situations, one of whom—Fatima—has the ability to reward those who remember her story and the stories and names of the nine other women mentioned within. By presenting the unmistakable message that one's situation can be improved through remembrance of the suffering of past women, the story teaches its reciters that remembering is an efficacious, powerful act.

The first woman in the story—the sister-in-law whose husband goes abroad to find work—is thus saved from a terrible situation by remembering another woman in a terrible situation, Fiza, the servant of 'Ali and Fatima, who also lacked resources but whose faith calls down a feast from heaven.[62] The second woman in the story—the severe woman who refuses the *laḍḍūs* offered by her young sister-in-law—is not, of course, blameless. In refusing the *laḍḍūs* she fails to participate in the vital work of remembering the suffering of the ten virtuous women. While the disrespect that this woman shows her sister-in-law as well as the ten virtuous women certainly reads as an action worthy of punishment, it is notable that the text offers no explicit equation of the woman's subsequent suffering with punishment. Rather, her pitiful state is the natural and inevitable consequence of her own failure to participate in the remembrance of the suffering of past women as well as her failure to rejoice with her sister-in-law on the occasion of her husband's return.

Because of her unwillingness to participate in remembrance, she herself becomes a polluting force: the story repeatedly emphasizes, for example, that she washes her hands before handling food that has been prepared for her, and yet her touch destroys food, making it absolutely clear that she is corrupt in her very being. Nothing is amiss in the human or the natural world: the fields offer up bounty that the obdurate sister-in-law and her husband cannot consume, and while both she and her husband are received with hospitality by the ruler and, to a lesser extent perhaps, by the husband's sister, they are unable to enjoy the offerings of a properly functioning social order until she actively recalls the suffering of the ten virtuous women.

By the story's logic, the only way to maintain one's prosperity is to remember the suffering of others, and this is why she suffers so severely.

This is not simply a story in which those relating it are inspired to hope for a deserved reward from Fatima and the others, nor is it a tale that turns on divinely ordained punishment. Rather, by remembering the suffering of the ten virtuous women, reciters of the tale ensure that they did not suffer in vain. By extension, they become part of the community of sufferers, and as such they become future beneficiaries of recitation of "The Tale of the Ten Virtuous Women." Owing to its form as a narrative within a narrative within a narrative, the story demonstrates and reinforces the notion that recitation itself is a fundamental efficacious act: in both cases, women who recite "The Tale of the Ten Virtuous Women" are removed from wretched situations. In remembering those who should be remembered, like the women in the story, the reciter *herself* takes on the role of a protector of the ten virtuous women. By the very act of recitation or the act of listening to the recitation, each woman who participates in the reading is *herself* ensuring that the suffering of the women in the story has not been forgotten, and thus each woman ensures that none of the ten virtuous women suffered in vain. In this way pilgrims to Ḥusain Ṭekrī who read the tale find themselves reciting a story in which they are essentially major characters: they tell one another their own story, bearing witness to their own situation, thus saving *themselves* as they save the ten virtuous women.

Why exactly individuals find remembrance effective, necessary, and powerful is a complicated and much-discussed issue. In the Shiʿa context, itself very influential at Ḥusain Ṭekrī, it is commonly believed that martyrs have the ability to intercede on behalf of petitioners, and this belief likely fuels interest in reading these stories at Ḥusain Ṭekrī. Indeed, the status of Ḥusain Ṭekrī's saints, whether read as angry ghosts who suffered an untimely death, Muslim martyrs, or martyrs for the Goddess, is a significant source of their appeal.

The power and necessity of remembering past suffering is a central feature of contemporary Indian Shiʿa practice, and the Shiʿa influence at Ḥusain Ṭekrī is partially responsible for the culture of reading "The Tale of the Ten Virtuous Women" that has developed there. Martyrdom and suffering are easily experienced in a nonsectarian way, and rituals that are built around these phenomena are therefore easily shared across religious traditions. A Shiʿa woman from Bombay whom I know quite well once said to me in passing, "I think that Catholics must be very heartless people." When I asked her what she meant, she explained that in her neighborhood in Bombay (Santa Cruz East), the Catholic population staged Easter passion plays. This young woman said that *she* couldn't watch the crucifixion without tears coming to her eyes, and she could not understand how the Catholics could watch the play without shedding a tear.[63]

Beyond these points of doctrine and common belief, of course, is the simple fact that, by definition, forgotten events are meaningless. As a young Shi'a woman from Delhi once explained to me, performing *mātam* was necessary in order to ensure that all believers keep in mind the horrible suffering and mortality that combat entails. She very astutely pointed out that most Americans would be unable to give exact dates, let alone numbers dead, for any American military conflicts, and she suggested that this lack of remembrance was the reason that the American government was inclined and able to enter so many military conflicts rather than recognizing war as an absolute last resort.

The efficacy of remembrance sits in interesting and occasionally awkward relationship with more orthodox formulations of power and legitimacy; thus, the severe sister-in-law whose tale comprises the second half of "The Tale of the Ten Virtuous Women" reads *namāz* to consecrate the ground on which she makes the *laḍḍus*. This consecration of the ground through *namāz* has two precedents in the text: in part through Fatima's explicit instructions to the first young woman, whose husband went abroad to find work, the frame story has already established *namāz*-consecrated ground as the ideal ground on which to make an offering to the ten virtuous women. In the same way, before the story proper begins, the text instructs its readers to perform two *rakāt*s of *namāz*. Again, the actions of the characters of the story mirror one another and are finally reflected in the actions of the reciter herself. In all three cases the conventional orthodox Muslim activity of performing *namāz* is preparatory, creating the conditions necessary for the efficacious act of remembering to have its naturally beneficial effect.

Similarly, while it is true that the story ends with a request that Allah forgive any sins that the reciter has committed and grant her requests, this petition has little to do with the actual economy as it has been revealed in the story, in which remembering is the powerful and efficacious act. Rather, it seems that Allah is mentioned only to lend an orthodox sheen, necessary by some estimations, to actions that are certainly condemned by some Muslims.[64] The invocation of the Qur'anic description of Mary at the beginning of the discussion of the ten virtuous women seems to perform a similar function: if the Qur'an itself sings the praises of Mary, it cannot be wrong for the reciters to recall the self-sacrificing and virtuous actions of similarly virtuous women, even if they are not explicitly mentioned in the Qur'an. The text thus places a story in which remembering and recitation are clearly the powerful actions into a legitimizing frame consisting of the two mainstays of mainstream orthodox Islamic thought: the absolute omnipotence of God and of the Qur'an. The real economy of the text, however, is based on the idea that the act of suffering itself is incredibly powerful, a force whose power is accessible only if it is remembered. By this logic, nothing is more powerful than a suffering individual who actively and empathetically recalls the suffering of past individuals. In its approach to the perennial religious questions of why suffering exists and what can be done about it—questions that are also central to the plight of those with ḥāẓirī—"The Tale of the Ten Virtuous Women" answers that suffering cannot be eliminated, but it can be harnessed and its power redirected.

Through recitation, the reciter and the listeners, who together create transreligion and transcaste actual communities, also become part of the imagined community represented by the lineage of the ten virtuous women. The cross-tradition recitation of this story is aided by the fact that the story is also masterfully nonsectarian. Whether this nonsectarianism is purposeful or not is debatable, but in any case, remarkably, nowhere in the text are the words "Hindu," "Muslim," or "Islam" used. Rather, the heroine is described as a "believer." It is true that the Urdu word in this case is *mominā,* which explicitly refers to a Muslim believer.[65] In India, the title *momin,* "believer," was widely adopted by low-caste weavers, so it is possible that in this story *mominā* connotes low-caste status.[66] Further, it is important to bear in mind that nearly any word has the capacity to take on new connotations depending upon the inclinations and aspirations of its user. Thus, for example, while Babli regularly used the term *kāfir* (unbeliever) to refer to anyone who lacked love for Husain, *kāfir* is more commonly used to refer to non-Muslims, particularly in elite or textual traditions. In any case, in contrast to Indian Muslims who identify as Sayyid (a descendant of Muhammad, and therefore potentially readable as person with extra-subcontinental origins), the woman, because she is described as a "believer," is almost certainly a convert, and therefore she has purely subcontinental origins. Both women in the story are distinguished primarily by their remembrance of the ten virtuous women rather than their religious pedigree, and Fiza, their counterpart in the time of Muhammad, is similarly distinguished by faith and good intentions rather than by lineage.

The ease with which "The Tale of the Ten Virtuous Women" crosses religious boundaries is also influenced by local culture: in form and, to a lesser extent, in substance, the tale is reminiscent of the Rajasthani Hindu Mother

Ten's stories (literally, "Condition-Mother," but translated as "Mother Ten" because of the homonymy in Hindi between the words for "condition" and "ten"), recited by women in Rajasthan to honor the goddess Daśā Mātā over a ten-day period between the Hindu festivals of Holī and Gaṇgaur. In these stories, devotion to Daśā Mātā, when combined with the ingenuity of the stories' heroines, leads to prosperity and the transformation of difficult situations.[67] Further, the form of "The Tale of the Ten Virtuous Women," like that of Mother Ten's stories, participates in the sort of vow-based religion widely practiced by women throughout the subcontinent, as it inspires a commitment to reading the story for ten days in hopes of a reward.[68] The similarities between the two no doubt also contribute to the cross-tradition appeal of "The Tale of the Ten Virtuous Women."

Each Muslim saint shrine is a unique mixture of pan-Islamic, pan-Indian, and local narratives and rituals. By virtue of both its Rajput and its Shi'a influences, Ḥusain Ṭekrī's culture is particularly influenced by the concept of martyrdom. While Ḥusain Ṭekrī was founded in a Sunni Muslim princely state and has historically been administered by a Sunni *mutavallī* who is a descendant of the *nawāb*s of Jaora, it has almost since its inception enjoyed the patronage of Shi'a communities from Bombay. Shi'a patronage of the site is significant and ongoing, and Shi'a practices form an important part of Ḥusain Ṭekrī's everyday public ritual life: *majlis* are commonly sponsored and recited in the rauẓas' courtyards, and throughout the year Shi'a communities sponsor small funeral processions on the death anniversaries of many martyrs. These processions involve a jasmine-bedecked coffin, standards with the symbols of the Five Pure Ones (a *panja*) and 'Abbas (a water skin), and a group of individuals performing *mātam*.

Hindu participation in *mātam* and Shi'a processions is common at Ḥusain Ṭekrī.[69] In this context, a common formal arena for cross-tradition exchange derives from the Shi'a tradition of singing *fariyād,* a genre of mourning and petition songs. It is common for Shi'a women at Ḥusain Ṭekrī to gather in one of its several privately owned Shi'a-administered *imāmbāṛās* as well as the rauẓas to sing these songs. As they sing they seek the help of the martyrs, proclaiming their helplessness and their hope that the martyrs will intercede on their behalf. Often *fariyād* are simple invocations of the various saints' names with a chorus that asks the saint to relay the petitioners' request for help to God, accompanied by the rhythmic beating of the breast, which is a common form of *mātam,* particularly among women. In both private Shi'a *imāmbāṛā* settings as well as at the rauẓas, *ḥāẓirīwāle* gather in front of the singers. During *fariyād* they generally manifest a range of ḥāẓirī practices, most commonly shaking the body, head, and hair, breathing heavily or rhythmically, or crying out in anger and pain.

Through their actions, those in ḥāẓirī bear witness to the presence of the saints, and those singing the *fariyād* bear witness to the suffering that the assembled group of women is enduring. In this context, too, there is an understanding that those who sing contribute to the recovery of those with ḥāẓirī. In the following discussion of *fariyād,* offered by a Shiʿa woman from Lucknow whose *fariyād* sessions Priya frequented, the relationship between mourners and *ḥāẓirīwālī* is made particularly explicit:

Shiʿa woman: The meaning of *fariyād* is simply, "Oh, Maulā, I'm troubled, I'm lost; please come and help me . . . *fariyād* is read at every rauẓa at Ḥusain Ṭekrī: the hours of Maulā ʿAli's court are from 12 to 1 in the afternoon, and Maulā ʿAbbas's hours are from 12 to 1 at night. And Bībī Sakina's hours are in the early evening—at sunset *[magrib].*

Carla: What do you mean, "They're present?"

Shiʿa woman: Their courts are in session, so they all come themselves at these times . . . *[pause for loud ambient ḥāẓirī]* I've been given special authority from Maulā, and because of this authority, I can't go to any dirty or impure place . . . I have authority to recite *fariyād* and do *mātam.* If someone is troubled, and they're so troubled that they are helpless, and can't even pray, and are weak, then immediately the order comes to me that I should do *mātam.* And it's understood that from where I've stood and read *fariyād* and done *mātam,* I've given Maulā an application, an emergency application. *[Here I clarify to be sure I've understood her properly]* I've told him that so-and-so is troubled; it's like emergency work . . . That's it, I read *fariyād,* and their *faislā* happens right away. But, I only recite *fariyād* when I receive an order from Maulā: I never recite it by my own choice. *[pause for more loud ambient ḥāẓirī]*

Carla: So how do these people know to find you? Do they come to you and say, "I'm suffering and I need your help?"

Shiʿa woman: No, no one talks to me like that. Maulā shows them in a dream; he shows them me doing *mātam* and reciting *fariyād,* and they see that this is a very honorable thing, and that a *faislā* will come from it. What do I know about other people's problems? So Maulā himself gives orders: he might say to install an *ʿalam,* and I raise an *ʿalam* [banner of one of the saints], and the *faislā* happens; or he might say to raise a *tābūt* [coffin], and the martyrdom of the *imāms* is also present in this, and so this too can bring about a *faislā* . . . the reason is, when an *ʿalam* or a *tābūt* is raised, then Maulā himself comes.

Carla: He himself comes?

Shiʿa woman: That's right: because of the events of Karbala, when we cry and recite *fariyād,* Blessed Fatima herself comes to collect our tears, and she

> uses them to soothe the wounds that her son suffered at Karbala. And so that means whenever she comes—well, whenever a really powerful and great individual comes to a place, whether you're reading *fariyād,* or you're troubled, or you're helpless, the cure will fit the problem. If there's someone with a lot of money, and they come and pray, they'll give the money [to someone who needs it], and if there is some doctor there, and there's some patient, the doctor can help the patient by giving him medicine—everything is possible when a great and powerful individual is present. If someone has a terrible and powerful spirit *[rūḥ]* that is tormenting them, well, Maulā's sepoys will be commanded to take it away and lock it up in his prison.[70]

Like many religious healers, this woman insists that she is simply an instrument of healing, and in keeping with the widely recognized distinction between miracles and magic, she regards her power as borrowed rather than the result of her own efforts. In contrast to magicians, who engage in the selfish, magical manipulation of the elements to steal from others, she wields this borrowed power in order to facilitate the equitable distribution of resources.

Most significant in this discussion of the nature of power and legitimacy at Ḥusain Ṭekrī, however, is the fact that like the story of the ten virtuous women, it is the act of remembering itself that is every bit as necessary and powerful as the suffering of the martyrs. Further, remembrance of the martyrs has two desirable effects: Husain's pain is lessened through the application of tears, and the suffering of petitioners is reduced through redistribution of resources. Again, remembrance is a means for restoring balance in one's community. Further, it is particularly meaningful that those who believe the story of Fatima's use of tears understand that they are aiding her in her work as a mother and caregiver: the measure of the success of one's treatment at Ḥusain Ṭekrī is, after all, the extent to which one is able to perform one's familial duties.

The discourse of family at Ḥusain Ṭekrī is probably the most common means by which pilgrims create and cultivate explicit cross-tradition and cross-*jāti* relationships with one another. Bilkis, whose daughter-in-law's ḥāẓirī was discussed in chapter 4, related an experience that she and her son had at the shrine of Sailani Bābā, where they were resident before the daughter-in-law's case was transferred to Ḥusain Ṭekrī. While at Sailani Bābā's dargāḥ they encountered a young Hindu woman with ḥāẓirī. As it turned out, her home was relatively near their village. This young woman had no one taking care of her, and one day, during ḥāẓirī, her possessing spirit (which Bilkis referred to as a *"śaitān")* ripped off the markers of her status as an auspicious married woman *(suhāg),* in this case, her bangles and *maṅgal sūtra,* or necklace worn by married Hindu women. Bilkis's son rescued these ornaments, and thereafter, along with two other men, he assisted in the care of this woman during her ḥāẓirī. Bilkis emphasized that this woman would regularly fall unconscious for an hour, and, because she was alone, it was very important that someone take care of her. Later, Bilkis continued, Sailani Bābā declared the young woman and the three young men brothers and sisters. Perhaps because early in the conversation I had asked if this involved any sort of gift giving, Bilkis also elaborated that each of the "brothers" was commanded to give their sister a gift. The first "brother" tied a *ta'vīẕ* on his "sister"; the second put a ring on her finger; and the third, Bilkis's son, put bangles on her wrists and gave her something for her hair. The gifts' protective and auspicious powers could not be more obvious: these "brothers" are restoring this woman to a condition from which she can once again attain a state of *suhāg,* or auspicious wifehood, a state that will be protected by the *ta'vīẕ.*[71] Bangles connote wifehood and beauty; a ring connotes wealth, status, and possibly Western notions of marriage; and, because women's hair is so commonly understood as the means by which a *pret* attaches itself, an item to care for the hair suggests that this woman is no longer the victim of a *pret,* or that she ought not to be tormented by a *pret* any longer. Finally, Bilkis added, Sailani Bābā had promised that he would cause all of them to meet during the fire walk at his dargāḥ—a reunion for this newly created family.[72] This Hindu woman subsequently developed a possession-based healing practice of her own, and, Bilkis added, it was because of this new kinship between her son and this woman that they sought the guidance of this woman in addressing the daughter-in-law's problems.

This notion of found family, widely used or assumed by pilgrims in describing or enacting their relations with one another, is also instigated by the relationships that pilgrims have with the martyr-saints of Ḥusain Ṭekrī. In mourning the martyrs out of love for them, pilgrims at Ḥusain Ṭekrī effectively forge familial relationships with one another, and by extension with the saints themselves, since mourning and remembering the deceased is primarily the work of family members of the deceased. At Ḥusain Ṭekrī the saints are not simply remembered as individual heroes battling evil forces, but rather as members of a single family, many of whom die trying to defend one another. The tragedy of their deaths is emphasized through description of the suffering that their death causes other members of the family.

Pilgrims' conceptions of family relationships with the saints have many variations. A woman from Kuwait who had suffered with *jādū*-induced ḥāẓirī following her husband's death once explained to me, during a much longer interview, that one of the turning points in her healing process had been the advice given to her by a Shiʿa cleric. He explained to her that as a Sayyid, she had extremely powerful ancestors who could help her if she sought their intercession, by which he meant that she could seek intervention from the Shiʿa *imāms*. She had thus visited the tomb of the Eighth Imām in Iran and then worked her way to Ḥusain Ṭekrī, which she had heard about from an Indian who lived in Kuwait. The martyrs of Karbala and the Shiʿa *imāms* were particularly powerful sources of intercession in this woman's life in part because they were her ancestors.

The nature of the relationships in this found family is also expressed through a devotion-based idiom. Along these lines, the term *Husainī* is used to describe any individual—irrespective of religious background—who mourns the death of Husain and his companions at Karbala. Thus, during a major Shiʿa-organized Muharram procession, a young Shiʿa woman emphatically explained to me that everyone who was participating in the procession was a "Husainī." The term also makes an appearance in *The Relationship between Hindus, Hindu Deities, and Imām Husain* (a booklet sold at Ḥusain Ṭekrī), which notes a community of "*husainī hindu*[s]" in Lucknow who "every year, during Muharram, mourn the death of Husain in the manner of Shiʿa Muslims."[73] While I did not find this term to be common at Ḥusain Ṭekrī, I never met anyone who strongly disagreed with the sentiment that those who love Husain and mourn his death could be called "Husainī." In any case, in participating in a public mourning procession together, individuals of diverse religious backgrounds place themselves in kinship relationships with one another.

It is worth noting that these found family relationships, while clearly important because they allow pilgrims to integrate and incorporate difference in a manner that I have suggested is central to the healing process, do not involve the sort of financial responsibility and dependency that is a ubiquitous feature of biological family life. While it is something of a commonplace in the anthropological study of religion that relationships are created and sustained through the act of giving gifts, it does seem that at Ḥusain Ṭekrī these found family relationships and friendships are both unencumbered (and unsubstantiated) by traditional family financial ties (particularly the gift giving associated with weddings) and sustained by the exchange of intangible rather than tangible gifts, such as the exchange that happens between *ḥāẓirīwāle* and *fariyād* reciters (a song-ḥāẓirī exchange), or between the reciter and listeners of "The Tale of the Ten Virtuous Women" (recitation-listening exchange). Other major forms of exchange at Ḥusain Ṭekrī are similarly founded on the giving and receiving of intangibles: the *ḥāẓirīwāle* and the saints (body-violence exchange), for example, or the inhalation of lobān by pilgrims (an exchange between smoke and presence at the shrine).[74] My own observations and experiences as well as pilgrims' self-consciously articulated analyses of their experiences all suggest that these and other exchanges at Ḥusain Ṭekrī create and sustain relationships that are transformative and powerful, and yet these relationships are often formalized by nothing more than declarations of familial relationship and actions of devotion.

These relationships seem to be substantiated with the giving of a tangible gift only when the two parties are ready to go their separate ways. Thus, for example, two Shi'a sisters from Lucknow sent Priya a letter and earrings upon their return to Lucknow, and when I left Ḥusain Ṭekrī after my follow-up research Priya and others offered me small gifts and meals.[75] The point here seems to be that the relationship between pilgrims—based almost entirely on the exchange of intangibles—has done all its healing *before* the tangible gifts are given. While these material gifts are necessary to make the found family relationships meaningful outside Ḥusain Ṭekrī and dargāḥs in general, during the healing process at the shrines themselves relationships can be initiated, maintained, and sustained through the exchange of intangibles.

In part because pilgrims to dargāḥs often seek the intercession of saints, dargāḥ culture in the subcontinent does not and has not existed in a perfectly harmonious relationship with self-proclaimed orthodox and reform tendencies within the tradition.[76] While in reality the level of exchange between the "Sufi" and "legal" institutions of the greater Islamic tradition is such that the distinction between the two is largely a false one, derived from ideology rather than history, late nineteenth- and twentieth-century India witnessed the birth of reform movements that sought to discredit the notion that saints had the ability to intercede on behalf of petitioners.[77] For reformers, at stake was a vision of an "Islamic" community purged of corrupting "Hindu" influence. These various reform movements also reflected sectarian rivalry between Shi'a and Sunni groups as well as a desire to replace popularly circulating "superstitious" stories about *bhūt* and *jinn* with "orthodox" Islamic doctrine. Not surprisingly, given the above discussion of the powerful cross-tradition attractiveness of discourses of suffering and martyrdom, some texts distributed by the major Islamic reform movement Tablighi Jama'at emphasize the suffering of the Prophet and his companions; Metcalfe has suggested that these texts were created to compete with the popularity of Shi'a mourning practices and rituals.[78] Thus, it is clear that the efficacy of stories of suffering in creating feelings of community was recognized by the writers of these countertexts, and that they used these stories in their effort to promote a version of Islam "purified" of corrupting elements, including Hinduism and Shiʿism.

In addition to texts that encourage remembrance of past suffering, at Ḥusain Ṭekrī today it is also possible to purchase a range of texts that are concerned with how to delineate Indian Islamic identity, but which actively and explicitly seek to integrate Hindus into a greater Islamic structure rather than distinguish "orthodox" Muslims and Muslim practice from a corrupting Hindu influence. This is not, however, an attempt founded upon contemporary Western notions of tolerance; the texts all clearly hold that truth is revealed via the universally recognized sources of Islamic authority (chiefly the Qur'an, the prophets, the Prophet Muhammad, and his immediate family). Rather, the two chief means used in these books to integrate Muslim and non-Muslim communities are the discourses of family and devotion. These discourses are dominant in both subcontinental and extra-subcontinental religious traditions. The texts' use of them suggests that cross-tradition exchange and incorporation are as reliant upon mutually recognizable structures of religious authority as they are upon particular stories and characters.

Three such texts available for purchase at Ḥusain Ṭekrī are *The Relationship between Hindus, Hindu Deities, and Imām Husain; Hindus' Love for Maulā ʿAli;* and, more iconographically, *Om and ʿAli.*[79] All three are published by Lucknow-based presses. *Hindus' Love for Maulā ʿAli* duplicates large portions of material from the other two texts.

The Relationship between Hindus, Hindu Deities, and Imām Husain and *Hindus' Love for Maulā ʿAli* are similarly inclined to document a devotion and connection based on family discourse between India and the major figures of early Islam. In fact, the major goal of *The Relationship between Hindus, Hindu Deities, and Imām Husain* seems to be establishing a link between Husain and India, the latter represented through the actions of both Indian rulers and Hindu deities. These relationships heavily rely upon the complementary concepts of devotion and family. The text notes that at the command of ʿAli, the students and disciples of Muhammad spread throughout the world. Eventually, "India's many sincere, loving, affectionate Hindus" become devoted servants of these "descendants of Muhammad." In this way, the text suggests, "the light of the Islamic religion *[islām dharm]* spread." Thus, the text concludes, "the relationship between Blessed Muhammad's descendants *[santān]* and the residents of India *[bhārtī nāgarik] must* be very profound and deep."[80] Furthering its case for the depth of the affection between Indians and Husain, the text continues by noting that when other parts of the Muslim world became inhospitable to Shi'a Muslims, the Shi'a community was able to safely seek refuge in Sindh, arriving, the text claims, in 145 Hijri. The text thus presents India as a place that allowed the Shi'a to save themselves.

Asserting the familial connection between "India" and Imām Husain, the text also offers a lineage *(silsilā):* after the retreat of the Shi'a community to Sindh, "Kāsim, son of Abraham, son of Ismail, son of Imām Ḥusain" also came to India in order to "save himself."[81] The text further elaborates that Husain himself expressed a desire to go to India because the Hindus of India "abhor violence."[82] Husain, the Shi'a text pointedly notes, knew that he would never find safety in a *Muslim* country; thus India, at that time a land without a Muslim population, was sure to be safe. The text notes that one Zain ul Abdin, a son of Husain, wrote a letter to the Indian king Chandragupta detailing Yazid's betrayal, and that the king sent an army to defend Husain, though they arrived after Husain and his companions had been martyred; again, the text emphasizes that (Hindu) India was more receptive to Islam than communities that contained Muslims.[83]

Likely in response to the sorts of nationalistic and communal discourses that have become increasingly dominant aspects of Indian life since the nineteenth century, the text, using the Islamic mechanism of *silsilā,* makes an effort to posit a connection between a person and a *nation,* thus including in its discussion of "Muhammad's relationship with India *[bhārat]*"[84] a description of a series of royal marriages: in the seventh century C.E., the Zoroastrian Iranian princess Mehr Bano, eldest daughter of a ruler named in the text as "Yajojard" (likely Yazdegerd III) marries the Ujjain-based king Chandragupta, and they produce a son named Samandr Gupta. After Yajojard is killed by an Arab army, his two remaining daughters are taken to Medina, and one of them, Shehar Bano, is married to Husain. Shehar Bano and Husain have a son, Zain ul Abdin. Thus, the Indian prince Samandr Gupta and the Arab prince Zain ul Abdin are first cousins, and this, the text concludes, further deepens the relationship between Imām Husain and India *(bhārat).* The choice of the term *bhārat* for "India" is probably not coincidental: it has a mythic connotation, unsullied by communal, historical entities such as "India" and "Pakistan."[85]

In addition to the discourses of devotion and family, the text's third means of creating a relationship between "India" and the martyrs of Karbala involves use of the Islamic trope of prophethood and the mechanism of prophecy. The remainder of the text chronicles many Hindu deities' foreknowledge of the events of Karbala. Section headings uncannily suggestive of tabloid headlines include "On Mount Kailash, what did Śrī Mahadevji say about Imām Husain?" "Śrī Rama's prophecy," "Guru Nanak's love of Husain," "Gandhi-jī and the disaster of Karbala," "Who taught the Buddha? And who helped him?" and "Śrī Krishna-jī's prophecy."[86] The text asserts, among other things, that 'Ali taught the Buddha in the Buddha's dreams, Guru Nanak went on the hajj,[87] several major Hindu deities predicted the coming of Muhammad and 'Ali, and Shiva and his wife Parvati recognized the future site of Husain's martyrdom because of the heat produced by that particular piece of earth. Like *The Relationship between Hindus, Hindu Deities, and Imām Husain, Hindus' Love for Maulā 'Ali* documents Hindu deities' prophecies about the coming of Muhammad, 'Ali, and Husain. Beyond this, it also documents contemporary instances of 'Ali appearing to devout Hindus—giving them *darśan* and granting their requests—because of their great devotion.

Compared with these two texts, *Om and 'Ali* seeks to strike an academic tone. Rather than emphasizing stories of non-Muslims' love of Husain and 'Ali or lineage-based relationships between Husain and "India," through a combination of the trope of prophethood, the mechanism of prophecy, and a pan–South Asian reverence for the power that is understood to be inherent in the written Arabic word, it seeks to prove that the syllable "Om" represents Hindus' own understanding of the pinnacle of their faith, and that the syllable is but another name for 'Ali. It establishes the nature of "Om" in part through quoting definitions given in several Sanskrit-English dictionaries published in the early decades of the twentieth century, first in English and then in Hindi, all of which suggest that "Om" be translated as a power or "hand" of god. The text then relates a lengthy sermon given by a Hindu sage many thousands of years ago that culminates in a prediction that:

> In the very distant future, in the final age, a great king of kings will be born who will perform every conceivable miracle. At his birth fire itself will be cooled. Idols will fall facedown; trees, rocks, and animals will do his bidding, and everything will come to him to offer respect. This great king's holy name will be "Mahāmatā." He will have the power to break the moon into two pieces with a flick of his finger. And along with this great king a prince will also be born. . . . Just as the supreme lord has many names, and just as this "Mahāmatā" has many names, so too this prince will have many names, and among his many names is "Om."[88]

Hindu "scripture" thus testifies, it seems, to the coming of Muhammad and, as we will see, 'Ali. Following this story, which *Om and 'Ali* cites as coming from the May 1827 edition of a Delhi-based periodical titled *Risāl e Sarasvatī, Om and 'Ali* moves from supporting its argument through the mechanism of prophecy to the pan–South Asian belief in the power inherent in Arabic script. Thus, as proof of the relationship between Om and ʿAli, the text suggests that that the stylized Devanagari Om, ॐ, bears a remarkable, even prophetic, resemblance to the Urdu/Persian ʿAli, علی.

After demonstrating the global implications of this correspondence by documenting instances of the recitation of "Om" in China as well as a Japanese temple that venerates a written word that looks like the Urdu/Arabic word *haidar*,[89] the text concludes with a dialogue between a Pandit and an interlocutor named Mool Chand. In this section Mool Chand bests the Pandit in debate, proving that in Vedic literature, it is predicted that "Om" will be born in the land of "Arabā." The implied meaning, of course, is that Hindu scriptures have predicted the birth of ʿAli.[90] Interestingly, this debate's source is cited as *"sanātana dharm pracārak, Lahore, 16 baisākh, 1682."* If genuine, it was likely originally written to discourage temple worship and ritual and to emphasize the "eternal" elements of the greater Hindu tradition that had, Sanātana Dharma missionaries felt, been obscured by ritual and idolatry. All of the sources that this text uses to make its case for global predictions of ʿAli's arrival and supremacy derive from Protestant and nineteenth-century notions of "religion" as a rational belief; thus, *Om and ʿAlī* holds that the true meaning of scripture has been obscured by centuries of meaningless, mechanical, irrational ritual.

In all three of these texts, then, non-Muslims and non-Muslim "scriptures" are integrated into Muslim communities through the discourses of devotion and family; from an explicit, orthodox Islamic perspective, the arguments' legitimacy derives from their use of the tropes of prophecy and prophethood. In addition to the pan-Islamic trope of prophethood, the Shiʿa doctrine according to which the twelve *imāms* are created from preexisting divine light is similarly useful in allowing ʿAli in particular to communicate with Hindu deities, themselves understood to be messengers from God.[91]

This use of prophethood is also common in casual conversations with Muslims of diverse backgrounds, who were keen to explain to me the reason Hindus were attracted to Muslim places. In independent conversations with me, the Sunni *mutavallī* of Ḥusain Ṭekrī, Haji Sarwar Ali Khan and the Itna ʿAsharī Shiʿa *imām* of the Ḥusain Ṭekrī–affiliated *imāmbāṛā* in Bombay both explained that in Islam, although there have been 124,000 *paigambar*, or messengers, only a fraction of these are named in Islamic sources.[92] Thus, they independently concluded, the Hindu deity Krishna was likely a *paigambar*. This theory is part of a larger Indian Muslim acceptance of the reality and power of Hindu deities. They do not take the position that Hindu deities do not exist; rather, some Hindu deities are understood to be *paigambar,* and others, particularly the Goddess in her bloodthirsty forms (chiefly the fearsome goddess Kālī, as she is depicted in popular lithographs) are understood to be demons.[93]

Attempts to integrate Hindu deities into a larger Islamic framework are also common in everyday conversations. I was present for one of these conversations that took place in a shop near the rauẓa of 'Abbas that is owned and operated by a Hindu family. The shop carries *ta'vīẕ,* semiprecious stones, plastic alternatives to semiprecious stones, pictures of the rauẓas and other major Indian dargāḥs, rings for "fashion," copper and brass rings for stomach health, ingenious handmade metal miniatures of common household objects (sold, I was told, as toys; the miniature tiffin is a wonder), shiny stickers emblazoned with prayers written in Urdu and Arabic, ropes, chains, locks, plastic containers for water and kerosene, brilliant mirror-art depictions of dargāḥs and the much-venerated Horse of Karbala Zuljenah (a.k.a. Dum Dum), and metal *zarīḥ* that are handmade by 'Abid Husain, whose sister's home houses a Ḥusain Ṭekrī–affiliated *imāmbāṛā.* Because this shop sells his *zarīḥ,* 'Abid visits it several times a year. During one of 'Abid's visits, likely due in part to my extended presence in the shop one day as we waited out a downpour, the two men got into a conversation in which they emphasized the tolerance that they felt was evident in the culture of Ḥusain Ṭekrī. In one of his extended musings on the relationship between Hindus and Muslims, 'Abid turned to the subject of Krishna and his likely status as one of the 124,000 *paigambar.* Literal readings of some of Krishna's exploits, however, presented a challenge to his interpretation: what of the well-known story of Krishna stealing the *gopīs*' clothing while they were bathing in the river? 'Abid reasoned that no *paigambar* could have behaved so lasciviously, concluding that this particular story had to have been created and propagated by those who wished to give Hinduism, and Krishna in particular, a bad name. Such was 'Abid's defense of Krishna's power and legitimacy. The shop owner kept silent throughout this speech, his expression offering no clues as to what he thought of his friend's exegesis. In pan-Islamic stories about prophets, these human messengers from God, after an initial period of testing, failure, and/or self-doubt, become virtuous exemplars whose lives are to be admired and imitated. In this case, if Krishna is indeed a prophet, his actions must be worthy of emulation. In converting Krishna from a god to a human messenger of God, some of his actions were also necessarily reinterpreted.

Husain Ṭekrī is an otherness-centered culture: otherness itself is what makes Ḥusain Ṭekrī powerful. The other can be a source of danger, illness, or healing, and the other can be encountered in communities that are both actual (through readings of "The Tale of the Ten Virtuous Women," recitation of *fariyād,* and helping others through their *khulī ḥāẓirī*) and imagined (through participation in the circulation of rumors, the practice of *khulī ḥāẓirī,* and participation in the discourse of *jādū*). The actual communities, within which healing occurs, have power and meaning because they exist in constant tension with the imagined communities. Because Muslim saint shrines are the only pan-Indian places that have the necessary conditions to host extremely diverse groups of people, more than any other type of place in India, they offer pilgrims the environment and the language necessary to harness this otherness and to use it as a potent force in both narratives of healing and healing practices.

Ḥusain Ṭekrī's pilgrims are keenly aware of otherness, and they make explicit and unconsidered use of it. Negotiation of otherness sometimes involves self-conscious attempts to acknowledge and then overcome it. At other times, the otherness serves as a necessary discursive reality that can make sense of the baffling and painful situations in which many pilgrims find themselves. The resultant notion of community that is common at Ḥusain Ṭekrī (and, given the interchangeability of dargāhs in the healing processes of pilgrims, is likely common at many Muslim saint shrines, especially, perhaps, those associated with martyrs or acts of asceticism on the part of a Muslim saint) is certainly not one built on a state of Turnerian communitas: constant awareness of difference is foundational to pilgrims' experiences and narratives of illness and healing. Liminality in the strictly Turnerian sense is similarly not quite representative of pilgrims' feelings of displacement, though liminality in a broader sense is characteristic of several aspects of Ḥusain Ṭekrī's culture, chief among them passing and anonymity. The discourses that actively and explicitly seek to eliminate religious difference are the texts and oral traditions that are the most removed from individual narratives of healing and recovery, and in these cases, the motivation derives from a desire to make sense of the apparent mixture of religious traditions and groups without abandoning notions of "Hindu" and "Muslim" as fundamental, fixed elements of individual identity. Only those invested in making larger political or ideological arguments would feel the necessity to keep these categories foundational and unchanging.

CONCLUSION

The Powerful Ephemeral

Dargāḥ Culture in Contemporary India

> A long time ago there was a king who had some kind of disease. A Hindu religious professional *[ved, paṇḍit]* or someone like that told him that if he bathed in the blood of 101 happily married couples *[joṛā]* he would be healed. The king set about gathering the 101 couples and put them all in a jail guarded by a sepoy who turned out to be none other than Band Choṛnewāle Bābā himself. Band Choṛnewāle Bābā reasoned that it wasn't good for 101 couples to die to save one man, and so he freed all the couples (hence his name). When the king found out he was furious, and he ordered Band Choṛnewāle Bābā beheaded. Band Choṛnewāle Bābā accepted this sentence, saying that if the king bathed in his blood he would be healed, which in fact turned out to be exactly what happened.

So goes one version of the tale of Band Choṛnewāle Bābā, whose humble roadside *cillā* graces the outskirts of Jaora.[1] This short story encompasses nearly everything that I have sought to argue about dargāḥ culture's unique ability to facilitate healing. Like stories about the founding of dargāḥs and stories about the ghosts that cause pilgrims' *jādū*-based illnesses, the story of Band Choṛnewāle Bābā reflects tensions between Hindu and Muslim and ruler and ruled. The happy couples languishing in the king's jail suffer unjustly, as do the *ḥāẓirīwāle* who self-identify as innocent *(maʿṣūm)*. Like the sacrifices of Muslim martyrs and Rajput heroes, Band Choṛnewāle Bābā's asceticism and selfless martyrdom are powerful enough to free the innocent and restore the health of the sick. In this way, the act of martyrdom, nonnarratively evoked in the burning and consumption of lobān that is common at dargāḥs throughout India, has local resonance as well as pan-

Islamic currency. As in the healing process of those with ḥāẓirī, the healing of the king has a physical and a social dimension: he is saved and, because he is the head of the community, the community is saved as well. Similarly, the freedom of the 101 couples has a social and a personal dimension: their individual lives are saved, and their potential to continue society through the families that they will eventually create is also preserved. Band Choṛnewāle Bābā's act of self-sacrifice is prompted by his keen sense of justice; as I have shown, much of dargāḥs' authority derives from pilgrims' understanding that they have entered a case in a court presided over by a judge whose commands *(ḥukm)* are manifest in the violence of *khulī ḥāẓirī.* And finally, this story of Band Choṛnewāle Bābā is itself a fragment, one of the countless tales of Sufi saints that, by virtue of its form, can be mobilized in a particular context to meet a particular goal, whether that goal is the construction of a narrative of healing or the narrative of a book.

Using Ḥusain Ṭekrī and some of its satellite sites as a case study, I have shown the ways in which Indian dargāḥs function as simultaneously local and cosmopolitan places, and I have shown that their efficacy as places of healing derives from this dual nature. Through shared practices that I have categorized as efficacious owing to their participation in either the power of asceticism or devotion and a shared collection of narrative forms that are part of dargāḥ culture, pilgrims to dargāḥs are provided with the tools and conditions necessary for constructing a narrative of healing that sustains them through the crises that bring them to the shrines. I have also suggested that these practices and narratives afford pilgrims the possibility of eventually becoming healers themselves.

In asserting the localness of the shrines as one aspect of their appeal and authority, I have shown that this localness is most ably demonstrated by the way in which shrines mark places where the power of the saint has been transferred to the land itself. In the case of Ḥusain Ṭekrī, the power of the saint is contained within water sources that are ascribed a supernatural origin. More generally, a *cillā* may possess a geographical feature that evidences the presence of the saint. This is the case, for example, at the roadside *cillā* of Bābā Farīd, whose actual tomb is in present-day Pakistan. This *cillā,* which is about a one-hour ride from Jaora, is known as the place where Bābā Farīd undertook a forty-day period of asceticism.[2] People say that the heat generated when Bābā Farīd suspended himself in a nearby stepwell and twirled around at the end of a rope resulted in all the trees in the area twisting, mirroring the saint's actions. To this day these strikingly gnarled trees surround a shrine that has been erected in his memory. In addition to these two ways in which a Muslim saint's visit can imbue the land with power, any conventional dargāḥ marks a transference of power from the saint himself to the earth in which the body of the saint is interred.

The land thus bears witness to and contains the power of the saint, making the authority of any shrine in part necessarily local. As a result, there is both reason for and benefit in making a pilgrimage to a distant dargāḥ. The local aspect of shrines' authority is further compounded by the culture of the region in which they are located. In the case of Ḥusain Ṭekrī, I have suggested that Rajput hero narratives and the valorization of martyrs to the Goddess contained therein likely shape the culture of the shrines as well as Rajput perspectives on their efficacy and legitimacy.

I have also argued that the power of Muslim saint shrines and similarly ambiguously Islamic places derives from their cosmopolitan character, which develops from several related factors. In an earlier period the Sufi institution of *silsilā,* or lineage, linked shrines in networks that connected the subcontinent with Persia, Arabia, and northern Africa. In the contemporary period, shrines previously unconnected by the mechanism of *silsilā* have become affiliated in part because of shared rituals, vocabulary, and action, much of it drawn from the language of the court. There is a complementary language of healing, to be sure, but it is telling that the speech of pilgrims in *khulī ḥāẓirī* is infused with legal terms: dargāḥs function as courts in both the royal and the legal sense of the English term, and the healing process relies upon this dual character. In participating in the legal culture of the shrines, the pilgrim comes to understand herself as part of a global community, allowing her to develop an experience of selfhood that transcends *jāti-* or family-based identities.

The cosmopolitan character of Sufi saint shrines also derives from the widely held understanding that the realm of a saint can potentially expand endlessly through the devotion of his followers. Recall, for example, the rather lengthy newspaper headline cited in the first chapter of this book: "One way, a dargāḥ and the other way, Hanumān jī / Hindu worship and Muslim worship happen side by side / In the village of Lālākheṛī, the court of [Sufi saint] Tāj ud Dīn / A rare example of Hindu-Muslim unity."[3] Tāj ud Dīn's grave is not actually located in Lālākheṛī; his tomb is in Nagpur and the dargāḥ in Lālākheṛī exists because his devotees have erected a shrine in his memory. It is suggestive that the Hindi headline uses the term "court" *(darbār)* to describe the space in which this "Hindu-Muslim unity" occurs, echoing in some ways the Islamic concept of a *wilāya,* or the "realm" of a Sufi saint. In the contemporary period, the court of a Sufi saint is conceptualized as a kingdom capable of accommodating buildings and institutions identified with both Hindu and Muslim communities.[4] Tāj ud Dīn's kingdom extends as far as its furthest devotee, even if that devotee lives in the tiny village of Lālākheṛī. The specifically Shi'a culture of *imāmbāṛās* possesses a similar ability to extend wherever the martyrs of Karbala are remembered and mourned. As a place built to commemorate the martyrs of Karbala, Ḥusain Ṭekrī is part of this kingdom.

Finally, although the above factors create the sense that a visit to a dargāḥ connects the individual with a cosmopolitan community variously conceptualized as a network or a realm, it is important to remember that the cosmopolitan culture of Ḥusain Ṭekrī and dargāḥs in general is also a product of the diversity of the pilgrims who visit the shrines seeking access to this powerful network. Such diversity among dargāḥ pilgrims does not, however, indicate a softening, blending, or elimination of religious difference. On the contrary, part of dargāḥs' healing power derives from the fact that they are experienced as places where the dangerous other is encountered, encompassed, and exorcized bodily, narratively, and socially. Similarly, the power of the saints, whether as angry, empathetic martyrs, powerful ascetics, or the enraged untimely dead, is regionally influenced. The openness, connectedness, and general messiness of dargāḥs together comprise their strength.

Everything that I have suggested is powerful about ambiguously Islamic places is also fleeting. The narrative forms discussed in chapter 2 derive their meaning from the context in which they are uttered and their efficacy from their fragmented, anecdotal, and open-ended nature. Meaning is created in these fragments, not in the dominant narrative of healing. The ephemeral nature of the smoke of lobān is a simple physical fact. In the inherently transitory nature of *khulī ḥāẓirī,* as with all forms of spirit possession and exorcism, the power of possessed speech and the actions of a possessed body cannot be effectively transferred to another medium; the only trace of the power of the act is the body itself, which is understood to be powerful in direct proportion to the amount of violence and impurity it has overcome. *Gum ḥāẓirī* by definition cannot be observed; the pain in the body of the victim is hidden. The rumor-based and imagined communities of transgressive and dangerous others are also ephemeral, and the actual communities that are created by pilgrims at Ḥusain Ṭekrī through shared ritual readings, meals, and places of residence change constantly as pilgrims come and go. None of these phenomena are purchased; they are not, after all, objects, and they consequently fail to leave a trace in a money-based economy. At Muslim saint shrines there is no single ritual specialist to be interviewed, no definitive canon to be interpreted, and no elaborate ritual to read. Perhaps this is why there are so few ethnographic studies of Indian dargāḥs, and even fewer that seek to elucidate their power as places of healing despite the fact that dargāḥs are everywhere in India and patronized by everyone. Perhaps, too, this is why they are so powerful.

APPENDIX A

Tārīkh e Yūsufī

The Tārīkh e Yūsufī, an Urdu history of the Princely State of Jaora, contains the oldest account of the founding of Ḥusain Ṭekrī.

First: During the reign of Nawāb Muhammad Ismail Khan, [there was] a strange incident. In 1304 Hijri [1886], it happened that there was a rare concurrence of the Hindu festival of Daśahrā and the eighth day of Muharram. The keepers of the *ta'ziyas* said, "We will not allow Rāmlīlā processions to pass in front of the *ta'ziyas* on the day of Daśahrā." In response, the government issued a warning, stating, "Do not interfere in the traditions of the Hindus, and Hindu rites ought not to disturb Muslims" *[hindū rasūm musalmānon men dakhl na den]*. But the Muslims didn't heed this warning. Two days earlier, from the time that the image of Ravana had been erected, a regiment of Central India English mounted troops from the cantonment at Agra had arrived to keep an eye on the commotion. After gathering their collaborators, they went and stood directly in front of the *ta'ziya*s for all to see. The *ta'ziya* bearers were very unhappy at this turn of events, and so later in the evening they went and immersed their *ta'ziya* in the river. And so there was a huge uproar, with weeping and wailing, and all the shops in the city were closed. But because of the presence of the English mounted troops, there was no possible way for riots to start. But the next day, on the ninth of Muharram, the *nawāb,* out of the kindness of his merciful heart, commanded that the *ta'ziya* bearers be brought into his care, and he himself gave the instructions that gratified the *ta'ziya* bearers, and he distributed around two hundred rupees among them, so that by the ninth day of Muharram, after a full day [of work], the *ta'ziya*s were once again properly prepared.

But at this very moment, people from the village of Rozana were on their way from Jaora. About two miles north [of Jaora] these people truly saw, with their own eyes, that the *ta'ziya* of the city of Jaora, accompanied by people on horses and people on foot, was moving steadily toward the north. And in absolute truth, in between the city [of Jaora] and the village of Rozana, the *ta'ziya* was placed on a small hill that sits on the edge of the border of the Brahmin village [of Rozana]. After a few minutes, they moved from that place toward the east, in the direction of the River Maleni. In no time at all, everyone in the city had heard about this series of events, and a huge crowd of people had gone and gathered on this small hill. And acknowledging that this place was blessed and the abode of blessed Imām Husain, the lord of this life and the life to come, they introduced the custom of offering *fātiḥa* and *nazr* and *niyāz* and giving hundreds of rupees in alms in the name of the departed souls of the *imāms*. On this hill, a well that had been dry for a long time spontaneously filled with water, even though it wasn't the rainy season, and after this happened, people had even more faith in the place.

Second: The commotion concerning bright torches that appeared each night spread in all directions.

Third: Often, it happens that patients find healing in the water of that well, and so followers of Allah began to spread out into every district and quarter. Thousands and thousands of people came from far and wide—from Lucknow, Azimabad [Patna], Surat, Bombay, Hyderabad, the Deccan, and many other places and countries, and their wishes and prayers began to be granted and fulfilled. Because of this miraculous and singularly rare event, this city of Jaora became exalted throughout India, and among every sort of community in the vicinity, these places became known as Blessed Jaora and the Blessed Hill of Husain *[jāvra sharīf o ḥusain ṭekrī sharīf]*. Because of the great faith that he himself had in this rare event, praise be to God, with a feeling of deep loyalty, the *nawāb* took it upon himself to maintain this wonderful and blessed place.

APPENDIX B

Ḥusain Ṭekrī Kyā Hai?

Ḥusain Ṭekrī Kyā Hai? *(What is Ḥusain Ṭekrī?), a Hindi/Urdu guidebook for pilgrims, contains a recent version of Ḥusain Ṭekrī's origin story.*

WHEN AND HOW WAS ḤUSAIN ṬEKRĪ MADE?

It has been more than one hundred years since Ḥusain Ṭekrī was established in the midst of dense jungle. When Ḥusain Ṭekrī wasn't here, people were afraid of passing the place where it would be, since it was a dense jungle. But since the residence of the Prophet's grandson Imām Husain came here, the jungle has become settled and crowds of people fill it from all sides. The sick, the incurable, and the troubled come here, and having become happy, they go.

The miracle of Ḥusain Ṭekrī happened on the tenth of Muharram, 1886. The *ta'ziya* of Jaora was in the historic *imāmbāṛā* until the evening of the tenth of Muharram, when it was lifted and taken in the midst of a procession to Karbala. This *ta'ziya* was commissioned with great purity and faith by Dādā Mukīm Khān [a brother of one of the nawābs of Jaora]. The *ta'ziya* was fairly large and heavy, requiring the efforts of sixty to seventy men to lift it. In 1886 the *ta'ziya* was in the *imāmbāṛā*, just as it always was. On the tenth of Muharram Rāmlīlā happened, and for this reason two processions were on the road at the same time—one the *ta'ziya* and the other Rāmlīlā. But the *ta'ziya* procession was at Phūṭi Baurī intersection, and the Hindu brothers couldn't pass until the Muslim brothers went ahead. In those days it was very cold, and therefore the *ta'ziya* bearers had set the *ta'ziya* at the intersection and lit a fire to stay warm. But the excellent Hindus couldn't advance until the *ta'ziya* procession advanced, and for this reason the Hindus asked the Muslims to move the *ta'ziya* procession away from the intersection. There were words between them. Knowing people thought, "God forbid this get out of hand." Therefore, they decided to tell the whole story to the ruler of the kingdom, and to do as he said. Both groups reached Muhammad Ismail Khan. He listened to both sides' stories and told the Muslims to let the Rāmlīlā procession pass. The Muslims respected the king's statement, but they were secretly chagrined. They were not happy with this decision of the king. Having resolved to be patient, they moved to the side and sat next to the *ta'ziya*. From another direction, the Hindus lifted their Ram display and began to move forward. When they came to the *ta'ziya*, they beheld a strange sight. They had never seen a miraculous sight such as this, whether they were Hindu or Muslim. Every one of them was in wonder at what was happening. What had happened was the *ta'ziya* that normally took sixty to seventy people to lift was moving, by itself, up in the air a few feet and then, slowly, moving forward. The *ta'ziya* came to the *imāmbāṛā*'s courtyard and stopped.

Having seen this miracle, the *ta'ziya* bearer's eyes became wet with tears. Everyone began kissing the *ta'ziya*. And the sound of "Yah Husain! Yah Husain!" rang in the air. The news of this miracle spread like wildfire. This was the first miracle that happened in Jaora.

Some people came from the village of Rozana to participate in the *ta'ziya* procession. When they were near Mehaṁdī Well, they saw a strange sight. Mehaṁdī Well was located in dense jungle; people saw lights in this jungle, and from the dense jungle lights came dazzling light. Every tree in the jungle was easily illuminated by the light. At first people were afraid and thought to themselves, "What is going on in this jungle? Even during the day people are afraid to come here; who would come at night?" Still, some people took the name of Maulā on their lips and went forward. They saw that the *ta'ziya* of Jaora was present. Here and there near the *ta'ziya* they saw veiled people whose faces radiated light, and it was from this light that the jungle was illuminated. Some people saw this and stopped, but those people who wanted to see more went forward. They saw a beautiful old man with a radiant face who was seated in one place. In front of him, water was coming up from the ground as if from a pump, and he was using the water for *vuzū* [the mandatory washing performed before *namāz*].

Some people saw another old man with a luminous face offering *namāz* on a nearby hill on the place where the standard *[parcam]* of Imām Husain now waves and the rauẓa of Imām Husain now stands.

People had never seen anything like this before; after consulting with one another, they decided that the *nawāb* should be told about what had happened. It was late at night by that point, though, so everyone went home. First thing in the morning, they arrived at Nawāb Ismail Khan's bungalow. There were women and children in this group. They told the *nawāb*'s servants that they had come to see the *nawāb* because they had seen a strange sight on a hill the previous evening. They [the servants] told the *nawāb*, and he told them to see to it that the people were seated comfortably with his permission. Immediately upon meeting the *nawāb*, the people told him about the miraculous things that they had seen. After listening carefully to what the people said to him, the *nawāb* said that he had seen in a dream exactly what the people had seen with their own eyes. It was also told [in the dream] that eyewitnesses would come and tell about this place. The *nawāb* said that this brilliant-faced old man had also said that he should go to this place and protect it. The *nawāb* sent the people to this place with his servants, and he himself arrived there soon thereafter. When the people arrived, the jungle was filled with a wonderful smell. It was revealed in a dream that "an enclosure should be created up to the point where the good smell has spread [because] we are pleased with this place." The *nawāb* also enclosed the place where water bubbled up from the ground. He made a big well at this place. The place was named Jhālrā Sharīf [Blessed Spring].

Some people came running from a hill and arrived in the presence of the *nawāb*. When the *nawāb* came to this hill with the people, there was an unearthly sweet smell in the air—better than aloe wood and ambergris. The *nawāb* gave the order to enclose the entire area. Since this miracle happened on the tenth of Muharram and that day is the day of Imām Husain's martyrdom, the hill was associated with Husain and named Husain Hill. The *nawāb* appointed a man to take care of the place and to administer lobān in the morning and evening.

THE CONSTRUCTION AND TRADITION OF THE *RAUẒAS*

The *nawāb* gave this holy place protection, but he did not build the rauẓas. One reason for this was the fact that he was given a command to protect this place, not to build rauẓas on it.

The command to build the rauẓas was given to Ḵẖojā Janab Ismail Muhammad. He had a leather business for which he traveled a lot. It is said that during the year in which the miracle of Ḥusain Ṭekrī happened, he [Ismail Muhammad] saw a messenger of God in a dream. This messenger told him that his work took him near Ḥusain Ṭekrī on a regular basis, and that he should go to the *nawāb,* and with the *nawāb*'s permission, he should build a rauẓa with his own money on the place the miracle had happened. At the place where water bubbled up from the ground he should build a rauẓa to Ḥaẓrat ʿAbbas, and on the sweet-smelling earth, the rauẓa of Imām Husain.

Considering his present situation, Ismail Muhammad said that he didn't have that much money. He was informed that his business was about to become exceptionally profitable, and the moment he met with these profits he was to go and build the rauẓas. Nine days after the dream he made a big profit from Surat. However, he didn't remember his dream. One reason that he didn't remember his dream was he had neglected to tell his wife and children about it, who would have reminded him if they had known.

Some days after the dream, a beautiful child came into Ismail Muhammad's office and asked him about the construction of the rauẓas and reminded him of the call to build the rauẓas. The child said that "even having met with success in commerce, you haven't seen to the construction of the rauẓas. This is the work of Imām e Mazlūm [the wrongfully oppressed *imām*], and if you don't properly observe the tradition, in the place of profit and usefulness, difficulty after difficulty will follow." Having said this, the child left.

Having heard what the child had to say, Ismail Muhammad was amazed because he hadn't told anyone about the dream. Immediately after seeing the child, he [Ismail Muhammad] went out to ask how he [the child] knew about this tradition. Outside he asked people about the child, but people told him that no child had passed near them. In any event, immediately after this incident Ismail Muhammad went home. He told his wife and his children about the dream. His wife Musammat Rahmat Bai was very impressed by the dream. Everyone made a very quick decision to visit Ḥusain Ṭekrī. Some days later, Ismail Muhammad, together with his wife and children, arrived at Ḥusain Ṭekrī. First of all, he saw to it that the rauẓa building process was started. After the rauẓas of Imām Husain and Ḥaẓrat ʻAbbas were built, he also saw to it that an inn was built for pilgrims. There are fifteen rooms in this inn, and to this day it is known as Ismail Sarai. There is not a set tradition for the time that the rauẓas were prepared. But in the history of Jaora it is written that the construction commenced in 1888.

Ismail Muhammad's death happened at Ḥusain Ṭekrī itself, and his grave is near the rauẓa of Imām Husain. His death occurred in 1340 [1921/1922].

Notes

PROLOGUE

1. A Shiʿite icon of a five-fingered hand, said to represent the *panj-e-pāk,* or Five Pure Ones: Muhammad, ʿAli, Hasan, Husain, and Fatima.

2. The name of the horse Husain rode at Karbala; its riderless return following the martyrdom of Husain is popularly understood to be the way that Husain's family learned that he had been killed.

3. Mastān Bābā, whose name likely derives from *mastānā,* meaning "drunken," died in the late 1990s. He was well known in Udaipur, and he figures prominently in the healing process of another pilgrim, whose story will be related in subsequent chapters.

4. In most cases, this is a Qur'an whose Arabic has been transliterated into Devanagari, sometimes with an accompanying interlinear translation into the vernacular.

5. A non-allopathic healer commonly faces a life-threatening situation or illness before becoming a healer him- or herself. See, for instance, Michael Taussig, *Shamanism, Colonialism, and the Wild Man: A Study in Terror and Healing* (Chicago: University of Chicago Press, 1987).

6. As I will explain in the following chapter, the term "saint," used throughout this book for revered Muslim individuals referred to with a wide range of titles and terms, is purposefully chosen.

7. According to Platt's Urdu-English dictionary, the Urdu term *zarīḥ,* commonly used to refer to a railing or latticework surrounding a temple or tomb, is "probably a corruption of [the Arabic] *ẓarīḥ.*" John T. Platts, *A Dictionary of Urdū, Classical Hindi, and English* (New Delhi: Munshiram Manoharlal, 2000). In India, the term is also used to refer to models of the tombs of the martyrs of Karbala made of precious metals and jewels. When writing the word *zarīḥ,* native Urdu speakers at Ḥusain Ṭekrī employed a range of spellings, including *jarī and zarī.* For more

on the usages of *zarīḥ,* see Frank J. Koram, *Hosay Trinidad: Muḥarram Performances in an Indo-Caribbean Diaspora* (Philadelphia: University of Pennsylvania Press, 2003), 68, 278.

INTRODUCTION

1. Subcontinental Muslim healers and teachers are known by a variety of honorifics with deep roots in the greater Islamic tradition. See the glossary for a fully elaborated list of terms.

2. They may connote temporal power to some pilgrims, since *k̲h̲wājā* has an older meaning of a wealthy individual, and *walī* also carries the meaning of a master or prince.

3. Husain, ʻAbbas, and ʻAli are, respectively, the grandson of the Prophet Muhammad, the half brother of Husain, and the son-in-law/cousin of the Prophet Muhammad. All three are foundational figures for centuries of Islamic discourse.

4. While Ḥusain Ṭekrī has a clear historical connection with the Shiʻa K̲h̲oja community, the name Imām Husain is commonly used by Sunni, Shiʻa, and Hindu pilgrims and therefore encompasses both the specific Shiʻa meaning of a successor to the Prophet Muhammad and the pan-Islamic meaning of a religious leader and/or the leader of common prayer in a mosque.

5. Muzaffar Alam, *The Languages of Political Islam: India 1200–1800* (Chicago: University of Chicago Press, 2004).

6. Joyce Burkhalter Flueckiger, *In Amma's Healing Room: Gender and Vernacular Islam in South India* (Bloomington: Indiana University Press, 2006).

7. Peter van de Veer, *Religious Nationalism: Hindus and Muslims in India.* (Berkeley: University of California Press, 1994), 205.

8. Harvard University's Pluralism Project's ongoing mapping of the American religious landscape does not include any dargāḥ-like institutions in its exhaustive listing of American religious spaces, though it does note the graves of several recognized Sufi saints. See www.pluralism.org. Further, no dargāḥ-like spaces are discussed in the essays contained in Barbara Daly Metcalf, ed., *Making Muslim Space in North America and Europe* (Berkeley: University of California Press, 1996).

9. In contrast, there are sources in which Muslim writers belonging to the educated elite consider their relationship with Hindus and Hindu India. See Carl Ernst, "India as a Sacred Islamic Land," in *Religions of India in Practice,* ed. Donald S. Lopez Jr. (Princeton, NJ: Princeton University Press, 1995), 556–63; and "Admiring the Works of the Ancients: The Ellora Temples as Viewed by Indo-Muslim Authors," in *Beyond Turk and Hindu: Rethinking Religious Identities in Islamicate South Asia,* ed. David Gilmartin and Bruce B. Lawrence (Gainesville: University of Florida Press, 2000), 98–120.

10. Christian W. Troll, ed., *Muslim Shrines in India: Their Character, History, and Significance* (New Delhi: Oxford University Press, 1989). It is important to state explicitly that in what follows, the term *subcontinental* is purposefully chosen; using *Hindu* in this context would be imprecise.

11. P. M. Currie, *The Shrine and Cult of Muʻīn al-dīn Chishtī of Ajmer* (New Delhi: Oxford University Press, 1989).

12. *Jāt* is a caste group.

13. This seeking of subcontinent-based (if not -derived) legitimacy is typical of many major Muslim saint shrines in India; thus, it is commonly asserted that seven journeys to one of the major Indian dargāḥs is "worth" one hajj. Similarly, the dargāḥ of Hazratbal in Kashmir sought to attain the status of Medina by becoming the home of a hair of Muhammad. For information on Hazratbal, see Muhammad Ishaq Khan, "The Significance of the Dargah of Hazratbal in the Socio-Religious and Political Life of Kashmiri Muslims," in *Muslim Shrines in India: Their Character, History, and Significance,* ed. Christian Troll (New Delhi: Oxford University Press, 1989), 172–88. Ḥusain Ṭekrī is also home to a hair of the Prophet Muhammad, which is displayed once a year on the occasion of his birthday. The hair is said to have been a gift from the Begum of Bhopal during the time Jaora was still a princely state.

14. Richard M. Eaton, "The Political and Religious Authority of the Shrine of Bābā Farīd," in *Moral Conduct and Authority: The Place of Adab in South Asian Islam,* ed. Barbara Daly Metcalf (Berkeley: University of California Press, 1984), 333–56.

15. Carl W. Ernst, *Eternal Garden: Mysticism, History and Politics at a South Asian Sufi Center* (Albany: State University of New York Press, 1992). The argument about the appeal of Muslim shrines to non-Muslims occurs in chapter 11.

16. While it is true that Husain is commonly understood to be a particularly Shiʿa object of veneration, it is also clear that publicly mourning his death was and is a major Indian Sunni activity. In Jaora, each Sunni Muslim community has its own *taʿziya,* as does the Sunni royal family of Jaora itself. Thus the Sunni *nawāb*'s alignment with Husain is not as unusual at it may initially seem.

17. On a practical level, Ḥusain Ṭekrī continues to exist because at the time of Independence, its lands were *waqf* property rather than the property of the *nawābs*.

18. *Darbār,* from the Persian *darbār; ʿadālat,* from the Persian *ʿadālat,* derived from the Arabic *ʿ-d-l,* to act equitably.

19. Throughout this book I have almost always transliterated Islamic religious terms from the Urdu rather than the Hindi. However, in the case of *faislā,* I have opted for transliteration from the Hindi because it accurately reflects the pronunciation common among pilgrims at Ḥusain Ṭekrī.

20. The left arm and wrist are not used because they are considered impure. While most pilgrims tie the cord themselves, the religious healers who commonly populate dargāḥs may also perform this action on behalf of their clients.

21. *Fariyād* is another common term for this sort of petition, but in my experience it was not frequently used at Ḥusain Ṭekrī.

22. The consequences of a king's loss of political power in a colonial South Indian Hindu context are explored in Nicholas B. Dirks's seminal *The Hollow Crown: Ethnohistory of an Indian Kingdom* (New York: Cambridge University Press, 1987).

23. The function of dargāḥ as a stand-in for an actual government court is demonstrated by Nasim's case, which will be related in chapter 2.

24. Anand Vivek Taneja, personal communication, October 12, 2008. Taneja's own work on the dargāḥ of Feroz Shah is not yet published.

25. The *New York Times* ran a story about a Lebanese man convicted of sorcery in Saudi Arabia. Because the Saudi constitution is the Qur'an itself, and because the Qur'an condemns magic, the man was sentenced to death. The conviction, how-

ever, rested upon his confession, which some argued was coerced and therefore not valid. See Michael Slackman, "TV Mystic Lingers in Saudi Jail," *New York Times,* April 24, 2010.

26. Liebeskind's discussion of three Indian Sufi orders demonstrates that dargāḥs' traditional sources of authority and power were significantly eroded in the modern period as a result of Indian reform movements, which urged Muslims to learn from primary source texts rather than align themselves with saints, and as a result of land reform and Partition, which devastated dargāḥs' networks and sources of income. See Claudia Liebeskind, *Piety on Its Knees: Three Sufi Traditions of South Asia in Modern Times* (New Delhi: Oxford University Press, 1998).

27. Marshall G. Hodgson, *The Venture of Islam, Volume 1: The Classical Age of Islam* (Chicago: University of Chicago Press, 1974), 59.

28. Talal Asad, *Genealogies of Religion: Discipline and Reasons of Power in Christianity and Islam* (Baltimore, MD: Johns Hopkins University Press, 1993), 53–54.

29. The contemporary commonplace within academia that static, rigid notions of East and West are ideologically driven fictions can be traced to Edward Said's classic *Orientalism* (New York: Pantheon Books, 1978). Influential anthropologists whose work has been criticized for presuming a static, universal, and/or atemporal form of Islam include Geertz, Mernissi, Combs-Schilling, and Gellner. See Clifford Geertz, *Islam Observed: Religious Development in Morocco and Indonesia* (Chicago: University of Chicago Press, 1968); Fatima Mernissi, *Beyond the Veil: Male-Female Dynamics in Modern Muslim Society* (Bloomington: Indiana University Press, 1987); Elaine Combs-Schilling, *Sacred Performances: Islam, Sexuality, and Sacrifice* (New York: Columbia University Press, 1989); Ernest Gellner, *Muslim Society* (Cambridge: Cambridge University Press, 1981).

30. Foucault's influence on this kind of discourse-focused scholarship is paramount. Michel Foucault, *The Order of Things: An Archaeology of the Human Sciences* (New York: Vintage Books, 1994); and *The Archaeology of Knowledge,* trans. A.M. Sheridan Smith (New York: Pantheon Books, 2002). For a recent lucid explanation of the impact of discourse-centered scholarship on the study of Islam and an excellent example of this type of scholarship, see Michael Lambek, *Human Spirits: A Cultural Account of Trance in Mayotte* (Cambridge: Cambridge University Press, 1981).

31. See, for example, Daniel Varisco, *Islam Obscured: The Rhetoric of Anthropological Representation* (New York: Palgrave Macmillan, 2005); John R. Bowen, *Muslims Through Discourse: Religion and Ritual in Gayo Society* (Princeton, NJ: Princeton University Press, 1993); Abdul Hamid el-Zein, "Beyond Ideology and Theology: The Search for an Anthropology of Islam," *Annual Review of Anthropology* 6: 227–54.

32. Talal Asad, "The Idea of an Anthropology of Islam," Occasional Papers Series (Washington, DC: Georgetown University Center for Contemporary Arab Studies, 1986).

33. Varisco, *Islam Obscured,* 154. See also Brinkley Messick, *The Calligraphic State: Textual Domination and History in a Muslim Society* (Berkeley: University of California Press, 1993).

34. Problematic analysis of Islamic discourse is reliant upon either implicit or explicit variations on the phrases "Islam and . . . " and "Islam is . . . ". In academic

writing, such paradigms are often adopted for political reasons (with forms as diverse as discourses of human rights and neo-conservative "civilizational" arguments) and as such are shaped by a popular, media-based conversation that necessarily uses the essentialist category "Islam" in order to participate in the globalized discourse that currently dominates popular culture. Additionally, insofar as it relies upon the content of the written Islamic canon (most basically, *sira*, hadith, and Qur'an) for its formulation of "Islam," some of this scholarship also reflects a disciplinary tendency to identify religion with written text.

35. Qur'an 7:109–126; 10:79–81; 20:65–70; 20:43–47. Qur'an 2:102 is also a significant verse in Qur'anic discussions of sorcery and magic, but again, neither the verse nor its content was discussed by Muslim pilgrims, either in conversations with me or in conversations among themselves to which I was privy.

36. See, for example, the account in the hadith collection *Sahih Bukhari*, volume 4, book 54, number 490.

37. The extent to which pilgrims are relating stories that they originally encountered in teachings by Muslim religious authorities is difficult, if not impossible, to trace at a place like Ḥusain Ṭekrī because it does not have a universally recognized *imām*. (It does, however, have an officially appointed *imām*, though he does not speak to the general population of pilgrims on a regular basis.)

38. Richard Bulliet, *Islam: The View from the Edge* (New York: Columbia University Press, 1994).

39. Messick, *The Calligraphic State*, 26.

40. Graham Dwyer, *The Divine and the Demonic: Supernatural Affliction and Its Treatment in North India* (London: Routledge Curzon, 2003).

41. Tony Stewart, *Fabulous Females and Peerless Pirs: Tales of Mad Adventure in Old Bengal* (New York: Oxford University Press, 2004); Peter Gottschalk, *Beyond Hindu and Muslim: Multiple Identity in Narratives from Village India* (New York: Oxford University Press, 2000). See also the table of contents of Donald S. Lopez Jr., ed., *Religions of India in Practice* (Princeton, NJ: Princeton University Press, 1995), which arranges its various articles according to both genre and tradition.

42. Two recent significant works on religious identity in modern India include Harjot Oberoi, *The Construction of Religious Boundaries: Culture, Identity, and Diversity in the Sikh Tradition* (Chicago: University of Chicago Press, 1994); and Gyanendra Pandey, ed., *Hindus and Others: The Question of Identity in India Today* (New York: Viking, 1993).

43. Respectively, Barbara Daly Metcalf, *Islamic Revival in British India: Deoband: 1860–1900* (Princeton, NJ: Princeton University Press, 1982); Peter van der Veer, "Playing or Praying: A Sufi Saint's Day in Surat," *Journal of Asian Studies* 51, no. 3 (August 1992): 545–64.

44. J. J. Roy Burman, *Hindu-Muslim Syncretic Shrines and Communities* (New Delhi: Mittal Publications, 2002); Yoginder Sikand, *Hindu-Muslim Syncretic Shrines in Karnataka* (Bangalore: Himayat, 2001).

45. Susan Bayly, *Saints, Goddesses, and Kings: Muslims and Christians in South Indian Society: 1700–1900* (Cambridge: Cambridge University Press, 1989); Peter Gottschalk, *Beyond Hindu and Muslim;* Anna Bigelow, "Sharing Saints, Shrines and Stories: Practicing Pluralism in North India" (PhD diss., University of California, Santa Barbara, 2004), 2.

46. Shail Mayaram, "Beyond Ethnicity? Being Hindu *and* Muslim in South Asia," in *Lived Islam in South Asia: Adaptation, Accommodation, and Conflict,* ed. Imtiaz Ahmad and Helmut Reifeld (New Delhi: Social Science Press, 2004), 18–39; Yoginder Sikand, "Shared Hindu-Muslim Shrines in Karnataka: Challenges to Liminality," in *Lived Islam in South Asia: Adaptation, Accommodation, and Conflict,* ed. Imtiaz Ahmad and Helmut Reifeld (New Delhi: Social Science Press, 2004), 116–86; Dominique-Sila Khan, "The Graves of History and the Metaphor of the Hidden Pir," in *Culture, Communities and Change,* ed. Varsha Joshi (Jaipur: Institute of Rajasthan Studies, Rawat Publications, 2002), 154–72.

47. Sikand, "Shared Hindu-Muslim Shrines," 175.

48. Desiderio Pinto, S.J., "The Mystery of the Nizamuddin Dargah: The Accounts of Pilgrims," in *Muslim Shrines in India: Their Character, History, and Significance,* ed. Christian Troll (New Delhi: Oxford University Press, 1989), 112–24.

49. Paul Jackson, S.J., "Perceptions of the Dargahs of Patna," in *Muslim Shrines in India: Their Character, History, and Significance,* ed. Christian Troll (New Delhi: Oxford University Press, 1989), 98–111.

50. Mumtaz Currim and George Michell, photographs by Karoki Lewis, *Dargahs: Abodes of the Saints* (Mumbai: Marg, 2004).

51. Carl W. Ernst and Tony Stewart, "Syncretism," in *South Asian Folklore: An Encyclopedia,* ed. Peter J. Claus, Sarah Diamond, and Margaret A. Mills (New York: Routledge, 2002), 586–88.

52. Jackie Assayag, *Au confluence de deux rivière: Musulmans et Hindous dans le sud de L'Inde* (Paris: Presses de l'École Francaise d'Extrême Orient, 1995), trans. by Latika Sahgal as *At the Confluence of Two Rivers: Muslims and Hindus in South India* (Delhi: Manohar, 2004), 121.

53. See for instance Victor Turner, *The Ritual Process: Structure and Anti-Structure* (Chicago: Aldine Publishing Company, 1969).

54. Shail Mayaram, "Spirit Possession: Reframing Discourses of the Self and the Other," in *La possession en Asie du Sud: parole, corps, territoire,* ed. Jackie Assayag and Gilles Tarabout (Paris: Éditions de l'École des hautes etudes en sciences socials, 1999), 123–24; Lambek, *Human Spirits.*

55. With her permission, I am using Maya's real name. At their request, I am not using Priya or Babli's real names. I am also not using Nasim's real name. Although she gave me permission to use it, as our relationship developed, she shared some personal stories with me that she seemed to want to remain private. I believe that when she gave me permission to use her real name, she had forgotten that she had told me these stories. Therefore, I have chosen to protect her privacy by giving her a pseudonym.

56. Marcel Mauss, *The Gift: Forms and Functions of Exchange in Archaic Societies,* trans. Ian Cunnison (Glencoe, IL: Free Press, 1954).

57. The standard gifts offered at dargāḥs include sweets, rose petals, incense, perfume, and sheets. In yet another instance of the shared identity of Hindu goddesses and Muslim saints, coconuts are also offered on occasion. Nearly all the makeshift shops at Ḥusain Ṭekrī deal primarily in these items.

58. Pierre Bourdieu, *Outline of a Theory of Practice* (Cambridge: Cambridge University Press, 1977); Catherine Bell, *Ritual Theory, Ritual Practice* (New York: Oxford University Press, 1992).

59. Bell, *Ritual Theory,* 81. A similar perspective on ritual, drawn from fieldwork conducted in Southern India, has been advocated by Nicholas B. Dirks, "Ritual and Resistance: Subversion as Social Fact," in *Contesting Power: Resistance and Everyday Social Relations in South Asia,* ed. Douglas Haynes and Gyan Prakash (Berkeley: University of California Press, 1992), 213–38.

60. The discussion of spirit possession and ritual in Elizabeth Fuller Collins, *Pierced by Murugan's Lance: Ritual, Power, and Moral Redemption among Malaysian Hindus* (Dekalb: Northern Illinois University Press, 1997), provides a clear, thorough description and endorsement of this perspective on ritual, contrasting it in particular with the views of Foucault, whose arguments about individuals being products of systems of power are well known.

61. See, for example, Isabelle Nabokov, *Religion against the Self: An Ethnography of Tamil Rituals* (New York: Oxford University Press, 2000); Graham Dwyer, *The Divine and the Demonic;* Bruce Kapferer, *The Feast of the Sorcerer: Practices of Consciousness and Power* (Chicago: University of Chicago Press, 1997).

62. Sudhir Kakar, "Some Unconscious Aspects of Ethnic Violence in India," in *Mirrors of Violence: Communities, Riots, and Survivors in South Asia,* ed. Veena Das (New Delhi: Oxford University Press, 1990), 135–45.

63. Mayaram, "Spirit Possession."

64. For a discussion of the supernatural threat posed by untouchable communities, see William Sax, *God of Justice: Ritual Healing and Social Justice in the Central Himalayas* (New York: Oxford University Press, 2009).

65. Mayaram, "Spirit Possession," 124.

1. PLACE: THE MAKING OF A PILGRIMAGE AND A PILGRIMAGE CENTER

1. Catherine B. Asher, "Mapping Hindu-Muslim Identities through the Architecture of Shahjahanabad and Jaipur," in *Beyond Turk and Hindu: Rethinking Religious Identities in Islamicate South Asia,* ed. David Gilmartin and Bruce B. Lawrence (Gainesville: University Press of Florida, 2000), 121–48.

2. Owing to prolonged drought in this part of Madhya Pradesh, they have little choice. As was documented in a *New York Times* series, India has serious water shortage problems. Somini Sengupta, "In Teeming India, Water Crisis Means Dry Pipes and Foul Sludge; Thirsty Giant / First of Three Articles," *New York Times,* September 29, 2006. As it was, any resident of Jaora who could not afford to drill a well had to purchase water from tanker trucks.

3. In India, Bohra are a *jāti*-based group of Shi'a Muslims. In public space they are often immediately identifiable by their style of dress.

4. There are still Hindu Chippas.

5. Ghulam Chippa, "Chippa Community Web page," available at www.chippa.com.

6. I am fortunate to have found Khadija and her family. Their home, while bursting at the seams and chaotically filled with young children, was a great source of information and refuge.

7. In everyday conversations about religion and Islam, *sabr* is also one of the most talked-about and revered qualities of the Prophet Muhammad. More collo-

quially, the Chippa driving slogan, which was written on the trucks in Devanagari, might be translated as "Easy does it."

8. Sikand, *Hindu-Muslim Syncretic Shrines*. For a discussion of the similar function of goddesses and Sufi saints, see Bayly, *Saints, Goddesses, and Kings*.

9. This was particularly true in the wake of the 1992 destruction of the Babri Masjid in Ayodhya.

10. Umesh Sharma, "Ek tarif dargāḥ, to dūsrī tarif hanumān jī / pūjā aur ibādat hotī hai sāth-sāth / hiṇdū-muslim ektā kī anūṭhī misāl lālākheṛī meṁ tājuddīn bābā kā darbār," *Dainik Bhāskar* [Daily Sun], August 20, 2005, Indore Edition.

11. On dargāḥs as participant in geographies of communalism, sometimes in rivalry with Hanumān or Goddess temples, see Khan, "Graves of History," and Philip Lutgendorf, "My Hanuman Is Bigger Than Yours," *History of Religions* 33, no. 3 (February 1994): 211–45. Anna Bigelow and Shail Mayaram have argued that dargāḥs offer pilgrims a means to overcome communalism. Mayaram sees dargāḥ-based spirit possession practices in particular as potentially community-building and tradition-transcending activities; Bigelow suggests that the ritual lives of dargāḥs and the narratives that they inspire can provide vital peace-making power in times of heightened communal tensions. See Mayaram, "Spirit Possession," and Bigelow, "Sharing Saints."

12. At the time of writing, the *waqf* board had filed a series of lawsuits against a number of lodge owners and private homeowners in hopes of reclaiming *waqf* land. The main issue seems to be that the previous management sold land that was actually part of the *waqf* trust and therefore not saleable. Shop and lodge owners were therefore understandably defensive when answering questions about their businesses' histories.

13. British records in the National Archives of India indicate that Jaora was a major opium-producing region until Independence. It is possible that this is still the case, but I have no evidence to confirm or deny such an assertion, though it may be worth noting that a common brand of matches for sale in Jaora features a photo collage of mature opium pods and fields of poppies. Additionally, it was rumored that dealers smuggled drugs out of Jaora in vehicles used to deliver the corpses of pilgrims who died at Ḥusain Ṭekrī to their families. The theory was that no policeman would have the fortitude to search the makeshift body bags used to transport the deceased.

14. Safdar Rizvi, *Husain Ṭekrī kyā hai?* (Hindi edition) (Delhi: Rahat Process, 2001, 2003).

15. For calculating the dates of Muharram and Daśahrā in 1885, 1886, and 1887, I have used Edwin M. Reingold and Nachum Dershowitz, "Calendrica," available at http://emr.cs.uiuc.edu/home/reingold/calendar-book/Calendrica.html. My calculations aside, the coincidence of Muharram and Daśahrā during 1885, 1886, and 1887, and the resultant communal tension throughout the subcontinent, are attested to in multiple sources. See, for example, *Gazetteer of the Nellore District: brought up to 1938* (Madras: Government of Madras Staff, 1942), 272.

16. Lt. Col. H. A. K. Gough to Chief Secretary, Jaora, June 20, 1920. Records of the Southern Central India States and Malwa Agency; Malwa Political Agency, Part 1, 1860–1931, File 107/1921, S. No. 789. National Archives of India, New Delhi.

17. Claim of the Thakur of Shujaota to a Well and Land around It on Mandsaur-

Ratlam Road. 1908 Central India Agency, Malwa Agency Office, File no. 390-D. National Archives of India, New Delhi. The British took great care in keeping meticulous records of the dispute, perhaps because of Jaora's role as a major producer of opium.

18. *Niyāzmand ne sunā hai ki ḥusain ṭekrī sharīf ko vas'at dene ke liye ārāẓī kī zarūrat hai. chunkī niyāzmand ko ḥaẓrat imām husain alehalsalām se khās 'aqidat hai isliye is kār e k̲h̲air men sharik honā chātā hun tāki bā's k̲h̲air va barkat ho.* Thakur Rup Singh of Shujaota to Nawab of Jaora, May 7, 1920. Records of the Southern Central India States and Malwa Agency; Malwa Political Agency Part 1, 1860–1931, File 107/1921, S. No. 789. National Archives of India, New Delhi.

19. Bayly, *Saints, Goddesses, and Kings.*

20. On the K̲h̲ojas in the nineteenth century, see Amriṭa Shodhan, *A Question of Community: Religious Groups and Colonial Law* (Calcutta: Samya, 2001); and Teena Purohit, "Formations and Genealogies of Ismaili Sectarianism in Nineteenth-Century India" (PhD diss., Columbia University, New York, 2007).

21. This quote is paraphrased.

22. Because the Aga Khan's arrival in Bombay precipitated a great deal of debate about whether or not he should have access to the K̲h̲oja community's property and wealth, it is very possible that, if Ismail Muhammad were among those who rejected his leadership, he would have been interested in finding another place to store his wealth and another religious institution to which he could make his offerings.

23. As for why he gifted the rauẓa, there are many reasons that make sense. It might have functioned as an institution to store funds, but in any case, it conforms to the broad pattern of offering a gift to a religious institution as a way of expressing gratitude for prosperity. It also may have been a way of soliciting saintly protection against those jealous enough of his success to perform magic.

24. Metcalf, *Islamic Revival.* Also see David Lelyveld, *Aligarh's First Generation: Muslim Solidarity in British India* (Princeton, NJ: Princeton University Press, 1978).

25. This donation is mentioned in the documents about Ḥusain Ṭekrī that have been compiled by the current management of the *waqf* board. Although I have not seen the original documentation regarding the donation (and there is a very good chance that none exists), there is no reason to doubt that the story is true. In the context of a larger interview conducted shortly before his death, Ẕākir Mohib, who was certainly in his eighties, explained to me that a branch of Habib Bank had actually been opened in Jaora before 1947, but it had not survived Partition, since the founding family went to Pakistan.

26. After Partition, Jaora ceased to be a Muslim princely state, but, as is the case with many dargāḥs throughout India, shrines that enjoyed royal patronage could continue to exist because their land and other holdings were held in *waqf.* In this way, while Muslim rulers and communities lost financial resources during Partition, dargāḥs were able to retain their property and endowments.

27. The K̲h̲ojas who today serve as facilitators of the annual fire walk *mātam* identify as followers of the Aga Khan, and they do not have overly friendly relations with the Ithna 'Ashari K̲h̲oja descendants of Ismail Muhammad, whom I interviewed in Bombay and who used to take a much more active role in the ritual life of Ḥusain Ṭekrī. The Nizari Ismaili community's building of the two new shrines is also a clear assertion of their custodianship of the shrines.

28. On the hereditary nature of the administration of dargāḥs, see Currie, *The Shrine and Cult;* Tahir Mahmood, "The Dargah of Sayyid Salar Mas'ud Ghazi in Bahraich: Legend, Tradition, and Reality," in *Muslim Shrines in India,* ed. Christian W. Troll (Delhi: Oxford University Press, 1992), 24–44; and Peter van der Veer, "Playing or Praying."

29. On the administration of the Chishtī dargāḥ in Ajmer, see Currie, *The Shrine and Cult,* particularly chapters 7 and 8.

30. Ibid., 154.

31. The branch of the *waqf* board to which Ḥusain Ṭekrī is accountable is in Bhopal.

32. Sarwar 'Ali Khan and the previous *mutavallī* are descendants of the last *nawāb* of Jaora, but they are not his sons. The ambiguity resulting from this situation prompted some significant conflict immediately prior to my arrival, and the details of the conflict—other than that it was couched in terms of a heredity-based right to serve as *mutavallī*—were not plainly stated.

33. Because it was not central to my project, I did not request copies of the records upon which the report was based. It is also unlikely that I would have been afforded access.

34. I have calculated this concurrence using Reingold and Dershowitz, "Calendrica."

35. The story of competing Muharram and Daśahrā processions has wide currency. See C. J. Fuller, *The Camphor Flame: Popular Hinduism and Society in India* (Princeton, NJ: Princeton University Press, 1992).

36. Versions of these two stories are contained in the contemporary guidebooks by Safdar Rizvi, *Ḥusain Ṭekrī Kyā hai* (Urdu and Hindi versions); and Moḥammad Afaq Ahmet, *Mojizā e Husain Ṭekri Sharīf* [The Miracle of Ḥusain Ṭekrī] (Mumbai: Khurśid e Jehrā Publications, 2001), in Hindi.

37. Many individuals who are critical of the new management at Ḥusain Ṭekrī claim that the well dried up when they started selling the water. It is true that the water is now sold at the shrines, whereas the lobān is free.

38. Whatever the miraculous dimensions of this story may be, it may have some mundane basis as well. An elderly resident of Ḥusain Ṭekrī once explained to me that as a young boy he would often skip school because he could make money selling this sugar to rich pilgrims from Bombay. On our way through the fields surrounding Ḥusain Ṭekrī, he showed me the place on a stray sorghum stalk where he said this sweet substance accumulates. Sorghum, which until recently was a major crop of Ḥusain Ṭekrī's *waqf* lands, contains a sweet white sap. Sorghum used to be a much more common crop in Jaora and the surrounding village, popular because of its drought resistance, but in recent years, because of improved irrigation technology, it has been abandoned in favor of water-hungry but far more profitable crops.

39. The guidebook *Mojizā e Husain Ṭekrī Sharīf* notes that the rauẓa of 'Ali was built in 1995. Ahmet, *Mojizā,* 46.

40. A family that lived near the rauẓa of Fatima related—with affectionate amusement—that during Muharram this old woman was a loud and enthusiastic *ta'ziya* procession of one.

41. Also pronounced *mehdī.*

42. This book is based upon research completed in late 2005. Since then, in keeping with the dynamic quality of dargāḥ culture, Ḥusain Ṭekrī's geography, administration, and ritual life have undergone some changes. The most significant change to the site's geography is Laṅgar House, constructed on private land directly across from the rauẓa of Fatima; this impressive facility is managed by Shahroo Mohsin, a businessman from Agra. Speaking with me in fall 2010, he explained that he has been coming to Ḥusain Ṭekrī since childhood and, having become financially successful, wanted to offer something to this special place. Mohsin told me that the Laṅgar House, which feeds at least 1,500 people a day, is funded exclusively by his own private income.

Mohsin's presence at Ḥusain Ṭekrī has not been uncontroversial. An ongoing legal battle between Mohsin and former *mutavallī* and member of the Jaora royal family Sarwar 'Ali Khan has resulted in the installation of an interim *mutavallī*. The case is complex and involves the question of the hereditary nature of the post; it also addresses the issue of whether or not Mohsin had the legal right to operate wheeled carts that dispense drinking water to pilgrims on land owned by the *waqf* board. Mohsin, who is Shi'a, suggested that Khan's opposition to his humanitarian projects was rooted in a dislike of Shi'ites; for his part, Khan, who is Sunni, insisted that he has no issues with Shi'ites and is instead concerned about the security of the site and the potential for a hostile, sectarian takeover funded, perhaps, by donations from abroad (e.g., Iran).

A recent and significant change to Ḥusain Ṭekrī's everyday life is that the rauẓa of Bībī Fatima is now completely enclosed and its gates are locked at night. This has significantly curtailed its nightlife, though every evening a handful of determined pilgrims can still be seen sitting on the road outside the gate performing the range of activities—offering prayers, reading stories, holding *mātam* sessions, and having ḥāẓirī—that used to take place inside. Finally, while much of Ḥusain Ṭekrī's ritual life remains the same as it was during the period of my research, on a recent visit to the rauẓa of 'Ali, I noticed lobān being administered first to those waiting outside its courtyard and only then being brought inside to be offered to those lined up there. I was told that this is done so that the handicapped—and especially those in wheelchairs provided by Laṅgar House—can benefit from the communal distribution.

2. PEOPLE: THE TALE OF THE FOUR VIRTUOUS WOMEN

The chapter epigraph is from Hayden White, *The Content of the Form: Narrative Discourse and Historical Representation* (Baltimore, MD: Johns Hopkins University Press: 1987), 4.

1. White, *Content of the Form*, 24.

2. On the use of narrative to utilize a violent past for present purposes, see also Shahid Amin, *Event, Metaphor, Memory: Chauri Chaura 1922–1992* (Berkeley: University of California Press, 1995).

3. The tenuousness of this link is attested to by the fact that many pilgrims appear to "regress"; that is, they arrive at a narrative only to find, through *khulī ḥāẓirī*, that elements of the narrative are either untrue or incomplete.

4. Given my regular experience of being suddenly and seemingly randomly given

new pieces of information by my primary informants, it is likely that, by accident or by design, there are elements of every story that are never shared.

5. This and all translations from the Hindi and Urdu are my own. Ellipses are used throughout for dialogic purposes. Unbracketed ellipses indicate pauses or tapering off into silence on the part of the speaker; bracketed ellipses indicate that I have eliminated interruptions from the television, phone calls, visitors, or my own attempts at clarification of a particular word. (Maya, for instance, is a native Sindhi speaker and missing her front teeth, which sometimes made her Hindi pronunciation challenging for me to understand.) My recorded interviews did not generally take place in what could be considered a controlled environment.

6. There are many homes housing *zarīḥ* that are maintained as places of healing by individuals who have been healed at Ḥusain Ṭekrī. Maya is referring to a well-known shrine of this kind in Udaipur.

7. *Ham* literally means "we," but it is often used colloquially to mean "I." Here this could be the usage, or Maya could be referring to herself *and* Husain/ʿAbbas.

8. Babli is not her real name, though it is the nickname she uses at Ḥusain Ṭekrī. She gave me permission to use this name but not her given name. Babli claimed to know about Maya's practice but not to have met her. She also claimed to be twenty-five, offering this age on a survey about lobān that I distributed. I have been told that it is not uncommon for Indian parents to register their children for school using an age a few years younger than the actual age; this ensures a larger window of opportunity for marriage and employment opportunities. It is not clear whether Babli really believes she is twenty-five or consciously misrepresented her age.

9. In a typical conversation that I often had about American education, for example, a working-class Muslim friend of mine responded to my statement that in America, parents often begin saving for their children's college education soon after they are born by observing that in India, parents begin saving for a girl's dowry and wedding soon after her birth. This friend was in the process of arranging a marriage for his sister, which was not actually going very well because she, unlike most young women of her *jāti,* had a B.A.

10. The reaction to being recorded varied widely. Some pilgrims were grateful for the opportunity to share their experience of suffering with the world; some did not give me permission to record our conversations because they feared that the recording would be used in magical spells to further harm them; and still others refused to be recorded because they feared that what they said would be heard by members of other religious communities or the site's administrators.

11. For another version of this story, see chapter 1.

12. The name is so paradigmatically common, in fact, that it was mocked in the 2005 Bollywood male-female buddy movie *Bunty aur Babli.* In naming the hero and heroine thus, the film cleverly positions them as representatives of the anonymous lower-middle-class Generation Xers of contemporary urban India. The commonness of their names is highlighted when, in a panicked moment, the male lead conceals their true identities by saying that he is Bunty and his female companion is Babli. She later reprimands him, saying that the name Babli makes her sound like some chubby, nondescript, completely ordinary girl.

13. Literally, daughter of a king. In this case, Fatima.

14. Initially, when the subject of Mastān Bābā came up, Babli assured me that

she had been interviewed by lots of people "like me" while sitting at Mastān Bābā's dargāḥ, and she emphasized that because of her experience she would certainly be willing and able to offer me the information I needed about Ḥusain Ṭekrī.

15. *Salwar* is usually the name for the long, loose, drawstring-waist pants that form the bottom half of the Indian *salwar kameez*. In this case, however, the term was being used in its generic sense, to refer to the bottom half of the outfit. *Cūrīdār*, literally "having bangles" (presumably a reference to the gathering around the lower leg), is a particular style.

16. On the interchangeable nature of Hindu goddesses, see, for example, Katherine Erndl, *Victory to the Mother: The Hindu Goddess of Northwest India in Myth, Ritual, and Symbol* (London: Oxford University Press, 1993); and Stanley N. Kurtz, *All the Mothers Are One: Hindu India and the Reshaping of Psychoanalysis* (New York: Columbia University Press, 1994).

17. Sāī Bābā's official religious identity is debatable, and the recent tendency to swathe his images in saffron robes has done much to minimize his (likely) Muslim roots. This aside, both his life story and his appearance maintain some popular Islamic elements.

18. *Laṅgar* refers to the free food that is distributed at dargāḥs and other religious venues.

19. Food available to pilgrims at a Muslim shrine. It is understood to have been blessed by the saint.

20. A small cake of sugar or molasses covered with sesame seeds, commonly distributed at dargāḥs and *imāmbāṛās*.

21. Babli's version of the story gave me the impression that she had been garlanded by Mastān Bābā many times.

22. Mahatma Gandhi popularized this term, literally "people of God," to refer to untouchables, or *dalits*.

23. When I asked her how she knew all these stories, Babli told me that she learned this and other stories from books about Muslim martyrs readily available for purchase at Ḥusain Ṭekrī.

24. At my informant's request, I am not using her real name.

25. Likely this is an *imāmbāṛā;* Priya did not know if Salim was Shi'a or Sunni.

26. *Is ma'ṣūm ko leke jāungā*. Typically, as the masculine conjugation of '*jāungā*' indicates, possessing spirits are the opposite gender of their hosts.

27. Forty days after the tenth of Muharram, Chehlum (literally, "fortieth") is the largest festival at Ḥusain Ṭekrī. A Ḵẖoja Shi'ite community from Bombay facilitates the fire walk, which they refer to as *āg kā mātam* (fire mourning). More generally, the word *cehlum* refers to an observance carried out forty days after an individual's death.

28. *Faislā,* or ruling, is the main term for final resolution of the problems that have brought the pilgrim to Ḥusain Ṭekrī.

29. Here she used the phrase "*mentally disturb zyādā rehtī thī.*"

30. *Ham ko nahī lagtā thā ki is ko kisī ne kuch kiyā*. In discussions of magic, the word *jādū* is rarely used. Rather, the stock phrases "someone did something" or "someone had something done" are common.

31. Respectively, these are the beginning of the Arabic phrase "in the name of God, the merciful and compassionate" and a prayer pronouncing blessings for the

Prophet Muhammad. The former precedes all but one of the chapters in the Qur'an and is commonly recited before undertaking something.

32. In Sagar, this major dargāḥ is a *cillā* of Tāj ud Dīn Bābā, whose *mazār* (grave) is in Nagpur, Maharashtra. Tāj ud Dīn Bābā is a well-known saint who dates from the British period; recall, also, the newspaper headline's reference to another *cillā* of his in a village near Jaora. Pīlī Goṭī literally means "yellow stone."

33. Technically, *dev uṭhānī gyāras.*

34. Yā Sīn is the thirty-sixth sura, or chapter, of the Qur'an. This popular sura is commonly recited for blessing and is also recited for the dead.

35. This Arabic-derived Urdu word also has a legal connotation of evidence.

36. *Bolā, maulā tu ne is se pardā rakh diyā, maiṁ us se be'izzat karnā chatā thā, us kī be'izzatī karnā* [sic] *chatā thā. Yeh bolā. Yeh bayān huī, bas.*

37. Some non-Muslim women, most notably Rajputs, practice purdah and veiling. However, their style of veiling differs from that of Muslim women and is easily distinguishable from it.

38. Once I asked Sakina-Nasim whether or not my book on Ḥusain Ṭekrī would be finished quickly. Her response was that I shouldn't wander so much, and that if I wrote the book thoughtfully *(dimāg se, socne se),* it would be finished quickly. The response is notable for its judicious mix of sound advice, optimism, and lack of an unequivocal statement about when the book would actually be finished.

39. From the Arabic *izār,* the name of the lower portion of the garment worn by pilgrims on the hajj. In Urdu (according to Platt's Urdu-English dictionary), *izār* simply means drawers or trousers with a drawstring waistband. Nasim's pronunciation of *izār* as *ijār* reflects a common tendency in some forms of spoken Hindi to substitute a *j* for *z.*

40. In Arabic, the tile of the poem is "Qasīdā al-burdā." See also Ali Asani's translation of the popular Sabri Brothers *qawwālī* that extols the virtues of Muhammad's cloak. Ali Asani, "In Praise of Muhammad: Sindhi and Urdu Poems," in *The Religions of India in Practice,* ed. Donald Lopez (Princeton, NJ: Princeton University Press, 1995), 159–86.

41. Here the word for "incense" is *agarbattī,* not lobān.

42. That is, she had a problem that needed resolution.

43. That is, someone had hired a magician to do magic.

44. Often when people tie strings on the shrines to make petitions at Ḥusain Ṭekrī, they take a portion of the string and tie it around their necks.

45. Nasim had chosen the rauẓa of 'Ali because it tends to have very few people in it late in the afternoon, but there were still enough people to make it difficult to talk privately. Because she was sharing a small room with her two young patients, sitting there was not an option either. The near impossibility of being alone is a commonplace of middle- and working-class Indian life. The significance of this fact, particularly in relation to discourses of magic, will be discussed in later chapters. Certainly, living with the Chippas, I was alone only when I was bathing, using the toilet, or sleeping. In most working-class homes no one would have the opportunity, or perhaps even the desire, to sleep in a room by oneself, and I was often asked how I could not feel frightened sleeping alone.

46. By "similar shrines" I mean a range of Muslim saint shrines encompassing

conventional dargāḥs and places as diverse as Maya's rooftop shrine *(baiṭhak),* the Bombay-based Ḥusain Ṭekrī–affiliated *imāmbāṛā,* and the *cillā* of Pīlī Goṭī in Sagar.

3. ABSENCE: LOBĀN, VOLUNTEERISM, AND ABUNDANCE

1. Lobān is technically the incense itself and not its smoke, but at Ḥusain Ṭekrī the term is used to refer to the smoke.

2. See Flueckiger, *In Amma's Healing Room.* The text addresses the broader subject of Islamic healing traditions in a South Indian context.

3. Extremely popular, the Ayat al-Kursī is written in full on a large sheet of silver that forms the center of the *zarīḥ* in the rauẓa of 'Ali.

4. *Naẕar* and *naẕarana* are, respectively, the local pronunciations of *naẕr* and *naẕrana.*

5. The *ṣalvāt* is a recitation of blessings on Muhammad and his descendants.

6. The assistant is usually a long-term pilgrim whose recovery has advanced to the point where he can be trusted with the lobān.

7. Sometimes, despite the rules, *ḥāẓirīwāle* enter the rauẓas. As a weary rauẓa attendant explained to me, it is impossible to control the actions of every pilgrim.

8. Occasionally individuals report conscious memory of things said in ḥāẓirī, but these are particular cases, each with a logic that takes as given that normally no memory from ḥāẓirī remains. Otherwise, individuals learn about revelations in ḥāẓirī through the reports of their caretakers and others.

9. There are, of course, South Asian religious festivals that resist everyday social order—*holī,* for example—but in these cases, identity is not erased but reversed. In this way, such festivals are only meaningful in relation to established social structures. The meaning and power of lobān, however, is not connected to everyday society. On *holī* as a reversal of social order, see McKim Marriott, *Village India: Studies in the Little Community* (Chicago: University of Chicago Press, 1955).

10. It is certainly true, however, that people take unburned lobān home with them, and pilgrims who are too ill to come to the shrines are served by self-appointed pilgrims who collect the remains of the hot coals from the main shrines and distribute lobān to those unable to leave their lodge rooms. As at the rauẓas, in these cases lobān is burned for the benefit of not only the individual but also his or her family members, the home or shop of the pilgrim, or the saints of Ḥusain Ṭekrī themselves, who are honored in Shi'ite households' *imāmbāṛās* and in small home shrines built by Hindu devotees. In other words, lobān is always consumed communally.

11. Smoking cigarettes is also understood to break a Muslim's Ramadan fast. In Hindi, a cigarette is "drunk": *pīnā,* or "to drink," is the verb used to express cigarette consumption.

12. For Hindus, observation of the Ramadan fast is most often meant to serve as a sign of gratitude or penance.

13. The belief that string is corruptible seems be somewhat widespread. One Saturday in Bombay I asked my rickshaw-wālā why he had refused to buy a fresh lemon and green hot pepper combination from one the vendors who work at busy intersections. The combination of a lemon and a pepper is widely understood to

fend off the evil eye and malevolent influence, which is much more pronounced on Saturday owing to the influence of Śani, or Saturn. He replied that the vendor had joined the pepper and lemon with string rather than wire, thus rendering the object possibly impure and therefore ineffectual.

14. For a recent treatment of *prasād* as a major category of South Asian civilization, see Andrea Marion Pinkney, "The Sacred Share: Prasada in South Asia" (PhD diss., Columbia University, New York, 2008).

15. I am extremely grateful to the administrators of Ḥusain Ṭekrī—particularly Ḥusain Ṭekrī's *mutavallī* and advocate, Haji Sarwar 'Ali Khan, and Mr. M.K. Taimuri, *waqf* board representative for Ḥusain Ṭekrī—for their gracious help in making this survey possible, and specifically for permission to survey the residents of the *waqf*-administered lodges.

16. In 2004–2005, the most expensive of the private lodges, by way of contrast, cost 4,000 rupees a month. A midrange private lodge offered small rooms with attached baths for 800 rupees a month.

17. *Lobān lene ke ṭhīk pehle / ke daurān / ke ṭhīk bād, āp ko kaisā mahsūs hotā hai?*

18. *Khushī, ḍar, behośī, udāsī, śānti, ārām, āśā / ummīd, krodh / gussā, kuch nahīṁ, kuch aur.*

19. This is out of the ninety-one surveyed. The numbers reflect the fact that some would describe more than one stage of the process of consuming lobān in physical terms.

20. The remaining responses, not noted above, were either "nothing" *(kuch nahīn)* or no response. I distinguished those respondents who offered no answer at all from those who chose "*kuch nahīn*" because in everyday speech the phrase usually means "nothing to speak of" or "nothing special" and does not indicate the total confusion about or disapproval of the question that prompted no response at all.

21. I am aware that analysis of the whole notion of individual "experience," religious and otherwise, has been critiqued and rejected by many. The critique turns on the notion that scholars of religion have often assumed that a ritual or narrative can be "read" to ascertain the nature of the inner experience of those involved on the grounds that both the experience and the rituals and narratives derive from the same historical, social, and linguistic processes. According to this line of reasoning, the paradox is that the experience itself is nondiscursive, and as such cannot be meaningfully reflected in any discursive form, be it ritual or academic narrative. One of the least desirable consequences of the combination of these two assumptions is the way that they allow a scholar to appropriate the "experience" in the service of one ideology or another. Taking this line of reasoning further, Robert Sharf has argued that ineffability itself is not a "delimiting characteristic" or a "phenomenal property," making it essentially off-limits to scholars of religion. See Robert H. Sharf, "Experience," in *Critical Terms for Religious Studies,* ed. Mark C. Taylor (Chicago: University of Chicago Press, 1998), 94–116.

It follows that anything that is by its nature nondiscursive would lose its original character when introduced into discourse of any kind. However, in the case of lobān, what this critique misses, I think, is the fact that the *physical* experience of taking lobān *is* discursive because it involves a consciousness of bodily sensations and, in many cases, a discourse in which the possessing spirit cries out that he or she is burning in the lobān. The physical act of taking lobān *is* a meaningful, individual, and discursive experience—the sensations of burning and erasure and the sweet smell together constitute what people find transformative and beneficial. The ritual and the individual experience *are the same,* and both are discursive by virtue of both the individual's awareness of his or her body and, often, the possessing spirit's reaction to the smoke of lobān, and both therefore can be read discursively. As for the post-lobān unconsciousness experienced by many, it is meaningful to them because it is nondiscursive, and there is no reason to make it anything more than that in their analysis or my own.

22. See Murphy Halliburton, "The Importance of a Pleasant Process of Treatment: Lessons on Healing from South India," *Culture, Medicine, and Psychiatry* 27, no. 2 (June 2003): 161–86, for a discussion of the categories of pleasant and unpleasant in Ayurvedic, allopathic, and "religious" contexts in Kerala.

23. Around the month of Muharram, tension erupted between the Shi'ite community from Bombay, which wanted the rauẓas kept open late for various commemorative events, and the Jaora-based Sunni administrative committee, which held that late-night activities at the rauẓas were disrespectful. This situation had a number of unspoken elements, chief among them contemporary Sunni disapproval of *mātam* and the weariness of the rauẓa attendants.

24. The actual date of the concurrence of the two festivals was likely the eighth of Muharram.

25. A *ta'ziya* is a model of one of the tombs of the martyrs of Karbala that is used in Indian Muharram processions.

26. This is the well that is now enclosed in a building built into the wall surrounding the courtyard of the rauẓas of 'Abbas and Sakina. Its water is pumped into Ḥusain Ṭekrī's public bathhouse.

27. *'Ud,* an Urdu word also used to describe the wooden containers in which incense used to be burned, before metal ones replaced them.

28. Rizvi, *Ḥusain Ṭekrī* (Hindi edition), 12–16.

29. For example, when the Sunni management of Ḥusain Ṭekrī found out that members of the Bombay Shi'ite community had instituted their own lobān in the *imāmbāṛā* that they maintain on the grounds of Ḥusain Ṭekrī, they vowed to put a stop to it immediately.

30. The chapter on this subject is titled "Husain Ṭekrī duniyā kā sab se baṛā ruhānī hospital," or "Ḥusain Ṭekrī: the world's biggest spiritual hospital."

31. The link between memory and smell is well established. See Howard Eichenbaum, Andrew P. Yonelinas, and Charan Ranganath, "The Medial Temporal Lobe and Recognition Memory," *Annual Review of Neuroscience* 30 (2007): 123–52. Special thanks to Dr. Amar Sahay of Columbia University for this citation.

32. The exchange of lobān and other dargāḥ-specific products adds another dimension to my suggestion that dargāḥs' authority in the contemporary period comes from the very fact of their perceived participation in a subcontinent-wide network of Muslim saint shrines.

33. My initial transcription and translation of this song was completed in 2001 in collaboration with Dr. A. N. Singh, then director of the American Institute of Indian Studies Hindi language program. I subsequently revised the translation in light of interactions with Mr. Khan and other members of the Ḥusain Ṭekrī community in 2003. If any errors remain, I of course take full responsibility.

34. Rizvi, *Husain Ṭekrī* (Hindi edition), 21–22.

35. It is possible—though very unlikely, given the context—that Hindu pilgrims understand these lyrics as "you called me here, if that's not fate, what is?" or "if that's not a religious duty, what is?" rather than "if that's not grace, what is?" since "*karam*" is a spelling/pronunciation variation on "*karm/karma*," a Sanskrit-derived term commonly used to describe actions and consequences of actions (including religious actions) that together constitute one's fate. These understandings of *karm* do not necessarily conflict with the meaning of the Arabic-derived *karam* if Maulā's generosity is understood to be foundational to the larger workings of the universe represented in the concept of *karm/karma*.

36. Gayatri is not her real name.

37. *Challā* is literally a ring or a circular object. Here the term seems to have been logically extended to refer to the fact that the string encircles the *jālī* and the neck or arm of the individual.

38. Rizvi, *Husain Ṭekrī* (Hindi edition), 25–26.

39. It is never tied to the left arm, as it is considered impure.

40. Because I went to Ḥusain Ṭekrī every day I often served as *challā* courier for friends from Jaora and Bombay. I would tie one length of string and deliver the other to the petitioner. Tying *challā* need not lead to a long-term stay at Ḥusain Ṭekrī; it is necessary in order to stay, but it does not require residency.

41. For example, Ḥusain Ṭekrī's major ritual event—a fire walk—takes place forty days after the tenth of Muharram; many Sufi meditation practices are forty days in duration; and a popular collection of prayers to the Hindu deity Hanumān, the Hanumān Cālīsā, contains forty verses.

42. As anyone who has visited any of the grand tombs of Indian Sufi saints and Muslim emperors has the opportunity to notice, the honeycombed stone latticework on the tombs' windows actually creates enough resistance to amplify the slightest movement of the air into a perceptible breeze, even on a hot summer day. This effect does not, alas, seem to exist at Ḥusain Ṭekrī, since the screens on the rauẓa windows are cast concrete or metal and not particularly thick.

4. PRESENCE: THE WORK AND WORKINGS OF ḤĀẒIRĪ

1. Not coincidentally, *court* is a term very commonly used by pilgrims to describe both Ḥusain Ṭekrī and a network of dargāḥs and similar shrines spread throughout India. As well as the English word *court*, the Urdu *'adālat* is also popular, as is the Urdu *darbār*. It is also, of course, possible that the word *court* was frequently employed with me because I am an "*aṁgrez*" (literally, "English," but a term commonly applied to Europeans and those of European descent).

2. Assayag documents instances of the saint speaking through the voice of the victim. Assayag, *Au confluence de deux rivière*, 118.

3. Gazetteers of the Bombay Presidency from 1883 and 1889 note the practice of *khulī ḥāẓirī*: "It often happens that a spirit [. . .], in spite of the frequent punishments and castings out, does not leave, or departs but for a moment to at once return. . . . [T]he man possessed by one of these stubborn spirits is seen dragged by unwillingly as if by an unseen agent to a post where without any visible cord his

hands seem to be bound and he to writhe and rave as if under severe corporal punishment." Quoted in Beatrix Pfleiderer, "Mira Datar Dargah: The Psychiatry of a Muslim Shrine," in *Ritual and Religion among Muslims in India*, ed. Imtiaz Ahmad (New Delhi: Manohar, 1984), 224.

4. There are claims that at certain dargāḥs this type of violent interrogation is sometimes enacted by a flesh-and-blood judge. *The Milli Gazette*, a reform-oriented Muslim newspaper, ran a critical, expose-style article on dargāḥ culture. The article noted that in some instances shrine caretakers beat the pilgrims. M. H. Lakdawala, "Mumbai's Babas Thrive on Misery," *Milli Gazette* 3, no. 23 (December 1–15, 2002), available at www.milligazette.com/Archives/01122002/0112200276.htm.

5. See Vincent Crapanzano, "Spirit Possession," in *Encyclopedia of Religion*, ed. Mircea Eliade (New York: Macmillan, 1987), 14: 12–19.

6. See Michael Taussig, *The Devil and Commodity Fetishism in South America* (Chapel Hill: University of North Carolina Press, 1980), *Mimesis and Alterity: A Particular History of the Senses* (New York: Routledge, 1993), and *Shamanism, Colonialism;* Frederick Smith, *The Self Possessed: Deity and Spirit Possession in South Asian Literature and Civilization* (New York: Columbia University Press, 2006); Michael Lambek, *Knowledge and Practice in Mayotte: Local Discourses of Islam, Sorcery and Spirit Possession* (Toronto: University of Toronto Press, 1993); Mary Keller, *The Hammer and the Flute: Women, Power and Spirit Possession* (Baltimore, MD: Johns Hopkins University Press, 2002).

7. The seminal work of T. K. Oesterreich, *Possession, Demoniacal and Other: Among Primitive Races, in Antiquity, the Middle Ages, and Modern Times,* trans. D. Ibberson (New York: R. R. Smith, 1930), reflects this assumption.

8. Smith, *The Self Possessed.* Similarly, Jordan Paper has argued that Confucianism, Taoism, and Buddhism are categories of religion imposed from the outside and suggested that Chinese religion is best conceptualized as a unitary system built around the sharing of food offerings. Jordan Paper, *The Spirits Are Drunk: Comparative Approaches to Chinese Religion* (Albany: State University of New York Press, 1995).

9. Thomas J. Csordas, "Elements of Charismatic Possession and Healing," *Medical Anthropology Quarterly* 14, no. 4 (June 1988): 121.

10. Freudian analysis of possession and exorcism has, as Fred Smith notes, fallen out of fashion in the past ten years, owing in large part to increasingly widespread acceptance of the charge that a Freudian perspective is too culturally specific to be applicable in non-Western contexts. See Frederick Smith, "The Current State of Possession Studies as a Cross-Disciplinary Project," *Religious Studies Review* 27, no. 3 (July 2001): 203–12. Gananath Obeyesekere's *Medusa's Hair: An Essay on Personal Symbols and Religious Experience* (Chicago: University of Chicago Press, 1991) has been criticized in this regard.

11. Jackie Assayag, "But, They Do Move . . . Religion, Illness and Therapeutics in Southern India," in *Managing Distress: Possession and Therapeutic Cults in South Asia,* ed. Marine Carrin (Delhi: Manohar, 1999), 30–50.

12. Franck Rollier, "Walking Round on the Straight Path in the Name of the Father: A Study of the Dispossession Trance at Murugmalla," in *Managing Distress: Possession and Therapeutic Cults in South Asia,* ed. Marine Carrin (Delhi: Manohar, 1999), 68.

13. Pfleiderer, "Mira Datar Dargah."

14. Ibid., 222.

15. Y. J. Shobha Devi and G. S. Bidarakoppa, "Jod Gomaz Dargah as a Healing Centre," In *Managing Distress: Possession and Therapeutic Cults in South Asia,* ed. Marine Carrin (Delhi: Manohar, 1999), 90–115.

16. Bālājī is the infant form of the Hindu god Hanumān.

17. It is worth noting that the time for *peśī* is initiated by *pūjā,* complete with *ārati* (offering of light) and bell ringing and cries of victory to Bālājī. As was noted earlier, goddess temple–based exorcism often simultaneously functions as *pūjā.*

18. Dwyer, *The Divine and the Demonic,* 111.

19. Comfort, coolness, lightness.

20. Dwyer, *The Divine and the Demonic,* 5.

21. Ibid.

22. Ibid., 109.

23. Sudhir Kakar, *Shamans, Mystics, and Doctors: A Psychological Inquiry into India and Its Healing Traditions* (New York: Knopf, 1982), 53.

24. Ibid., 24.

25. Researchers love the Bālājī temple. Their attraction to it possibly warrants further research.

26. Antti Pakaslahti, "Family-centered Treatment of Mental Health Problems at the Balaji Temple in Rajasthan," in *Changing Patterns of Family and Kinship in South Asia,* ed. Asko Parpola and Sirpa Tenhunen, *Studia Orientalia* 84: 129–66.

27. Ibid., 161–63.

28. During my time at Ḥusain Ṭekrī I did meet several people who remembered what they said during ḥāẓirī, but these individuals were a small minority, and in at least one case the individual had actually prayed for and been given the ability to remember his ḥāẓirī, in order, he said, to help him understand what had happened to him.

29. More generally, Western therapeutic methods can be broadly classed as behavioral, cognitive, and emotional. Of these, behavioral therapies are least focused upon insight and share some characteristics with ḥāẓirī, particularly the idea that one's outlook can be changed by changing one's behavior.

30. Interestingly, the *dybbuk* of the Jewish tradition behaves in a manner similar to that of the *pret.*

31. Felicitas Goodman, *How About Demons?: Possession and Exorcism in the Modern World* (Bloomington: Indiana University Press, 1988), offers many case studies and examples of the distinction between haunting and possessing spirits in contemporary Western contexts.

32. See the discussion of Bourguignon's work in Lila Shaara and Andrew Strathern, "A Preliminary Analysis of the Relationship between Altered States of Consciousness, Healing, and Social Structure," *American Anthropologist* 94 (1992): 147–48. See also Erika Bourguignon, *Possession* (San Francisco: Chandler and Sharp, 1976).

33. Dwyer's glossary contains several words for "spirits" and "magic" in common circulation at the Bālājī temple in Rajasthan. See Dwyer, *The Divine and the Demonic,* 161–64. Jonathan Parry has also offered an account of different varieties of malevolent spiritual presences, all of which share the characteristic of having

died a bad death. See Jonathan P. Parry, *Death in Banaras* (Cambridge: Cambridge University Press, 1994), 230.

34. Dwyer, *The Divine and the Demonic,* 155.

35. For a more sustained discussion of contemporary rural Hindu understandings of the relationship between notions of karma and the veneration of ancestors, see Ann Grodzins Gold, *Fruitful Journeys: The Ways of Rajasthani Pilgrims* (Berkeley: University of California Press, 1988).

36. Parry also notes this term; see Parry, *Death in Banaras,* 230.

37. The reasonably successful 2004 Bollywood film *Bhūt* concerns a Bombay apartment that is haunted by the ghost of its previous resident, a young woman who was murdered by a sexually predatory neighbor. The new female resident of the apartment is eventually possessed, *Exorcist*-style, by the spirit of the murdered woman.

38. Vomiting objects like these is also widely cited as evidence for Ḥusain Ṭekrī's miraculous efficacy. In the 2003 edition of one of Ḥusain Ṭekrī's guidebooks, the author falsely claimed that I had seen such miracles, stating, "Carla Bellamy, an American youth *[sic],* has said that there is no place on earth like Ḥusain Ṭekrī. Before coming here she had never seen bones, pieces of broken glass, and blades, etc. come from people's mouths. . . . [S]he has seen patients with ḥāẓirī and she has seen such things come out of these patients that have an extremely harmful effect on the body, and yet the patient is unharmed." Rizvi, *Ḥusain Ṭekrī* (Hindi edition), 88.

39. Beatrix Pfleiderer's psychoanalytically oriented study of the dargāḥ of Mīrā Dātār in Gujarat, itself often visited by patients at Ḥusain Ṭekrī, also contains reference to patients using the trope of magic from Africa, which suggests that this notion predates the very recent advent of satellite TV in India. However, in her analysis of healing at Mīrā Dātār, Pfleiderer mistranslates "*jādū*" as "miracle," making it difficult to be certain if her work in this case is a reliable description of the conversation in which *jādū* is mentioned. Pfleiderer, "Mira Datar Dargah."

40. In describing his wife's situation, this man used the relatively rare Arabic-derived Urdu word *k͟hābiṣ,* which can be translated as "evil spirit," "miser," or "impure."

41. What was spoken in *khulī ḥāẓirī* was sometimes incomprehensible to me owing to the use of local dialects or languages other than Hindi (mainly Gujarati or Punjabi), or because of the extreme emotion with which the words were spoken. In these cases, if I asked others to translate, they would almost always shrug and say that they could not understand what was being said either.

42. *Jādū* is the word used for both "magic" and "spell."

43. One lakh = 100,000 rupees.

44. No pilgrim ever volunteered why this particular tree was used, and the tree is also completely absent from the several guidebooks for pilgrims readily available at Ḥusain Ṭekrī. Many elements of the site's landscape (chiefly its wells, but also its land) are imbued with different kinds of power, though this tree lacks an association with any of the miracles that have rendered the land and some of the wells of Ḥusain Ṭekrī sacred. In recent years another tree at Laṅgar Kuāṁ (literally, "blessed food-giving well"), still living and growing close to a well near the rauẓa of 'Ali, has become a popular place to nail lemons and have ḥāẓirī. This tree also lacks a story explaining its efficacy. In any case, it seems that this simple ceremony of binding the spirit in the lemon only punctuates the work that has been

accomplished in ḥāẓirī, the consumption of lobān, and the other major healing practices common at Ḥusain Ṭekrī.

45. Because, for cultural reasons, it was not possible for me to develop time-intensive long-term relationships with male practitioners of ḥāẓirī, it is difficult to know if men ascribe any particular meaning to the covering of their faces after a bout of *khulī ḥāẓirī.*

46. The power of the caretakers' actions extend beyond the bouts of *khulī ḥāẓirī.* Priya's mother suffered terrible stomach problems during her time at Ḥusain Ṭekrī, and Babli's father, afflicted with a heart condition that took his life between my initial and follow-up research, was unable to access good medical care while chaperoning Babli at Ḥusain Ṭekrī. In these and other cases, the *ḥāẓirīwālā* or *ḥāẓirīwālī* would express gratitude for his or her caretaker in conversations with me.

47. In this case the *pret* used masculine conjugations of verbs, indicating a male speaker.

48. It is entirely possible that many years ago Maya was given a specific narrative that she, like the young Hindu woman quoted above, had no reason to repeat outside the realm of Ḥusain Ṭekrī. Even if this is the case, however, it is noteworthy that many of Maya's recollections of her time at Ḥusain Ṭekrī involved her fearsome ḥāẓirī.

49. These are, respectively, the masculine and feminine forms of the adjective.

50. Maya once mentioned that she hadn't had her youngest daughter, Pinky, weighed at Ḥusain Ṭekrī. When I asked why, she replied that, as the youngest of many daughters and arriving after a long-awaited son, Pinky was not exactly *requested,* and so there was no reason to offer thanks for her at Ḥusain Ṭekrī.

51. These are the central concerns of Keller, *The Hammer and the Flute,* as well as the concerns of the many scholars whose work she surveys.

52. According to J. J. Roy Burman's *Hindu-Muslim Syncretic Shrines and Communities,* this dargāḥ is located in the village of Pipalgaon in Chikhli Taluka of Buldhana district in Maharashtra. Bilkis, however, said that Sailani Bābā's dargāḥ is located in Madhya Pradesh. It is possible that she is speaking of a *cillā* of Sailani Bābā; it is also possible that we misunderstood one another or, because Buldhana borders Madhya Pradesh, perhaps Bilkis mistakenly thought the dargāḥ was actually in that state. According to Burman's text, this dargāḥ is known throughout Maharashtra as a place for healing illnesses caused by *pret.* Burman, *Hindu-Muslim Syncretic Shrines,* 105–8.

53. Of course, it is always a family member or neighbor who pays to have magic performed.

54. When Maya used lemons for this purpose she would often hold them over the head of the seated victim. She once explained to me that she performed this procedure away from her home because it was dangerous: the spirits could escape and enter her home. Maya said she would generally throw the lemon along the side of the road when she was finished.

55. Commonly, when making this gesture the individual will repeat *"tobā,"* an Arabic-derived Urdu word that can be translated as "heaven forbid."

56. See, for example, Paula Richman, ed., *Many Rāmāyaṇas: The Diversity of a Narrative Tradition in South Asia* (Berkeley: University of California Press, 1991).

See also Paula Richman, ed., *Questioning Ramayanas: A South Asian Tradition* (Berkeley: University of California Press, 2001).

57. Kavita, Shobha, Shobita, Kanchan, and Sharada, "Rural Women Speak," *Seminar* 342 (February 1988): 41.

58. Of course, no source of legitimacy and authority is completely immune to disbelief and rejection; the more it becomes reliant upon narrative, the more debatable it becomes. Thus, I never encountered anyone at Ḥusain Ṭekrī who doubted the reality or the power of the violent, transgressive actions of ḥāẓirī if the actions were directly observed.

59. This idea that possession can be understood as work, participating as a "real" player in "real" economies, is also seen in Keller, *The Hammer and the Flute,* 105–24.

60. This somewhat contradicts Babli's story of being cursed in a previous life, but even in that case, there is a sense that magic is an aberration, a human interference with *qismat* and *karma,* since Babli's action of saving a child should have caused her to reap great karmic rewards.

61. This woman's family asked me to stop recording her ḥāẓirī. I thus lack a recording of the entire ḥāẓirī session, but I recorded these terms in my field notes.

5. PERSONAE: TRANSGRESSION, OTHERNESS, COSMOPOLITANISM, AND KINSHIP

1. See, for example, Gottschalk, *Beyond Hindu and Muslim;* Antonio Rigopoulos, *The Life and Teachings of Sai Baba of Shirdi* (Albany: State University of New York Press, 1993); David Gilmartin and Bruce Lawrence, eds., *Beyond Turk and Hindu: Rethinking Religious Identities in Islamicate South Asia* (Gainesville: University Press of Florida, 2000).

2. Starting with Dumont's seminal *Homo Hierarchicus,* which assigned caste a central role in Indian self-conceptualization, many subsequent discussions of Indian selfhood and the place of group identity in self-identity have sought to disprove or nuance Dumont's claims. E. Valentine Daniel, *Fluid Signs: Being a Person the Tamil Way* (Berkeley: University of California Press, 1984), is an influential and self-conscious attempt to move discussions of South Asian selfhood away from notions of caste as foundational. See also Nabokov, *Religion Against the Self,* 13–15, for discussion and modification of Marriott and Inden's discussion of "dividual" personhood in South Asia. McKim Marriott and Ronald Inden, "Toward an Ethnosociology of South Asian Caste Systems," in *The New Wind: Changing Identities in South Asia,* ed. Ken David (The Hague: Mouton, 1977), 227–38. See also William Sax, *Dancing the Self: Personhood and Performance in the Pāṇḍav Līlā of Garhwal* (Oxford: Oxford University Press, 2002); Arjun Appadurai, "Is Homo Hierarchicus?" *American Ethnologist* 13, no. 4 (November 1986): 745–61 and Flueckiger, *In Amma's Healing Room.*

3. Benedict Anderson's seminal work *Imagined Communities* argues that a rise in literacy in vernacular languages and widely circulated print media contributed to the emergence of nationalism in the formerly colonized world. Benedict Anderson, *Imagined Communities: Reflections on the Origin and Spread of Nationalism* (London: Verso, 1991).

4. It is true that these are my categories, derived from my observation of Ḥusain Ṭekrī's pilgrims. On the subject of the appropriateness or usefulness of such categories, I agree with Dumont when he writes, "We must take pains not to introduce any concept whatsoever into the description which is not, either 1, that of the people themselves, or 2, shown necessary by direct analysis of the material, even if it is not present in the consciousness of those concerned. We differ from certain analysts in stating that 2 is as legitimate as 1—because, among other things, religion entails a certain non-consciousness by definition. There have been too many attempts to 'explain' rituals by the explanations which can be obtained from the actors; a ritual would not be a ritual if one knew perfectly well why one performed it." Louis Dumont, *A South Indian Subcaste: Social Organization and Religion of the Pramalai Kallar,* trans. M. Moffat (New York: Oxford University Press, 1986), 348.

5. Race is a problematic and, in contemporary Western academic discourse, somewhat dated concept. Here I use the term as a reflection of the reality that in India the color of my skin is immediately identified as that of an *aṁgrez,* and thus I am identified as an *aṁgrez* (a common northern Indian pronunciation of the word *English*).

6. The level of regulation of Indian dargāḥs varies greatly. In some cases women cannot enter the main shrine that houses the tomb of the saint, and in some cases they can. Also, sometimes the courtyard has a separate area for women, and sometimes it does not.

7. There are exceptions to this tendency, often involving a temple built to honor a goddess who has become associated with a Muslim saint. See Sikand, *Hindu-Muslim Syncretic Shrines,* especially pp. 9–10 and 31–32.

8. Further, it is true that as pilgrims get to know one another all sorts of complicated conflicts and alliances are created, but even in these cases, in my experience, conflicts and cliques are largely based on personal reasons, not caste- or class-based ones.

9. For a relatively recent discussion of the social impact of Hindu and Muslim rumor-based fears of one another, see especially chapters 4 and 5 of Sudhir Kakar, *The Colors of Violence: Cultural Identities, Religion, and Violence* (Chicago: University of Chicago Press, 1996).

10. The authors of *Witchcraft, Sorcery, Rumors, and Gossip* suggest that rumor may prompt accusations of "witchcraft" or function as a form of witchcraft itself. I argue here that the latter phenomenon is strongly present at Ḥusain Ṭekrī. See Pamela Stewart and Andrew Strathern, *Witchcraft, Sorcery, Rumors, and Gossip* (Cambridge: Cambridge University Press, 2004).

11. For another example of the significance of the means of disposing of corpses to Hindu-Muslim notions of community identity, see Kakar, *The Colors of Violence,* 97. In this quotation, a Hindu man expresses a desire that his *jāti* begin to burn their dead in part because of pressure from Hindus who wonder why they bury their dead like Muslims.

12. March 22, 2003.

13. In India, Bohra are a *jāti*-based group of Shi'a Muslims. In public space they are often immediately identifiable by their style of dress.

14. Academic year in Udaipur, 2000.

15. May 5, 2003.
16. Spring 2003.
17. April 9, 2003.
18. March 20, 2003.
19. May 8, 2003.
20. July 24, 2003. *Sayyid* is a title given to those who are descended from the Prophet Muhammad.
21. September 26, 2003.
22. November 15, 2003.
23. September 19, 2003.
24. March 20, 2003. This idea was often articulated by both Hindus and Sunnis.
25. November 26, 2003. Remarkably, Kakar records an almost identical rumor, though his source is a Pardi Hindu. Though now resident in Hyderabad, Pardi Hindus originally migrated from the northwest and speak a Marwari-Rajasthani dialect. See Kakar, *The Colors of Violence,* 105.
26. In conversations about magic, one oft-cited show was *Kyā hādsā kyā hakīkat* (Coincidence or Truth?).
27. William Sax has documented untouchable communities' mobilization of the deity Bhairav to seek justice in the wake of abuse from members of dominant caste groups. See Sax, *God of Justice.*
28. Here Halima used the English term *dracul-type.*
29. While the word *aṁgrez* almost certainly derives from the term *English,* in practice it is a common Hindi term for anyone who looks European, whether or not they are from England or speak English.
30. Here this woman's husband explained that Fatima often visits people in their dreams.
31. This detail was almost certainly offered in order to explain why this young woman began to have ḥāẓirī, since she came to Ḥusain Ṭekrī without any suspicion that magic was the cause of her problems. Normally, as was discussed in earlier chapters, a string needs to be tied and a request made before a person can have ḥāẓirī, but in this case, because she did not suspect that magic had been performed, she did not tie a string. Again, the flexibility of ritual activity and interpretive possibilities available at Muslim saint shrines is evident.
32. It is somewhat unusual for ḥāẓirī to entail the presence of those who hired the magicians, but clearly it is within the realm of possible interpretations of the practice.
33. It is true that "Christian" is sometimes used to denote Europeans or anyone who looks Western European, but here it seems that the religious meaning is operative, since the *ta'vīẕ* is buried in a Christian cemetery.
34. In my time at Ḥusain Ṭekrī I did not find any completely consistent set of beliefs about the nature of magicians, though the Aghori and practitioners of Tantra were popular choices among both Hindus and Muslims. This makes sense given the above-demonstrated tendency of individuals to construct the fearsomeness of others based on improper maintenance of living and dead bodies: Aghori and other Tantric practices involve use of bodily products that are universally understood to be polluting, and thus considered to impart an influence that will render prayers or rituals invalid. I was also occasionally told that Muslim practitioners of *abjad*

would harness the power of their recitations for magical purposes, or that they would make *ta'vīz* that involved dangerous manipulation of Qur'anic verses.

35. This actually begs the question of why a Hindu would visit a place that is potentially haunted by a polluting Muslim spirit. In part, as has been documented, the power of Muslim saints derives in part from their transgressiveness.

36. Khan, "The Graves of History."

37. For a discussion of Arabic and Urdu writing in popular Islamic healing practices, see Flueckiger, *In Amma's Healing Room,* particularly chapter 2.

38. Gottschalk, *Beyond Hindu and Muslim.*

39. Van der Veer, "Playing or Praying."

40. Flueckiger, *In Amma's Healing Room.*

41. This Hindu family was under the care of a Shi'a Muslim man named Salim (not the same Salim mentioned by Priya), whom I met during my first visit to Ḥusain Ṭekrī in 2000. Salim often serves as a guide for visiting families from his hometown. It is likely that his presence during the interview made the family particularly disinclined to say anything potentially derogatory about Islamic places like Ḥusain Ṭekrī. This is not to imply that the family did not have a deep and positive relationship with Ḥusain Ṭekrī. Indeed, the father of the family attributed his success in abandoning the consumption of alcohol to the power of Ḥusain Ṭekrī.

42. Sunila is not her real name. "Udichi Brahmin" means, literally, "northern Brahmin." I am not certain what additional or specific meaning this might have.

43. In the course of her interview she also explained that the *pret* engaged in *cheṛ-chāṛ* (touch-touching), which seems to be a somewhat common term for sexual teasing or attacks. For part of our interview two men sat and listened, and this, she later explained, made it difficult for her to explain the exact nature of the torment.

44. Sunila understood her body to have been magically filled with many offending presences, including *jinn, ātmā,* and different kinds of animals. The terminology she used to describe the animals' presence was *caukī,* literally, "sitting place": *"mere ūpar gāy kī [caukī], bhais kī, hathī kī, gaḍhe kī, kutte kī, kabūtar kī, bandar kī, nāg kī, chipkalī kī . . .* " (cow *caukī,* and also the *caukī* of water buffalo, elephants, donkeys, dogs, pigeons, monkeys, snakes, and salamanders . . .).

45. *Aur is meṁ, maiṁ saphal huī huṁ, par purī saphalī nahīṁ huī, purī saphalatā mujhe nahiṁ milī.* The term *saphal,* literally, "fruitful" or "profitable," reinforces the notion that at Ḥusain Ṭekrī it is *labor* that produces results.

46. The impressive optimism and strength that Sunila expresses here is common among pilgrims at Ḥusain Ṭekrī.

47. While there are too many instances of this phenomenon to mention, a few major examples include: the universal valorization of the long-suffering Sītā as an ideal wife and the concept of *strīdharm* (women's religious duty) more generally; *satī* as a widely recognized means for a woman to express her devotion to her husband: Rakhi, the immensely popular pan-Hindu celebration of sisters' duty to protect brothers; Karva Chauth, the widely observed pan-Hindu pre-sunrise to sunset fast observed by women to ensure their husbands' long life; Śrāddha, or the annual veneration of deceased ancestors, which is conducted in the home by a hired pandit but which entails a great deal of food preparation and housecleaning by the wife; and, finally, the publication in English of books like Om Lata Bahadur, *The Book of Hindu Festivals and Ceremonies* (New Delhi: UBS Publishers' Distributors,

1997). Books like this seek to educate a young generation of diasporic Hindu women of their duty to maintain an authentic and meaningful Hindu culture abroad. In all of these instances a woman's religious duties are intimately related to her role as a protective and supportive sister, mother, or wife. To be clear, this is not to suggest that "Hinduism" oppresses women. It is only to note that it would be very difficult for a Hindu woman to conceive of a Hindu identity that did not entail commitment to family life.

48. Though it did not occur to me to ask for the name of their town, because they said that their *jāti* was Caran and that they were from Rajasthan, I assumed that they were talking about the town of Deshnok, near Bikaner in northeastern Rajasthan. The town of Deshnok is directly connected by rail to both Ajmer and Jaora. The rat-populated temple there is that of the goddess Karni Mātā.

49. See Lindsey Harlan, *The Goddesses' Henchmen: Gender in Indian Hero Worship* (New York: Oxford University Press, 2003), 118–20; also see Alf Hiltebeitel, *Rethinking India's Oral and Classical Epics: Draupadi among Rajputs, Muslims, and Dalits* (Chicago: University of Chicago Press, 1999), 108–9.

50. For an analysis of the effect of mass transportation on Hindu pilgrimage practices, see Gold, *Fruitful Journeys,* especially chapter 5. In my time at Ḥusain Ṭekrī, though most pilgrims I met had heard of the site either in a dream or by word of mouth, people occasionally cited television specials or newspaper articles in which it had been featured. While I was there at least two television news teams visited to do stories on the site, in one case including its resident researcher in their interviews. Several newspaper stories about Ḥusain Ṭekrī were also published during my tenure there, for which I was also interviewed. Urban reporters clearly delighted in the generally fantastic and strange atmosphere of Ḥusain Ṭekrī, and my presence there made the entire spectacle all the more entertaining: lots of "crazy" people, among them an earnest minidisc recorder–toting foreign lady. For its part, the management of Ḥusain Ṭekrī, which aspired to make the site as well recognized nationally as the Chishtī *dargāḥ* in Ajmer, was confident that this press coverage would increase pilgrim traffic.

51. It is important to note that many non-Muslims have relationships with Muslim saint shrines that date back for many generations. It is clear that at Ḥusain Ṭekrī some of these generational relationships begin as the result of a family member being healed at the site. In other words, in some cases a healing relationship with the shrine may precipitate a kinship-based one.

52. Recall that the first time I met Priya she left one of these gatherings to speak with me, ignoring the protestations of the group.

53. Vernon Schubel has translated and analyzed many similar Shiʿa women's devotional stories. He also discusses, but does not translate, "The Tale of the Ten Virtuous Women." See Vernon Schubel, *Religious Performance in Contemporary Islam: Shiʿi Devotional Rituals in South Asia* (Columbia: University of South Carolina Press, 1993).

54. A story called the "Ten Virtuous Women" recited by a Shiʿa family during a private session differed from the story that is translated in this chapter. However, in basic message and form it is very similar to the version translated here, which was recited by Babli at the rauẓa of Fatima. In the story recited by the Shiʿa family, a woman lacking resources is rewarded for remembering the suffering of an ear-

lier generation of women (including Fatima and others), and those who temporarily keep this woman from performing the ceremony properly are punished by loss of home and family, which are only restored when "The Tale of the Ten Virtuous Women" is properly recited. As in the version of the story Babli read, prosperity derives from the woman's act of recitation and remembrance rather than from her father, her husband, or the local ruler.

55. While the script of the translated text is Devanagari, the language is Urdu derived from Persian and Arabic, which makes for difficult transliterations into the Roman alphabet. Throughout, the transliterations from the Hindi reflect the Devanagari edition available at Ḥusain Ṭekrī. This means that they may not have the diacritics that they would have had if the text been written in an Arabic-derived script.

56. In the Devanagari, the word is *isrāīl.*

57. The counting of the women here is somewhat confusing because the text is structured around associated narratives while at the same time occasionally offering catechismlike lists that do not reflect the sequence of the stories in the text as a whole. Here the text takes as a given that the four women are Mary, Fatima, Asiya, and Hagar, but the subsequent counting of them and the relating of their stories is not clearly organized. Hence Hagar is number two in the list of women, but as their stories are told she is referred to as the fourth woman. The assumed larger sequencing is basically this: Mary's story is told and then Fatima is introduced, but her story is saved for later. Next Asiya's story is related. Hagar is brought in as the fourth, even though she is mentioned as the second in a list that explicitly begins with Fatima as the first wife but actually begins with the Qur'anic description of Mary.

58. In Urdu, Zam Zam. This is the name of a well that exists in present-day Mecca. Drinking from it is a common (but not required) part of performing the hajj.

59. A formulation commonly used in Shi'a communities: Muhammad, 'Ali, Hasan, Husain, and Fatima. Here, a reference to the family.

60. In Urdu, *ṣugarā,* "little"

61. In preparation for making the offering that is the culmination of the tenth day of the story-reading cycle. The offering must be made in a state of ritual purity.

62. In fact, in the story, Fiza actually proves to be an *abler* provider than 'Ali himself, since 'Ali was forced to borrow food to feed his family.

63. For a discussion of various religious uses and interpretations of weeping, see John Stratton Hawley and Kimberley C. Patton, eds., *Holy Tears: Weeping in the Religious Imagination* (Princeton, NJ: Princeton University Press, 2005). Taken as a whole, the book itself makes a convincing case for the translatability of weeping across religious traditions.

64. In a subcontinental context, seeking intercession of Muslim saints is explicitly condemned by the influential Tablighi Jama'at. See van der Veer, "Playing or Praying."

65. In Urdu the word for "believer" is *mūmin,* derived from an Arabic root meaning "to feel or be secure."

66. Because the term *mominā* may also mean a female of the Muslim weaver *jāti,* it would also identify the protagonist in the story as a woman who converted to Islam from a *jāti* that is considered fairly low in the Hindu caste hierarchy. Julahas, a low-caste community of weavers, started taking *momin* (a vernacular form of mūmin) as a title in the nineteenth century. It subsequently became so popular that now many Ashraf Muslims avoid the (formerly common) name Momin lest

they be mistaken for low-caste weavers. The biggest Julaha political organization of the twentieth century was the All-India Momin Conference, which opposed the Muslim League in its demand for Pakistan.

67. My choice to refer to these stories as "Mother Ten's stories" follows the translation of Ann Grodzins Gold, "Mother Ten's Stories," in *Religions of India in Practice,* ed. Donald S. Lopez Jr. (Princeton, NJ: Princeton University Press, 1995), 434–48.

68. Selva Raj and William Harman, eds., *Dealing with Deities: The Ritual Vow in South Asia* (Albany: State University of New York Press, 2006).

69. The phenomenon of Hindu participation in *mātam* has also been documented by David Pinault in *The Horse of Karbala: Muslim Devotional Life in India* (New York: Palgrave, 2001). Pinault did not interview these Hindus or speculate as to why they participate. See also the forthcoming work of Mahboob Ali "Afsar" Mohammad on non-Muslim participation in Shi'a rituals.

70. Individuals commonly used the English-origin word *sepoy* to describe the invisible agents of the saints. When pressed for another term, some use the word *farishtā,* often translated as "angel," or *muwakkil,* best translated as "deputy."

71. Ambient street noise in this recording makes it impossible for me to be absolutely certain, but it seems that once in her description of this young woman Bilkis referred to her as these three men's *jalan bahin,* or "burning sister." Because Bilkis sometimes referred to Sailani Bābā as *jalan bābā,* it is likely that this description of the kinship relationship was offered in order to indicate that the kinship relationship was created by Sailani Bābā. *Jalan* is commonly used to describe Muslim saints' temperament; they are easily angered, which, as has been discussed, is part of their power. Recall also that *pret* often lament their "burning" state during the dispensation of lobān.

72. *Bābā milvā denge*, or Bābā will make sure we find one another.

73. Z. Hasanain, *Imām husain se hinduoṁ va un ke devtāoṁ kā sambandh* [The relationship between Hindus, Hindu deities, and Imām Husain] (Lucknow: Husain Book Agency, 1999), 31.

74. It is of course true that the reading of "The Tale of the Ten Virtuous Women" entails sharing *laḍḍūs*, and it is also true that the found family relationship between Bilkis's son and the young Hindu woman eventually involved small gifts after the young Hindu woman was healed. However, there are many relationships that are not substantiated in this way.

75. Before leaving I also taught Priya and her mother how to knit socks.

76. The question of which social, economic, and political factors informed this theologically articulated debate, while important, is not relevant to this discussion.

77. On such reform movements, see Metcalf, *Islamic Revival.*

78. See Barbara Daly Metcalf, "Living Hadith in the Tablīghī Jama'at," *Journal of Asian Studies* 52, no. 3 (August 1993): 584–608.

79. Hasanain, *Imām husain;* Z. Hasanain, *Maulā 'alī se hinduoṁ kā prem* [Hindus' love for Maulā 'Ali] (Lucknow: Husain Book Agency, 2001); Hakim Sayyid Mahmud Gilani, *Om aur 'alī* [Om and 'Ali], trans. Haidar Mehdi (Lucknow: Abbas Book Agency), n.d.

80. Hasanain, *Imām husain,* 5.

81. Ibid.

82. Ibid., 6. The Hindi here is *"bhārat meṁ hindū hinsā se ghṛṇā kartā hai."*

83. This detail echoes popular retellings of the Muslim tradition that some members of some of the early Muslim community sought protection in the Christian kingdom of Ethiopia.

84. Hasanain, *Imām husain,* 5.

85. This story does not correspond with the actual dates of Chandragupta and his son.

86. Hasanain, *Imām husain,* 16, 18, 21–22, and 24–25.

87. This journey is also attested to in Sikh scripture.

88. Gilani, *Om aur ʿalī.* The text has been translated into Hindi. I was unable to determine the original language. This text and the others were likely written by members of the Indian Ismaili community; many of its ideas and strategies are similar to those common in the Ismaili community.

89. *Haidar,* an Arabic-derived Urdu word for "lion," is another epithet for ʿAli. In its discussion of China and Japan, the text cites English-language travel literature.

90. Gilani, *Om aur ʿalī,* 40–48.

91. The text refers to Hindu deities as *avatāra* and *devtā,* thus using Hindi words that clearly maintain the sense that they are deities.

92. This extra-Qur'anic notion of the 124,000 *paigambar* is widespread in India and the rest of the world. On India see Flueckiger, *In Amma's Healing Room,* 175.

93. This latter interpretation of the goddess Kālī was elaborated upon by a Shiʿa hotelier from Hyderabad in the context of a much larger English-language interview in which he detailed his own exploration of *abjad* and his wife's Ḥusain Ṭekrī–derived charismatic healing practice.

CONCLUSION

The epigraph is my own English summary of an interview with an employee of Ḥusain Ṭekrī originally recorded in Hindi on September 17, 2003. The name Band Choṛnewāle Bābā (literally, "Imprisonment Opening Father") was used by my informant, and so I have reproduced it here. I have also heard the variation Bandī Choṛ Bābā applied to this saint.

1. On a later visit, I heard another version of this story from a shrine attendant. This version was similar to the one related above but concludes with the defeat of the king rather than his recovery.

2. *Cillā,* derived from the Persian *cihal,* literally means "forty days." Sufi meditation practices often span this period of time.

3. Sharma, "Ek tarif dargāh."

4. Up through the British period, a saint's *wilāya* could reflect both political and religious authority; see Eaton, "The Political and Religious Authority," 341.

Glossary

The following Urdu terms are commonly used for Muslim healers, leaders, and spiritual mentors whose memories and/or graves are objects of veneration in India. Unless otherwise indicated, definitions are based on John T. Platts, A Dictionary of Urdū, Classical Hindī, and English *(New Delhi: Munshiram Manoharlal, 2000).*

AULIYĀ: A plural noun meaning friends (of God); saints, holy men, prophets, apostles; a saint *(walī)*. From the Arabic *walī.*

BĀBĀ: Father; grandfather, old man; sir; sire; a *saṅyāsī* or *faqīr.* From the Sanskrit *vaprā* or *vapraḥ;* also Persian *bābā,* or father.

BĪBĪ: Lady, dame, madam; wife; mistress; a term of endearment.

ḤAẒRAT: Excellent, highness. From the Arabic *ḥaẓra* and Persian *ḥaẓrat.*

IMĀM: One who is followed or imitated; exemplar, guide, leader, head of a religion; patriarch; priest; minister or reader of a mosque. From the Arabic *imām.*

ḴH̱W̤ĀJA: Lord, master, owner; a man of distinction; a respectable man, a gentleman; a rich merchant. From the Persian *ḵẖwāja.*

MAULĀ: Lord, master, ruler; a patron; a judge; magistrate; the Supreme Lord; a manumitted slave, freedman. From the Arabic abstract verbal noun "to be near."

PĪR: An old man; a saint; a spiritual guide or father; a priest; founder or head of a religious order. From the Persian *pīr.*

SARKĀR: Chief, master, lord; superintendent, supervisor, overseer, agent; landlord.

SHĀH: King. From the Persian *shāh.*

SHAHĪD: A witness; one who is slain in the cause of religion; to come by one's death unjustly; to fall desperately in love. From the Arabic *shahīd.*

SHĀHZĀDĪ: Literally, daughter of a king; princess. From the Persian *shāhzādī.*

WALĪ: A singular noun meaning a master, lord, prince, governor, defender; a friend, a favorite (of God or a king); a saint; a servant or slave. In contemporary spoken Hindi and Urdu, *walī* is liberally applied to any venerated Muslim individual.

Bibliography

Ahmad, Imtiaz, and Helmut Reifeld, eds. *Lived Islam in South Asia: Adaptation, Accommodation, and Conflict.* New Delhi: Social Science Press, 2004.

Ahmet, Mohammad Afaq. *Mojizā e Husain Ṭekrī Sharīf* [The Miracle of Ḥusain Ṭekrī]. Mumbai: Khurśid e Jehrā Publications, 2001.

Alam, Muzaffar. *The Languages of Political Islam: India 1200–1800.* Chicago: University of Chicago Press, 2004.

Amin, Shahid. *Event, Metaphor, Memory: Chauri Chaura 1922–1992.* Berkeley: University of California Press, 1995.

Anderson, Benedict. *Imagined Communities: Reflections on the Origin and Spread of Nationalism.* London: Verso, 1991.

Appadurai, Arjun. "Is Homo Hierarchicus?" *American Ethnologist* 13, no. 4 (November 1986): 745–61.

Asad, Talal. "Anthropology and the Analysis of Ideology." *Man* 14, no. 4 (December 1979): 607–27.

———. *Genealogies of Religion: Discipline and Reasons of Power in Christianity and Islam.* Baltimore, MD: Johns Hopkins University Press, 1993.

———. "The Idea of Anthropology of Islam." Occasional Papers Series. Washington, D.C.: Georgetown University Center for Contemporary Arab Studies, 1986.

Asani, Ali. "In Praise of Muhammad: Sindhi and Urdu Poems." In *The Religions of India in Practice,* edited by Donald Lopez, 159–87. Princeton, NJ: Princeton University Press, 1995.

Asher, Catherine B. "Mapping Hindu-Muslim Identities through the Architecture of Shahjahanabad and Jaipur." In *Beyond Turk and Hindu: Rethinking Religious Identities in Islamicate South Asia,* edited by David Gilmartin and Bruce B. Lawrence, 121–48. Gainesville: University Press of Florida, 2000.

Assayag, Jackie. *Au confluence de deux rivière: Musulmans et Hindous dans le sud de L'Inde.* Paris: Presses de l'École Francaise d'Extrême Orient, 1995. Translated by Latika Sahgal as *At the Confluence of Two Rivers: Muslims and Hindus in South India*. Delhi: Manohar, 2004.

———. "But, They Do Move . . . Religion, Illness and Therapeutics in Southern India." In *Managing Distress: Possession and Therapeutic Cults in South Asia*, edited by Marine Carrin, 30–50. Delhi: Manohar, 1999.

Assayag, Jackie, and Gilles Tarabout. *La possession en Asie du Sud: parole, corps, territoire*. Paris: Éditions de l'École des hautes etudes en sciences socials, 1999.

Babb, Lawrence A. *The Divine Hierarchy: Popular Hinduism in Central India*. New York: Columbia University Press, 1975.

Bahadur, Om Lata. *The Book of Hindu Festivals and Ceremonies*. New Delhi: UBS Publishers' Distributors, 1997.

Bayly, Susan. *Saints, Goddesses, and Kings: Muslims and Christians in South Indian Society: 1700–1900*. Cambridge: Cambridge University Press, 1989.

Behl, Aditya. "Introduction." In *Madhumālatī: An Indian Sufi Romance*, by Mīr Sayyid Manjhan Shaṭṭārī Rājgīrī, translated by Aditya Behl and Simon Weightman, xi–xlvi. New York: Oxford University Press, 2000.

Bell, Catherine. *Ritual Theory, Ritual Practice*. New York: Oxford University Press, 1992.

Bhoot. Directed by Ram Gopal Varma. Mumbai: Dream Merchants Enterprise, 2003.

Bigelow, Anna. "Sharing Saints, Shrines and Stories: Practicing Pluralism in North India." PhD diss., University of California, Santa Barbara, 2004.

Boddy, Janice. "Spirit Possession Revisited: Beyond Instrumentality." *Annual Review of Anthropology* 23: 407–34.

Bourdieu, Pierre. *Outline of a Theory of Practice*. Cambridge: Cambridge University Press, 1977.

Bourguignon, Erika. *Possession*. San Francisco: Chandler and Sharp, 1976.

Bowen, John R. *Muslims Through Discourse: Religion and Ritual in Gayo Society*. Princeton, NJ: Princeton University Press, 1993.

Bulliet, Richard. *Islam: The View from the Edge*. New York: Columbia University Press, 1994.

Bunty aur Babli. Directed by Shaad Ali. Mumbai: Yash Raj Films, 2005.

Burman, J. J. Roy. *Hindu-Muslim Syncretic Shrines and Communities*. New Delhi: Mittal Publications, 2002.

Carrin, Marine, ed. *Managing Distress: Possession and Therapeutic Cults in South Asia*. Delhi: Manohar, 1999.

Chippa, Ghulam. "Chippa Community Web page." Available at www.chippa.com (accessed November 1, 2006).

Collins, Elizabeth Fuller. *Pierced by Murugan's Lance: Ritual, Power, and Moral Redemption among Malaysian Hindus*. Dekalb: Northern Illinois University Press, 1997.

Combs-Schilling, Elaine. *Sacred Performances: Islam, Sexuality, and Sacrifice*. New York: Columbia University Press, 1989.

Crapanzano, Vincent. "Spirit Possession." In *Encyclopedia of Religion*, edited by Mircea Eliade, vol. 14, 12–19. New York: Macmillan, 1987.

Crapanzano, Vincent, and Vivian Garrison. *Case Studies in Spirit Possession*. New York: John Wiley and Sons, 1977.

Csordas, Thomas J. "Elements of Charismatic Possession and Healing." *Medical Anthropology Quarterly* 14, no. 4 (June 1988): 121–42.

Currie, P. M. *The Shrine and Cult* of Muʿīn al-dīn Chishtī of Ajmer. New Delhi: Oxford University Press, 1989.

Currim, Mumtaz, and George Mitchell, photographs by Karoki Lewis. *Dargahs: Abodes of the Saints.* Mumbai: Marg, 2004.

Daniel, E. Valentine. *Fluid Signs: Being a Person the Tamil Way.* Berkeley: University of California Press, 1984.

Dirks, Nicholas B. *Castes of Mind: Colonialism and the Making of Modern India.* Princeton, NJ: Princeton University Press, 2001.

———. *The Hollow Crown: Ethnohistory of an Indian Kingdom.* New York: Cambridge University Press, 1987.

———. "Ritual and Resistance: Subversion as Social Fact." In *Contesting Power: Resistance and Everyday Social Relations in South Asia,* edited by Douglas Haynes and Gyan Prakash, 213–38. Berkeley: University of California Press, 1992.

Dumont, Louis. *Homo Hierarchicus: The Caste System and Its Implications.* Translated by Mark Sainsbury, Louis Dumont, and Basia Gulati. Chicago: University of Chicago Press, 1980.

———. *A South Indian Subcaste: Social Organization and Religion of the Pramalai Kallar.* Translated by M. Moffat. New York: Oxford University Press, 1986.

Dwyer, Graham. *The Divine and the Demonic: Supernatural Affliction and Its Treatment in North India.* London: Routledge Curzon, 2003.

Eaton, Richard M. "The Political and Religious Authority of the Shrine of Bābā Farīd." In *Moral Conduct and Authority: The Place of Adab in South Asian Islam,* edited by Barbara Daly Metcalf, 333–56. Berkeley: University of California Press, 1984.

———. *The Rise of Islam and the Bengal Frontier, 1204—1760.* Berkeley: University of California Press, 1993.

Eichenbaum, Howard, Andrew P. Yonelinas, and Charan Ranganath. "The Medial Temporal Lobe and Recognition Memory." *Annual Review of Neuroscience* 30 (2007): 123–52.

el-Zein, Abdul Hamid. "Beyond Ideology and Theology: The Search for an Anthropology of Islam." *Annual Review of Anthropology* 6: 227–54.

Erndl, Katherine. *Victory to the Mother: The Hindu Goddess of Northwest India in Myth, Ritual, and Symbol.* London: Oxford University Press, 1993.

Ernst, Carl W. "Admiring the Works of the Ancients: The Ellora Temples as Viewed by Indo-Muslim Authors." In *Beyond Turk and Hindu: Rethinking Religious Identities in Islamicate South Asia,* edited by David Gilmartin and Bruce B. Lawrence, 98–120. Gainesville: University Press of Florida, 2000.

———. *Eternal Garden: Mysticism, History, and Politics at a South Asian Sufi Center.* Albany: State University of New York Press, 1992.

———. "India as a Sacred Islamic Land." In *Religions of India in Practice,* edited by Donald S. Lopez Jr., 556–63. Princeton, NJ: Princeton University Press, 1995.

Ernst, Carl W., and Tony Stewart. "Syncretism." In *South Asian Folklore: An Encyclopedia,* edited by Peter J. Claus, Sarah Diamond, and Margaret A. Mills, 586–88. New York: Routledge, 2002.

Ewing, Katherine. *Arguing Sainthood: Modernity, Psychoanalysis, and Islam.* Durham, NC: Duke University Press, 1997.

Flueckiger, Joyce Burkhalter. *In Amma's Healing Room: Gender and Vernacular Islam in South India.* Bloomington: Indiana University Press, 2006.

Foucault, Michel. *The Archaeology of Knowledge.* Translated by A. M. Sheridan Smith. New York: Pantheon Books, 1972.

———. *The Order of Things: An Archaeology of the Human Sciences.* New York: Pantheon Books, 1971.

Freeman, Richard. "Dynamics of the Person in the Worship and Sorcery of Malabar." In *La possession en Asie du Sud: parole, corps, territoire,* edited by Jackie Assayag and Gilles Tarabout, 149–82. Paris: Éditions de l'École des hautes etudes en sciences socials, 1999.

Fuller, C. J. *The Camphor Flame: Popular Hinduism and Society in India.* Princeton, NJ: Princeton University Press, 1992.

Gazetteer of the Nellore District: Brought up to 1938. Madras Government of Madras Staff, 1942.

Geertz, Clifford. *Islam Observed: Religious Development in Morocco and Indonesia.* Chicago: University of Chicago Press, 1968.

Gellner, Ernest. *Muslim Society.* Cambridge: Cambridge University Press, 1981.

Gilani, Hakim Sayyid Mahmud, *Om aur 'Alī* [Om and 'Ali], Translated by Haidar Mehdi. Lucknow: Abbas Book Agency, n.d.

Gilmartin, David, and Bruce B. Lawrence, eds. *Beyond Turk and Hindu: Rethinking Religious Identities in Islamicate South Asia.* Gainesville: University Press of Florida, 2000.

Gold, Ann Grodzins. *Fruitful Journeys: The Ways of Rajasthani Pilgrims.* Berkeley: University of California Press, 1988.

———. "Mother Ten's Stories." In *Religions of India in Practice,* edited by Donald S. Lopez Jr., 434–48. Princeton, NJ: Princeton University Press, 1995.

Goodman, Felicitas D. *How About Demons?: Possession and Exorcism in the Modern World.* Bloomington: Indiana University Press, 1988.

Gottschalk, Peter. *Beyond Hindu and Muslim: Multiple Identity in Narrations from Village India.* New York: Oxford University Press, 2000.

Halliburton, Murphy. "The Importance of a Pleasant Process of Treatment: Lessons on Healing from South India." *Culture, Medicine, and Psychiatry* 27, no. 2 (June 2003): 161–86.

Harlan, Lindsey. *The Goddesses' Henchmen: Gender in Indian Hero Worship.* New York: Oxford University Press, 2003.

Hasanain, Z. *Imām husain se hinduoṁ va un ke devtāoṁ ka sambandh* [The relationship between Hindus, Hindu deities, and Imām Husain]. Lucknow: Husain Book Agency, 1999.

———. *Maulā 'Alī se hinduoṁ kā prem* [Hindus' love for Maulā 'Ali]. Lucknow: Husain Book Agency, 2001.

Hawley, John Stratton, and Kimberley C. Patton, eds. *Holy Tears: Weeping in the Religious Imagination.* Princeton, NJ: Princeton University Press, 2005.

Haynes, Douglas, and Gyan Prakash, eds. *Contesting Power: Resistance and Everyday Social Relations in South Asia.* Berkeley: University of California Press, 1992.

Hiltebeitel, Alf. *Rethinking India's Oral and Classical Epics: Draupadi among Rajputs, Muslims, and Dalits.* Chicago: University of Chicago Press, 1999.

Hodgson, Marshall G. *The Venture of Islam, Volume 1: The Classical Age of Islam.* Chicago: University of Chicago Press, 1974.

Jackson, Paul, S.J. "Perceptions of the Dargahs of Patna." In *Muslim Shrines in India: Their Character, History, and Significance,* edited by Christian Troll, 98–111. New Delhi: Oxford University Press, 1989.

Kadri, Khalil Muhammad. *Bahiśtī Zevar.* Translated by Tanvīr Fāruqī. Delhi: Jasīm Book Depot, 1997.

Kakar, Sudhir. *The Colors of Violence: Cultural Identities, Religion, and Violence.* Chicago: University of Chicago Press, 1996.

———. *Shamans, Mystics and Doctors: A Psychological Inquiry into India and Its Healing Traditions.* New York: Knopf, 1982.

———. "Some Unconscious Aspects of Ethnic Violence in India." In *Mirrors of Violence: Communities, Riots, and Survivors in South Asia,* edited by Veena Das, 135–45. New Delhi: Oxford University Press, 1990.

Kapferer, Bruce. *The Feast of the Sorcerer: Practices of Consciousness and Power.* Chicago: University of Chicago Press, 1997.

Kavita, Shobha, Shobita, Kanchan, and Sharada. "Rural Women Speak." *Seminar* 342 (February 1988): 40–44.

Keller, Mary. *The Hammer and the Flute: Women, Power and Spirit Possession.* Baltimore, MD: Johns Hopkins University Press, 2002.

Khan, Dominique-Sila. "The Graves of History and the Metaphor of the Hidden Pir." In *Culture, Communities and Change,* edited by Varsha Joshi, 154–72. Jaipur: Institute of Rajasthan Studies, Rawat Publications, 2002.

Khan, Muhammad Ishaq. "The Significance of the Dargah of Hazratbal in the Socio-Religious and Political Life of Kashmiri Muslims." In *Muslim Shrines in India: Their Character History, and Significance,* edited by Christian Troll, 172–88. New Delhi: Oxford University Press, 1989.

Korom, Frank J. *Hosay Trinidad: Muḥarram Performances in an Indo-Caribbean Diaspora.* Philadelphia: University of Pennsylvania Press, 2003.

Krengel, Monika. "Spirit Possession in the Central Himalayas. *Jāgar*-rituals: An Expression of Customs and Rights." In *La possession en Asie du Sud: parole, corps, territoire,* edited by Jackie Assayag and Gilles Tarabout, 265–88. Paris: Éditions de l'École des hautes etudes en sciences socials, 1999.

Kuch Kuch Hota Hai. Directed by Karan Johar. Mumbai: Dharma Productions, 1998.

Kurtz, Stanley N. *All the Mothers Are One: Hindu India and the Reshaping of Psychoanalysis.* New York: Columbia University Press, 1994.

Lakdawala, M. H. "Mumbai's Babas Thrive on Misery." *Milli Gazette* 3, no. 23 (December 1–15, 2002).

Lambek, Michael. *Human Spirits: A Cultural Account of Trance in Mayotte.* Cambridge: Cambridge University Press, 1981.

———. *Knowledge and Power in Mayotte: Local Discourse of Islam, Sorcery and Spirit Possession.* Toronto: University of Toronto Press, 1993.

Lelyveld, David. *Aligarh's First Generation: Muslim Solidarity in British India.* Princeton, NJ: Princeton University Press, 1978.

Liebeskind, Claudia. *Piety on Its Knees: Three Sufi Traditions of South Asia in Modern Times.* New Delhi: Oxford University Press, 1998.

Lopez, Donald S., Jr., ed. *Religions of India in Practice.* Princeton, NJ: Princeton University Press, 1995.

Lutgendorf, Philip. "My Hanuman Is Bigger Than Yours." *History of Religions* 33, no. 3 (February 1994): 211–45.

Mahmood, Tahir. "The Dargah of Sayyid Salar Mas'ud Ghazi in Bahraich: Legend, Tradition and Reality." In *Muslim Shrines in India: Their Character, History and Significance,* edited by Christian Troll, 24–43. New Delhi: Oxford University Press, 1989.

Marriott, McKim, ed. *Village India: Studies in the Little Community.* Chicago: University of Chicago Press, 1955.

Marriott, McKim, and Ronald Inden. "Toward an Ethnosociology of South Asian Caste Systems." In *The New Wind: Changing Identities in South Asia,* edited by Ken David. 227–38. The Hague: Mouton, 1977.

Mauss, Marcel. *The Gift: Forms and Functions of Exchange in Archaic Societies.* Translated by Ian Cunnison. Glencoe, IL: Free Press, 1954.

Mayaram, Shail. "Beyond Ethnicity? Being Hindu *and* Muslim in South Asia." In *Lived Islam in South Asia: Adaptation, Accommodation, and Conflict,* edited by Imtiaz Ahmad and Helmut Reifeld, 18–39. New Delhi: Social Science Press, 2004.

———. "Spirit Possession: Reframing Discourses of the Self and the Other." In *La possession en Asie du Sud: parole, corps, territoire,* edited by Jackie Assayag and Gilles Tarabout, 101–32. Paris: Éditions de l'École des hautes etudes en sciences sociales, 1999.

McGregor, R. S., ed., *The Oxford Hindi-English Dictionary.* Oxford: Oxford University Press, 1993.

Mernissi, Fatima. *Beyond the Veil: Male-Female Dynamics in Modern Muslim Society.* Bloomington: Indiana University Press, 1987.

Messick, Brinkley. *The Calligraphic State: Textual Domination and History in a Muslim Society.* Berkeley: University of California Press, 1993.

Metcalf, Barbara Daly. *Islamic Revival in British India: Deoband: 1860–1900.* Princeton, NJ: Princeton University Press, 1982.

———. "Living Hadith in the Tablīghī Jama'at." *Journal of Asian Studies* 52, no. 3 (August 1993): 584–608.

———. *Perfecting Women: Maulana Ashraf 'Ali Tanawi's Bihishti Zewar: A Partial Translation with Commentary.* Berkeley: University of California Press, 1990.

———, ed. *Making Muslim Space in North America and Europe.* Berkeley: University of California Press, 1996.

———, ed. *Moral Conduct and Authority: The Place of Adab in South Asian Islam.* Berkeley: University of California Press, 1984.

Nabokov, Isabelle. *Religion against the Self: An Ethnography of Tamil Rituals.* New York: Oxford University Press, 2000.

Oberoi, Harjot. *The Construction of Religious Boundaries: Culture, Identity, and Diversity in the Sikh Tradition.* Chicago: University of Chicago Press, 1994.

Obeyesekere, Gananath. *Medusa's Hair: An Essay on Personal Symbols and Religious Experience.* Chicago: University of Chicago Press, 1991.

———. "Psychocultural Exegesis of a Case of Spirit Possession in Sri Lanka." In *Case Studies in Spirit Possession,* edited by Vincent Crapanzano and Vivian Garrison, 235–94. New York: John Wiley and Sons, 1977.

Oesterreich, Traugott Konstantin. *Possession, Demoniacal and Other: Among Primitive Races, in Antiquity, the Middle Ages, and Modern Times.* Translated by D. Ibberson. New York: R. R. Smith, 1930.

Pakaslahti, Antti. "Family-centered Treatment of Mental Health Problems at the Balaji Temple in Rajasthan." In *Changing Patterns of Family and Kinship in South Asia,* edited by Asko Parpola and Sirpa Tenhunen. *Studia Orientalia* 84: 129–66.

Pakeeza. Directed by Kamal Amrohi. Mumbai: Mahal Pictures Pvt. Ltd., 1971.

Pandey, Gyanendra, ed. *Hindus and Others: The Question of Identity in India Today.* New York: Viking, 1993.

Paper, Jordan. *The Spirits Are Drunk: Comparative Approaches to Chinese Religion.* Albany: State University of New York Press, 1995.

Parry, Jonathan P. *Death in Banaras.* Cambridge: Cambridge University Press, 1994.

Pfleiderer, Beatrix. "Mira Datar Dargah: The Psychiatry of a Muslim Shrine." In *Ritual and Religion among Muslims in India,* edited by Imtiaz Ahmad, 195–233. New Delhi: Manohar, 1984.

Pfleiderer, Beatrix, and Virchand Dharamsey. *Die besessenen Frauen von Mira Datar Dargah: Heilen und Trance in Indien.* Frankfurt: Campus Verlag, 1994.

Pinault, David. *Horse of Karbala: Muslim Devotional Life in India.* New York: Palgrave, 2001.

Pinkney, Andrea Marion. "The Sacred Share: Prasada in South Asia." PhD diss., Columbia University, New York, 2008.

Pinto, Desiderio, S.J. "The Mystery of the Nizamuddin Dargah: The Accounts of Pilgrims." In *Muslim Shrines in India: Their Character, History, and Significance,* edited by Christian Troll, 112–24. New Delhi: Oxford University Press, 1989.

Platts, John T. *A Dictionary of Urdū, Classical Hindī, and English.* New Delhi: Munshiram Manoharlal, 2000.

President and Fellows of Harvard College and Diana Eck. "The Pluralism Project at Harvard University." Available at www.pluralism.org (accessed November 1, 2006).

Purohit, Teena. "Formations and Genealogies of Ismaili Sectarianism in Nineteenth-Century India." PhD diss., Columbia University, New York, 2007.

Raj, Selva, and William Harman, eds. *Dealing with Deities: The Ritual Vow in South Asia.* Albany: State University of New York Press, 2006.

Rājgīrī, Mīr Sayyid Manjhan Shaṭṭārī. *Madhumālatī: An Indian Sufi Romance.* Translated by Aditya Behl and Simon Weightman. New York: Oxford University Press, 2000.

Ramanujan, A. K. "Is There an Indian Way of Thinking? An Informal Essay." *Contributions to Indian Sociology* 23, no. 1 (1989): 41–58.

Reingold, Edwin M., and Nachum Dershowitz. "Calendrica." Available at http://emr.cs.uiuc.edu/home/reingold/calendar-book/Calendrica.html (accessed November 1, 2006).

Richman, Paula, ed. *Many Rāmāyaṇas: The Diversity of a Narrative Tradition in South Asia.* Berkeley: University of California Press, 1991.

———, ed. *Questioning Ramayanas: A South Asian Tradition.* Berkeley: University of California Press, 2001.

Rigopoulos, Antonio. *The Life and Teachings of Sai Baba of Shirdi.* Albany: State University of New York Press, 1993.

Rizvi, Safdar. *Husain Ṭekrī kyā hai?*. Hindi edition. Delhi: Rāhat Process, 2001, 2003.
———. *Ḥusain Ṭekrī kyā hai.* Urdu edition. Delhi: Rāhat Process, 1998.
Ṛollier, Franck. "Walking Round on the Straight Path in the Name of the Father: A Study of the Dispossession Trance at Murugmalla." In *Managing Distress: Possession and Therapeutic Cults in South Asia,* edited by Marine Carrin, 51–73. Delhi: Manohar, 1999.
Said, Edward. *Orientalism.* New York: Pantheon Books, 1978.
Saunders, Lucie Wood. "Variants in *Zar* Experience in an Egyptian Village." In *Case Studies in Spirit Possession,* edited by Vincent Crapanzano and Vivian Garrison, 177–92. New York: John Wiley and Sons, 1977.
Sax, William Sturman. *Dancing the Self: Personhood and Performance in the Pāṇḍav Līlā of Garhwal.* Oxford: Oxford University Press, 2002.
———. *God of Justice: Ritual Healing and Social Justice in the Central Himalayas.* New York: Oxford University Press, 2009.
———. *Mountain Goddess: Gender and Politics in a Himalayan Pilgrimage.* New York: Oxford University Press, 1991.
Schömbucher, Elizabeth. "'A Daughter for Seven Minutes': The Therapeutic and Divine Discourses of Possession Mediumship in South India." In *La possession en Asie du Sud: parole, corps, territoire,* edited by Jackie Assayag and Gilles Tarabout, 33–60. Paris: Éditions de l'École des hautes etudes en sciences socials, 1999.
Schubel, Vernon. *Religious Performance in Contemporary Islam: Shi'i Devotional Rituals in South Asia.* Columbia: University of South Carolina Press, 1993.
Sengupta, Somini. "Braids of Faith at Baba's Temple: A Hindu-Muslim Idyll." *New York Times,* March 17, 2006.
———. "In Teeming India, Water Crisis Means Dry Pipes and Foul Sludge; Thirsty Giant / First of Three Articles." *New York Times,* September 29, 2006.
Shaara, Lila, and Andrew Strathern, "A Preliminary Analysis of the Relationship between Altered States of Consciousness, Healing, and Social Structure." *American Anthropologist* 94 (1992): 145–60.
Shafiq, Khwaja Muhammad. *Ĕ'jāz e Ḥusain* [The miraculous cure of Husain]. Hyderabad, 1945.
Sharf, Robert H. "Experience." In *Critical Terms for Religious Studies,* edited by Mark C. Taylor, 94–116. Chicago: University of Chicago Press, 1998.
Sharma, Umesh. "Ek tarif dargāh, to dūsrī tarif hanumān jī / pūjā aur ibādat hotī hai sāth-sāth / hiṇdū-muslim ektā kī anūṭhī misāl lālākheṛī men tājuddīn bābā kā darbār." *Dainik Bhāskar* [Daily Sun], August 20, 2005, Indore Edition.
Shobha Devi, Y. J., and G. S. Bidarakoppa. "Jod Gomaz Dargah as a Healing Centre." In *Managing Distress: Possession and Therapeutic Cults in South Asia,* edited by Marine Carrin, 90–115. Delhi: Manohar, 1999.
Shodhan, Amrita. *A Question of Community: Religious Groups and Colonial Law.* Calcutta: Samya, 2001.
Sikand, Yoginder. *Hindu-Muslim Syncretic Shrines in Karnataka.* Bangalore: Himayat, 2001.
———. "Shared Hindu-Muslim Shrines in Karnataka: Challenges to Liminality." In *Lived Islam in South Asia: Adaptation, Accommodation, and Conflict.* Edited

by Imtiaz Ahmad and Helmut Reifeld, 166–86. New Delhi: Social Science Press, 2004.

Slackman, Michael. "TV Mystic Lingers in Saudi Jail." *New York Times,* April 24, 2010.

Smith, Frederick. "The Current State of Possession Studies as a Cross-Disciplinary Project." *Religious Studies Review* 27, no. 3 (July 2001): 203–12.

———. *The Self Possessed: Deity and Spirit Possession in South Asian Literature and Civilization.* New York: Columbia University Press, 2006.

Stewart, Pamela J., and Andrew Strathern. *Witchcraft, Sorcery, Rumors, and Gossip.* Cambridge: Cambridge University Press, 2004.

Stewart, Tony. *Fabulous Females and Peerless Pirs: Tales of Mad Adventure in Old Bengal.* New York: Oxford University Press, 2004.

Sweetser, Anne Thompson. "The Power to Heal: Medicine and Society in the Pakistani Himalayas." PhD diss. Harvard University, Cambridge, MA, 1992.

Tārīkh e Jaora. Government Press Jaora: Directorate of Education for Jaora State, 1947.

Tārīkh e Yūsufī. Agra: Riyaz ul Hind Press, 1889.

Taussig, Michael. *The Devil and Commodity Fetishism in South America.* Chapel Hill: University of North Carolina Press, 1980.

———. *Mimesis and Alterity: A Particular History of the Senses.* New York: Routledge, 1993.

———. *Shamanism, Colonialism, and the Wild Man: A Study in Terror and Healing.* Chicago: University of Chicago Press, 1987.

Troll, Christian W., ed. *Muslim Shrines in India: Their Character, History, and Significance.* New Delhi: Oxford University Press, 1989.

Turner, Victor. *The Ritual Process: Structure and Anti-Structure.* Chicago: Aldine Publishing Company, 1969.

van der Veer, Peter. "Playing or Praying: A Sufi Saint's Day in Surat." *Journal of Asian Studies* 51, no. 3 (August 1992): 545–64.

———. *Religious Nationalism: Hindus and Muslims in India.* Berkeley: University of California Press, 1994.

Varisco, Daniel. *Islam Obscured: The Rhetoric of Anthropological Representation.* New York: Palgrave Macmillan, 2005.

———. "Metaphors and Sacred History: The Genealogy of Muhammad and the Arab 'Tribe.'" *Anthropological Quarterly* 68, no. 3: 139–56.

White, Hayden. *The Content of the Form: Narrative Discourse and Historical Representation.* Baltimore, MD: Johns Hopkins University Press, 1987.

Wilce, James. "Discourse, Power, and the Diagnosis of Weakness: Encountering Practitioners in Bangladesh." *Medical Anthropology Quarterly* 11, no. 3 (September 1997): 352–74.

Index

Page references in italics refer to illustrations.

auspiciousness: of married women, 161, 204–5; pan-Indian trope of, 68
Ayat al-Kursī (text), 96, 241n3

bābās (saints), 3
Babli (pilgrim), 22, 23; age of, 238n8; death of father, 122; dreams of, 66; education of, 59, 61; experience of *ḥāẓirī*, 62–63, 65, 67, 142; healing process of, 67–68, 69; identity of, 232n55; on *kāfir*, 201; knowledge of Islam, 61, 93; on lobān, 103, 108; and Mastān Bābā, 63–69, 238n14, 239n21; narrative of, 59–70; nickname of, 60, 238nn8,12; previous life of, 249n60; recitation of "The Tale of the Ten Virtuous Women," 190, 191, 253n54; wearing of locks, 124, 125
Babri Masjid (Ayodhya), destruction of, 234n9
badnāmī (disgrace), 160
Bai, Musammat Rahmat, 225
Bālājī (Hanumān), 136, 246n16; temple of, 246nn25,33
*balā*s (evil spirits), 140–41
Band Choṛnewāle Bābā, martyrdom of, 215, 216
bathing: commands involving, 124; in dirty water, 148, *156*, 156–59; spirit possession during, 122
Bell, Catherine, 26, 27
Bhairav (deity), 251n27
Bhūt (movie), 247n37
Bidarakoppa, G. S., 136
Bigelow, Anna, 234n11
Bilkis (pilgrim), 248n52; narrative of, 154–55, 158–60, 204–5, 255n71
bodies: of *ḥāẓirīwāle*, 133; improperly maintained, 180–81, 251n34; as legitimating agents, 162–63
Bohra (Shi'as), 32, 177, 233n3, 250n13
Bombay: Catholics of, 199; Ḥusain Ṭekrī *imāmbāṛā* at, 211; Islamic boundaries in, 37; Shi'ite community of, 53, 199–200, 202, 239n27, 243n29
Bourdieu, Pierre, 26
Bourguignon, Erika, 139, 246n32
breathing, in South Asian literature, 102
Bulliet, Richard, 16–17
Bunty aur Babli (movie), 238n12
Burman, J. J. Roy: *Hindu-Muslim Syncretic Shrines and Communities*, 248n52
burqas, Hindu women's, 80–81

Cābuk Sharīf, 62, 63; *ḥāẓirī* at, *131*
caste, 249n2; flexibility concerning, 172; justice involving, 251n27
chains, wearing of, 94, 124. *See also* locks
challā (strings), 244nn37,39–40; binding to Ḥusain Ṭekrī through, 122–23; corruptibility of, 241n13; healing through, 122; on *jālī*, 121, *123*, 129; proxy use of, 123; tying of, 94, 121–23, 229n20
Chandragupta, King, 209, 256n85
Chehlum (festival), 239n27
Chippa, Ghulam, 32
Chippa, Khadija, 32–33, 233n6
Christianity, threats from, 180, 251n33
*cillā*s (sacred places), xix; Band Choṛnewāle Bābā's, 215; geographical features of, 216–17; of Tāj ud Dīn, 84, 240n32
*cīl*s (kite, a bird of prey), Hindu goddesses as, 187, 188
Collins, Elizabeth Fuller: *Pierced by Murugan's Lance*, 233n60
communities: creation through suffering, 207–8; cross-traditional, 191; dead souls from, 179–81, 184; untouchable, 28, 233n64. *See also* *jāti*s
communities, imagined, 213; at Ḥusain Ṭekrī, 173–74; role of media in, 174; role of rumor in, 175–76, 218
communities, pilgrims', 182; of *dargāḥ*s, 33, 183, 234n11; of Ḥusain Ṭekrī, 48, 127, 171, 172–73, 213, 218
corpses, improperly disposed of, 181, 250n11
Csordas, Thomas J., 134
culture, South Asian: abundance in, 113; heat in, 109; magic in, 133; milk in, 113; *prasād* in, 242n14; purity in, 133; selfhood in, 135, 136, 139, 140, 162; solitude in, 240n45; spoken word in, 18; voluntary discipline in, 131; in Western diaspora, 6; xenophobia in, 176. *See also* religious identity, South Asian

identity: individual and group, 172, 173, 249n2; pilgrims' construction of, 22, 120–21, 175–76; role of festivals in, 241n9. *See also* community; religious identity; selfhood
illness: communal nature of, 137; magical and mundane, 169. *See also* suffering
imām (honorific), 3
imāmbāṛās (shrines), xix; of Bombay, 211; *ḥāẓirī* at, 135; of Ḥusain Ṭekrī, 46; of Jaora, 44; police investigations of, 12; Shi'ite, 218, 241n10; singing *fariyād* at, 202
imāms: authority of, 3; of Ḥusain Ṭekrī, 231n37; Shi'a, 3; twelve, 211
individuals, commodification of, 140
innocence: of *ḥāẓirīwāle,* 153, 154, 164, 167–68; nature of, 167–68; pilgrims', 120, 164; during spirit possession, 120
Islam: authority in South Asia, 8; court culture of, 5; discourse-centered scholarship on, 230nn30,34; discursive tradition of, 13–14; extra-subcontinental influences on, 4–5; forms of authority in, 18; founding texts of, 13; Hindus' practice of, 61, 71, 81–82, 157, 187; legal institutions of, 207; local cultures and, 13; reform movements in, 207, 230n26; relationship to Hinduism, 207–12; remembrance in, 201; role of Arabic script in, 17; static form of, 230n29; Sufi institutions of, 207
Ismail, Nazim, 37
isnād (chain of transmission), 17
isolation: divine revelation during, 171; of spirit possession, 133, 173; vulnerability to magic during, 170–71
Ithna 'Asharis, 37, 235n27
izārs (garments), 240n39

Jackson, Paul, 20
jādū (magic), 146, 247n42; of loneliness, 171; pilgrims on, 164; *prets*' speech concerning, 149; reasons for, 165. *See also* magic
jālī (latticework): association with air, 128; *challā* on, 121, *123,* 129; clinging to, 94, 126–27, *127,* 170; community around, 127; current in, 126
Jaora (Madhya Pradesh), xviii; Chippa Muslim community of, 32–33; *dargāḥs* of, 235n26; drought in, 233n2; Hindu temples of, 32, 33; Husain's visitation to, 110–11, 156, 171; *imāmbaṛas* of, 44; map of, *xxii;* mosques of, 32; old town, 31; opium production in, 234n13; outskirts of, 34; railway connections of, 31; religious tolerance in, 33; role in creation of Pakistan, 38; shrines of, 9, 33, 44; suburbs of, 31; Sunnis of, 37, 40, 229n16; *ta'ziyas* of, 44
jātis (birth-based communities), 32; Chippa, 23, 32, 233n4; reincarnation into, 187; threats from, 29, 233n64; untouchables, 179
jealousy, in *ḥāẓirī* narratives, 138–39, 141, 165
jinn, 162; agency of, 143; possession by, 56, 84
justice: involving caste, 251n27; from saints, 92, 148; through *ḥāẓirī,* 133, 148, 163–64; Western, 148

kāfir (unbelievers), 201
Kakar, Sudhir, 137
Kālī (goddess), 161, 212, 256n93
kām (labor): in healing, 95. *See also* labor, pilgrims'
Karbala, Shi'ite stories about, 60. *See also* martyrs, Muslim: of Karbala
karma, 140; and ancestor veneration, 247n35; and *qismat,* 249n60
Karni Mātā (goddess), 253n48
Karva Chauth (fast), 252n47
Keller, Mary: *The Hammer and the Flute,* 248n51, 249n59
k̲h̲ābīṣ (evil spirit), 247n40
k̲h̲ādims: ancestry of, 41; of Mu'īn āl-dīn Chishtī *dargāḥ,* 39
Khalifat committee, 37
Khan, Chunnu, 114–16, 121
Khān, Dādā Mukīm, 223
Khan, Dominique-Sila, 182–83
Khan, Ismail 'Ali, *nawāb,* 111; grave of, 41
Khan, Muhammad Ismail, *nawāb,* 221, 224; grave of, 9
Khan, Sarwar 'Ali, Haji, 9, 40, 41, 211, 236n32, 237n42

TEXT
10/13 Sabon

DISPLAY
Sabon

COMPOSITOR
Integrated Composition Systems

INDEXER
Roberta Engleman

CARTOGRAPHER
Bill Nelson

PRINTER AND BINDER
Thomson-Shore, Inc.